Canada's Department of External Affairs

Volume 1 The Early Years

1909–1946

CANADIAN PUBLIC ADMINISTRATION
SERIES
COLLECTION ADMINISTRATION PUBLIQUE
CANADIENNE

J. E. Hodgetts, *General Editor/Directeur général*
André Gélinas, *Directeur associé/Associate Editor*

The Institute of Public Administration of Canada
L'Institut d'administration publique du Canada

This series is sponsored by the Institute of Public
Administration of Canada as part of its constitutional
commitment to encourage research on contemporary
issues in Canadian public administration and public
policy, and to foster wider knowledge and understanding amongst practitioners and the concerned citizen.
There is no fixed number of volumes planned for the
series, but under the supervision of the Research
Committee of the Institute, the General Editor, and
the Associate Editor, efforts will be made to ensure
that significant areas will receive appropriate attention.

L'Institut d'administration publique du Canada com-
mandite cette collection dans le cadre de ses engage-
ments statutaires. Il se doit de promouvoir la recherche
sur des problèmes d'actualité portant sur l'administration publique et la détermination des politiques
publiques ainsi que d'encourager les praticiens et les
citoyens intéressés à les mieux connaître et à les
mieux comprendre. Il n'a pas été prévu de nombre
de volumes donné pour la collection mais, sous le
direction du Comité de recherche de l'Institut, du
Directeur général, et du Directeur associé, l'on
s'efforce d'accorder l'attention voulue aux questions
importantes.

An edition in French is distributed under the title
*Le français dans les airs: le conflit du bilinguisme
dans le contrôle de la circulation aérienne au Canada*
by les Presses de l'Université du Québec

**L'Analyse des politiques gouvernementales:
trois monographies**
Michel Bellavance, Roland Parenteau et Maurice Patry
(Published by les Presses de l'Université Laval)

**Canadian Social Welfare Policy:
Federal and Provincial Dimensions**
Edited by Jacqueline S. Ismael

**Maturing in Hard Times:
Canada's Department of Finance through
the Great Depression**
Robert B. Bryce

Pour comprendre l'appareil judiciaire québécois
Monique Giard et Marcel Proulx
(Published by les Presses de l'Université du Québec)

Histoire de l'administration publique québécoise 1867-1970
James Iain Gow
(Published by les Presses de l'Université de Montréal)

**Health Insurance and Canadian Public Policy:
The Seven Decisions That Created the Canadian
Health Insurance System and Their Outcomes**
Malcolm G. Taylor

**Canada and Immigration:
Public Policy and Public Concern
Second Edition**
Freda Hawkins

**Canada's Department of External Affairs:
The Early Years, 1909-1946**
John Hilliker

An edition in French has been published under the title
Le ministère des Affaires extérieures du Canada, 1909-1946: Les débuts
by Les Presses de l'Université Laval

Canada's Department of External Affairs

Volume 1   The Early Years, 1909–1946

JOHN HILLIKER

The Institute of Public Administration of Canada
L'Institut d'Administration publique du Canada

McGill-Queen's University Press
Montreal & Kingston • London • Buffalo

ISBN 0-7735-0736-1 (cloth)
ISBN 0-7735-0751-5 (paper)

Legal deposit first quarter 1990
Bibliothèque nationale du Québec

Published by the Institute of Public Administration of Canada in co-operation with the Academic Relations Division, External Affairs and International Trade Canada, and the Canadian Government Publishing Centre, Supply and Services Canada.

Printed in Canada on acid-free paper

Canadian Cataloguing in Publication Data

Hilliker, John, 1935–
Canada's Department of External Affairs
Contents; v. 1. The early years, 1909-1946.
Includes bibliographical references.
ISBN 0-7735-0736-1 (bound) —
ISBN 0-7735-0751-5 (pbk.)
1. Canada. Dept. of External Affairs—History.
2. Canada—Foreign relations administration.
I. Title.
JL103.E8444 1990   354.71061   C89-090394-8

64136

A French translation of this book, entitled *Le ministère des Affaires extérieures du Canada, 1909–1946: Les débuts*, has been published by Les presses de l'université Laval (ISBN 2-7637-7208-0).

This history is dedicated to
the memory of
John W. Holmes.

Contents

Preface

AS THE SOURCE REFERENCES in this book indicate, the history of Canadian external policy before 1946 has received extensive study, especially in recent years. Many of the works published on the subject have touched on the process whereby that policy was made, but nowhere has there been an examination of the Department of External Affairs similar to that afforded to some other branches of government, including two, the Department of Trade and Commerce and the Department of Finance, which have been closely involved in Canada's relations with other countries.

Throughout the period 1909–46, the department came under ministers whose main responsibilities lay elsewhere: the secretary of state until 1912 and the prime minister thereafter. Direction by the prime minister was a source of prestige and of influence on government operations generally, but pressure to assist with his domestic requirements could also create diversions from the department's concentration on its foreign-policy mandate. Helping to relieve the latter burden was the appointment of Arnold Heeney in 1938 as principal secretary to the prime minister and in 1940 as clerk of the privy council and secretary to the cabinet. As the department's foreign-policy agenda became increasingly heavy during the Second World War, responsibility for the prime minister's other requirements was assumed more and more by his own staff. By 1946 the time had come to recognize this development with the creation of a separate portfolio of external affairs.

The growth and character of the department in the years covered by this volume were determined also by the attitudes and objectives of successive under-secretaries and other senior officials and by the politics of the day, and even more perhaps by the demands of Canada's changing international position. In the regime of Sir Joseph Pope, the first under-secretary (1909–25), Canada's status in dealing with other countries was semi-colonial; the department therefore had a restricted mandate and remained unimpressive in size. Pope had no desire to push for greater responsibilities either for his country or for his department, which therefore was ripe for change when, after the First World War, Canadians were increasingly restless under the remaining ties with London.

The relationship with the United Kingdom and its empire was one of the major preoccupations of Pope's successor, O. D. Skelton (under-secretary 1925–41), who saw his department as a vital instrument in the assertion of Canadian autonomy. Two of Skelton's objectives were establishment of a network of diplomatic missions in other parts of the world, as evidence of Canada's independence, and creation of a foreign service of high quality able on its own to serve the country's interests in international negotiations. At the same time, Skelton was cautious about undertaking commitments abroad, especially in response to the crises of the 1930s in Europe and Asia, which he did not consider to be of direct interest to Canada and which he knew were unwelcome to the government of the day because of the potential for political division at home. Under Skelton's direction, the policy agenda remained limited, the department compact, and the organizational structure simple, with responsibility heavily concentrated in the under-secretary.

Skelton set aside his preference for non-involvement in great power relations on the outbreak of the Second World War, and he and his department were major contributors to the government's war effort. Prior to Skelton's death in 1941, however, there was little growth in the department's resources and virtually no change in its operation. Those took place under his successor, Norman Robertson (under-secretary 1941–46), who was part of a third generation of departmental leadership brought in since the late 1920s and itself testimony to Skelton's effectiveness as a recruiter. Under Robertson's direction, the department, reflecting the importance of Canada's contribution to the allied cause, was an assertive promoter of the national interest across a much broader range of international issues than hitherto. At the same time, resources were increased substantially despite wartime restrictions, and the department for the first time was organized systematically, an important consequence being some devolution of authority from the under-secretary to his senior colleagues. Thus by the end of the war the department was positioned to deal with the expanded range of interests and the new responsibilities arising from Canada's enhanced position in the world. The continuing adaptation of this growing and increasingly complex department, under a minister of its own, over the years 1946–68 will be the subject of volume II.

Acknowledgments

RESEARCH FOR AN ADMINISTRATIVE HISTORY of the Department of External Affairs was begun in 1978 in the former Historical Division by a team working under the direction of Don Page. The members of the team whose work contributed to this volume and the periods or subjects for which they were given responsibility were the following:

Gaston Blanchet	1919–1939
E.A. Kelly	Financial administration
F.J. McEvoy	1909–1921
Don Page	1939–1945
Louise Reynolds	The role of women

In 1983, the secretary of state for external affairs created an editorial board, drawn from the department's serving and former officers, the universities, and the foreign policy community, to oversee production of an official history for publication in the Canadian Public Administration Series of the Institute of Public Administration of Canada. According to its guidelines, the board's mandate was "mainly advisory," with "authority to solve such problems of emphasis, interpretation, style and content as may arise." The following were members of the board while the volume was under consideration:

John Holmes (chair)
André Bissonnette (vice-chair)
Arthur Blanchette
Ralph Collins

Louis Delvoie
Lawrence Dickenson
Professor André Donneur
Professor David Farr
Louise Fréchette
Dwight Fulford
John Graham
Gary Harman
Alex Inglis
Michael Kergin
Pamela McDougall Mayer
Robert Reford
Basil Robinson
Sen. John Stewart
Richard Tait

The text prepared by Dr Page on the basis of his team's research has been an important resource in the preparation of the present book. I am grateful to him for his continuing interest in the project and to all members of the team for their research.

A special debt of gratitude is owed to Arthur Blanchette. As a result of his commitment, while director of the former Historical Division, to completion of a departmental history, the project was securely established in its present form. Following his retirement he was an unfailing source of encouragement and wise counsel and made a continuing contribution to the research for this volume and to the initial drafting of certain sections of the text.

Much additional research was done to produce the present volume. My principal associate in this task was Mr McEvoy, whose contribution, which can be found in all parts of the book, I gratefully acknowledge. Valuable assistance at this stage was also provided by Anne Hillmer and Mr Kelly.

The dedication of this book is an indication of the importance of John Holmes's contribution. The members of the editorial board fulfilled their mandate with supreme tact, never imposing judgments on the author. They constituted a valuable source of advice and encouragement in the writing of the history. Final approval of the text rested with the general editor of the Canadian Public Administration Series, Professor J.E. Hodgetts, whose comments on the manuscript at various stages were of great help both in developing themes and in correcting points of detail. The Institute of Public Administration, and especially its assistant executive director, Maurice Demers, were of inestimable help with the arrangements necessary to bring this book to publication. John Parry was most helpful and considerate in preparing the manuscript for the press. I wish to thank as well

Dr Norman Hillmer, for reading the entire text and making valuable suggestions for improvement.

No restrictions were placed on access to any of the documentation needed for this volume, and the department co-operated fully in meeting all requirements. The research could not have been carried out without extensive help from the staffs of the department's Records Information Management Division, the departmental library, and the National Archives of Canada. Also of much help were archivists at the Public Record Office in London, the National Archives in Washington, DC, the Archives of Ontario in Toronto, and six universities: Acadia, Bishop's, British Columbia, Queen's, Toronto, and York. I also much appreciate the kindness of the owners of the various private collections cited and of those persons who were interviewed. Word processing of the manuscript through its many versions was handled with care and patience by Gail MacDonald.

The photograph of Norman Robertson is from the department's collection. All others are from the Documentary Art and Photography Division, National Archives of Canada. The National Archives copy negative number (prefixed by C or PA) and, where known, the name of the photographer are indicated for each picture.

Lord Grey (PA 42405)

Sir Wilfred Laurier (W.J. Topley: PA 27977)

Charles Murphy
(PA 42173)

W.J. Roche (PA 25974)

Sir Robert Borden (PA 27011)

Arthur Meighen (C 691)

William Lyon Mackenzie
King (C 42725)

R.B. Bennett (C 687)

Sir Joseph Pope
(W.J. Topley; PA 110845)

O.D. Skelton (C 2126)

Norman Robertson
(Department of External
Affairs, photo collection)

The Trafalgar Building (PA 8934)

The East Block in 1912 (PA 42791)

Canada House, London, c. 1925 (PA 127557)

The legation, Washington (PA 127561)

The legation, Paris (PA 127556)

The legation, Tokyo (PA 120404)

xxviii

The Imperial Conference, London, 1926. Left to right: Vincent Massey, W.L. Mackenzie King, Ernest Lapointe, Peter Larkin (C 9061)

The Canadian legation staff, Tokyo, 1929. Left to right: K.P. Kirkwood, H.L. Keenleyside, Herbert Marler, J.A. Langley (PA 120407)

The League of Nations, 1928. Left to right:
O.D. Skelton, Philippe Roy, Sen. Raoul Dandurand,
W.L. Mackenzie King, Charles Dunning, Walter
Riddell (C 9055)

The San Francisco conference, 1945. Front row, left to right: Louis St Laurent, W.L. Mackenzie King. Second row, left to right: Warwick Chipman, Hume Wrong, Norman Robertson, Charles Ritchie (C 22720)

Part One

**Beginnings:
To 1926**

Chapter One
External Relations
to 1909

GOVERNMENTS IN CANADA HAVE ALWAYS had to pay close attention to external relations because of the importance of such concerns as trade, settlement, and the definition of boundaries. Long before the Department of External Affairs came into being, in 1909, various mechanisms for the conduct of such relations had been developed. Those that most affected the work of the future department took shape mainly after about 1840, as a result of two crucial changes in British imperial policies: gradual withdrawal of military forces from North America and adoption of the principle of free trade. These changes required the colonies to become more self-reliant in their relations with the United States, assuming more responsibility for their defence while at the same time looking for reciprocal trading relationships to make up for the loss of privileged access to the British market. It was natural, therefore, for the colonies to want to extend responsible government, which was developing at the same time, into external relations, still considered to be under the jurisdiction of London.

Responsibilities of the colonial governments

The British North American colonies gained the right to frame their own customs tariffs when the British Parliament passed the Enabling Act in 1846. This statute, complementing British adoption of free trade, allowed the colonies to abolish the element of British preference in their tariff duties. The United Province of Canada used this concession to fashion a tariff that suited its economic interests. Thus it offered free trade to the other British North American colonies (1850), introduced protective duties on foreign and British manufactured imports (1859), and moved to provide preferential treatment for natural products coming from the United States, as embodied in the provisions of the celebrated reciprocity treaty, in force from 1854 to 1866.

The colonies, although they took the initiative in pressing for reciprocity with the United States, were given only a limited role in negotiation of the treaty. This was undertaken by the governor general, Lord Elgin, meeting with the US secretary of state. During final stages of negotiations in Washington, in May 1854, Elgin was advised by Francis Hincks, premier of Canada, and by E. B. Chandler, leader of the government in New Brunswick. A representative from Nova Scotia was not on hand because of a misunderstanding. During these years the United Kingdom steadfastly refused, however, to accept the colonies' contention that they had a right to participate in commercial negotiations. The colonies used the 1854 advisory precedent when they turned to search for markets overseas after the United States abrogated the reciprocity treaty following cross-border tensions during the Civil War. In 1866, the governments of Canada, Nova Scotia, New Brunswick, and Prince Edward Island sponsored a trade commission that visited the Caribbean and Brazil. Although barred from negotiating treaties, the commissioners, under instructions from their governments, had authority "to inquire, to furnish information, to report, and to make recommendations to their respective governments."[1]

The proximity of the United States gave the colonial governments an interest in certain matters affecting the legal status of residents: extradition, naturalization, and passports. Jay's treaty of 1794 had provided for the mutual exchange of criminals, but after the expiry of the relevant clause in 1807 there was a long period of confusion resulting from British slowness in making arrangements with other states for extradition. It was not until the Webster-Ashburton treaty of 1842 that there was again an Anglo-American agreement that could serve as a basis for colonial action, and by the time of Confederation there were effective arrangements with only two more countries, France and Denmark.

The colonies were constrained as well by positions taken in London on naturalization. The local legislatures, almost from their creation, had claimed the power to naturalize resident aliens. In the judgment of the imperial Parliament, however, the status of British subject was effective only within the borders of the colony that conferred it. For travel in the United States, a naturalized person might obtain a certificate of nationality (in effect, a form of passport) from the mayor of the local town. Natural-born British subjects did not require passports in the United States; if venturing farther afield, residents of the colonies obtained the necessary documentation from the Foreign Office in London or from their country of origin.[2]

Decision-making, administration, and representation

Although limited, the responsibilities of the colonies for external relations were sufficient to require a well-understood, if simple, procedure for dealing with them. Practice in the United Province of Canada, whose civil service was to be the model for the new dominion, may serve as an example.

The governor general decided whether matters should be dealt with locally or in London. To meet new border regulations introduced by the United States as a result of the Civil War, he also assumed jurisdiction over the issuance of passports, which he signed. Applications were forwarded to him through a network of agents established for the purpose. The conduct of correspondence with Whitehall and with agents of the British government abroad, most notably in Washington, was the concern of the civil secretary. By 1867, this official was considered part of the personal staff of the governor general, not the senior civil servant in the colony with powers of direction and co-ordination over the departments of government. The latter function was performed before 1867, in a rudimentary way, by the provincial secretary.[3] Here was the point of contact, albeit not fully developed, between the governor general's office and the ministry in the assignment of tasks arising from the external interests of the colony.

For representation of its external interests, the colonial government relied on the diplomatic and consular services of the United Kingdom. The participation of the local government remained limited. The colonials who took part in the reciprocity negotiations with the United States did not enjoy plenipotentiary powers, and the idea of a resident spokesman for commercial interests was discouraged by the British, who argued that the task might better be left in the care of the mother country.[4]

The proscription on representation abroad did not apply to London, where it had become usual by the eighteenth century for the American and the West Indian colonies to maintain agents to represent their interests and conduct business affairs for them. Starting with Nova Scotia in 1762, the northern dependencies followed suit. They did so mainly on an ad hoc basis, for they had little incentive to establish permanent agencies. By comparison especially with settlements in Australasia, missions from British North America could reach the mother country with ease, and changing priorities in Britain after the American revolution meant that there was less to be gained from permanent representatives established

5

to promote the interests of the remaining North American colonies.[5]

The most urgent preoccupation of the governments of those colonies was the attraction of British settlers. In 1840, an emigration agent, Dr Thomas Rolph, was sent to England to publicize the attractions of the province of Canada. His mission was short-lived, and for a number of years the main colonial concern was not recruitment so much as lack of control over the quality of immigrants. The problem was finally solved between 1848 and 1854, when the British government gave up its involvement in response to vigorous colonial complaints. In the province of Canada, immigration came under the jurisdiction of the Bureau of Agriculture (given departmental status in 1862). Starting in 1854, the bureau began sending emigration agents overseas on recruiting trips once more, to continental Europe as well as Britain, and these were soon joined by representatives of private enterprise.[6]

For a limited range of other matters of interest to the colonial and foreign governments, communication was possible through consular officers appointed by the latter, under writs of exequatur (certificates of recognition) granted by the British authorities. Career consuls were full-time officers in the service of their country of origin. Depending on the importance of their posts they were designated consul general, consul, or vice-consul. Honorary consuls were generally appointed when a career officer was not required or could not be afforded. They were residents of the colony, often engaged in trade, and could be either citizens of the appointing country or British subjects.

The first US consulate was opened in Halifax in 1833 as a result of east coast shipping problems, and from 1850 onward various European governments began to appoint consuls in Montreal and elsewhere. Early Colonial Office Lists reveal that, by 1860, consular representation had become quite developed in the colonies, spanning the continent from Halifax, where the United States maintained a career consulate and Denmark and Austria-Hungary honorary consuls, to Vancouver Island, where the kingdom of Hawaii was represented by an honorary consul. Full-time consular representation, concentrated in the major cities, was maintained by Argentina, Belgium, France, certain Hanseatic towns, Italy, and the United States, which had such representation not only in the main cities but in some border towns as well. On occasion consuls were called upon to represent the interests of other countries in their areas. Thus, for instance, the services of the French consul in Quebec were available to the governments of Denmark and the Hanseatic towns.

The consulates were concerned primarily with shipping questions, commercial relations, and the welfare of their nationals, who sometimes experienced unusual problems: in 1857, a resident of Montreal requested assistance from the US consulate to expedite the delivery of slaves he had purchased. They could also serve discreetly as sources of information for their home governments and play a role in negotiations involving Canada. Consular officials assisted in bringing about a customs accord between Canada and France in 1863, based on the Anglo-French commercial treaty of 1860. But care had to be exercised to avoid any suggestion of aspiration to diplomatic status, which, London was quick to indicate, could lead to problems with the mother country.[7]

THE EFFECT OF CONFEDERATION, 1867–1873

The union of Canada, Nova Scotia, and New Brunswick in 1867 did not require substantial modification of these procedures. External affairs did not receive much attention in the discussions preceding Confederation, and the British North America (BNA) Act of 1867 (now the Constitution Act, 1867) conferred only limited authority in this sphere. The powers of the dominion Parliament included regulation of trade and commerce and defence, but there was no suggestion that Canada should act as an independent entity in external affairs. The emphasis rather was on upholding obligations to which it was committed as part of the British Empire. "The Parliament and Government of Canada," section 132 of the act stated, "shall have all powers necessary or proper for performing the Obligations of Canada or of any Province thereof, as Part of the British Empire, towards Foreign Countries arising under Treaties between the Empire and such Foreign Countries." The new dominion might have autonomy at home, but in its relations with other countries it was still a colony, with the conduct of its external affairs firmly in the hands of the British Foreign Office.

Channels of communication

As in the pre-Confederation province of Canada, the governor general, with an office in the East Block of the Parliament Buildings in Ottawa, was central to the conduct of external relations. All external questions passed through his office, and he decided which to refer to London and whom to involve locally. His role, however, had declined by the time of Confederation. In part this was a consequence of the advance of colonial self-government, which had already reduced his authority in domestic affairs to a nominal level. Also important was the laying of the transatlantic cable in 1865, since speedier communication with London restricted the personal initiative that had earlier been possible because of the time lag between Canada and Britain. Nevertheless, the governor general remained a central figure in the conduct of foreign policy, more so than his counterparts in the other colonies which much later became self-governing. The reason was Canada's geographical position, which gave the governor general, in conjunction with the British minister in Washington, a special role to play in the relationship with the United States.[8]

The governor general, it has been said, was "the human link in the imperial chain."[9] Messages were sent and received through his office and coded and decoded there. At one end of the chain was Whitehall, where the Colonial Office received communications, referred them if necessary to other departments, such as the Foreign Office (which might in turn involve an embassy abroad), the Board of Trade, or the Admiralty, and sought to compose a reply that would be acceptable in both London and Ottawa. The other end of the chain was the Canadian government. The formal link between the governor general and his ministers was the Privy Council. This body, chaired by the governor general, seldom met, its business being conducted by the committee of council (in practice, the cabinet). When the governor general referred an incoming message to the council, it was considered by the cabinet and sent to the appropriate department for action. The department's report, submitted in due course to the cabinet by its minister, then became the basis of a minute of the council and subsequently of the reply to the original communication. When large issues of imperial policy were raised, the procedure gave the Canadian government the opportunity, by order-in-council, to inform London of the local conditions that ought to be borne in mind. On minor issues, the procedure might be circumvented by direct reference of an issue by the governor general to the minister concerned. Direct communication was also possible at times in transactions involving the United States, although in theory they were supposed to pass from one end of the chain to the other. Thus, on less important items, the governor general and the British minister in Washington might communicate with each other, with the latter keeping the Foreign Office informed.

While there was no department of government specifically charged with handling external affairs, the secretary of state, as successor to the pre-Confederation provincial secretary, became the focal point. The secretary of state was the minister locally responsible for correspondence regarding the appointment of foreign consuls, extradition, and passports. He frequently took charge of arrangements for official visits and ceremonies. In collaboration with Government House, the secretary of state's department handled protocol and honours and advised the provinces on such matters. It was through the governor general and the secretary of state that Canada was notified of and invited to participate in international conferences and given instructions on the application of British policy or the implication of treaties affecting Canada. Other departments seeking to do business with or to obtain redress from foreign governments sent their requests through the secretary of state to the governor general and thence to London.

The secretary of state was responsible for transmission of petitions from Canada to London. Departments of government, although they rarely did so, could use this channel to request information through the British diplomatic service about the actions of foreign governments. The process also operated in reverse: it was the secretary of state who responded to inquiries about Canada from other governments, via their representatives in London. This function of the secretary of state also made it possible for individual Canadians and organizations with interests abroad to call upon the services of British offices around the world. The opportunity thus afforded was of value, for example, to Canadian churches, because of their extensive missionary activity.[10]

Through the governor general's office the secretary of state had limited access to British information on a variety of international issues about which the governor general received copies of Foreign and Colonial Office correspondence. In the years immediately following Confederation, Canadian interest in such material was modest. As the country's external interests expanded, however, and Britain became more involved in foreign disputes having a bearing on Canada, this source of information became more important.

Extradition, naturalization, and consular services

Within the administrative context described here, Confederation was followed by an increase in local responsibility for certain legal procedures involving relations with other countries. One of the most important, because of the proximity of the United States, was extradition. In the first session of Parliament after Confederation, a new extradition act covering all the provinces was passed, but its effect was undermined by British legislation in 1870; the possibility of conflict was not removed until 1882, when application of the British act was suspended in Canada. Thereafter, extradition was governed in Canada by local legislation passed in 1877 and amended in 1882.[11]

The questionable status of British subjects naturalized in Canada took longer to resolve, for it was not until 1914 that the British Parliament passed an act declaring naturalization in a dominion to be effective throughout the empire and the world. Persons naturalized in Canada, however, continued to receive passports issued in the dominion. Starting in 1893 the document was available to those born there as well, although a different form had to be used until the question of naturalization was resolved. These passports were issued under the authority of the governor general, but the work involved was carried out in the Department of the Secretary of State.

Also subject to change after Confederation was the position of foreign consuls. Writs of exequatur continued to be granted in London, provided that the Canadian government had no objection. But after 1872 appointments not requiring exequatur no longer had to be referred to London for approval. They could be handled by the Canadian government alone, with only notification being made to the Foreign Office.[12]

For consular assistance abroad, Canadians relied on British representatives, whose services the government in Ottawa expected to receive without cost to itself. This assumption applied even to the provision of financial assistance to Canadians who ran out of funds while outside their country's borders. Before Confederation the province of Canada had steadfastly refused to sanction payments to such distressed Canadians, except for merchant seamen, unless the government had given its approval in advance. With only a few exceptions, the government of the new dominion maintained this policy. Even if Ottawa did pay, it was always with the proviso that such expenditures were "not considered a legitimate charge on the revenues of the Dominion."[13] For some time the British tolerated this position because the number of such cases was not large, but in 1890 the Foreign Office instructed its consuls to refuse further relief. The Canadian government then accepted responsibility for distressed Canadians except in the United States, presumably in the belief that they could manage somehow to get home or obtain assistance from relatives in Canada. This solution was not achieved without a certain amount of strain between Ottawa and London: "We have been at Canada for more than 20 years on this subject," was the weary comment of a member of the Colonial Office in closing the file.[14] Still free of charge were the many other services that travelling Canadians could use through the world-wide network of diplomatic and consular offices maintained by the British.

Policy-making, representation, and negotiation

Useful as these British services might be, Confederation had given the government of Canada a range of external interests that could no longer be fully served within the limitations of colonial status. The work of defining these interests and of devising means to deal with them was principally that of the politicians rather than of the public service. The latter was small, with around 350 officers and clerks in Ottawa immediately after Confederation. By the standards of its day, the early Canadian public service was not lacking in capability, and it included men of imagination and distinction in its senior ranks, but their interest was excited mainly by domestic needs. The politicians, in contrast, were well supplied with ideas of their own on external relations, as indicated by the attention given to tariffs, defence, and immigration in the party platforms for the election of 1867.[15]

The emergence of these subjects in the election campaign was of much importance for the way external relations would be conducted afterward. From the time of Confederation, various branches of government had an interest in external policy, which became entrenched as time went on and had to be accommodated after a department of external affairs was created over forty years later. An equally important circumstance to be taken into account after 1909 was the dominant position in the determination of external policy established by the first prime minister, Sir John A. Macdonald, and consolidated in the years that followed.

In Macdonald's opinion there were two key external relationships for Canada, those with the United States and the United Kingdom. In dealing with the former, he wanted Canada to have a distinct personality, but, in view of the disparity in power, he recognized that it also needed the support of Britain. For practical as well as sentimental reasons, therefore, he favoured the imperial tie, but he wanted something better than colonial status: not subordination but partnership, as "an autonomous nation within the British Empire, linked to the United Kingdom by ties of interest as well as by a common crown."[16] Such a vision encouraged him to take important initiatives in the management of relations with both the United Kingdom and the United States.

To further his objectives in the United Kingdom, Macdonald needed a representative with impressive credentials. There was also a continuing need to attract settlers. Immigration being a responsibility shared, according to the BNA Act, by the federal and provincial governments, emigration agents sent to Britain before Confederation remained in place. In 1868, the Dominion Office of Immigration (reporting to the Department of Agriculture until 1892 and then, until 1917, to the Department of the Interior) was opened in London, and soon afterward other such offices were established in continental Europe and the United States. In the United Kingdom, the dominion office was intended to consolidate the Canadian presence, but the first chief agent, William Dixon, did not assert his authority. Partly for that reason, and partly because of the narrowness of his mandate, the office did not meet Macdonald's broader representational requirements.[17]

In 1869 Macdonald found the appropriate representative in his former minister of finance, Sir John Rose, who had left the cabinet to go into banking in the British capital. Although Rose's position was informal, he received his authority by order-in-council, which described him as "a gentleman possessing the confidence of the Canadian Government with whom Her Majesty's Government may properly communicate on Canadian affairs.''[18] In many ways, he performed functions that were to become the stock in trade of Canadian diplomats. On matters of vital concern, he was supposed to act only on instructions from Ottawa. The promotion of emigration formed part of his brief, and his aid was sought by the agents in Britain in dealing with problems of special importance. In London he could exert informal influence on politicians and officials, and in Ottawa his reports helped to keep the government abreast of developments in the British capital. Although he dealt on some matters with the minister of finance and his reports were circulated through the secretary of state's department, much of his communication was with Macdonald. His activity, therefore, helped to establish the prime minister's dominant position in the conduct of external relations.[19]

The importance of prime ministerial control became apparent in the context of Anglo-American negotiations to settle differences outstanding after the Civil War. A number of the issues were primarily of concern to Canada, where the government sought to exert pressure on the United States by withholding licences to fish off the east coast. The vigour with which the policy was pursued was due in part to Macdonald's prolonged absence from the capital as a result of illness, giving the minister of marine and fisheries, Peter Mitchell, a free hand in an important area of external relations. He had the wherewithal to make Canada's presence felt, since the government had decided to fit out a marine police of six cruisers. As a result, Mitchell's policy was a cause of consternation in London, and Macdonald, when he returned to duty, concluded that it ought to be modified. "I must," he observed, "take the subject into my own hands."[20]

So he did. East coast fishing and Canadian-American relations generally were in his control when the major cross-border problems were referred to a joint high commission in Washington in 1871. Macdonald was named one of the commissioners on the British side, the first Canadian, indeed the first representative of a British colony, to have plenipotentiary powers in negotiations affecting his country. The significance was not lost on Lord Monck, who had been governor general at the time of Confederation. "The man who has created a 'Dominion'," wrote Monck to Macdonald, "is to be trusted with the care of its external interests and I hope the experiment on your part of diplomacy in leading strings will convince you that you are nearly strong enough to work alone."[21]

The results of the experiment were not pleasing to Macdonald, for he did not secure his primary aim, restoration of reciprocity in return for Canadian concessions on fisheries and other matters. Part of his problem was persuading the British delegation to accept his position, which he sought to do by securing cabinet backing for stiff-necked resistance to concessions. To produce the required messages, he sent two sets of communications to Ottawa. One, which he discussed with the British commissioners, reported on developments and asked for guidance. The other, dispatched in secret, indicated the instructions that he wanted to receive from the cabinet.

The effort failed, because Macdonald had no independent means of confidential communication with his colleagues in Ottawa. Messages sent in cypher were kept secret from the Americans but not from the British. They were available to the governor general in Ottawa, Lord Lisgar, who freely communicated their contents both to London and to the British side in Washington. The other British commissioners, therefore, were aware that the Canadian government's resistance to concessions was at least partially created by Macdonald and hence not as impressed as he wished by his claims about Canadian opposition to the treaty.[22] Dependent on the British for the tools of diplomacy as well as for representational status, the prime minister was less effective abroad as a spokesman for Canada's interests than he was at home.

NEW DIRECTIONS CONFIRMED, 1873–1878

As supporters of a closer definition of Canadian interests within the empire, the Liberal government of Alexander Mackenzie, which came to power in 1873, was committed to the effort to improve the country's position in dealing with other states. It was somewhat bolder in this regard than its predecessor, on occasion transacting business in Washington without going through the intermediary of the British legation (despite the consternation of the latter) and using the consular channel for commercial discussions with France.[23] In London, the position of Sir John Rose, who enjoyed Mackenzie's confidence, was given more formal status with the title of financial commissioner for the dominion of Canada. A new office, general agent for the dominion and superintendent of emigration, was created and awarded to a British member of Parliament with Canadian connections, Edward Jenkins. He was expected to enhance the Canadian position and to establish his authority over the other agents in the country. He turned out, however, not to be very useful to Canada, partly because he lacked diplomatic skills and partly because his position in Parliament shifted from the government to the opposition side. Eventually downgraded as a result of an economy drive in Ottawa and a disagreement with the minister of agriculture, Jenkins resigned and was replaced by an official with the rank of chief clerk in the Canadian public service.[24]

At home, Mackenzie, like Macdonald, kept control of external policy in his own hands, thereby avoiding commitment to the ideas of some of the more adventurous members of his government. He also kept a close watch on negotiations with the United States, though not a participant himself. As the Canadian representative to take part, alongside the British minister, in discussions arising from the treaty of Washington, Mackenzie chose his friend Sen. George Brown, proprietor of the Toronto *Globe*, who was given plenipotentiary powers. Other Canadians who became involved had to conform to the requirements of the prime minister and his representative. When the minister of marine and fisheries, Albert Smith, began to interfere in the negotiations after Mackenzie had permitted him to go to Washington, he was chastised, probably at Brown's instigation, and soon returned to Canada. All instructions, Smith was told, must come from Ottawa.[25]

INCREASING CANADIAN RESPONSIBILITY, 1878-1896

As a result of Mackenzie's actions, the dominant position of the prime minister in the conduct of external relations was well established when Macdonald returned to power in 1878. With a tenure lasting until his death in 1891, Macdonald had ample time to shape the way in which the external policies of Canada were formulated. In the course of doing so, he brought about a number of advances in Canada's capacity to look after its relations with other countries.

Commercial negotiations and representation abroad

Anxious to find new markets for Canadian products to help to compensate for the failure to gain freer access to the United States, Macdonald took up an idea that had originated with Mackenzie—the dispatch of Alexander Galt (a former minister of finance and negotiator on fisheries with the United States) to Europe for commercial discussions with the governments of Spain and France. The objective, it has been suggested, was not only to broaden the range of Canada's trade but also to assert a stronger national presence in the conduct of external relations. Partly because of difficulties with the British, the mission was not a success in either regard. An agreement was not achieved with France until 1893, and none was reached with Spain.

However, progress was made during this period in relieving the self-governing colonies of the provisions of commercial treaties that the United Kingdom had made in the past, and was still making, on behalf of the empire. The inconvenience of soliciting colonies' views as to whether a pending British treaty should be applied to them was solved by the Colonial Office devising an article that enabled them to be exempted from the provisions of a current treaty if they desired. The procedure was worked out and put into practice after 1878.[26]

Galt's problems in the negotiations with France and Spain were one reason the Canadian government decided to seek more formal representation in London than was provided by Sir John Rose, but the move was intended also to serve the prime minister's broader objective of "the extension of colonial responsible government into the hitherto unoccupied territory of foreign affairs."[27] In 1879 a ministerial delegation visiting London gave the British authorities notice of the Canadian government's intentions. What they envisaged was the appointment of a "resident minister" who would look after all Canadian interests in Britain. In the prime minister's view, the proposed appointment was "quasi-diplomatic" and "a very important step towards asserting the importance of the Dominion of Canada as a portion of Her Majesty's Empire."[28]

The British were willing to accept a Canadian representative but objected to the diplomatic status implied by the title resident minister. Macdonald accepted the British terms in order to avoid a quarrel that might get the new office off to a bad start, and in due course the two sides agreed on the designation "high commissioner," the title used to this day. The new representative, observed the prime minister confidently, would give "a higher status to Canadian commerce and more direct means of communication with the various nations."[29]

One result of the Canadian legislation of 1880 creating the new office was the displacement of Rose, who resigned his position as unofficial Canadian representative. He did continue to work, however, on instructions from Ottawa and in co-operation with the high commissioner, on specific financial matters concerning Canada. The post of high commissioner went to Galt. His instructions emphasized the activities of his office that were most important to development in Canada, particularly emigration: he was named chief emigration agent, and this was to be his first priority. On this subject he was responsible to the minister of agriculture, and he dealt with the minister of finance regarding matters related to that portfolio. On other aspects of policy and administration the formal channel of communication was the secretary of state, but it was common for ministers and their deputies to ignore this route. A substantial private correspondence developed with the prime minister, further reinforcing his leading role in the conduct of external relations. The governor general, too, had to be borne in mind. Galt's instructions were submitted to the Marquis of Lorne, who sent a copy to the colonial secretary. The governor general also insisted on seeing copies of all correspondence with the high commissioner. As a result, Galt on more than one occasion found himself at a disadvantage in dealing with British officials who had advance notice of the positions he planned to take.[30]

Galt remained in London until only 1883. He was not happy in the job, partly for reasons that were to become familiar to the future Canadian diplomatic service. British reluctance to concede the appearance of diplomatic rank created problems of status and precedence that were to plague high commissioners for many years to come. Ottawa also created problems. Galt was disappointed by the lack of response from headquarters to the reports that he sent on developments in Britain. He was dissatisfied as well with the remuneration authorized for his position ($10,000 per annum plus $4,000 for dwelling and contingencies at the time of his appointment), which was insufficient to cover the representational side of his functions and created a situation that for a long time made the representation of Canada the preserve of the wealthy. "To succeed in influencing public opinion and the government in favour of Canada . . . it is essential that one should meet in society the large landlords, the leaders of the Conservative Party and generally members of both Houses," Galt observed. "This cannot be done by staying at home."[31]

The credibility and influence of the high commissioner's office were much enhanced under Galt's successor, Sir Charles Tupper, a member of Macdonald's cabinet. So influential did Tupper become that, in 1890, Macdonald noted that "the colonial ministers have begun to treat the colonial representatives as diplomatic agents rather than as subordinate executive officers, and to consult them as such."[32] The high commissioner had extensive meetings with British officials and direct correspondence with the colonial secretary and the Foreign Office (despite the reservations of the latter). He publicized Canadian products, gave speeches promoting the dominion, and invited the public to learn more about it in a library and reading room at his office. He developed contacts with other colonial representatives, among whom he assumed the leading role, and, on an unofficial basis, with members of the diplomatic corps in London.

The high commissioner's staff was small, consisting in 1895 of only a secretary, an assistant secretary, and four clerks, but it produced enough work to require expansion in the secretary of state's department in Ottawa. The high comissioner increasingly became the effective channel of communication between the governments of Canada and Britain, in preference to the traditional route via the governor general.[33] The office was also a reflection of Canada's unique position in the empire; other colonies of settlement might have resident representatives, known (since 1865, when the title was used by South Australia) as agents general, but Canada was the only one to be represented by a high commissioner, with the enhanced status that Tupper achieved, until after the turn of the century.

The appearance of agents general was of considerable interest to the high commissioner, for the provinces were attracted by this form of representation: Nova Scotia opened an office in 1885, and New Brunswick followed two years later. The principal interests appear to have been emigration and trade. With the same title as the sole representatives of other dependencies, they assumed the right to deal with the British government through the colonial secretary. Tupper did not raise difficulties but assisted the agents general in securing the facilities and privileges to which they felt entitled.

Provincial initiative had more effect on the federal government at this time in another capital, Paris. There in 1882 the government of Quebec established a representative, Hector Fabre, a former journalist and senator. The federal authorities soon afterward, in the words of a report on the origin of the office, "availed themselves of Mr. Fabre's presence in Paris to utilize his services." According to his instructions, Fabre was to concern himself with emigration and trade, to follow any directions he might receive from the high commissioner in London, and to report to Ottawa through the secretary of state. The British government does not seem to have been consulted about the appointment, but there was little reason for it to be concerned, for the title used (first agent and later commissioner) had no diplomatic pretensions.

In practice, Fabre was more active in cultural affairs, promoting liaison between French-speaking Canadians and France, than in emigration and trade work. While the dominion Department of Finance paid his salary, Fabre's connection with Ottawa became decidedly tenuous. There was never, observed the report, "any certainty as to which Department of the Canadian Government his office was attached"; his status was always "more or less undefined and unsatisfactory."[34]

Failure to define more precisely the government's expectations of the office in Paris was no doubt related to Macdonald's scepticism about Canadian representation abroad, except in London. The advantage to be gained from drawing on British prestige and powers of enforcement, at no cost to Canada, far outweighed any irritations that might arise between the two countries, he observed when the subject came up in Parliament in 1882. Being "cast upon our own resources . . .," he said, "would be an injury, a destruction, a ruin of Canada."[35] This applied even to the United States. "I greatly doubt the expediency of having a Canadian permanent minister at Washington," Macdonald stated. "The present system of uniting the British minister ordinarily appointed with a Canadian whenever a question affecting Canada arises works more satisfactorily than the proposed change."[36]

International and intra-imperial diplomacy

As the Canadian frequently united with the "British minister ordinarily appointed," the high commissioner in London became a kind of ambassador at large for Macdonald's government. It was Tupper who was responsible for the negotiations that produced the commercial agreement with France in 1893. Although nominally between that country and Britain, the agreement was exclusively concerned with Franco-Canadian tariff relations. Tupper and the British ambassador, Lord Dufferin, signed on behalf of the queen, and in due course the agreement was approved by the Canadian Parliament. Thus by 1893 Canada could claim the right to negotiate commercial agreements for itself, although in form its representatives were still under imperial auspices and associated with British diplomats. This achievement in turn made an important contribution to the completion of fiscal autonomy and the attainment of treaty-making powers for Canada, well in advance of other British colonies.[37]

During this period Canadian representatives also began to appear at international conferences. The first at which the Canadian government was represented in its own right was probably a monetary conference in Paris in May 1881. Galt and Tupper both attended but, at their request, with only "limited powers," in order to avoid committing the dominion to the decisions of the conference; they were not issued with formal letters of credence. Two years later, Tupper took part in an international conference on submarine cables, this time with credentials on behalf of Canada, although he was not a full plenipotentiary in the diplomatic sense. He used his enhanced authority to promote the interests of dependent territories and, on one occasion, disagreed openly with the British delegation. "I feel some pride," he reported to Macdonald, "that Canada took her place on an equal footing with all the other Powers."[38]

Tupper's satisfaction notwithstanding, Canada could expect only a limited role in international conferences so long as it lacked full control of its external relations. More of substance, meanwhile, was likely to arise at colonial conferences, the first of which met in London in 1887, the year of Queen Victoria's golden jubilee. The invitation did not specify that prime ministers or members of their cabinets were expected to attend the London meetings, and, with Parliament in session in Ottawa, representation at that level would have been difficult. The Canadian representatives were the railway builder and surveyor Sandford Fleming (an advocate of a Pacific cable, a subject of interest to Canada that was slated for discussion) and Sir Alexander Campbell, formerly postmaster general and newly appointed lieutenant-governor of Ontario. They had only restricted authority. On one of the most important subjects on the agenda, defence, they were specifically instructed to make no commitments, because of the government's concern to avoid involvement in overseas operations in which there was no direct Canadian interest. Thus, even though not present himself, Macdonald established the precedent, carefully followed by his successors, that the Canadian contribution to imperial conferences was a matter for the prime minister to control.

Trade and Commerce and the Colonial Conference of 1894

Maintenance of prime ministerial control over the conduct of external relations was in some doubt after Macdonald's death in 1891, for the governing party was subject to "confusion and lack of direction"[39] and underwent four changes of leadership by 1896. The institutional structure, meanwhile, became more diffuse, when legislation to create the Department of Trade and Commerce, which had been passed in 1887, was proclaimed on December 5, 1892. The principal external activities of this department were trade promotion and the development of shipping, for the negotiation of commercial agreements remained with the minister of finance. Because of high-tariff policies in the United States, the new department concentrated on seeking opportunities within the empire, in the process creating a new form of Canadian representative abroad. In 1892 the department secured the services of residents of the West Indies as part-time commercial agents on honoraria of $250 per year. In the following year, the first minister of trade and commerce, Mackenzie Bowell, visited Australia, in the hope of promoting the Canadian Pacific Railway and a new transpacific shipping service as inducements to trade with Canada. One result of this excursion, two years later, was the appointment to Sydney of the first full-time trade commissioner sent out from Canada, John Short Larke.[40]

On his visit to Australia, Bowell promoted the idea of a conference of colonies interested in the Pacific trade. In 1894 the Canadian government, apparently without consulting London, called them together in Ottawa. The conference, which favoured tariff preferences among the colonies and relief from obligations imposed by some British commercial agreements, caused concern to the government in London. The colonial secretary, Lord Ripon, not only rejected these proposals but, in a circular dispatch, reminded the colonies of their subordinate status in international affairs. "To give the Colonies the power of negotiating Treaties for themselves without reference to Her Majesty's Government," Ripon asserted, "would be to give them an international status as separate and Sovereign States, and would be equivalent to breaking up the Empire."[41] Thus within a few years of Macdonald's death there was the possibility that another of his achievements, the development of Canadian means for the achievement of external objectives, would suffer reverse.

EXPANDING EXTERNAL INTERESTS, 1896–1909

The election of 1896 restored the balance in the management of external relations that had been eroded after Macdonald's death. The new prime minister, Wilfrid Laurier, reasserted the authority of his office, and the Liberal party which he headed, historically cool to imperial control, was disposed to resist constraints imposed by London. There were powerful reasons, moreover, for Laurier to assert himself in this sphere of activity. In English Canada, imperial sentiment was strong, under the stimulus of such events as Queen Victoria's diamond jubilee in 1897 and the South African war of 1899–1902. This was a development requiring a careful balancing act in view of Quebec's much more reserved attitude toward the empire. At the same time, there was a need for the settlement of outstanding issues with the United States, brought to the fore by the discovery of gold in the Yukon, whose border with Alaska was ill-defined and a potential cause of difficulty between the two countries.

Joseph Pope and external relations

Although the public service was still not a rich source of policy advice, there was within it a man who was to be of great value to Laurier in the conduct of external relations, the under-secretary of state, Joseph Pope. As a result of the capability that he demonstrated in service to Laurier, Pope would be the logical choice to head the Department of External Affairs when it was created in 1909.

Pope had gone to Ottawa in 1878 as private secretary to his uncle, James Colledge Pope, minister of marine and fisheries in Macdonald's government. The younger Pope quickly came to the attention of the prime minister, in due course becoming his private secretary. In this capacity until Macdonald's death, Pope dealt regularly with the principal political figures in the dominion. "There was scarcely a person in all Canada, prominent in church or state," he recalled later, "with whom I was not at some time or other brought into contact."[42]

Following Macdonald's death, Pope took up the position of assistant clerk of the privy council. He gained entry into the field of diplomacy in 1893, when Charles Hibbert Tupper (son of the high commissioner) took him to Paris as his private secretary for arbitration of a dispute with the United States over sealing in the Bering Sea. There Pope won praise from the British attorney general, Sir Charles Russell, for "the zeal, ability and . . . industry with which you did all that lay in your power to secure and defend the interests of Canada."[43]

In one of the last acts of the outgoing government in 1896, Pope was appointed under-secretary of state. That he retained his position after the

Liberals took office no doubt owed a good deal to his close personal ties with the Lauriers. Although privately in sympathy with the Conservative party and a biographer of Macdonald, Pope embraced the ideal of the impartial and permanent civil service. He was scrupulously non-partisan in the conduct of his official duties, for example abstaining from voting in the election of 1900.[44]

As under-secretary of state, Pope had charge of much of the correspondence dealing with Canada's external relations. He soon gave evidence of reliability in dealing with foreign representatives who had troublesome subjects on their minds. In the spring of 1897, he received a visit from a Vatican official, Mgr Merry del Val, who had been sent to Canada to investigate the Manitoba schools question. "I was not in a position to afford him any information on the subject of his mission," Pope recorded. "My personal sympathies on this question were opposed to those of the Government of the day, yet loyalty to them, as well as ordinary prudence, restrained me from opening my lips on the subject."[45] As a result of his involvement in the Bering Sea arbitration, Pope was of particular value to Laurier in dealing with relations with the United States. He was not the only official interested in external relations, however, since some subjects, such as trade and immigration, were already the responsibility of other departments.

Jurisdictional problems in London

The existence of several centres of authority in Ottawa created problems of co-ordination in doing business with other governments. In London, disagreement arose over the respective roles of the high commissioner and home departments in dealing with federal agents stationed abroad. Lord Strathcona, who, as Sir Donald Smith, succeeded the elder Sir Charles Tupper as high commissioner in 1896, was more insistent upon his authority than his predecessors had been. The trade and immigration services and the provincial representatives were all affected.

During these years the commercial service expanded considerably and acquired greater organizational formality. In 1907 the designation trade commissioner was formally adopted for all Canada-based officers serving abroad full-time; collectively they were known as the Trade Commissioner Service, with a superintendent based in Ottawa; and the term *commercial agent* was reserved for part-time representatives. By 1911 there were twenty-one trade commissioners and five part-time agents, representing Canada in South Africa, Australasia, the United Kingdom, continental Europe, Japan, China, Newfoundland, the West Indies, the Bahamas, and Latin America.

The presence after 1903 of commercial representatives in Britain (where the work had been previously done by emigration agents) led Strathcona to raise the question of jurisdiction. The Department of Trade and Commerce did not accept Strathcona's suggestion that the agents be placed under his direct control, but it did instruct them to follow his guidance as far as possible and to send him copies of their reports and expense accounts. This arrangement was particularly hard on the representative in London, Harrison Watson, whose establishment was nominally a branch of the high commissioner's office. At Strathcona's insistence, all correspondence between Watson and his department had to go via the office of the high commissioner, with the result, complained the department, that "Mr. Watson's energies were stifled to his own chagrin and regret."[46]

A similar problem arose as a result of the efforts of the minister of the interior, Clifford Sifton, to recruit immigrants. Since his campaign led him into direct correspondence with his department's agents in Britain, strain developed with the high commissioner. At its worst, the situation produced rival agents competing for immigrants in the same part of the British Isles, one loyal to the high commissioner and the other to the minister in Ottawa. The creation in 1899, at Strathcona's suggestion, of a position on his staff—inspector of agencies in Europe—with responsibility for the service in Britain and on the continent was not much help, for the incumbent, W. T. R. Preston, did not get along with the high commissioner. In 1903 Preston was removed from the high commissioner's office and placed in charge of an agency independent of it, as Canadian commissioner of emigration in Great Britain and Europe. Although the high commissioner did subsequently resume at least nominal authority over the emigration agents and could use his influence and prestige to promote their work, he ceased to be directly involved in this activity.[47]

The number of provincial representatives in London increased rapidly after Strathcona became high commissioner, with British Columbia deciding to appoint an agent general in 1901, Prince Edward Island in 1902, and Ontario and Quebec in 1908 (although the last did not fill the office until 1911). Strathcona took the position that only he had the right to deal with the Colonial Office and therefore objected when the government of British Columbia in 1908 sought recognition of the right of its agent general to the same relationship.

The high commissioner's position was upheld by Laurier and the Colonial Office. One reason, it has been suggested, was the appearance in London of high commissioners representing other dominions, the first being from New Zealand in 1905. But not all agents general were treated the same, for those from the Australian states, whose constitutional relationship with their central government was different from that of the Canadian provinces, were still allowed to deal with the British authorities.

As a result, Strathcona's policy caused considerable discontent in the Canadian provinces, whose governments felt that their representatives had been placed at a competitive disadvantage.[48]

The prime minister and imperial relations

While these differences of opinion might lead the high commissioner's office and other branches of government in Canada to work at cross purposes in specialized areas of activity, no such confusion was permitted on the larger subject of Canada's overall relationship with the empire. That was a matter over which Laurier, like Macdonald before him, retained personal control. He had good reason to do so, for the imperialist sentiment evinced by the Conservative government of Lord Salisbury, which came to power in Britain in 1895, was bound to make the issue sensitive in Canada. This was particularly true of the colonial secretary, Joseph Chamberlain, who held the office until 1903 and who occupied a more powerful place in the government than was usual for that position. Chamberlain in 1897 provided the welcome news that the British government was willing to be flexible about the application of its commercial agreements with other countries, as requested by the Colonial Conference of 1894, but his enthusiasm for a more highly centralized empire required close attention from a prime minister wishing to reconcile divergent views of the imperial relationship within Canada.

Laurier had to deal with these issues at colonial conferences in 1897, 1902, and 1907. The first was held in the year of Queen Victoria's diamond jubilee, also the occasion for Laurier's knighthood and Strathcona's elevation to the peerage. The Lauriers had a prominent place in the jubilee celebrations. In their honour, the high commissioner and his wife contributed a brilliant late-evening reception at the Imperial Institute on Dominion Day, featuring a musical program including one of Queen Victoria's favourite singers, the Canadian soprano Emma Albani (later Dame Emma).

The conference of 1897 was strictly private, and the structure encouraged the prime minister to keep Canada's participation under his personal control. It was the first such gathering specifically intended for the heads of colonial governments, and only they were admitted to the sessions. Ministers were permitted to attend the sessions in 1902, but only when subjects concerning them were under discussion.

Pope had a modest involvement in preparations for the third conference, of 1907, providing a document on which a change in the designation of future gatherings from "colonial" to "imperial" was based. The two ministers in Laurier's party, Louis-Phillipe Brodeur (Marine and Fisheries) and Sir Frederick Borden (Militia and Defence), participated, but only in discussions relevant to their portfolios. The prime minister of Australia tried to secure the admission of a senior official to the conference sessions, but he was defeated by the Colonial Office, with the support of Laurier.

The Colonial Conference of 1907 made a number of decisions that regularized procedures for the future. Meetings were to take place every four years and thenceforth to be chaired by the British prime minister rather than the colonial secretary. It was accepted that ministers might normally attend future meetings and that each participant might have two speakers per session. Ministers might on their own also attend subsidiary conferences; the first of these, concerned with defence, took place in 1909, with Brodeur and Frederick Borden representing Canada. But for full-scale imperial conferences the chief representative was still to be the prime minister, who accordingly retained his pre-eminent place in the imperial relationship.

The joint high commission and the Alaska boundary award

Laurier also kept a close eye on relations with the United States but allowed a more subsantial role to cabinet members most closely associated with the subjects under discussion. Public servants, notably Pope, also played a prominent part in dealing with these matters.

In 1898–99, the outstanding differences with the United States were considered by a joint high commission. This marked an important step forward in the conduct of Canadian external relations, especially by comparison with the Washington conference of 1871. The deliberations opened at Quebec, before moving on to Washington. Four members of the British delegation were Canadian: Laurier, Sir Louis Davies (minister of marine and fisheries), Sir Richard Cartwright (minister of trade and commerce), and John Charlton. The last, although not a cabinet minister, had been member of Parliament for Norfolk North, Ontario, for more than thirty years and was included because of his knowledge of the lumber trade, in which he had interests on both sides of the border. The premier of Newfoundland was also a member. Only the chairman, Lord Herschell, was from the United Kingdom. On the advice of the Foreign Office, the Canadians received their instructions not from London but from Ottawa. They kept in close touch with their cabinet colleagues, enabling a minister such as Sifton (interested in the Alaska boundary) to influence the proceedings.

The preparation of the Canadian case was assigned to a team of public servants. Background on the Atlantic fisheries, the Bering Sea, the Alaska boundary, and trade was requested from Pope, R. N. Venning, chief clerk for fisheries in Marine and Fisheries, W. F. King, dominion astronomer, and James G. Parmalee, deputy minister of trade and commerce. Pope in addition was named one of the secretaries of the delegation, along with Laurier's protégé Henri Bourassa, who had been elected to Parliament for the first time in 1896.

The team's work was only a limited success. The Alaska boundary, complained Herschell, "had not been thoroughly studied or thought out by any Canadian official."[49] But Pope made a good impression. He was responsible for the arrangements that enabled the delegation to work effectively. It was important, Laurier had told Davies, "to give him [Pope] quietly the general supervision of all the routine business connected with the different subjects which we will have to deal with. He can do it quietly without making himself obstrusive [*sic*] to anybody."[50] Pope lived up to expectations, arranging telephone and telegraph service, organizing the provision of press clippings to keep the delegates informed, booking hotel accommodation in Washington, and handling accounts.

Pope's involvement in Canadian-American relations continued as a result of the failure of the joint high commission to resolve the issues before it. He was one of the key participants in the Anglo-American tribunal in London that settled the Alaska boundary in 1903. To a substantial degree because of his resourcefulness, the Canadian case was much better prepared than it had been for the joint high commission. Not much had been done, however, to anticipate the US arguments and plan a strategy for dealing with them. One reason, it has been suggested, was deficiency in government organization in Ottawa: the lack of a foreign office specifically responsible for "studying all the ramifications of the question."[51] Because of dissatisfaction with the award, considerable support could be expected in Canada for the view that the episode demonstrated the need for greater local control over external relations.

Laurier caught the mood when he declared in the House of Commons "that so long as Canada remains a dependency of the British crown the present powers that we have are not sufficient for the maintenance of our rights. It is important that we should ask the British parliament for more extensive power, so that if we ever have to deal with matters of a similar nature again we shall deal with them in our own way, in our own fashion, according to the best light that we have."[52] This statement alarmed the governor general, Lord Minto, who observed that "such an arrangement would really mean independence."[53] It fascinated the US consul general in Ottawa, who reported a current of opinion that "Canada should in the future insist upon the exclusive management of all international questions which relate exclusively to Canada, without British interference or control."[54]

Yet no dramatic action followed. One reason may have been doubt about public support once the first reaction to the Alaska boundary award was past. Another may have been the lack of civil servants experienced in diplomacy. But the most convincing explanation is perhaps that offered by O. D. Skelton in his biography of Laurier: "Nothing was more foreign to Sir Wilfrid's ruling bias than to urge any policy on a general and theoretical ground; not until a concrete issue arose would the demand for wider powers be renewed. When the occasion did arise, in the Waterways treaty with the United States, in the trade conversations with European powers, in the immigration negotiations with Japan, Canada's control over foreign affairs was to be quietly, un-dogmatically but surely and steadily advanced."[55]

Trade and immigration

In its commercial negotiations, Laurier's government built on the precedents established by Galt and Tupper and on decisions taken by the unofficial colonial conference in Ottawa in 1894. The government also took advantage of the presence of foreign consular representatives in Canada to hold discussions that circumvented British channels. The governor general, Lord Minto, complained about lack of consideration, and the authorities in London argued that Canada was giving foreign consuls practically diplomatic status and threatening the diplomatic unity of the empire. Laurier, however, contended that, when territorial and commercial interests were involved, Canada's claim to treaty-making power was "right, just and should be granted."[56]

Commercial negotiations overseas proceeded more smoothly. In 1907, London was informed that Canada wished to negotiate a new trade agreement with France and also to seek one with Italy. The foreign secretary, Sir Edward Grey, told the embassies in Paris and Rome that the Ripon circular of 1895 might be disregarded, and he assured Laurier privately that Canadians could negotiate a treaty so long as the British ambassador was one of the signers. Nothing came of the Italian project, but the negotiations in Paris, conducted by the Canadian minister of finance, W. S. Fielding, with the assistance of his deputy and the minister of marine and fisheries, Brodeur, were successful, producing a treaty signed by Fielding, Brodeur, and the British ambassador in Paris, Sir Francis Bertie.

Also leading to a Canadian initiative were relations with Japan. In British Columbia there was mounting discontent over immigration from China, Japan, and India, which culminated in race riots in 1907. Dealing with Japan was particularly delicate, since it was in alliance with Britain. The federal government was interested in developing commercial links with Japan, and in 1907 Parliament approved the application to Canada of the Anglo-Japanese treaty of commerce and navigation negotiated in 1894 and 1895. The resultant failure of Ottawa to ban Japanese immigration was highly unpopular in British Columbia. In the election of 1908, it was the most important issue in the province, where the Liberals took only two of the seven seats.

The federal government dealt with the situation by sending the postmaster general, Rodolphe Lemieux, to Tokyo in 1907 to arrange a "gentlemen's agreement" whereby the Japanese themselves would limit emigration to Canada.[57] Lemieux was accompanied by Pope, whose responsibility was to prepare précis of conversations with the Japanese. The Canadians had the active assistance of the British ambassador, Sir Claude Macdonald, but co-ordination with Ottawa was not ideal. Some confusion arose because of misunderstanding as to what promises had been made to Laurier by the Japanese consul general in Canada, prompting the Colonial Office to comment pointedly on "the danger and inconvenience of allowing consular officers to discharge semi-diplomatic functions."[58]

As negotiations continued, the Canadian government was not kept fully up-to-date, for Lemieux sent only brief summaries of developments by telegram, leaving the detailed explanations of his actions to follow by mail. The attitude in Ottawa therefore was not sympathetic when the agreement negotiated by Lemieux differed in some of its clauses from the cabinet's directions. Although Pope wrote to Laurier in defence of the draft,[59] Lemieux was recalled and the agreement was rejected by the prime minister. One more to the cabinet's liking was reached subsequently, the details of implementation being worked out in Ottawa with the Japanese consul general.

Dealing with the United States

Remaining for settlement was a heavy agenda of outstanding items with the United States. Laurier, somewhat cool toward that country since the Alaska boundary award, was less vigorous than he had been in dealing with these problems. The governor general, Lord Grey, in contrast, was much interested in a comprehensive settlement, as was Elihu Root, who became US secretary of state in 1905. The process was aided by James Bryce, British ambassador (as the position had become in 1893) from 1907 until 1913. Making their task difficult was the lack of a central clearinghouse for external issues in Canada, which complicated the already circuitous process of communication with the United States on major issues, via the governor general and London.

The handling of these matters might have been facilitated by the presence of a Canadian representative in Washington. Grey suspected that there were such representatives there from time to time, but on missions informal and indeed clandestine in nature. The practice, he observed in 1906, was undesirable:

Laurier, not feeling in touch with the British machinery entrusted with the duty of fighting his battle for him, sometimes has secret agents of his own at Washington and is always suspected by our Embassy at Washington of working behind their backs. Now this is obviously an evil state of things, and you will I feel sure agree with me that it is desirable to bring my Ministers and the British Embassy into closer touch and to establish a feeling of mutual goodwill and confidence with the object of securing a good working relationship between Ottawa and our Embassy at Washington.[60]

Grey would have liked to have a Canadian attached to the British embassy as an adviser to the ambassador on Canadian issues. Both the Foreign and Colonial offices, however, opposed his suggestion. The colonial secretary, Lord Elgin, affirmed that "the Imperial Government still remains in charge of the foreign relations of even the greatest of the colonies, and I think the argument for the staff of the Embassies remaining wholly Imperial is of the strongest."[61]

Some other means therefore had to be found to deal with Canadian relations with the United States, especially those that were of no direct concern to the United Kingdom. One such was waterways which flowed along or across the border. The matter first received attention at a conference on irrigation in Albuquerque, New Mexico, in 1895, at which Mexico and Canada as well as some American states were represented. Organizational change was slow to follow, but in 1905 Canada and the United States joined in the International Waterways Commission, on which each country had three members. This body had the power merely to make recommendations to the two governments, but four years later, under the terms of the boundary waters treaty, it was supplanted by the International Joint Commission, which could make decisions regarding the level and flow of boundary waters. In accordance with the usual practice, the boundary waters treaty was between the United Kingdom and the United States, but negotiations on the British side were conducted by the chairman of the Canadian section of the waterways commission, George Gibbons, and membership of the International Joint Commission was confined to Canadians and Americans, again three to a side.[62] Much of the commission's work was technical and involved matters of detail, but the subject-matter was a major component of Canada's external relations, which by the boundary waters treaty was transferred from British to Canadian hands.

Two other bodies created tentatively in 1908 were intended to regulate relations between the two countries: a highly successful boundary commission, finally made permanent in 1923, responsible for monuments demarcating the frontier, and a fisheries commission, which disappeared less than six years later, after the US House of Representatives failed to approve regulations it recommended. A similar fate met innovations that might have improved the capacity of the Canadian Parliament to deal with certain aspects of Canadian-American relations. In 1909 the House of Commons created committees on forests, waterways, and waterpower and on marine and fisheries, both of which had an interest in cross-border problems. Neither became very active, for the reason, it has been suggested, that the subjects they dealt with did not affect interest groups large enough to demand constant attention.[63]

Even if all the agencies devised to deal with specialized aspects of Canadian-US relations had been successful, they would not have been sufficient to introduce order into Canada's handling of the broad range of issues awaiting settlement between the two countries, let alone the dominion's expanding interests overseas. Nor was there adequate provision for this activity elsewhere in the machinery of government. Although Pope as under-secretary of state was the official through whom the ministry dealt with the governor general, he did not draw on the resources of his department for support in his various external activities. His role in assembling documents, drafting memoranda and dispatches, providing advice, and taking part in negotiations was a personal one that went far beyond the terms of reference of his official position. On his own, as Grey observed, Pope had become "the non-official Foreign Office of the Canadian Govt."[64]

Pope's long and varied experience in government enabled him to understand the intricacies and defects in the system for handling correspondence among departments and with the governor general. The Alaska boundary issue was particularly revealing of the problems involved. In preparing the Canadian case, Pope found himself building "bricks without straw." "You may be surprised at my requests for what are elementary papers," he warned John Anderson of the Colonial Office. "Alaska matters have always been referred to the Minister of the Interior, and though I say it with bated breath, never properly dealt with. We sadly lack system here."[65] When the proceedings of the tribunal came to an end, the minister, Sifton, was surprised to learn that Canada had no designated repository for the accumulated papers. It was left to Pope to try to be the unofficial keeper of whatever Canadian records these international negotiations required. Intolerant of confusion and muddle and anticipating more such negotiations, he was driven to try for improvement in the system and to recommend creation of a full government department responsible for the dominion's external affairs.

Chapter Two
Foundation of the Department: 1909–1911

Pope, Grey, and Bryce

THE IDEA OF A CANADIAN department of external affairs was suggested by a Winnipeg journalist, W. Sanford Evans, in 1901, but was not put forth within the government until somewhat later. The first to do so was Joseph Pope. The importance of the international negotiations of the previous two decades, Pope suggested to Laurier in 1904, warranted the keeping of records in a department "charged with all the matters of a quasi-diplomatic character."[1] Pope for one was weary of trying belatedly to collect documents dispersed over several departments. Besides the frustrations caused by delays in the retrieval of records, he found it embarrassing when he had to ask the British for copies of papers because nobody knew where to find originals that were supposed to be in Canada. Laurier, however, took no notice of these inconveniences.

While Laurier might ignore Pope's complaints, he could not overlook the problems of the civil service as a whole, which had suffered a decline in the quality of entrants since 1882.[2] As the years went by, Laurier had become less tolerant of lax administration, and he was under growing pressure to make improvements at all levels: attacks on patronage were features of the opposition's campaigns in the elections of 1904 and 1908 and of its criticisms of the government for various scandals in the parliamentary sessions of 1906, 1907, and 1908. To deal with the problem, the government in 1907 appointed a royal commission to study the civil service. The hearings of this commission provided the opportunity for Pope to return to his project of creating a department of external affairs.

Pope wrote the commmissioners a lengthy memorandum in which he pointed out the need for "a more systematic mode of dealing with what I may term, for want of a better phrase, the *external affairs* of the Dominion." After describing the existing procedure, he commented on the adverse effect of dispersing responsibility for external matters among a number of departments. "If it is an important despatch," he wrote, "the policy of the Government in regard to the principle involved is, no doubt, discussed and agreed to in Council; but the terms of the report are almost invariably left to the department to which the despatch was originally referred. Under this mode of dealing with official correspondence there is no uniformity of system or continuity of plan."[3]

Some time later, Pope revealed even more substantial flaws in the system. As time permitted, Laurier, as president of the privy council, would read out to the assembled cabinet ministers a few lines of even the most routine dispatches, which in 1908 numbered 1,596, until some clue to their contents was ascertained and they were directed to the appropriate ministers. Everything depended on the prime minister's memory when, months or years afterward, subsequent dispatches on the same subject were distributed. Since no records were kept of where documents went, it often took a reminder from the Colonial Office to get a civil servant onto the trail of an unanswered dispatch. And, because more than one department might be concerned with an issue, both knowledge and records tended to be scattered among officials who individually did not know how to respond. The results were haphazard files and undue reliance on the memory of a few public servants.

Pope also expressed concern, in his memorandum to the commissioners, that "in Downing Street, Canadian dispatches are noted for diversity rather than for elegance of style." He therefore recommended that all dispatches be referred to one department, whose staff would be trained in the study of diplomatic questions and the conduct of correspondence. If a new branch of government could not be created, he suggested this work should be done under the aegis of the secretary of state, who would then preside over a department dealing with both internal and external affairs.

Pope's ideas received little consideration from the commission, which was concerned mainly with the appointment, promotion, and classification of public servants. Outside the commission, however, others in positions of power shared Pope's dissatisfaction with the prevailing confusion. In the cabinet, after his experience in Tokyo and later attempts to obtain documents from the British government, the postmaster general,

Rodolphe Lemieux, complained about the inadequacy of the Foreign Office as a source of information. "If my suggestion had been listened to years ago," Pope reminded Lemieux, "we should not have to ask anybody for these papers today, for we should have had them ourselves."[4]

The governor general, Lord Grey, and the British ambassador in Washington, James Bryce, also wanted change. Grey was "restless and interfering," an enthusiast who as governor general refused to be a figurehead.[5] Determined to play a first-hand role in the diplomacy of the period, in 1908 he made creation of a department of external affairs an objective.

In Washington, Bryce claimed that three-quarters of his embassy's workload concerned Canada. A forthright man impatient with delay, he set out to deal with Ottawa direct rather than through the circuitous procedure involving the Colonial Office, but he soon learned that speedier conduct of business did not necessarily follow. He had to cope with Laurier's inclination to procrastinate and his tendency under the strain of overwork to forget what position his government had previously taken on a question. In Ottawa, moreover, diplomatic correspondence often ended up in the hands of subordinate clerks where it could sit for weeks, sorely trying the patience of the American officials with whom the embassy had to deal. Bryce soon concluded, therefore, that Canada badly needed "a sort of Foreign Office" to which the various questions under discussion with the United States could be referred.[6]

Bryce raised the matter with Laurier and the governor general when he visited Ottawa in February 1908. Laurier promised to take action, much to Bryce's relief, "for the inconveniences of the present system or rather want of a system can hardly be overstated." Bryce also hoped that the head of the new department would visit Washington from time to time to consult the ambassador and that Canadian specialists would be sent there whenever necessary, "not merely to assist the Embassy but also to satisfy the Canadians that their cases are being fully stated and competently argued."[7] These ideas had the support of Grey, who wrote to the colonial secretary the following month about his difficulties with the existing system:

> There is no Department, no official through whose hands all matters dealing with External Affairs must go. Consequently, there is no record, no continuity, no method, no consistency. I have represented all this to Laurier, who agrees with every word I say. He regrets that he did not, when he came into office 11 years ago, create a Department. Well it is not too late now. Do it now, I urge. I fear that I must wait till after the elections, he replies. I trust I may be able to overcome this fatal procrastination. We only have three men in the Government Service

who have any knowledge of details connected with Canada's foreign relations. One drinks at times, the other has a difficulty in expressing his thoughts, and conversation with him is as difficult as it is to extract an extra tight cork, and the third is the Under-Secretary of State, Pope—a really first class official. Not a day should be lost in putting him in charge of a Department of External Affairs under Sir Wilfrid Laurier, and in a short time he would be able to train one or two young men who would take up his work after he has gone. He would have the papers on every question in good shape. Sir W. Laurier's work would be ever so much facilitated, and Canada would be prompt and satisfactory to deal with, instead of the swollen impossible cork, the extraction of which almost bursts a bloodvessel.[8]

The Colonial Office doubted that a new department alone would provide a complete solution. "One main cause of delay," it was observed there, "is perhaps to be found in the rule by which all political questions other than mere matters of routine are discussed and decided by the Cabinet of the Dominion." But, since this was "a system which is hardly likely to be altered at an early date,"[9] the colonial secretary, the Earl of Elgin, was inclined to agree that a department under the direct control of the prime minister would facilitate dealing with external questions.

A change in imperial organization also contributed to the need for a more efficient channel of communication between the United Kingdom and Canada. The Colonial Conference of 1907 had called for establishment of a permanent imperial secretariat for handling correspondence related to future conferences. After a visit to Ottawa from an official of that secretariat, Laurier created in the Privy Council Office an additional position of clerk for imperial and foreign correspondence. On April 21, 1908, William MacKenzie, a Liberal party stalwart and a member of the Press Gallery, was appointed to the position. Pope was not impressed. "This is carrying out my scheme in a fashion though not exactly in the way I intended," he observed. "I should not have thought that MacKenzie's training as a newspaperman was such as to fit him for the duties of a diplomatist, but the press of the country (and indeed, Sir Wilfrid Laurier) seem to think differently."[10] MacKenzie's position was seriously affected by this judgment of Pope's. Although MacKenzie remained in the Privy Council Office as a docketer and registrar of correspondence and was twice sent by Laurier's successor on important missions to Washington, Pope refused to include him in his plans.

Whatever his merits might have been, MacKenzie single-handed could not have met the expectations of those pressing for a full-fledged department of external affairs. Bryce, therefore, continued to experience difficulties in his attempts to get on with negotiations with the Americans.

The loss of time incurred in "this constant breaking the chain of negotiations and then trying to rivet the sundered links afresh . . . is so great that really nothing seems so urgent as to create at once the needed department," he complained to Grey.[11] But now a new colonial secretary, Lord Crewe, expressed the misgiving that such a department might detract from Britain's paramountcy in foreign relations:

> I shall rather dread the establishment of a regular Foreign Department with a minister all to itself, which might be likely to undertake, or at any rate to attempt, independent action in matters upon which we here, and the Foreign Office in particular, ought to have a preliminary word. On the other hand, if it were a question of fitting out the Prime Minister with a small Foreign Bureau containing one or two experienced permanent officials who would give their whole time to these questions and to nothing else, and who would be able to put pressure upon the Prime Minister to deal with such matters when they were urgent, instead of postponing them to other matters of domestic interest, I think that nothing but good could result.[12]

Grey informed the colonial secretary that everyone in the Canadian cabinet agreed that something had to be done and assured him that there need be no concern about independence. The minister of finance, W. S. Fielding, Grey reported, was prepared to support the project by finding the money for additonal salaries but was at the same time a staunch defender of the imperial connection. But even if Crewe were reassured, Laurier remained an obstacle to prompt action. The subject came to a head at the end of a long parliamentary session, and the prime minister would promise Grey only that he would take it up when the house reassembled after the election of 1908.[13]

Drafting the legislation

Once re-elected, Laurier kept his promise to Grey, informing Pope in September 1908 that cabinet had agreed to establish a department of external affairs and that Pope would be made its deputy head. "If they really mean this," Pope noted in his diary, "it is a welcome piece of news. To tell the truth I have been feeling discouraged and disheartened over the apathy with which my suggestions have been received."[14]

As early as January 1908 Pope had begun drafting a bill to establish a department, although he did not submit a text to Laurier until February 1909. Pope's draft, based on the situation as it had evolved under Laurier, provided in its key third clause that

The Secretary of State for External Affairs shall be charged with the direction of all matters relating to the external affairs of the Dominion, including the conduct and management, in so far as appertains to the Government of Canada, of such international and inter-colonial negotiations as are now pending, and others that may, from time to time, arise. All communications from the Secretary of State for the Colonies, or from any other authority within the Empire, or from His Majesty's Ambassador in the United States, or other member of His Majesty's diplomatic or consular service abroad, touching matters other than those of internal concern, shall be referred to the Secretary of State for External Affairs and be dealt with by him.[15]

Between February and the time the bill was presented to the House of Commons in early March, the Department of Justice made a number of changes in Pope's draft, which he did not see until they became public in Parliament. This development enabled the minister of justice, Allen Aylesworth, to become the primary influence on Laurier in the creation of the department. Aylesworth was well placed to take advantage of the opportunity, since he was a close friend of the prime minister and they had similar views on most issues of the day, especially imperialism. They were temperamentally and intellectually congenial, and Laurier trusted Aylesworth completely.[16] The latter, according to his testimony during debate on the external affairs bill, had been interested in international relations for some time, and he had had personal experience of the activity as a member of the Alaska boundary tribunal. Like Laurier, he had been disillusioned with British diplomacy as a result of the award.

One of the changes made by the Department of Justice in drafting the bill placed the proposed department under the secretary of state rather than the prime minister, as Grey and Pope would have preferred. Pope was later told by the secretary of state, Charles Murphy, that the alteration was a result of Aylesworth's influence. Although Pope had once been willing to contemplate placing external affairs under the secretary of state, he was disappointed by the decision to give the department less prestigious ministerial direction. All he could do, however, was denounce the course chosen as "a great mistake."[17]

There were other changes as well, the most important of which was the third clause, drafted by Aylesworth and differing substantially from Pope's version: "The Secretary of State, as head of the Department, shall have the conduct of all official communications between the Government of Canada and the Government of any other country, and shall be charged with such other duties as may, from time to time, be assigned to the department by order of the Governor in Council in relation to such external

35

affairs, or to the conduct and management of international or intercolonial negotiations so far as they may appertain to the Government of Canada.''

Pope disapproved of giving the secretary of state "the conduct of all official communications" with other governments because of the implication that Canada could carry on direct negotiations, thereby diminishing the imperial relationship. Grey too disliked the clause, which he regarded as "an improper attempt to shelve the governor general."[18] In its defence of the bill, the government insisted that no constitutional change was intended: officially at least, the creation of a department of external affairs was intended to improve the efficiency of Canada's government, not to assert its independence in international affairs, although Laurier and Aylesworth no doubt were aware that it could also assist the latter objective, a prospect that they would not have found unwelcome.

THE EXTERNAL AFFAIRS ACT OF 1909

Response to the bill

On March 4, 1909, the secretary of state, Charles Murphy, proposed that the House of Commons consider creation of a department of external affairs. Using notes prepared by Pope, Murphy asserted in his short opening speech that no abrupt departure from the status quo was involved, as no constitutional change or alteration in the position of the governor general was contemplated. The government's aim was merely "an improvement in the administration of that class of public affairs which related to matters other than those of purely internal concern."[19] This argument was reinforced by Laurier, who described the increasing volume of questions relating to external affairs. "We have," he contended, "attained such development as a nation that in order to deal with these matters, we must have a department for the purpose. It is not intended it shall be a very numerous department, a very heavy department . . . . But I think it is essential that we should have this department by itself, with nothing else to do but to give their special attention and all their attention, to these matters alone."

The principal spokesmen for the opposition were Robert Borden, leader of the Conservative party since 1901, and Sir George Foster, a former minister of finance (1888-96). Drawing attention to a feature already well established in the conduct of Canadian external relations, Borden gave it as his personal preference that, if the new department had to be created, it be placed under the prime minister. Foster dealt with another entrenched Canadian practice, the assignment of specific international issues to various domestic departments. In this regard, the crucial activity would be the drafting of replies to dispatches by trained officials of the new department. In Foster's view this function properly belonged to the minister of the department with substantive responsibility. That minister, he argued, "is the man who has to determine the policy and is the man who has to lay down the tenor of the despatch and submit it to his colleagues." "You may bring from that bureau [External Affairs]," he warned, "all that your new-fledged diplomats may pen on paper but the minister whose department is chiefly affected will say 'I do not agree with some parts of it, I will have to think it over' and then your merry-go-round starts again." If External Affairs were to do the drafting, Foster went on,

you must have a replica of every department of the government in the Department of Secretary of State [that is, External Affairs], men who are as able as the ministers of the departments are, men who are just as well up in their history as the ministers of the departments; consequently you are to have, if you are going to have an effective service, a very costly and numerous service. . . . I believe that difficulties and practical difficulties will be encountered in that respect which I doubt if the right honourable gentleman has thoroughly weighed. The objection I have to this system is that it is not effective unless you make a most thorough, expensive and expert system and have in the department some man who knows as much about every department in the government as does the responsible minister himself in reference to its history and circumstances. . . . No outside bureaucrat can have the atmosphere of the department who has not yet been brought up to the work and who does not know the history of it.

Because of the difficulty of co-ordinating the interests of various departments and the high degree of confidentiality that some subjects involved, Foster argued that external affairs should be dealt with by "a little body of expert clerks [attached] to the Privy Council," working under the direction of the prime minister.

In the debate that followed, Laurier went somewhat beyond the position that the new department was to be merely an administrative convenience. The department, he said, was to be "not only a clerical one. . . . There is to be a permanent official, the Under-Secretary of State for External Affairs, whose duty and business would be to keep posted from day to day on the external history of Canada as it progresses. . . . We want a department in which the history of all these despatches will be kept and followed from day to day." He was not troubled by the possibility of conflict with other branches of government, for it was his expectation that, "when a question had been the subject of communication from day to day or week to week for some time, the Department of External Affairs would probably be able to answer it on the spot without reference to any other department." Thus it would assume more than a post-office role.

Laurier acknowledged that it might be sufficient to assign external affairs to staff in the Privy Council Office or the Department of the Secretary of State, but he wanted to give the work "the dignity and importance of a department by itself, as is done in other countries." Although vague in defining what the limits of the activities of the new department would be, he knew that what his government was creating had more than administrative significance. Indeed, he indicated discreetly that this was his intention. "All governments," he asserted, "have found it necessary to have a department whose only business shall be to deal with relations with foreign countries, and in our judgement Canada has reached a period in her history when we should follow the example of other countries in that respect." The department was not to function as a true foreign office for some years, but Laurier arranged that the legislative authority to do so would already be in place when the time came.

To ensure this possibility, Laurier had to overcome opposition from the governor general (supported by Pope) to the third clause of the bill. As a civil servant, Pope did not act on behalf of Grey, but he did discuss the issue with W. H. Walker, a lawyer who was an experienced member of the governor general's staff. Pope chose to regard the provision that the secretary of state should "have the conduct of all official communications between the Government of Canada and the Government of any other country" as "a bit of clumsy drafting" and hoped that Walker would devise something better. Walker, however, saw no untoward implication, in view of the government's position that no change was intended in the functions of the governor general.[20]

Grey meanwhile believed that he had obtained a promise from Laurier to substitute the word "care" for "conduct" as the activity of the secretary of state. But Laurier neglected to have the change made during the course of the debate. He was under no political pressure to do so, since the opposition did not focus on the third clause, even though that clause could have been viewed as a means of developing and conducting an autonomous foreign policy. In fact, the debate in the House of Commons lasted less than two hours and involved no expression of divergent views of the country's international position.

By avoiding fundamental issues in the debate, the government undoubtedly expedited creation of the department, but with important consequences for its future development. The debate did little to clarify the role of the Canadian government, and hence of the administrative branch given responsibility for the subject, in the making of the country's foreign policy. Both the larger question of international autonomy and the smaller one of the responsibilities of the department, therefore, remained for pragmatic solution by ministers and their civil service advisers in response to changing international, imperial, and domestic circumstances. The same was true of the administrative requirements of the new department, even though they had been the focus of the debate. Spokesmen for the government, it appears from what they said, had not given much thought to how they proposed to go about reforming the system, and the comments of the opposition were not sufficiently persistent to force them to make more detailed plans.

The lack of controversy in Parliament carried over to the reception of the legislation by the press. No comment at all appeared in the major French-language newspapers, and only seven of the largest English-language dailies published editorials on the subject. Such scant attention suggests that the debate had not stirred much interest in the country at large, but the editorials did ventilate the administrative and constitutional considerations underlying the external affairs bill.

The *Winnipeg Tribune* was the bluntest opponent, claiming on March 5 that there were already too many departments in Ottawa and too many "idle men" working in them. The Ottawa papers followed the same theme, with the *Journal* of March 8 reluctantly accepting the new department as a clerical body as long as responsibility for handling foreign correspondence remained with the prime minister. The *Citizen* of March 6 was prepared to approve the designation of an official responsible for international matters, but not a department.

The watchdog of imperial interests, the Toronto *Mail and Empire*, did not see the department as a step toward Canadian nationhood and therefore (on March 5) expressed no objection to its collecting and collating documents. The enthusiastic reception given by the *Montreal Daily Star* on March 5 and the Regina *Morning Leader* on March 10 was in marked contrast, for they did regard the department as an instrument of self-reliance. "That business is bound to grow as our external relations become more ramified and important," commented the *Star*, and "it is only a question of time in any case until we shall have to get not only a department but a Minister to deal with it. Then there is the effect upon our people of calling their attention strikingly to the fact that this country has far-reaching 'external relations'. We are far too prone to take a parish view of our responsibilities and we cannot have the fact brought home to us too forcibly that we are in touch with the world."

The constitutional implications of the legislation were not lost upon official foreign observers stationed in Canada. The French consul general in Montreal, Joseph de Loynes, interpreted the creation of the department as a step affirming Canada's "indépendance diplomatique."[21] In Washington, a report from the US consul general in Ottawa, J. G. Foster, was put before the secretary of state, with comments by one of the assistant secretaries drawing attention to both the administrative convenience and the constitutional development likely to result from the work of the new branch of government: "This is an interesting matter. Such a measure could hardly have been adopted without the approval of the Home Government. It is a step toward an international relation of Canada to foreign powers, like that which Egypt possesses under the Sultan's decree of autonomy. The right of Canada to negotiate treaties directly with foreign states has been discussed in the Canadian Parliament, and talked of in London, as a solution to the difficulties growing out of the present dilatory conduct of even trifling matters through the Circumlocution Office in London."[22]

The governor general, too, was aware of the possible constitutional importance of the bill. He was troubled in particular by the effect that creation of the department might have on his own position, because of Laurier's failure to amend the third clause to give the secretary of state the "care" rather than the "conduct" of international communications. Discreetly aided by Pope, Grey continued to press for the change.

When the bill had passed second reading in the Senate, Grey decided to remind Laurier of his promise. He also saw Murphy and Aylesworth and was assured by all three that an amendment would be forthcoming. Yet a few days later the bill passed the Senate without change. Grey then pressed for an amending act. Laurier responded with the assurance that the government had had no ulterior motive and that it had "no thought of interfering with the well-settled principle that the Governor General has the conduct of foreign and imperial relations." Since both houses had already passed the legislation, he was disinclined to put forward an amendment immediately, instead offering the prospect of a bill during the next session of Parliament. Although still unsatisfied, Grey had to accept Laurier's assurances and agree to give assent to the bill.[23]

Grey's anxieties were not taken very seriously in London, where a Liberal government had come to power in 1905. Although determined not to concede control over foreign policy to the dominions, this government was not committed, as its predecessor had been, to imperial centralization. It had also recognized the distinction between the self-governing dominions and the crown colonies by creating a Dominions Department within the Colonial Office in 1907.[24]

A sanguine view of the legislation received encouragement in London from *The Times*. Reporting on February 19, 1909, the newspaper's correspondent in Canada treated its intent as administrative improvement rather than constitutional change. The object as he saw it was "practically to create a clearing house between all the branches of the Canadian public service and the Colonial Office."

A similar view prevailed in the Colonial Office, where the question of "conduct" was treated as academic. "There is," an official stated, "a great deal of fuss here about nothing.''[25] The Colonial Office acquiesced in Grey's desire to strike an agreement about an amending bill but did not want a serious quarrel with Laurier. The British government was not inclined to offer a public challenge to the Canadian position when Sir Gilbert Parker, an Ontario-born member of Parliament at Westminster and a promoter of imperial unity, asked about the effect of the proposed department of external affairs on the authority of the British government. "This Department," replied the prime minister, Herbert Asquith, "is merely intended—like the Corresponding Department of the Commonwealth Government [of Australia]—to conduct correspondence with the Secretary of State for the Colonies, and His Majesty's Ambassador at Washington, and with the several departments of the Canadian Government. . . . No suggestion has been made by the Canadian Government for the increase of their powers in dealing with external affairs.''[26]

The bill assented to and sustained

The bill establishing the Department of External Affairs received royal assent on May 19 and took effect on June 1, 1909. With the help of Pope, Grey then set about getting the change he wanted. When Parliament reassembled in the autumn of 1909, Pope raised the issue of amendment with his minister, Murphy, but the latter was opposed to concessions. The proposed change, he said, would make the department "a mere filing office" and would draw undesirable attention to a branch of government "not popular with some of my colleagues, and still less so with many of the Government supporters.''[27] In due course, he advised Laurier to let "sleeping dogs lie." Since it was Grey who was most concerned about this issue, Murphy suggested, Laurier could safely await his departure from Canada within a few months, in the expectation that his successor "will never dream of raising such an objection.''[28]

Laurier followed Murphy's advice, and Grey left Canada without securing the protection he wanted for the role of the governor general in external affairs. The best he could do was to ensure that the holder of the office be kept abreast of the dossier. When he informed Bryce that he (Bryce) could correspond with the department, Grey insisted on receiving copies on the ground that his good offices could be used to push things along in the proper direction. Bryce agreed, assuring Grey that the "really important correspondence" would continue to be directed to the governor general.[29] That was the most Grey's successors could expect, for the amending legislation was never introduced.

Either as an administrative device or as a potential instrument for enlarging the involvement of a dominion in international affairs, the Canadian Department of External Affairs had no true equivalent elsewhere in the self-governing territories of the British Empire. The Australian department of the same name was not a counterpart. It had some responsibilities not possessed by the Canadian, most notably for relations between the central government and the Australian states, and its overseas links were more limited, being confined mainly to the imperial channel with London. Although a department of external affairs was established in New Zealand in 1919, the purpose was mainly to administer the League of Nations mandate over Samoa. A department of external affairs was not established in the Union of South Africa until 1927. In Canada, by contrast, the government from 1909 had the means not only to enhance its efficiency in handling external relations but also to increase its authority over them as the opportunity arose.

ORGANIZING THE DEPARTMENT

The minister and the under-secretary

Realization of the new legislation's potential would be determined by the use made of it by governments and their officials. From the first, it was clear that the pace would be set by the prime minister. The secretary of state's jurisdiction proved to be something of a smoke-screen, for Laurier continued to dominate the formulation of foreign policy and established a close and direct relationship with the new department. Thus from the start the department depended for credibility on its ability to serve the objectives of the prime minister, and it may have gained a certain cachet from the special relationship that developed.

But there was also, as Pope had expected, a disadvantage resulting from the act, which did not provide for designation of a secretary of state for external affairs. Although Murphy, on Laurier's instruction, signed over that title,[30] he had been sworn in only as secretary of state. As a result, there was no one clearly identified in cabinet or in public as the ministerial spokesman for the Department of External Affairs. Whatever Laurier's intention, therefore, External Affairs was vulnerable to treatment as an appendage of the Department of the Secretary of State rather than as a branch of government like the others, equal in standing to such prestigious ministries, founded at Confederation, as Finance and Justice.

In this situation, the new department's effectiveness depended heavily on its deputy minister, designated under-secretary of state for external affairs at the suggestion of Pope. There had never been much doubt that Pope would be the first to hold the office. A vigorous fifty-four and the beneficiary of long experience of Canada's external relations, Pope could slide easily into his new position and become the architect of the department. The task would receive his undivided attention, since he gave up his position as permanent head of the Department of the Secretary of State when he took over External Affairs.

As an upholder of the imperial connection and of Grey's interpretation of the role of the governor general, Pope was not likely to exploit the autonomist implications of the External Affairs Act. Nor was he likely to become a source of serious rivalries with other branches of government. He did not display much interest in activities that were the preserve of other departments, such as trade relations and immigration, and so had little incentive to challenge their authority. He also had a rather narrow conception of his own department's role. He saw it not as a producer of policy initiatives but as a repository of knowledge and an instrument for the implementation of ministerial directives. He was, in short, well suited to creating and running a department assigned a limited range of external activities, the objectives and scope of which were determined by ministers in response to evolving needs and opportunities.

Pope's appointment was announced on June 2, 1909. On the same day, Grey warned Bryce against expecting too much right away from the new department: "No room has yet been assigned to the office. Mr. Pope has not even got a table to write on, or a chair to sit in; no cupboards in which to put his papers and his books, and as he is a gentleman who moves with dignity and deliberation some time must elapse to enable him to settle down comfortably in the midst of his new surroundings, before he is in a position to tackle the business of his office."[31] Pope had reservations about Laurier's desire that the department be launched as soon as possible. "I have not sufficient clerical assistance . . . ," he complained to Murphy on June 30, 1909. "We have to design books, forms and in fact to think out a whole system in detail."[32] The prime minister's wish, however, was not to be denied, with the result that Pope had to design his department, find resources for it, establish its relationship with others, and superintend its substantive work, all at the same time.

Pope's first problem in carrying out these tasks was with his minister, Murphy. The latter was a man of combative temperament and not particularly respectful of the eminence that his under-secretary had gained over the years. "Mr. Murphy," Pope complained to his diary in March 1910, "has directed that all despatches from the G[overnor] G[eneral]'s office be sent to *him* instead of to me. I have never experienced such a lack of confidence from my chief before and I am old to begin."[33] More important, however, was the relationship with the prime minister, because of the close attention Laurier paid to the external affairs dossier. According to Pope,

all important subjects of negotiation were laid by me before the prime minister, according to Sir Wilfrid's instructions. He discussed them with me, and when he had decided on a line of action (which might or might not be in accordance with the view of the Department immediately concerned, or perhaps before the despatch had reached that department) I would, after acquainting that department with the Prime Minister's wishes, prepare a report to be signed—not however by the Prime Minister, but by the Secretary of State, whose first knowledge of the subject was thus a cut and dried report set before him to sign.[34]

Laurier's support helped to establish the credibility of External Affairs with other departments. As the civil servant responsible for a new and untried branch of the administration, Pope had to deal with challenges to his authority after his appointment as under-secretary of state for external affairs. These were no doubt encouraged by the comparatively humble standing of Pope's nominal chief: "Some of the Ministers, or at any rate their Deputies," the under-secretary observed in concluding his reflections on his relationship with Murphy and Laurier, "did not relish the idea of reporting to the Governor-in-Council through . . . a Junior Minister." Gradually, however, as it became apparent that Pope had the backing of the prime minister, all but one of the other deputies became co-operative. The exception was the most junior, Thomas Mulvey, Pope's successor as under-secretary of state.

Mulvey had arrived in Ottawa after six years as assistant provincial secretary of Ontario. Pope did not take easily to this newcomer sitting in his old chair, behind his old desk, issuing orders in areas of responsibility that had been Pope's for the previous thirteen years. Their correspondence is filled with objections by each to alleged encroachments on his jurisdiction by the other. "I think perhaps the root of the difficulty," Pope told Mulvey, "is to be found in the erroneous view generally held in this community that the office of the Secretary of State is necessarily one and indivisible; . . . and that the office of the Secretary of State of External Affairs is, if not exactly subordinate, at any rate, a lesser dignity which has been evolved from the former."[35]

The irritant between Pope and Mulvey that was most important for the Department of External Affairs involved communication with the lieutenant-governors of the provinces. Murphy, with the backing of Mulvey, insisted on having all correspondence routed through himself, producing a cumbersome procedure for responding to provincial needs. When he had been under-secretary of state, Pope had had the authority to deal expeditiously with those provincial interests that might be affected by the international aspects of his office. Now the task was complicated by the requirement to work, as a matter of form, through another branch of the federal government.

Apart from losing the right to correspond with provincial governments, Pope's authority as under-secretary of state for external affairs does not seem to have suffered from his disagreements with Mulvey. Pope brought with him to External Affairs the various diplomatic tasks that he had performed in his former capacity and added some new ones appropriate to this specialized branch of government. Passport issuance was transferred to External Affairs. Research for the production of dossiers of confidential documents consumed a good deal of time. Pope continued to be an important participant in international negotiations involving Canada, and his department's role as a channel of communication gave it an interest in commercial relations, immigration, and defence, although they were the primary responsibility of other departments.

The staff

The staff assigned to deal with these activities would not be large. Up until 1908, the standard departmental organization provided for a deputy minister, principal and chief clerks, and junior clerical help, with most employees in the last category performing routine tasks. The Department of the Interior had 642 employees in Ottawa in 1909, but many other departments were very small. Trade and Commerce had a total headquarters staff of 25, Secretary of State before External Affairs was created had 34, Justice had 49, and even Finance had only 123, of whom 30 were located outside the capital.[36] External Affairs would be very much at the bottom of the range: during debate in the House of Commons, Laurier, Murphy, and Aylesworth had variously estimated total strength at three to five.

Pope did not demand a large staff, but he did make it a condition of his appointment that Walker of the governor general's office join him as his assistant. Walker's experience in handling correspondence in the governor general's office and his knowledge of treaties made him a valuable asset to Pope. He could manage affairs when Pope was absent. Next to Pope, Walker had a better appreciation than anyone in the civil service of how external business should be conducted. But impressive though they might be, Walker's qualities did not bring him instant promotion when he joined External Affairs. While Pope wanted him designated assistant under-secretary, Murphy would not sanction the change. For the time being, therefore, Walker's rank was chief clerk, the same as it had been in the office of the governor general; advancement to assistant under-secretary came only in 1912. From the time he entered the department, however, he was clearly second in command, although another chief clerk, A. Brophy, was transferred from Secretary of State and remained with External Affairs until 1911.

While Pope and Walker attended to the larger issues, there was a small support staff to deal with matters of routine. These too were limited in scope. There was no provision for a Canadian system of confidential communication with government agents abroad. Until 1926, all official correspondence continued to pass through the governor general's office, where it was decoded or encyphered and registered. Nor was there a sophisticated filing system. Files under 566 titles were opened in 1909. According to the procedure instituted in that year and retained without change until 1940, they were not grouped according to subject but were simply numbered consecutively as they were created. If a topic had several subdivisions, the various parts of the file were differentiated by letter. In principle, new files were to be created annually, with the last two digits of the year added to the file number as a suffix. This practice, however, was not followed consistently, with the result that some file numbers remained active for many years after their creation.

Departmental operations of this kind were simple enough that Pope and Walker handled all business with the assistance of only three clerks, a number that later grew to seven. A variety of employees comprised the clerical grades in the public service, including secretaries, many of whom, according to the practice of the time, were male, and female copy-typists, or "typewriters," as Pope called them.[37]

The recruitment and management of staff at all levels were affected not only by the particular requirements of the Department of External Affairs but also by legislation governing the civil service as a whole. That legislation was changed in 1908 when the government, in response to the recommendations of the royal commission appointed the previous year, passed a civil service amendment act. This act sought to bring the "inside" (Ottawa-based) service more into line with the needs of a rapidly growing country in which the scope of government activity was expanding. Under its terms, the merit principle was made more effective for both appointments to and promotion within the inside service, a new system for the classification of positions was introduced, and a central personnel agency, the Civil Service Commission, was created to oversee the operation of these measures.

The legislation set aside the existing classification of the "establishment" or personnel of each department in favour of a new format that provided for three broad divisions, each with its own salary scale and each consisting of two subdivisions, A and B, of which the former had the higher level of responsibility. The first division consisted of the senior technical, administrative, and executive officers. In the second division were "certain other clerks, having technical, administrative, executive, or other duties which are of the same character as, but of less importance and responsibility than those of the first division." Clerks whose duties were "copying and routine work, under direct supervision,'' were in the third divison. Examinations for appointment to and promotion within the government service were to be set and administered by the Civil Service Commission, and new recruits were to be on probation for six months before their status became permanent.[38] As of March 31, 1911, Walker was in subdivision A of the first division, and Brophy was in subdivision B. The department's translator was in the second division, and the remaining three clerks were in the third.

Because Laurier's government was distracted in its last years by other matters, most notably the European naval crisis and its implications for Canada, the Civil Service Commission did not become fully operational until after the election of 1911. From the first, however, common attitudes about the personnel suited to government service had a major effect on recruitment to and working conditions in the department. Most affected were francophones and women.

Since the dominion public service had been based on that of the United Province of Canada, francophones were well represented at the time of Confederation. Their position, however, had eroded over the years.[39] Attempts to redress the balance had been insufficient to offset the disincentives of living and working in a predominantly anglophone environment. By 1909, few senior government officials displayed much concern that their operations should reflect Canada's dual cultural and linguistic heritage. English prevailed as the language of communication within the public service in Ottawa, not by law but by custom.

Pope was married to a francophone and could read and understand her language. But French was not much used in the department during its early years, even in correspondence with the Belgian and French consulates. Nor were there any French Canadians on the department's original staff. That a need was soon felt for some competence in French was indicated by the engagement early in 1910 of a clerk, J. A. Leblanc, who was later given the designation of translator. His, however, was strictly a technical position, not one that would provide for a French-Canadian point of view on the substance of the department's work. The only other employee with a French name to join the service at this time was a messenger, G. Champagne.

While the obstacles to the provision of satisfactory careers for francophones were unacknowledged, discrimination against women, especially at the higher levels, was overt. It was a broadly accepted fact of life in an environment that still accorded women only limited opportunities for professional advancement and the exercise of independent responsibility. And such opportunities as existed were more likely to be taken advantage of by anglophone than by francophone women, owing to the relatively few professional opportunities available to the latter.

At the time of Confederation there had been only one woman in the civil service, and by 1886 only twenty-four occupied permanent positions, all at very junior levels. But by the time the royal commission of 1907 was created, there were about 700 women in the inside government service, a significant proportion out of a total of some 3,000 employees. The commission, therefore, gave considerable attention to the role of women in the public service.

Almost unanimously, senior officials, including Pope, voiced disapproval of the employment of women, especially in managerial positions. Pope was prepared to acknowledge that some women performed better than expected at their jobs, but he was no enthusiast for the principle of female employment. "Speaking generally," he told the commissioners, "I do not think it desirable, though I know of several exceptions. But I am speaking of the general principle, because I find that as a rule women clerks claim the rights of men and the privileges of their own sex as well."[40]

Views such as these carried the day: the hearings were followed by action intended to stem the tide of women entering the public service. Salaries were raised and benefits increased to attract men, to whom appointments to the first and second clerical divisions were almost entirely limited. To inhibit the promotion of women, the third clerical level was "rigidly fenced off" from the second. A further study in 1912 reported that the strategy had been successful: fewer women had been appointed, the third division had been reduced in size, and the promotion of women had become much more difficult.

By the end of 1909 there were three women on the staff of External Affairs, all with English names and all in the lowest grade (the third division). Of the first female employees, one, Agnes McCloskey, was a notable exception to the belief that the careers of women in the public service were likely to be brief or at any rate undistinguished, for she remained in the department for nearly forty years and became a powerful force in its administration. In an interview with the *Christian Science Monitor* published on July 13, 1943, she said that, to get ahead in the public service, a woman must be ambitious, "not in a personal sense, but in reaching out to grasp what her Department stands for, how it links with other departments and what relation it has to the government of the country as a whole." In achieving her objective, she observed, a woman would benefit from "a natural flair for some phase of the job." Although she had been assigned to External Affairs as a typist, McCloskey's real métier was mathematics.[41] As a result, she soon began to help with the departmental accounts. With the expansion of the department's activities and resources over the years, this proved to be the basis of considerable author-

ity over the allocation of those resources and the operation of the department generally.

Versatility of the kind that Agnes McCloskey displayed was no doubt
important in the early days of External Affairs, in view of the small size
of the staff. But modest in number though it was, that staff was much
the most important resource of the department. Of the total budget of
$14,950 for 1909–10, $12,450 went for salaries, $1,500 for printing, and
$1,000 for sundries. Most of the allotment for sundries, it seems, went
to pay for temporary clerks or typists, when regular staff members went
on vacation.

Departmental salaries in 1909 were not lavish, but considering the purchasing power of the dollar at the time and the absence of personal income
tax, they were quite reasonable, especially for the higher ranks. Pope, as
a deputy minister, received $5,000 per annum. Walker, his senior assist-
ant, was paid $2,800 in his capacity as chief clerk and higher rates of pay
after his promotion to assistant under-secretary in 1912. These salaries
compare favourably, for instance, with those in the academic world of
the day. At Queen's University, a faculty dean could expect to receive
$2,500 per annum and a senior professor between $2,000 and $2,500.[42]
Salaries in the clerical grades in the department ran between $500 and
$2,800 per annum, depending on rank and seniority. Leblanc received $900
as a clerk-translator in 1910, and messengers were paid $800. Farther down
the scale were male secretaries, junior clerks, and female typists. The last
received the lowest rate: $500 in 1909, raised to $550 in 1910, with an
annual increment of $50.

Accommodation and working conditions

Guided as it was by conditions applicable throughout the government,
the allocation of salaries, like the staffing process generally, was quite
straightforward. The same could not be said of the search for office accommodation. This produced an interdepartmental struggle that exposed the
vulnerability of External Affairs as a new branch of government. For its
first few months the department had to operate under three different roofs
before finally coming to rest in quarters that were still regarded as
temporary and were in a second-rate location. This episode and its unsatisfactory outcome exasperated the governor general, disappointed the prime
minister, and almost broke Pope's heart with frustration and resentment.

Because the Department of External Affairs was so closely linked to
the secretary of state, to the prime minister, and to the governor general,
it had been generally assumed that Pope would be provided with offices
in the East Block of the Parliament Buildings. Here was the pivot of nation-

al government. The prime minister, the governor general, and several ministries had their offices there. The East Block was the meeting place for all official dignitaries from abroad. Both Laurier and Murphy had confirmed the department's right to a location there, but standing four-square in the preferred space was the deputy minister of Indian affairs, Frank Pedley, who refused to be budged in spite of personal appeals from the prime minister and the governor general. As an alternative, Murphy arranged to make his office available to Pope when he was out of town, but this solution was rendered unsatisfactory by stonemasons who were instructed to make structural changes in the windows during Murphy's absence.

Since Pope could not establish an operation in makeshift quarters within the space held by the Department of the Secretary of State in the East Block, he sought alternative temporary accommodation in the Trafalgar Building at the northeast corner of Bank and Queen streets. These rooms, however, were occupied by the Ottawa school board and could not be vacated and made ready for several months. Pope found some vacant rooms in the Centre Block that he was able to occupy until Parliament reconvened. By then it would be possible to settle into the Trafalgar Building.

On October 12, 1909, more than three months after it had begun its operations, the department finally moved into its own offices in the Trafalgar Building, with a staff slightly enlarged to handle the extra work that resulted from being located away from the East Block. Pope, Walker, and five clerks, along with numerous filing cabinets and the office library, occupied the second floor, and two female typists were installed on the fourth floor, where the lighting was better. The Trafalgar Building was poorly lit and insufficiently heated. It also accommodated a club whose meetings caused Pope to be concerned about the possibility of break-ins and noisy distractions for those working late in the day. Apart from the indignity of being placed above a barber shop and other commercial enterprises, which nourished Pope's fear that the department was being shunted out of the way, the location of the Trafalgar Building had numerous drawbacks. The offices in the East Block to which the department was so intimately tied were now five blocks away, necessitating a messenger service, since, among other things, the seal for all passport issuance remained there. Passports were still being signed by the governor general and sealed by his staff.

While Pope was resigned to the inconvenience, the governor general was not. The move had taken place during Grey's absence from Ottawa, and on his return the battle for space in the East Block resumed. Grey reminded Laurier that he had consented to the transfer of Walker only on condition that he be readily available for consultation; now "Mr.

Walker in his Bank St. office is almost as useless to my office as if he were in Calcutta." As well, the governor general complained, "the public convenience suffers if there is not easy access between the offices of the Secretary and the Under-Secretary of State. The work of my office and of your office is also retarded. My convenience, your convenience, and that of all the officials concerned, are injuriously affected."[43]

When Laurier procrastinated, Grey took matters into his own hands, calling in Frank Pedley and explaining that the "interests of the Crown" required him to surrender his offices and that no blame was to be attached to Pope. "The efficient service of the Crown," Grey urged, "should be properly provided for and that was a reason before which all private interests must bow."[44] After this encounter, Laurier finally ordered Pedley out, but Pope declined to be dislodged again.

A similar appeal was then directed by Grey to Pope. The latter, however, would not change his mind. Grey bitterly complained to Laurier:

I do not suppose a Governor General has ever put himself to so much trouble in order to protect a servant of the Crown, in the position of Mr. Pope, from possible injury resulting from a change called for in the Public Interest. . . . I feel that I shall have been, and shall continue to be, humiliated, if nothing is done. Apart from putting the Governor General in a false position, it would appear hardly credible that deference to Mr. Pope's feelings should be allowed to outweigh the acknowledged requirements of the Public Service, and I shall be greatly mistaken in my estimate of his character, if when the matter is put before him in this way, he does not agree with me.[45]

Pope had had enough of moving. Moreover, he did not want to prejudice his relations with Pedley and other deputy ministers who, he feared, would not give him much respect if it were known that he was responsible for disturbing one of his senior colleagues. Laurier acquiesced, and the matter lapsed, in anticipation that a proposed extension of the East Block could provide proper accommodation for all concerned. By the time Grey left Canada, in the autumn of 1911, he had forgiven Pope, but he still remembered the affair as "the greatest humiliation" he had endured during his seven years in office.[46]

Apart from the conditions in the Trafalgar Building, the Department of External Affairs proved to be an agreeable place of employment. In those early years no one could claim to be overworked. The daily routine was leisurely and often included a game of billiards or whist. Except for emergencies, Pope himself rarely arrived at the office before ten. A regular one-o'clock luncheon at the Rideau Club was followed by a siesta in a comfortable armchair before he returned to the office at four for another two hours. As long as the work was completed, he did not care if those who lived far from the office took an hour and a half to go home for lunch or left at four for a quiet stroll through the tree-lined streets. For six days a week it was a most satisfying life, with a generous annual vacation of three weeks.

GOING TO WORK

The confidential prints

Notwithstanding the relaxed working environment, the Department of External Affairs was no sinecure, as Pope's own activities reveal. He made it one of his first priorities to study how the British Foreign Office functioned and to compile as complete a set of records as possible. "I am naturally desirous," he wrote to one correspondent, "to carry the date of our beginning as far back as possible and I do not see why I should not start with . . . the Commission to Jacques Cartier from Philippe Chabot, Admiral of France, dated 30 October 1534."[47]

This procedure involved the acquisition of documents from various repositories. In 1910 Pope visited London to study the organization of the filing and registry systems of the Foreign Office and the Colonial Office and to acquire as many relevant documents as he could. His priorities were revealed in his interim report to Murphy:

> I have gone over many papers in the Library of the Foreign Office, and indicated a number of confidential prints dealing with various public questions in which Canada is interested, reaching back 70 or 80 years. I have asked for copies of these papers and my request is now under consideration of some of the numerous Under-Secretaries I have met. Some of the documents I don't think they will give me. Some they can't, for the reason that they have no copies, but I hope to secure a number of interesting and important papers. I am at the same time making researches in the Public Record Office, chiefly with regard to ancient Treaties affecting Canada.[48]

Pope's objective was not mere compilation of records, but preparation of a series of confidential collections for use by ministers and officials who had to make decisions bearing on international negotiations, similar to dossiers in the Foreign Office. The first of many such collections of documents, known as confidential prints, that Pope and Walker compiled was on inland fisheries, and another followed on the North American fisheries arbitration. Laurier seems to have been particularly appreciative of the results, on several occasions telling Pope that he regretted the series had not been started ten years earlier.[49]

The department and diplomacy

Pope was much more than a paper manager. The details of preparing the confidential prints were left to Walker, thereby enabling Pope to attend to diplomatic negotiations as he had done in the past. His expertise in dealing with the United States was recognized by the British ambassador in Washington, Bryce, who found him a "most efficient, and altogether reasonable and pleasant" associate.[50]

Pope's capacity for trans-border diplomacy was important in view of the lack of permanent Canadian representation in Washington. Bryce was prepared to welcome a Canadian as a member of his staff, but Laurier was not enthusiastic. When the question came up in the House of Commons, the prime minister asserted that such a step was not necessary because of the excellent job that Bryce was doing in handling Canadian interests. "I do not believe," he stated, "that if we had an attaché at Washington we could improve very much the conditions which exist at this moment."[51]

The most important issue in Canadian-American relations engaging Pope's attention after he became under-secretary of state for external affairs was pelagic sealing. At a time when such matters still were usually handled by cabinet ministers, Pope was named the Canadian participant in negotiations on the subject in Washington involving the United Kingdom, the United States, Japan, and Russia. Although Bryce was the chief British delegate, Pope was the more active person, since it was Canadian interests that required protection. His success in securing the concessions desired by Canada earned him warm praise from Grey, who was the prime mover in the award of a knighthood in recognition of Pope's achievement.[52]

Not all negotiations required travel abroad, for the consular community in Canada provided an important channel of communication with foreign governments. According to the External Affairs Act, the department was given responsibility for "the administration of all matters relating to the foreign consular service in Canada." Consular representatives, therefore, were requested to use External Affairs as their channel in approaching the various branches of the Canadian government.

By 1909 the names of 304 consuls general, consuls, and consular agents were listed as representing thirty-two countries in Canada; of the total, about one-third were employed by the US government.[53] Consular representation was concentrated mainly in Halifax, Montreal, Toronto, and

Vancouver, but seven countries maintained consuls in Ottawa as well: Argentina, Belgium, China, Denmark, Japan, Paraguay (honorary), and the United States.

Although the practice was still troubling to the British, the Canadian government continued to treat consulates as quasi-diplomatic missions on such subjects as tariffs and trade. Through this channel, tariff agreements were reached with Germany and Italy. In December 1910, Laurier informed the House of Commons that, because Canada had no diplomatic service, foreign consuls "by tolerance" were exercising semi-diplomatic powers and "many of the consuls have really performed diplomatic duties."[54] The increasing importance being accorded consular officials led the US consul general to suggest to Washington "the desirability of having someone at Ottawa in a semi-diplomatic position and with personal influence and acquaintance."[55]

A limited mandate

This recommendation was appropriate in view of Pope's standing in the small circle of deputy ministers of his day. According to one contemporary chronicler, he was known in official circles as "the man with a pull."[56] This arose not only from his role in the conduct of government business but also from his social position, for the Popes were frequent guests at Sunday afternoon tea with the Lauriers and the Greys.

Even so, there were limits to the under-secretary's "pull." His influence did not work, or perhaps was not exercised, when it came to getting proposals through the cabinet. A year after it had begun operations, Bryce observed to Grey that "the Department of External Affairs had not, so far, accelerated business."[57] The problem, he acknowledged, was not in the department but rather in Laurier's continuing tendency to procrastinate and in the government's adherence to the traditionally ponderous system of conducting business. Indirectly, however, his complaint was a comment on the limited effectiveness of the department, since these were the very obstacles to efficiency that it had been expected to overcome.

The substantive mandate of the department was quite limited. This was true even of the area of activity that was Pope's specialty, relations with the United States. Matters related to waterways that would otherwise have been a responsibility of the department had been assigned by the boundary waters treaty of 1909 to the International Joint Commission. The department handled the commission's correspondence with the provinces (through the secretary of state) and the prime minister. In conjunction with the British embassy in Washington, the department was also the channel for communication between the Canadian government and the US State Department about issues coming before the commission. The members of the commission, however, were paid by the Department of Public Works, and External Affairs had no continuing relationship with the substance of its work until 1912. Nor was the department given responsibility for the settlement of the North Atlantic fisheries question. This was handled by the minister of justice, Aylesworth, whose principal adviser was John S. Ewart, an Ottawa constitutional lawyer with strong autonomist views who came to advise a number of Liberal leaders.[58]

Through its under-secretary, External Affairs did deal with the substance of some issues that were mainly the responsibility of other departments, particularly the question of naval vessels on the Great Lakes. Pope also met with deputy ministers whose departments had interests outside Canada, such as F. C. T. O'Hara of Trade and Commerce. He did not challenge the maintenance of these departments' external interests, however, and for the most part External Affairs became involved only in a post-office capacity. Thus Canadian officials abroad, the greatest variety of whom were concentrated at the office of the high commissioner in London, continued to receive instructions from their several headquarters departments. There also was a good deal of correspondence on routine business between Canadian and British departments, either direct or with the assistance of the high commissioner, although on important questions of external policy the channel was now through External Affairs to the governor general and thence to the Colonial Office.[59]

Pope did endeavour to regularize communication between External Affairs and the office of the high commissioner in London, but, since the department was not given a supervisory role, it had no power to co-ordinate the flow of instructions and reports across the Atlantic. The office was asked to address to the under-secretary of state for external affairs "the more official and important communications which relate to matters of foreign or external concern," and it undertook as well to provide copies of all public statements that it issued. Correspondence having to do with routine matters, the interests of the provinces, and the library, however, was to continue to go to the under-secretary of state.[60]

The relationship with the commissioner in Paris was even more tenuous: no record of correspondence of any kind appears to have survived for this period. The lack of a co-ordinating agency in Ottawa no doubt contributed to the confusion over Canadian representation in the French capital after the commissioner, Hector Fabre, died in 1910. Both the commercial and the emigration agent claimed status as interim commissioner, and the rivalry was not solved by Laurier's appointment of Sen. Philippe Roy in May 1911 as Fabre's successor, with the new title of commissioner general. The emigration agent insisted on being called "under commissioner" in order to advance his status with the French government and to camouflage his real responsibility, since the active promotion of emigration was contrary to local law. Roy, in contrast, wanted to establish, under his own office, a publicity branch to promote trade, commerce, and investment and to leave emigration in the hands of steamship lines and fraternal societies. Further strains arose when he set up an office on his own in a dignified commercial section of Paris, apart from that maintained by the emigration agent in a more popular quarter.

Important as were the practical consequences of these gaps in its authority, the most telling comment on the position of the Department of External Affairs is perhaps its lack of involvement in the three major developments affecting Canada's relations with other countries at the close of the Laurier years. The department's main contributions to preparations for the Imperial Conference of 1911 were the circulation of correspondence and the arrangements for the compilation of confidential prints. The election of 1911 was one of the rare occasions in Canadian history when external relations figured prominently in the campaign, but the department had no involvement in the two issues that arose, naval policy and negotiations with the United States on the revived project of reciprocity. On the latter, Pope wrote to W. Griffith, secretary at the office of the high commissioner in London, "Neither I nor my department had anything whatsoever to do with the recent negotiations at Washington, and . . . we were not furnished with the scratch of a pen on the subject."[61]

The limited scope of the department doubtless reflected the intentions of the prime minister. Although Laurier had created the department both to promote administrative efficiency and to enhance the possibility of greater Canadian autonomy in international affairs, he was not an enthusiast for either needless innovation or avoidable foreign commitments. Thus he was likely to wait upon events rather than to create a larger place for the department within the structure of Canadian government. Nor would the initiative for fuller realization of Laurier's intentions come from Pope. After Laurier's defeat in the election of 1911, the role of the department was a matter to be determined by the new prime minister. It would depend both on how active a foreign policy he decided to implement and on where he looked for advice and for the resources to carry it out.

Chapter Three
Early Operations:
1911–1921

Robert Borden and external relations

THE GENERAL ELECTION OF SEPTEMBER 21, 1911, which brought the Conservatives under Robert Borden to power, was for a number of reasons of special importance for the Department of External Affairs. The controversies over naval policy and reciprocity had caused both political parties to deal with fundamental issues affecting Canada's external relations. The interest thus expressed was one to which the new prime minister had already given considerable attention while leader of the opposition, and it was sustained throughout his years in office and indeed afterward.

Borden was not likely, however, to exploit the autonomist implications of the External Affairs Act. While he favoured a more active role for Canada, he saw it taking place within the imperial context and so was not inclined to challenge the ultimate authority of London in matters of foreign policy. Nor was he at all committed to using the department as the instrument for achieving his most important policy goals. Rather, having been a critic of creating such a department, he might be inclined to use alternative resources, even while maintaining the administrative structure created by Laurier and seeking to put it to better use, especially in the day-to-day business of government.

Borden was at least as interested in Canada's external relations as Laurier, and he was more active. The reason lay partly in the deteriorating international situation and in Borden's insistence on viewing defence in a wider imperial context. Another important factor was Borden's determination to have Canada play a more active role in the Ottawa-Washington-London triangle. It had long been recognized that Anglo-American accord was the key to Canada's well being. Borden wanted to perform the function of linchpin, hoping to exploit Canada's ties of kinship with the United Kingdom and neighbourly dealings with the United States to make his country the interpreter between the two.

Effective participation in triangular diplomacy required a greater voice for Canada in determining imperial foreign policy, which in turn implied involvement in the empire's affairs to a degree that Laurier had always rejected. The entry fee, Borden hoped, would be paid through a contribution to imperial defence. "The great dominions, sharing in the defence of the Empire on the high seas," he declared, "must necessarily be entitled to share also in the responsibility for and in the control of foreign policy."[1]

When Borden formed his government, the secretary of state, W. J. Roche, a veteran politician from Manitoba, presided ex officio over the Department of External Affairs. Like Laurier, however, Borden kept the control of external relations in his own hands, with the result that Roche's role became largely a formality. Borden, therefore, did not object when Sir Joseph Pope, as under-secretary of state for external affairs, continued the practice of bypassing his titular chief and making representations to the prime minister.

The External Affairs Act of 1912

Within days of the election of 1911, the governor general, Lord Grey, told Bryce in Washington that he had advised the prime minister-elect that "it is imperative in the interests of the Crown that the External Affairs Department should be removed from the Secretary of State's Department to his [the prime minister's] own."[2] Once Borden had taken office, this advice was reinforced by Pope, who put forward a draft bill on which he and Walker had been working quietly since 1909.

Early in 1912, the new external affairs bill was introduced, affirming that "the Member of the King's Privy Council for Canada holding the recognized position of First Minister shall be the Secretary of State for External Affairs."[3] The change did not excite controversy in Parliament, where it appeared that all that was involved was a reallocation of portfolios, and the bill was quickly approved on February 6, 1912. Royal assent was given on April 1, at which time Borden was sworn in as secretary of state for external affairs. In this capacity, he had the "conduct" rather than the "care" of external relations, since the opportunity was not taken to make the amendment that Grey had wanted in the legislation of 1909. Now more than ever, therefore, the prime minister had the lead in matters of foreign policy.

The department under the prime minister

There was a need for the more vigorous direction that could be expected now that the external affairs portfolio was under the prime minister. It was no secret that, apart from such politically contentious issues as naval policy and reciprocity, foreign relations were of secondary importance in the government's deliberations. In 1911, an informed but anonymous observer had described the frustrations of conducting business not immediately affecting the internal affairs of the country:

> Not once, but repeatedly have I been told by foreign Consuls of the difficulty in bringing the Canadian Government to realise that questions respecting their various countries have present significance for Canada and may have very great future significance. They have complained that Ministers are so absorbed by the internal affairs of the country that they fail to regard anything external of importance enough to bestow any consideration or study upon it. The Consuls frequently express surprise at so much shortsightedness on the part of those in responsible positions, and at their utter lack of desire to learn of the conditions of foreign lands even when these might with care and understanding be turned to the advantage of Canada.[4]

At least one journalist recognized the potential importance of the department after it came under the prime minister's jurisdiction. The department, the writer acknowledged, was "seldom heard of, little figuring in the eyes of the public, bereft of the cynosure which patronage would place upon it, unpopular in that it is so severely diplomatic as to eschew popularity." But, although obscure, it was a "necessary berth" for the prime minister, and it was "the portfolio of development."[5]

There were drawbacks in being placed under the prime minister. With a heavy agenda of domestic politics, he could not be expected to devote more than a modest portion of his time to external affairs. Proximity to the prime minister also subjected the department to diversion by the domestic affairs in which he was involved. At a time when there was little provision for a staff to serve the prime minister, External Affairs was available as a source of personnel. Thus the department had the potential to become a talent bank for the government, as staff members, on the basis of experience gained and connections made at the centre, moved into senior positions elsewhere. While this function undoubtedly gave the department influence on activities outside its own mandate, it also could be a serious distraction, when a prime minister made heavy demands for assistance with his domestic responsibilities.

These problems took time to emerge, for the department's workload was not overly heavy before 1914, and neither Borden nor Pope forced the pace of change. Meanwhile, there were important advantages resulting from reporting to the prime minister. As Pope had pointed out beforehand, the act of 1912 brought the legislative basis of the department into line with practice. On important questions of policy, the department from the first had "usually been, . . . *as it must necessarily be*, under the head of the government." Thus the effect of the change was "merely to give legislative sanction to the actual conditions and thus ensure a more satisfactory administration of the department besides relieving the Under-Secretary from a position which in the past has been well nigh intolerable."[6] Not only was the strain with the Department of the Secretary of State relieved, but the prestige of External Affairs and its under-secretary was enhanced by association with the prime minister rather than with a junior minister whose main attention was elsewhere. The improved standing and influence, in turn, allowed easier access to the resources that the department needed to perform its functions and serve the prime minister effectively.

The most noticeable early result of becoming the prime minister's department was perhaps the resolution, to Pope's satisfaction, of the vexed problem of accommodation. On October 5, 1914, the department was transferred from the Trafalgar Building to the East Block, which was to remain its headquarters until 1973. Pope received Sir John A. Macdonald's old office, on the second floor under the tower at the southwest corner. Two adjacent offices overlooking the lawn accommodated the chief clerk, F. M. Baker, and the assistant under-secretary, Walker. The secretarial and clerical staff was housed in another four rooms across the corridor, overlooking the courtyard, and shortly after the move two more rooms became available on the top floor, also on the courtyard side. Next to External Affairs on the second floor were the offices of the governor general, and beyond them the rooms of the Privy Council.

While the move was made possible by the completion of an extension to the East Block, the department's claim on the space was strengthened by the need to be near the prime minister. Pope, moreover, was able to persuade Borden that External Affairs should be given offices that clearly marked it off from the Department of the Secretary of State. Thus in physical location as well as in leadership the separate identity of the Department of External Affairs was clearly established.

A second consequence of coming under the prime minister was an augmentation in personnel. This was stimulated not by the needs of the department but by those of the prime minister, who had no appropriation for employees except for a private secretary. The process started modestly in 1913 when a sum of $600 was provided in the departmental estimates for a private secretary to the secretary of state for external affairs; in fact, Borden used this vote to appoint two secretaries, Jocelyn (Joe) Boyce, formerly a clerk in the Privy Council Office, and A. W. Merriam of the Customs Department, from April 1 of that year. Although they were members of the department, Boyce later said that he did not really consider himself such until some years afterward, when he became its chief clerk. Political appointees who functioned as private secretaries to the prime minister were also on the department's payroll. In addition, the department provided clerks, stenographers, and messengers for the prime minister, to a total of ten people by 1921.

So far as the work of the department was concerned, the most important effect of being placed under the prime minister was to give it a closer relationship with the government's offices in London and Paris. This occurred at a time when both were experiencing important transitions in development as a result of organizational changes and when they were having to deal with new pressures created by the deteriorating situation in Europe.

The Canadian high commissioner in London had always been an appointee of the prime minister and continued until 1921 to report to him. The department, however, now for the first time had direct access to at least some of his reports, and, by virtue of its administrative role on behalf of the prime minister, it became more involved in routine operations in London. Those operations and the lack of co-ordination among various departmental agents working in Britain were an offence to Borden's views on sound and efficient administration.[7] The opportunity for improvement arose when Lord Strathcona, still in office at the age of ninety-three, died in January 1914. The prime minister then sent George Perley, minister without portfolio and his chief administrative trouble-shooter, to London to study the status and operations of the high commissioner's office. When war disrupted Perley's work, he was instructed to remain in London as acting high commissioner, a rank he had assumed in June.

A similar need for co-ordination and accountability existed in Paris, because of the disputes over jurisdiction between the commissioner general, Philippe Roy, and the commercial and emigration agents. These were resolved when Roy was given clear authority over commercial work in December 1911, and the emigration agent was withdrawn shortly after the outbreak of the First World War in 1914. In Ottawa, meanwhile, there was concern that the commissioner general might have conflicting interests, arising from his concurrent representation of the government of

Quebec and his retention of a directorship in a mortgage company that he had founded three years earlier to raise money in France for investment in Canada.

After Borden had inspected the situation himself on a visit to Paris in the summer of 1912, an agreement was worked out whereby Roy gave up his directorship and the representation of Quebec. In return, his salary was increased to $12,000, placing him a notch above the high commissioner in London ($10,000), the chief justice of Canada, and the lieutenant-governors of the provinces. Henceforth Roy, under the supervision of the prime minister, would give all his attention to representing the federal government. Since the prime minister had no mechanism for exercising his responsibility, jurisdiction over the office in Paris passed to the department at the beginning of 1913. The prime minister did not escape all involvement, however, even in matters of detail, for as secretary of state for external affairs he was now responsible for approving such minor items as the list of newspaper subscriptions for the office in Paris.[8]

Administration and work of the department

At headquarters, too, achievement sometimes fell short of the ideal. A counterpart to the poor drafting of Canadian documents in English, about which there had been complaint in London before the department was created, was the inadequacy of translations into French. When the external affairs bill was being considered in January 1912, a proposal was made by Raoul Dandurand, a Liberal senator with an established interest in international affairs, that "the deputy minister should have an assistant, a literary man of repute in the French language, to supervise all documents sent to foreign governments." He added that "such documents in the French language have been so queerly translated that high officials of the French Government have expressed a preference for English versions. . . . Coming from this bilingual country, I felt somewhat humiliated when I was in Paris to learn that documents emanating from the Federal Government of Canada were so badly translated that the French Government asked that the English version be sent instead."[9] No such appointment was made, but there was an effort at improvement. Additional junior personnel were taken on for translation, at times combining that activity with other duties, such as clerical, reference, and library work.

The department was more deeply affected by the new government's interest in civil service reform. Soon after the change of regime, studies of the civil service and government machinery by a British expert, Sir George Murray, were instigated at Borden's behest. Murray's call for more authority for deputy ministers, closer control of expenditures, use of written rather than oral communication to transact business, and a better classification system for civil servants might have led to major changes across the board had not war made problems more complicated and a general solution impossible.[10] But even though reform continued to be piecemeal, there were consequences of note for External Affairs, especially in classification of positions. It was as a result of the operation of this process that Walker was given the rank of assistant under-secretary.

Another change, the appointment in 1912 of a consulting engineer, brought closer involvement with the International Joint Commission and its responsibilities for resolving boundary waters disputes referred to it by the Canadian and US governments. In that year the prime minister decided that W. J. Stewart, chief hydrographer of the Department of the Naval Service, should be transferred to External Affairs to prepare and look after Canada's cases before the commission. Before the commission could undertake a case, the US State Department and External Affairs, through the British embassy, decided whether it should go forward and the terms of reference to be applied. This situation continued until 1923, when the minister of the interior was authorized to deal with all matters related to Canadian-American waters. At that time, Stewart and J. B. Challies, who also had been advising the secretary of state for external affairs, were instructed to report to the Department of the Interior.

Despite the administrative changes that took place after Borden came to office, the department did not take on many new responsibilities. An examination of the files opened in 1912 shows that it continued to be primarily a responsive operation, transmitting requests and information to other branches of government. For Pope and Walker, a good deal of time at first had to be spent on sorting out remaining jurisdictional problems with the Department of the Secretary of State and on the struggle for better accommodation that culminated in the move to the East Block. Otherwise, their main preoccupations continued to be building up documentation on external matters and overseeing the issuance of passports (about 300 per year). With relocation to the East Block, the governor general's signature on passports could at last be obtained without transporting them the several blocks from the Trafalgar Building.

The years 1912 and 1913, then, were quiet ones for the department. The days passed calmly and predictably. Pope's diary for weeks on end contains mainly the following terse notation: "To office. Evening at home." Lunch continued as a rule to be at the Rideau Club, or sometimes for variety at the Chateau Laurier Hotel, which was completed in 1912. The pace was sufficiently relaxed that, with Borden's acquiescence, Pope was able to take an extended holiday cruise to the Mediterranean in the spring of 1913, leaving Walker in charge during his absence.

In the capital, Pope's position was solidly entrenched within the local establishment. The social pace during 1912 and 1913 seems to have been both varied and lively. Entertainment at Government House was frequent, with the Popes regularly invited. They entertained quite actively on their own, often receiving and in turn being received by members of the consular corps. Pope was an avid card player, with a particular fondness for poker. So too were many members of the senior civil service and the consular corps, for whom he held poker evenings at his home. The Popes often dined with the Bordens and continued to see the Lauriers, whose house in Sandy Hill was quite close to their own.

For all Pope's security of position and his acknowledged expertise in matters concerning the department, he did not enjoy as close a relationship with Borden as he had with other prime ministers, nor was he always the most fruitful source of advice, particularly about unexpected problems in Canada's international relationships. By the time Borden became prime minister, the under-secretary had established a longstanding attachment to certain questions affecting Canada's external interests but was not always attentive to new challenges. He had also developed a passion for detail that sometimes caused him to expend a disproportionate amount of attention on minor matters at the expense of larger issues. He was relentless, for example, in opposing the flying of the red ensign in preference to the Union Jack and the use of the phrase "His Majesty's Canadian Government." "I venture to hope," he wrote to Borden with regard to the latter, "that this attempt to assert our equality with the ancient government to which we owe our political being, and which is clothed with a jurisdiction reaching round the world, will not secure your sanction. To my mind it is presumptuous, aggressive, and in the worst possible taste."[11]

Loring Christie joins the department

On major questions of external policy, Borden looked for advice and assistance not to the under-secretary but to the occupant of a new position in the department, that of legal adviser. The position was created to serve Borden's objective of improving the calibre of legal advice available to all departments of government. He asked Pope to acquire information on the work of the assistant under-secretary (legal) in the British Foreign Office, and in due course applications were solicited for a specialized clerical position in External Affairs, carrying a salary of $1,600. Borden himself was sufficiently interested in the project to interview several candidates from his own province of Nova Scotia. Other concerns, however, took precedence, and he let the matter rest without hiring anyone until another candidate, Loring Christie, appeared unexpectedly.

Christie, like Pope and Borden, was a Maritimer. Upon graduating from Acadia College in Wolfville, Nova Scotia, he was characterized by the secretary of the faculty as "a young man of splendid character and ability and in every way adapted for successful post-graduate work." He went on to Harvard Law School where he graduated among the top three in his class while also serving as editor in chief of the *Harvard Law Review*. After an unsuccessful attempt to find employment in Toronto, he entered a law firm in New York and from there joined the US Department of Justice, where he performed brilliantly, serving for a brief period as acting solicitor general. To meet the requirements of this position, he began reluctantly to take the first step toward naturalization as an American citizen. Without being solicited, a concerned friend in the British embassy in Washington asked Borden to help find Christie a position in a Toronto or Montreal legal firm.[12] Borden, who had not previously known of Christie, arranged to meet him. After the interview, Christie was appointed, while Pope was out of the country on his Mediterranean cruise, by an order-in-council of February 1913 as legal adviser in the Department of External Affairs at an annual salary of $3,000, with effect from April of that year.

Christie's job description was written by Walker, also a lawyer. He was

to have charge of the legal work of the Department of External Affairs; to advise the Government and the Department on questions of international law, the ratification, denunciation, and interpretation of treaties, and matters involving the Dominion's international and Imperial relations; to prepare the text for treaties, legislation and Orders-in-Council respecting Imperial and foreign affairs, and for Parliamentary material explanatory thereof; to prepare references to the International Joint Commission and similar arbitral tribunals, and to prepare the argument on behalf of Canada; to attend International and Imperial Conferences in an advisory capacity; to undertake confidential missions abroad as directed, and to perform other work as required.[13]

As legal adviser, Christie was the department's third ranking officer, after Pope and Walker. Pope was to continue to deal with US affairs, tariffs and trade, matters relating to protocol such as honours and official visits, and the consular corps. As deputy head, he was responsible for the department's administrative and financial affairs. Walker was concerned primarily with passports, consular work, naturalization questions, treaties, and production of confidential prints. He assisted Pope on administrative and financial subjects and acted for him during his frequent absences while on duty in Washington. On the basis of his job description, Christie had a clearly defined role. He soon discovered, however, that there were insufficient legal issues to occupy his time fully. Thus his "other work" and his "advisory capacity" became more important.

One of the first assignments given to Christie by the prime minister was to prepare a "Comparative Digest of Resolutions adopted at the Colonial and Imperial Conferences, 1887–1911." Had Pope or Walker been given the assignment, Borden would have received what the title suggested, a factual recapitulation of texts. Under Christie, and with Borden's approval, the digest became an appeal for greater imperial unity and enhanced Canadian influence through active consultation.[14] From Christie, it was apparent, Borden could receive imaginative advice for his personal use. Thus it developed that Christie worked really for Borden rather than for Pope. The papers he prepared for the prime minister were not sent to the under-secretary or to the department's files, unless Borden so directed. As a result, Pope was often unaware of Christie's ideas, and on more than one occasion he complained to Borden about the inconsistency this lack of knowledge produced in the department's work when the two were handling related matters.[15]

By his own admission, Christie was in an anomalous position. He was in the department but not of it. Even his physical location emphasized his unusual status. While the rest of the department was still in the Trafalgar Building, Christie had gone to an office in the East Block, near that of the prime minister. When External Affairs was transferred to the same location, Christie's office remained away from the others. This separation was an indication that Christie was assuming the role of the prime minister's personal adviser on general foreign policy and thus was not a departmental officer like the others.

Christie was a man of ideas, an intellectual in public life, who was passionately committed to the views he propounded. Canada in his view was neither a colony nor a possession but "a separate individuality [with] a will and power of her own, a self-respecting national consciousness— all manifested in a determination to recognize and shoulder her responsibility in the affairs of the world as a member of the family of nations which constitute the British Commonwealth."[16] Such a position accorded well with Borden's desire to acquire a voice for Canada in imperial affairs, and Christie was committed to the prime minister's conception of triangular diplomacy. Unlike Pope, therefore, Christie could help Borden to think through the issues and to articulate and apply his ideas as the occasion arose.

The department in 1914

By 1914, when all preconceptions about Canada's external relations were irrevocably challenged by the outbreak of the First World War, the department had grown modestly in size to fourteen employees, not counting the staff assigned to the prime minister. External Affairs' identity, independent of the Department of the Secretary of State, had been clearly established, its prestige enhanced through its association with the prime minister, and its involvement in the country's external relations enlarged. The department was in a better position than it would have been at its founding five years earlier to contribute to the country's war effort and to broaden its own scope somewhat in the process. But, as Borden's reliance on Christie made clear, External Affairs was by no means a sophisticated foreign office in embryo, able to offer the government comprehensive advice on major and unexpected issues. The department's work during the war and the immediate aftermath would be useful, but it would by no means be sufficient to meet all the government's external needs. Those that the department could not supply would continue to be met, as before the war, by other means, especially the personal collaboration between Borden and Christie.

THE DEPARTMENT AND THE WAR, 1914–1918

Wartime responsibilities

The basis for the department's involvement in new wartime duties was established well before the outbreak of conflict. At the close of 1913, the British secretary of state for the colonies had urged the self-governing dominions to follow the example of the Overseas Defence Committee in Britain by preparing a plan for handling anticipated hostilities. Borden therefore instructed Pope in early January 1914 to look after preparation of a war book, a task for which he was well suited because of his attention to detail and his broad knowledge of government operations. Departments were asked for suggestions about what measures would be required, and these were co-ordinated into a single operational plan by a committee of ten deputy ministers chaired by Pope.

The under-secretary's work brought him high praise from the prime minister[17] and ensured that the government was able to respond to the emerging crisis expeditiously, even though both the governor general and the prime minister were away from the capital in the summer of 1914. When advice to take precautions against a possible surprise action came from the Colonial Office on July 29, the governor general's secretary passed the message to Pope, who set the defence scheme in motion by notifying the key departments.

Numerous questions had to be dealt with that had never before confronted a Canadian government. What was to be done with enemy alien army reservists who wished to return to Germany? How were Canadians stranded in Europe to be looked after? What should be done about a German cruiser sighted off Newfoundland or the German and Austrian consuls residing in Canada? The lines of communication between London and Ottawa were heavily loaded as more instructions were received and requested in the pre-war hours. Then at 2:38 a.m. on August 2, 1914, came the message, "Call out Royal Naval Reserves." Precautionary measures were required to deter advance strikes such as a projected attack by Austrian steamship crews on a wireless station at Glace Bay. At 8:45 p.m. on August 4 the telegram announcing the outbreak of war arrived. The cabinet was assembled and a date, August 18, was set for the summoning of Parliament.

Leisurely hours of business immediately became a thing of the past. On the night of August 4, Pope recorded in his diary: "We are in for it now and all I hope is that the German War Lord will get a d—d good licking. Much excitement in the streets. I drove two of my lady typewriters to their homes about midnight."[18] The next day was equally busy with war preparations before he bicycled home at 11:30 p.m. Because of the time difference between London and Ottawa, telegrams from the Colonial Office requiring immediate attention arrived in External Affairs at all hours of the night. In addition, the department was the channel for keeping the British government informed of Canadian war activities and of new regulations required by the situation. While the time-consuming task of putting these messages into cypher and decyphering the replies was done in the governor general's office, Pope on occasion did the work himself in order to speed up the process.

Soon much of the activity sorted itself out, leaving External Affairs to function primarily as a post office, but the pressure of work remained heavy, and, particularly at first, there was a steady diet of new subjects to be mastered. Files had to be created for such topics as censorship, contraband, internees, and relief for Canadians abroad. The Russian consul general in Montreal placed thirty-one demands on the department during the first five months of the war. Some of the questions he raised were important and others trivial, but all were unfamiliar and time-consuming. They included complaints about the scale of relief available for unemployed Russian workers in Canada and the absence of a Russian representative from a luncheon of the Montreal Canadian Club, as well as requests for procurement of an ice-breaker, commutation of a death sentence, assistance to Russians wishing to join Canadian contingents, and a customs ruling on the export of an artillery gun.

A few months into the war, regular procedures and new channels had been established to handle the workload, relieving the necessity for much of the detailed co-ordination with imperial authorities and consular representatives that had been essential at the start. Before the war, Murray's report on the civil service had pointed out that ministers and their deputies were overloaded with minor administrative responsibilities, but no corrective action had been taken. Now wartime pressures forced a change. Pope placed more responsibility for the routine paper flow, parliamentary returns, and correspondence on the department's chief clerk, Baker. Much of Baker's responsibility for accounting in turn devolved upon his assistant, Agnes McCloskey, whose upward movement through the departmental administration gained momentum.

As a result of the war, the government had to give much more attention than formerly to the development of external policies and to negotiations with other states. The lead was taken by Sir Robert Borden (as he had become in June 1914). At home, Borden was required to justify the sacrifices demanded by the war. He could do so partly by denouncing the enemy, but he also had to respond to the growing conviction, stimulated by Canada's involvement in the war as a major contributor of men, wealth, and supplies, that the country had distinct interests of its own that deserved recognition from its allies. This he sought to achieve by enhancing Canada's standing within the empire. The principal focus of his attention, therefore, was London. There he assumed the role of chief exponent of his country's interests, dealing with the British prime minister and with the heads of government of the other dominions.

Personal diplomacy on the scale required by the war was not something Borden could handle unaided. Although Pope's wartime tasks included preparation of long-range studies,[19] he was not very well suited to provide the kind of all-round support that Borden required. That came much more readily from Christie, whose position as the prime minister's personal adviser on foreign policy was consolidated during the war.

Christie's assignments began at the outset of the war, when Borden requested help in preparing a public explanation of Canada's involvement, in the form of a justification of the British cause.[20] Despite the importance to the prime minister of such assistance, Christie, at the age of twenty-nine, was by no means content to remain on the home front. Like other men of his years, he was caught up in the enthusiasm of the war and wanted to see active service, but the request was denied. He did have opportunities to go overseas, but as a civilian, when he accompanied Borden to London, Paris, and the front in 1915 and to imperial meetings in London, with side trips to the front, in 1917 and 1918.

External relations

There was much for Borden to do in London on such matters of wartime business as finance and contracts, and he wanted to be admitted to the deliberations of the government there on vital issues concerning prosecution of the war. The replacement of Herbert Asquith as prime minister in 1916 by David Lloyd George made it possible for Borden to achieve the greater voice he desired.[21] In 1917, an imperial war conference was summoned to meet in London, and the prime ministers of the dominions were invited to meet, as the imperial war cabinet, with British ministers bearing the heaviest responsibility for the war effort. By this means Canada and other dominions, for the first time, were provided regularly with information on policy decisions in London and on developments reported by British diplomatic missions around the world. Thus began a system of access to the informational resources of the Foreign Office and the diplomatic service that was of much value to the department, especially during the years when its own sources of information were few.

For Borden, one of the most attractive features of the consultative process in London was the opportunity it gave him to advance his views on the future of the dominions within the empire. Particularly satisfying was the acceptance by the Imperial War Conference of a resolution arguing for a constitutional readjustment after the war that should be "based upon a full recognition of the Dominions as autonomous nations of an Imperial Commonwealth, and . . . should recognize the right of the Dominions and India to an adequate voice in foreign policy and in foreign relations, and should provide effective arrangements for continuous consultation in all important matters of common Imperial concern, and for such necessary concerted action, founded on consultation as the several Governments may determine."[22] The resolution, as a basis for a post-war British commonwealth of nations, contributed to the realization of Borden's objectives for the advancement of Canada's interests. His associate in developing the Canadian case was Christie, whose role was of major importance when the prime minister was in London.

Borden's frequent appearances in London—on four extended visits to Britain and continental Europe, for a total of about thirteen months, between 1915 and 1919—also affected the position of the two officially acknowledged participants in the Canadian relationship with the United Kingdom, the governor general and the Canadian high commissioner. Because the Canadian prime minister's personal role was enhanced, particularly by creation of the imperial war cabinet, the importance of the governor general as an intermediary with the British government declined. In 1918, political correspondence between Borden and the British prime minister ceased to be routed via the governor general. The high commissioner, too, tended to be overshadowed when Borden was in London. His office was much busier than it had been in peacetime, but increased activity did not necessarily indicate involvement in the top levels of decision-making. Indeed, the high commissioner's office was supplanted, to some extent, by other channels established to deal with particular aspects of wartime collaboration between Canada and the United Kingdom.

This was not what the acting high commissioner, Perley, had in mind. "The next few years," he told Borden in August 1914, "are going to be full of problems connected with the Empire and its future relationship and the difficult question of cooperation between its component parts and I cannot but think it will help very much the solution of these problems if Canada had a [cabinet] Minister in this office who would be in continual touch with the Government of Great Britain."[23] Perley was certain that, if the high commissioner were a member of the Canadian cabinet like himself, rather than merely a government official, he would carry more weight with the British authorities and have greater access to sensitive information. Internal minutes of the Colonial Office supported Perley's contention,[24] but Borden did not agree. Perley (knighted in the interim) therefore was not given permanent appointment as high commissioner until after he withdrew from the cabinet in 1917.

Perley's ministerial status, even though he was only acting high commissioner, enabled him to persuade the Colonial Office to provide him with copies of all dispatches being sent through the governor general to the Canadian government.[25] Some other departments in London, by contrast, bypassed his office on occasion in their dealings with the governor general.[26] Eventually the governor general became the channel for transmitting correspondence on policy issues, whereas much of the detail associated with troops and supplies was handled by the high commissioner. There were no hard and fast rules, however, as to what means were to be used. Thus, while the normal route for the Militia Department was through the office of the high commissioner, its minister often went direct to the War Office. The Department of the Naval Service, in contrast, worked through External Affairs, the governor general, and the Colonial Office in doing business with the Admiralty.

This variety in the channels of communication carried with it the danger of confusion, particularly while Col. Sir Sam Hughes (as he became in 1915), who paid little attention to established lines of authority, was minister of militia in Canada. In an effort to deal with these difficulties, Borden used Perley to intervene in relations between the British War Office and the Canadian Expeditionary Force and also as a source of advice in handling complaints from disgruntled members of that force. When Hughes was dropped from the cabinet in 1916, Borden accepted Perley's recommendation that the chief Canadian authority in Britain be a civilian. On October 27 of that year, a new department of government known as the Overseas Ministry was created, and on November 1 Perley, while still acting high commissioner, was placed in charge as minister of overseas military forces.[27]

This arrangement helped in the co-ordination of military and civilian work, but the load was too heavy for one man to carry for long. In 1918 the Canadian Overseas Military Headquarters was established as a section of General Headquarters under Brig.-Gen. J. F. L. Embury. Its role was to confer with General Headquarters on matters concerning the organization and administration of the Canadian forces and, after the war, to look after the demobilization of the Canadian Corps and the adjustment and settlement of Canadian affairs in France. Once this headquarters was established, there was no further need for External Affairs or the high commissioner's office to handle business in the United Kingdom on behalf of the Militia Department or the Department of the Naval Service.

Although it was only one of several channels of communication between the Canadian and British governments, the high commissioner's office played a changed and very busy role during the war.[28] At the outset the office was called on to make various financial arrangements with the Treasury Department in London. The office became heavily involved as well in arranging for British war purchases, in ensuring that British and allied authorities were aware of Canada's capacity to provide supplies, and in helping Canadian companies deal with the effects of British export controls on trade with third countries. The presence of large numbers of Canadian forces in Britain and at the front brought forth a never-ending flow of issues to be settled or investigated. There were also numerous miscellaneous tasks. These included arranging for gold, owed to the Bank of England from the United States and other countries, to be transferred to Canada for custody in the vaults of the Department of Finance; for soldiers to cast ballots in federal and provincial elections; and for visits to the front. Passport work increased so much as a result of the wartime requirements of other governments that a special staff had to be formed. By 1918, between 1,500 and 2,000 passports per month were being issued.

Further complicating the task of the Canadian representative in London during the war was renewed interest by the provincial agents general in opening up more direct lines of communication with the British government. On the death of Lord Strathcona, they reasoned that the time had arrived to redress their situation before a successor was appointed. After meeting with his counterparts, the agent general of Ontario, Richmond Reid, wrote to Borden on February 2, 1914, in search of a higher status that would allow them to bypass the high commissioner in bringing provincial matters to the attention of the British government. He pointed out that, when Ontario had opened its office in 1909, it had had a staff of three, but that by 1914 the number had grown to twenty-one and there were branches in Belfast and Glasgow as well. How could the high commissioner's office, with a staff of only seven, adequately advance the interests of Ontario as well as those of the other provinces? Another source of discontent was the more advantageous position of the agents general of the Australian states. Even the representative of Tasmania, Reid complained, received more recognition than did he and his Canadian colleagues. The same point was made in a joint submission from all the provincial representatives, transmitted through the premier of Quebec, which followed Reid's.

Borden's response to these requests came in the form of a memorandum on the subject prepared by Pope, who pointed out that the constitutional positions of the Australian states and the Canadian provinces were not analogous. The king appointed the governors of the Australian states, and they were entitled to correspond with the secretary of state for the colonies. Since the provincial lieutenant-governors could not communicate with the Colonial Office, it would be inconsistent to authorize their agents to do so. Nor did Pope admit any advantage in a multiple system of representation. He reaffirmed, rather, that there should continue to be a single channel of communication through the office of the high commissioner.

In the interest of prosecuting the war, the matter of provincial agents was held in abeyance, but it was not lost sight of. A belated response to Pope's memorandum came in July 1916 from the agent general of Alberta, John Reid (whose office had been created in 1913), through his premier. Reid rejected Borden's "gratuitous lecture on constitutional relations" as begging the question. No provincial agent general, it was claimed, ever dreamed of taking part in matters of state in London. What was desired was a better means of conducting business with British officials on matters that did not come within the purview of the high commissioner's office. Borden would promise only the high commissioner's assistance in the discharge of their duties by the agents general.

No more successful was another approach tried by the government of Nova Scotia after the war. A minute of council was forwarded by the lieutenant-governor asking the governor general to make representations to the Colonial Office toward recognition of the provincial agents general. The request was sent on to London but was turned down by the Colonial Office after Pope let it be known that the granting of such recognition would furnish the provinces with the means of embarrassing the federal government and lowering the status of the high commissioner.[29]

In Paris there were no such problems, since the government of Quebec had chosen to do without a representative of its own after Roy relinquished the post in 1913. His work as commissioner general of Canada was much increased by the war. At the outset of the conflict, he won the hearts of the French people for his dedication to his work. When Paris was menaced and practically deserted in September 1914, the only foreign government representative to remain at his post was Roy.[30] His primary responsibility later was to obtain French war contracts for Canadian businesses. He also handled numerous problems arising from the presence of Canadian soldiers in France. Toward the end of the war the staff of the office in Paris was doubled (to six, excluding Roy) to deal with these matters and to support a renewed effort to find more Canadian markets on the continent.

Wartime developments necessitated smoother and more effective means for representing Canadian interests in the United States, an endeavour in which Pope played an important role. He continued to deal with the fisheries questions which were his specialty and took on new tasks as well. In the early months of the war, for example, he spent much of his time assisting the British embassy in Washington in sorting out technical problems relating to US neutrality. The agenda given to him by Borden for a visit to Washington in June 1917 included use of Canadian military camps by US troops, provision of railway transport for troops, food control, suspension of coasting laws on the Great Lakes, acquisition of steel for the Canadian Car and Foundry Co., and arrangements for nickel shipments.[31]

In carrying out his work in Washington, Pope developed very close working relations with Bryce's successor as British ambassador, Sir Cecil Spring Rice, and with the governor general's secretary. On many issues these three, through informal discussions and correspondence, would decide on both the substance of recommendations and the best means of presenting them. When an approach had been settled in this way, it was ready to go forward to the prime minister in Ottawa or to the Foreign Office or the Colonial Office in London, depending on the subject. Thus before the ambassador sent a proposal through the usual British channels to Borden, he and Pope would work out the details, the timing for presentation, and the expected response.

Near the end of the war Spring Rice acknowledged that, had it not been for Pope, who had "the esteem and confidence of the State Dept. and all US officials," the complicated three-sided relationship could never have worked so well.[32] Pope, however, was not the only participant. Christie was an important source of ideas for explaining the empire's wartime objectives to Americans. Other prominent Canadians dealt with specialized requirements arising from the war. Together with the British embassy, they developed means of doing business in Washington outside the formal channels. These, according to Spring Rice, met with the approval of the US State Department, which was

> very willing that business should be transacted direct by the heads of the Canadian Departments concerned with the corresponding number in the American Government. The part that the Embassy plays is merely to inform the State Department and to stand aside until the negotiation is completed, or until an official communication from the Embassy

to the United States Government becomes necessary. Such official communication, of course, is communicated in copy to Ottawa and London. It has been the custom of the British Ambassador to go to Ottawa at least twice a year in order to confer with the Governor General and his Ministers, and to make verbal reports and explanations as to the business in Washington and the political situation.[33]

Successful though these informal arrangements were, they became insufficient to handle the growing range of Canadian interests as the war continued, particularly in view of concurrent pressures on the British embassy. By 1916 the embassy was swamped with war-related work and complained that it no longer had time to devote to Canadian issues. The Canadians, too, had reason for dissatisfaction, for the frequent turnover of junior personnel in the embassy made it impossible for the British to master these subjects in detail or to provide continuity in handling them. There was also concern in the Department of Marine and Fisheries that the embassy did not give it adequate advance warning of congressional bills affecting Canada.[34] Further problems were the declining influence of Spring Rice, who was unpopular with President Woodrow Wilson's government, and the proliferation in Washington of British wartime agencies that had no Canadian connections.

Borden's solution was to suggest appointment of a Canadian representative, independent of the embassy, with the title of high commissioner. Like earlier ideas about a Canadian presence in Washington, this one was troubling to the British authorities, and it came to naught, though not because of their objections. Rather, the person ultimately chosen for the post, John Douglas Hazen, the minister of marine and fisheries, declined the offer because of the cost of establishing himself in Washington.[35]

Relations with the United States became more complicated after that country entered the war on April 6, 1917, because of the number of new government agencies that sprang up there. This development shifted the centre of Canadian interest from the US State Department to other offices involved in procuring supplies. Among those affected was Sir Joseph Flavelle, chairman of the Imperial Munitions Board, established in Canada in 1915 to co-ordinate production of munitions and their shipment to the front, and responsible to the Ministry of Munitions in Britain. As early as May 1917 Flavelle decided that he needed a permanent representative in Washington to handle the business of his board. Others had similar requirements, including C. A. Magrath, who as fuel controller provided liaison with an American counterpart to ensure quick and efficient co-operation in an area of vital importance to Canada, half of whose coal came from the United States. In September, Magrath urged on Borden the need for "a man of exceptional ability" to serve in Washington as the direct representative of the prime minister.[36]

By October, Flavelle was telling Borden that, for his board to function effectively, a representative in Washington was essential. His choice was Lloyd Harris, an Ontario manufacturer who had handled munitions contracts and was familiar with relations between business and government. By mid-November Harris was in Washington as a lobbyist for Canadian manufacturers. He quickly realized that his work was greatly hampered by lack of formal authority. In January 1918, therefore, he urged Borden to create a Canadian war mission that would be the equivalent of purchasing offices established by other allied powers.

Harris's idea made good sense to Borden, but Pope had reservations. To the under-secretary, a permanent Canadian representative in Washington was not only unnecessary but an undesirable departure from imperial unity. He realized, however, that he could not speak out against a wartime necessity. "My chief apprehension," he confided to his diary, "is that this office might be a weapon in the future in the hands of men not so loyal to England as I am convinced Sir Robert Borden is. On that, however, we must take chances."[37] Officials in the Colonial Office had concerns similar to Pope's, but they acquiesced: they knew it was futile to oppose, and the office was to be only a temporary wartime operation.

The mission was established, with Harris as chairman, by order-in-council on February 2, 1918. The chairman was empowered to communicate with the prime minister on questions of importance and was to be kept informed of all Anglo-American negotiations in so far as they affected Canada. Under special direction from the prime minister, and in conjunction with the British ambassador, Harris was "to engage in negotiations with the Government of the United States relating to affairs which, while directly concerning Canada, may also affect the interests of the British Commonwealth as a whole."[38] These provisions made it clear that, despite the increase in his domestic preoccupations, the prime minister would continue to play the leading role on matters of war policy involving the United States. The responsibility of the department was to cover the cost of the office, even though the activities were largely commercial in nature.

The department had a similarly limited relationship with a bureau of information that the Canadian government established in New York. Financial administration of the bureau was the responsibility of External Affairs, but questions of policy came under the Privy Council Office. The department assumed supervisory responsibility after the war but never became involved in the substance of information work. The bureau was transferred to the Department of Trade and Commerce in 1921.

The effect of the war

While Borden gave a good deal of attention to the large issues of foreign policy during the war, he found as the conflict continued that he had little time for questions of lesser importance. Help in dealing with the latter resulted from the prime minister's decision, for the first time in Canadian history, to give some members of Parliament departmental responsibilities without making them members of the cabinet. In 1916 he created the post of parliamentary under-secretary of state for external affairs. The incumbent was to assist the prime minister in the administration of the department and, subject to his approval, to conduct official communications with foreign governments. He was also to preside over the department in the prime minister's absence. Held successively by Hugh Clark and F. H. Keefer, the post was of some benefit to Borden as a wartime expedient. In conformity with the legislation temporarily authorizing the government to pay the salaries of such positions, the office was terminated in July 1920.[39]

After formation of the Union government in October 1917, Borden considered giving up the external affairs portfolio. In his mind for the succession was Newton W. Rowell, formerly Ontario Liberal leader, whom Borden made president of the privy council and vice-chairman of the war committee of the cabinet and on whom he relied heavily for support and advice. Rowell shared the prime minister's outlook on external affairs and served as acting secretary of state for external affairs during some of the latter's lengthy absences. He also attended in 1918 the meetings of the imperial war cabinet and the Imperial War Conference. Pope got along well with him and pronounced him "the best I have ever served under, at all times accessible, courteous, patient, and one who quickly and decisively made up his mind, an invaluable quality in a minister."[40] Yet Borden failed to give Rowell ministerial responsibility for External Affairs. One result was to deprive the department of a vigorous administrative shake-up, for Rowell and Christie would have been prepared to introduce substantial changes in its mode of operation.[41]

Administrative improvement would have been timely, for the war had affected even routine operations in the department. The increased burdens had necessitated bringing in a host of temporary clerks, who were paid not out of the department's regular budget but from funds appropriated for exceptional expenditures, under the War Appropriations Act. The number of temporaries increased from four in 1916 to fifteen in 1917 and fifty-seven in 1918. Much of the clerical workload involved the issuance of passports. Whereas only 461 had been issued during the fiscal year 1914–15, by 1920–21 the number totalled 30,600.[42] The additional temporaries were required also to supervise the expenditures of the Canadian war mission in Washington, the information office in New York, and a number of new agencies in Ottawa. Among the last was the "Empress of Ireland" Relief Fund, established to compensate the families of passengers who had lost their lives when the vessel sank in the Gulf of St Lawrence on May 29, 1914. As well, the department had to deal with the stresses on the home front caused by the war. Staff was required, for example, to handle voluminous correspondence with people who sought exemptions from the prohibition on overseas travel in order to visit members of the armed forces stationed abroad.

The increase in personnel did not automatically lead to more efficient conduct of business, since it caused severe shortages of space which necessitated creation of new and inconvenient work places. When the department took over its rooms in the East Block in 1914 there was no provision in the original plan for the library, which had to be located on the third storey of another wing. Toward the end of 1916, additional clerks employed to work on passports were housed in the library, which for all practical purposes ceased to function. "I venture to think it specially unfitting," Pope wrote to Borden in 1917, "that the Department presided over by the Prime Minister, and which in other countries is always given prominence should be so circumscribed."[43] The under-secretary got nowhere, however, with a suggestion that he be given space in the East Block occupied by other departments. Rather, he was asked by the Department of Finance to give up his two passport rooms for three storage rooms in the attic, causing him to complain to the deputy minister of public works that "his Department is treated as if it were no account at all, while accountants and computers, who could account and compute just as well anywhere else, are luxuriously lodged."[44]

Nothing was done to alleviate the problem of insufficient and inadequately arranged quarters, even though attention was called to one of its major consequences. Complaints came from the public and from members of Parliament about the inability of the department to provide passports within a reasonable length of time. With the backlog getting worse as the number of applicants reached 3,000 per month in 1918, Pope pleaded with Rowell to intervene so that a number of rooms, recently given to women working in the Victory Loan campaign, could be converted into a passport office accessible to the public. In making his recommendation, Pope was not unmindful of the distraction created for the men of his own staff by these "young ladies of very youthful appearance."[45] But they turned out to make a better claim than he to their offices. The department therefore had to live with overcrowding until the demands of war subsided.

Apart from accommodation in Ottawa, many changes had taken place in the department's operations by the end of the war. An office was functioning in Washington with a staff of nine, and in London there were eleven, including the high commissioner. In Paris there had been an increase to eight, including the commissioner general. With the acquiescence of the Colonial Office, these establishments were dealing with officials of the host governments. At home, the number of departmental files being opened annually had increased vastly, from 1,362 in 1913 to 8,470 in 1918. The permanent staff had doubled to twenty-six (seventeen men and nine women), and at various times there were more than twice that number of temporaries.

Yet, although the department had taken on some new wartime functions, the change was more one of degree than of kind. There were still only three officers, Pope, Walker, and Christie, and only the last contributed to formulation of policy on major international issues. Much external business was conducted not by External Affairs at all but by ministers in charge of other departments, who were travelling abroad more frequently than before the war. Above all it was the prime minister who was in charge of foreign policy, and he exercised his authority more by virtue of that office than as secretary of state for external affairs. The department had more work to do and more resources to do it with, but its range of responsibilities remained virtually unchanged.

FALLING BEHIND THE TIMES, 1918–1921

The peace settlement

Canada's position in the imperial war cabinet and later at the peace conference in Paris on the post-war settlement was determined largely by Borden as head of his country's delegation, in consultation with those who accompanied him. He chose as his associates Sir George Foster (knighted in 1914), minister of trade and commerce; Arthur Sifton, minister of customs and inland revenue; and Charles Doherty, minister of justice. Christie was there to advise the prime minister, to keep Ottawa informed of what was transpiring, and to provide legal expertise. Also on the legal side was the judge advocate general, Lt.-Col. O. M. Biggar.

There was no advance planning, nor were there position papers or commentaries drawn up on the British and American proposals on the agenda. The foremost legal experts in the delegation, Doherty, Christie, and Biggar, tried their hands at some draft proposals but were at a disadvantage from a slow start and gave up when they realized that the British were not interested in late submissions.[46] Their work therefore became revising and copy-editing what others had initiated. As well, members of the delegation, together with a group of Canadian businessmen, headed by Harris of the war mission in Washington, were kept busy trying to promote

Canadian products and expertise for use in European reconstruction.

The dominions attended the Paris Peace Conference and signed the resultant treaties as part of the British Empire but had little influence on negotiations, which were dominated by representatives of the great powers. Borden thought that the enhancement of Canada's international status as a result of such participation was an important if limited advance. "Canada," he told his wife, "got nothing out of the war except recognition."[47] Pope was more negative. "I am one of those," he observed to Foster, "who do not see in what way Canada's international status has varied in the last half century."[48] As an upholder of the status quo in the imperial relationship, Pope was not displeased to come to this conclusion. This outlook was now well behind the times, and it was to keep him in a minor role in policy-making in the final years of his career.

The League of Nations

The most obvious post-war change in international diplomacy that required adaptation was the creation of the League of Nations—in which Canada was individually represented—as an instrument to promote and enforce international peace. The Canadian delegates to the first assembly in Geneva in 1920 were Doherty, Foster, and Rowell. Their position was prominent, for, in the absence of the non-member United States, they were expected by other countries to provide a North American point of view. The task was one they were well equipped to handle, as the most experienced and knowledgeable Canadian ministers on international affairs. The delegation was therefore able to function effectively without much help from the department: all Pope and Walker did was to package some documents related to its forthcoming activities.

Despite the prominent Canadian role in Geneva, Pope was not impressed. He believed it inappropriate to Canada as a member of the British Empire. "I think it is all absurd," he wrote upon their return, "and I am convinced that Canada's true policy just now is to develop her resources and to leave European questions such as the Bessarabian future &c to our Imperial statesmen and the trained experts of Downing Street." Pope was never bashful about declaring that he had not read the League of Nations covenant and did not believe in it.[49] Christie, in contrast, was concerned about the department's inability to serve a government committed to playing a more active international role. "Nothing could be more futile," he had noted earlier, "than to expect governments to act wisely and well if they are badly informed and advised, or badly served in the execution of policy."[50] Rowell, too, was aware of the department's deficiencies. As acting minister in 1920, he sent Christie to London. One of Christie's tasks was to determine the channels through which the British government and the dominions would work with the League's secretariat. Another was to study how the Foreign Office functioned, with a view to improving the organization of External Affairs.[51]

Representation in Washington

Borden rather than the department took the lead in plans for the future of the Canadian war mission in Washington. The mission had clearly established the advantage of a separate Canadian presence in the US capital, and neither Borden nor Christie was willing to see it disappear when the war ended. Borden ordered it continued until the peace treaty was signed, and he hoped thereafter to turn his attention to transforming it into a permanent mission. In his view it was "in effect, although not in form, a diplomatic mission."[52]

As in the past, the British Foreign Office was unenthusiastic about the prospect of a distinctive and prominent Canadian presence in Washington.[53] Eventually, however, it suggested that Canada appoint a minister responsible for Canadian affairs who would be second-in-command at the embassy and in charge in the ambassador's absence but not accredited separately to the US president. This proposition was accepted in Ottawa. On May 10, 1920, the acting prime minister, Sir George Foster, announced that a Canadian minister would be appointed to Washington. He would take his instructions from External Affairs, be second-in-command in the British embassy, and replace the ambassador when the latter was absent.

In Parliament, Laurier's successor (chosen in 1919) as leader of the opposition, Mackenzie King, denounced the measure as a fuzzy compromise. The whole reason for having a Canadian representative in Washington, he argued, was that the country had not been well served by British diplomats, who looked after their own rather than dominion interests. "Why not," he continued, "let the British diplomatists manage British affairs and let us manage our own affairs," instead of having a subordinate Canadian minister handling business for the mother country in the ambassador's absence? Conferences and a co-operative spirit between Britain and Canada were the only links required.[54] But the Liberals were not united on the issue, W. S. Fielding taking the position that there should not be an appointment of any kind. This conflict enabled Borden to dismiss their arguments. Yet he did not consolidate his success, for when he left office a few weeks later he had not appointed anyone to fill the new position.

Headquarters activities

Pope, meanwhile, had to spend much of his time on the continuing problem of delays in passport issuance, which by the beginning of 1919 he had come to regard as a "terrible affliction."[55] Because the difficulty arose in part from overcrowding, Pope had to find a new location for the Passport Office outside the East Block. Late in January 1919 the operation was moved to larger and better-organized offices nearby on Sparks Street.

Shortly afterward, the parliamentary under-secretary, F. H. Keefer, took over supervision of this activity. His reorganization of the office and its procedures brought noticeable improvement within three months. The number of applications handled doubled without an increase in staff being needed, and it became possible to issue a passport in less than forty-eight hours. According to Keefer, the revenue generated (approximately $100,000) covered not only the salaries of the staff involved ($39,000) but also the expenses of the rest of the department as well ($50,000).[56] When demand for passports declined somewhat in 1920, supervision of the operation was returned to a civil servant, John Connolly, recently demobilized from the armed forces.

Removal of the Passport Office from the East Block was contrary to Pope's preference for keeping the department together in a single location. Also subject to challenge was Pope's approach to one of his specialties, the arrangement of tours for imperial and foreign dignitaries, whom he often accompanied on their travels in Canada.

The most important of these post-war tours was that of the Prince of Wales (later King Edward VIII) in the summer of 1919. As under-secretary of state, Pope had successfully organized the tour of the prince's parents, King George V and Queen Mary, when as Duke and Duchess of Cornwall and York they had visited Canada in 1901. The Prince of Wales, however, turned out to have a different approach to the enterprise from his parents, with results disturbing to Pope. Pope considered the prince's preference for informal encounters with the general population to be undignified and possibly dangerous to the royal person. This reaction in turn helped produce tension between himself and the prince's party, which led to his being dropped, to his own relief, from part of the tour.[57] Although goodwill was restored, the episode was an indication that the world of ceremony, just like the world of policy, was changing. Here as well Pope's adherence to the preconceptions of an earlier generation limited his usefulness.

Another post-war challenge to Pope's conception of the proper way of doing things was in the realm of government organization. In 1919 the Civil Service Act was amended to give the Civil Service Commission far-reaching control over and ultimate responsibility for managerial decisions on appointments, promotions, salary scales, and classification.[58] The resultant interference by this agency in the department's operations was not welcomed by Pope. Remuneration, he thought, should be based on ability and aptitude rather than on position. Deputies, he argued, could run their departments more efficiently if left to their own devices. "The present inflexible, rigid, mechanical, iron-bound system," he complained, "destroys initiative, kills individual effort, is subversive of discipline, and tends to the creation of a Service the members of which rely more upon combination, intrigue and cabal among themselves to advance their interests, than upon honest hard work."[59]

Particularly troubling was the effect on the department of the reclassification of positions, carried out after completion of a controversial study by a firm of management consultants, Arthur Young and Co. of Chicago. Through appeals, most posts were eventually graded to the undersecretary's satisfaction, but some required special intervention. After some difficulty, Agnes McCloskey, who had become the department's chief bookkeeper, was designated departmental accountant grade 1, effective April 1, 1921. This position gave her a salary of $1,500, putting her in the middle of the range for senior clerks ($1,320–$1,680).[60] Walker, whom the commission downgraded, was restored to his former salary level ($4,000) after the prime minister became involved. Borden also secured Christie a raise, to $5,000 per year. Here, if it were required, was an indication of the comparative value placed on the department as an institution and on Christie as the prime minister's personal adviser: while Walker was second in command of the department, his salary was less than that of the legal adviser, nominally the third-ranking officer but in fact a more important contributor to the making of foreign policy.

The department in 1920

Borden, who resigned as prime minister and secretary of state for external affairs on July 9, 1920, had developed a robust view of the position he wanted his country to occupy in the world and had forged a set of policies to achieve it, but he had not applied himself so consistently to preparing an institutional framework to give them lasting effect. Nor was the deficiency supplied by the department. In Pope and Walker, External Affairs did not have the resources of leadership that might have enabled it to respond imaginatively to the challenges of the war and its immediate aftermath. Christie, who might have provided the department with initiative of its own, was not in a position to do so, since his main sphere of activity was in the service of the prime minister. By 1920 the prospects of administrative reinvigoration without a striking change in political leadership were probably less than they had ever been, for Borden was in poor health at the close of his years in office and Pope, weary after the heightened pace of activity since 1914, was intent upon returning to the pre-war status quo.

The more vigorous direction that the department required might have come from Rowell. He was perhaps best placed to make optimum use of the very different talents of Pope and Christie, for both regarded him as the ideal replacement for Borden as Conservative leader and secretary of state for external affairs. Rowell, however, decided that he could not work with Arthur Meighen, who was chosen to succeed Borden as Conservative leader and prime minister, and promptly left the government. His resignation of itself had a negative effect on the department, for it took place before Christie's report on his study of the British Foreign Office had been received. As a result, the idea of using the British model as a guide to the improvement of the department in Ottawa was dropped.[61]

Meighen and the department

The double duty of prime minister and secretary of state for external affairs was not one for which Meighen was well prepared, for he was a neophyte in international relations. His only previous involvement had been in 1917, when he had handled negotiations in London on Canadian railways. He had not participated in the debate in the House of Commons over the treaty of Versailles and the League of Nations covenant, and he did not see himself as an international statesman in the mould of Borden. Consequently, he relied even more heavily than his predecessor on Christie. As Meighen recalled many years later, "He was my principle adviser, and, indeed, under myself the Chief Officer of the Department of External Affairs."[62]

Thus Christie continued to play an important role in imperial and international conferences. In 1921, he worked closely with Meighen at the Imperial Conference in London and was Borden's right-hand man when the latter represented Canada in the British Empire's delegation at the Washington Conference on the Limitation of Naval Armament. In Washington, he also worked for Sir Maurice Hankey, the secretary to the British cabinet, in the delegation's secretariat. When Hankey returned to London before the conclusion of the conference, Christie was asked to head the secretariat. This assignment, observed Grattan O'Leary in the *Ottawa Journal* on January 28, 1922, was "a reminder to the Canadian public that the much maligned Civil Service contains officials who, in capacity, knowledge and experience, are equal to the best civil servants in the world."[63]

Meighen placed the office of the high commissioner in London under the jurisdiction of External Affairs, thereby meeting a long-felt need for centralized direction from headquarters, but was not an enthusiast for an expanded presence abroad. Representation in Washington, according to the British ambassador to the United States, was a matter about which Meighen had reservations. Meighen, the ambassador recorded, told him that "he was personally opposed to the idea of Canada being represented by a Minister at Washington''[64] and refrained from expressing his opinion at home only out of deference to Borden's views. Thus Meighen presided over not the enhancement but the downgrading of the Canadian presence in Washington: the war mission was wound up as of March 31, 1921, and its secretary, Merchant Mahoney, was retained as an agent of External Affairs in the US capital pending further arrangements. While not a member of the staff and having no diplomatic status, Mahoney did obtain an office in the British embassy, from which he provided information on commercial matters to the Canadian government.

The fate of the office in Washington was symbolic of Meighen's relationship with the department and its work during his eighteen months in office. His main concerns were domestic, leaving him little time for external affairs. For the most part, he continued the policies articulated by Borden and sustained his method of operation. The department, meanwhile, although it continued its modest growth, reaching a level of thirty-five employees in 1921, was getting weaker at the top. Pope, now sixty-seven, was ordered by his doctor at the end of the year to take an extended rest because of a heart condition.

By that time, it was clear that the Canadian government would soon need both more and better resources for the conduct of its external relations. In spite of the efforts of Borden and Christie, schemes for a united imperial policy-making mechanism had not borne fruit. Thus Canada, it seemed, would be obliged to find its own way in international affairs rather than relying on the collective resources of the empire: willy-nilly, it would develop the constitutional implications of the External Affairs Act of 1909. The Canadian government would have to develop more extensive resources of its own both for doing the country's business abroad and for gathering the information to meet its unique needs in decision-making. Such expansion, of course, would also require an increase in headquarters personnel. The need for growth in the senior ranks in Ottawa was already evident, for the department had been receiving since the war hundreds of reports on international issues from the British[65] and, more recently, others from the secretariat of the League. With only three officers in Ottawa, it could not be expected to put all this material to effective use.

The immediate problem facing the department, however, was that of transition. The external policies developed by Borden and sustained by Meighen were deeply rooted in the philosophy of the Conservative party. That meant that they might well be changed by a government with different priorities. The difficulty was not the prospect of change itself, but the lack of resources to bring it about smoothly. To a considerable degree, Christie had replaced Pope as a one-man foreign office, especially as a source of ideas and as a negotiator in the changed world of post-war diplomacy. But he had done so as a personal associate of two prime ministers, far removed from his departmental base. The question for the future was not Christie's integrity but how he would be perceived by a successor government. That such an issue arose was an indication of the state of development of the department when King took over after Meighen went down to defeat in the election of December 6, 1921.

Chapter Four
Skelton Takes Charge:
1921–1926

NEW LEADERSHIP AND NEW PRIORITIES

FOR THE FIRST TIME IN its history, Canada after the election of 1921 had a minority government, as a result of deep regional divisions within the country. With the support of 116 Liberals and one Independent Liberal, William Lyon Mackenzie King was one seat short of controlling the House of Commons. Arrayed against the government were 50 Conservatives, 64 members of a new agrarian party, the Progressives, and 4 others. Much of the government's energy, therefore, was devoted to the problem of survival. Although it had to deal with a number of international problems that arose during the period, it had little time for external initiatives, and the conditions that had produced the election result encouraged caution in this area of activity. Not only did the government have to devote time and attention to affairs close to home, but it also had to be mindful that some of the deepest causes of division arose from external commitments and interests. One major problem was the aftermath of the wartime conscription crisis in Quebec. Equally serious was disagreement over tariff policy between protectionist interests in central Canada and the Maritime and western provinces, which favoured reduction of trade barriers.

Under the new government, Canada's involvement in the wider world might be limited and the approach cautious, but already by 1921 it was clear that the course would be different. The country's international position had been enhanced by participation in the Paris peace conference and representation at the League of Nations. The Liberals wanted to go a good deal farther in the direction of independence than Borden had done. During its leadership convention in 1919, the party had strongly opposed central- ized imperial control of foreign policy and had demanded that any substantive change in Canada's relations with the empire be subject to parliamentary approval and confirmation by referendum. There was not complete acceptance at first of this position, for the debate in the House of Commons on approval of the peace treaties with Germany and Austria had seen the Liberals split into two main factions. Some, such as the former minister of finance, W. S. Fielding, who had come second in the leader- ship race, were close to the Conservatives: they argued in favour of the constitutional status quo and maintenance of a position of subordination in external affairs. Others, including Ernest Lapointe, who was to become King's Quebec lieutenant, asserted that Borden had not gone far enough. By the time the Liberals took office in 1921, the latter approach had won out, and the new government spoke from a viewpoint clearly different from that of its predecessor.

King had not taken part in the debate on the peace treaties. He had lost his seat in the election of 1911 and had not returned to the House until October 30, 1919. His position, however, was well established on the side of change. His views on external policy differed markedly from those of Borden and Meighen. It should be grounded, he argued, on national unity and its projection abroad—that is, it should be an extension of domestic policy and should not become a source of tension or divisive- ness. Imperial relations should be conducted according to the same prin- ciple. Thus King wanted to avoid automatic involvement in international crises facing the empire. Instead he came to favour a more autonomous position for Canada, which in turn would require more extensive resources for the conduct of external relations.

The Department of External Affairs, as King inherited it from Borden and Meighen, was not well equipped to take on an expanding role, even at the gradual pace dictated by the circumstances of minority government. It was, except for Christie, still much the same department as that created by Laurier and Aylesworth a dozen years earlier. Its officer strength of three had remained static for nearly a decade. Of the total personnel of thirty-five in Ottawa in 1922, more than half were doing passport work. Most serious of all, the under-secretary, Pope, was ill-suited to the require- ments of the new government. In failing health and out of tune with the times, he would not be much help in handling the most pressing issues of the day.

Much of Pope's work on protocol, government hospitality, and cere- mony gradually passed to Howard Measures, who joined King's staff in 1921. The other subjects on which the prime minister might find it useful to consult the under-secretary were decidedly limited. While Pope made a contribution to preparations for the prime minister's participation in imperial conferences in 1923 and retained an interest in some areas of policy, including aspects of the relationship with the United States, the under-secretary's range of activity seems to have been narrowing. "The Prime Minister and the Minister of National Defence left for Washington today to discuss with the U.S. Secy. of State the question of naval vessels on the Great Lakes [once one of Pope's subjects]," he noted on July 10, 1922. "The weather here is delightful."[1]

King therefore had to look elsewhere for advice on policy. One who was well qualified to help was Christie. At first King seemed to welcome the possibility, for he told Christie when they met that he wanted to carry on the relationship that had been established with Borden and Meighen. He therefore kept Christie from going to conferences in Genoa and Geneva in order to have him available for important work at home. To Christie's frustration, however, that work did not materialize very quickly. When it did, it turned out to involve not major policy issues but taking over from Pope the task of accompanying a visitor from India on a tour of Canada. Part of the problem was King's hesitation to trust someone who had been as closely linked as Christie with two Conservative prime ministers. But there was a deeper difficulty as well, for it is evident from his diary that King did not feel comfortable in Christie's presence and found conversation with him difficult. As a result, Christie was moved into an inferior office and left with little to do. After March 1922 he did not even have much of relevance to read, since he was denied access to Foreign Office cables. In May 1923, weary of underemployment, Christie resigned to join Dunn, Fisher and Co., the London financial firm of the Canadian millionaire Sir James Dunn.[2]

Following Christie's resignation, King began to exert gentle pressure on the under-secretary to think of retirement. The latter let it be known that he wanted to work until April 1, 1925, and, in order to maximize his income, to go on paid leave before finally retiring a year later. In the mean time, King, as he told the House of Commons in 1923, left the department to function as a post office for distributing dispatches.[3] As they had done for so long, Pope and Walker concentrated on the more routine aspects of external relations: passport and consular affairs, general administration, and, in Pope's case particularly, official visits and protocol matters.

Having decided, at least for the time being, not to look to the department for advice on foreign policy, King had to find an alternative. At first, he placed a good deal of reliance on his private secretary, Laurent Beaudry, and on O. M. Biggar, judge advocate general and later chief electoral officer, who had been in the Canadian party at the peace conference. Increasingly, however, King went outside the public service, turning to his friend John S. Ewart, who had been adviser to Laurier's minister of justice, Allen Aylesworth, during the arbitration on North Atlantic fisheries at The Hague in 1910. There was help within the cabinet, too, most notably from Ernest Lapointe, the Quebec lieutenant, who was minister of marine and fisheries and later minister of justice. Thus was formed a sort of surrogate department of external affairs after King came to office, but it existed very much on an ad hoc and part-time basis and so did not provide the kind of consistent and comprehensive support that the real thing might have done. King, in other words, was to a considerable degree on his own in dealing with foreign policy. Canada still had a one-man foreign office, in the person of the prime minister and secretary of state for external affairs.

SEEKING POLICY ADVICE

Help from outside the department

The first external problem that King had to deal with was the conclusion early in 1922 of the Washington Conference on the Limitation of Naval Armament, at which Borden continued to represent Canada as a member of the British Empire's delegation. Borden informed King that it would be impracticable to require that the agreement provide for approval by Parliament as the new prime minister had suggested. King was suspicious that Borden was deliberately trying to bypass Parliament and also feared that he might have committed Canada to something the government would not approve of. Considering his departmental advisers too close to Borden to give the advice he wanted, King turned to Ewart. With Ewart's assurance that he was doing the right thing, King instructed Borden that parliamentary approval would be required before acceptance of the agreement by the government.[4]

A more serious issue arose from conflict between Greece and Turkey as a result of the latter's dissatisfaction with the terms of settlement drawn up by the Paris Peace Conference—the treaty of Sèvres. The Greeks had the support of the United Kingdom, and in September 1922 a crisis developed over the Turkish threat to Chanak, an exposed British outpost on the Asian shore of the Dardanelles. The region was of no direct interest to Canada, and King, preoccupied with running a minority government, had paid little attention to the deteriorating situation there, nor had he received much information from the Foreign Office. He therefore was taken by surprise on September 16 when he learned, from a newspaperman in Toronto, that the United Kingdom was sounding out the possibility of obtaining a Canadian contingent in the event of war with Turkey.

If past experience, most recently the crisis over conscription in 1917, were a guide, the prospect of involvement in the Anglo-Turkish problem could be expected to cause difficulties in Canada; it therefore required the government's careful attention. Christie and Pope were both absent from Ottawa, and Beaudry had agreed to leave the prime minister's service for the position of editor in chief of the Quebec City newspaper *Le Soleil* on the day the crisis broke. Thus King had to do a good deal of the research and drafting himself.

Because the issue was potentially so divisive, King considered it important to consult the two cabinet ministers, Fielding and Lapointe, who most clearly represented the extremes of national opinion on the question of imperial solidarity, although both at the time were in Geneva at the League of Nations Assembly. Fielding favoured compliance with the British request. Surprisingly, Lapointe at first indicated that he did so as well. King then consulted Ewart and opted for delay. The government, he decided, should request fuller information, seek to put a stop to secret diplomacy, and leave it to Parliament to decide whether the country should go to war if need be in aid of the British. Cabinet agreed and King told the British prime minister, David Lloyd George, that public opinion required the prior approval of Parliament, which could not be obtained immediately since that body was not in session. Encouragement to hold to this course came from Lapointe, who now advised King not to act without parliamentary consent and to pay close attention to public opinion.

For King, public opinion quickly became cause for anxiety. The very possibility that he feared most seemed to be coming to pass as the country split over the issue. French-Canadian newspapers were united against participation, and English-language dailies made their decision along party lines. "Our policy," King wrote, "must be non-participation where we have had nothing to do with policy and no agreement."[5] In a dispatch that he wrote himself, he informed the British that Canada would adhere to a similar policy of non-involvement when time came for resolution of the problem after the fighting was over.

Although the Conservatives sought to exploit criticism of the government, King weathered the domestic storm. The crisis petered out after the opposing countries reached an armistice, which in due course led to a new peace settlement, the treaty of Lausanne, to replace the treaty of Sèvres. King developed the Canadian response to the new treaty without any departmental involvement, except for clerical assistance. He wanted no part of this treaty, especially since he had not had a hand in negotiations. With advice from Ewart and after further consultation with two of his ministers, Charles Stewart and Charles Murphy, King, with the approval of the cabinet, told the British that Canada could not be bound by the treaty unless it had been represented at all peace conferences with full powers, a Canadian had signed the agreement, Parliament had approved, and the king had ratified it at the request of the government in Ottawa. On Ewart's advice, King also suggested to the governor general that he sound out the British on the possibility of inserting a clause in all future treaties that would exempt the dominions from any obligations not explicitly approved by their parliaments. In the end, however, he accepted that signature on behalf of the king was binding on the whole empire, subject to the condition that the extent of Canada's obligation should be determined by the Parliament in Ottawa.[6]

If the Canadian government wanted to avoid automatic involvement in commitments such as those arising from the treaty of Lausanne, it needed acknowledgment that it was able to sign international agreements on its own. For King, therefore, there was now a real need to make good on a Canadian claim to independent treaty-making power. There was also an opportunity to do so, when the halibut fisheries treaty with the United States was ready for signature in 1923. Important though it was to the evolution of Canada's international position, this enterprise was one in which the department had little involvement of substance.

In December 1922 the governments of Canada and the United States had entered into negotiations to regulate the rapidly depleting halibut fishery in the North Pacific Ocean. On the Canadian side the negotiations were conducted mainly by experts from the Department of Marine and Fisheries. They were successfully concluded in early 1923, and a target date for the signing ceremony was set for March 1 in Washington. After consultations with his cabinet colleagues, most notably the minister of marine and fisheries, Lapointe, King decided that the treaty should be signed by Canada alone, on the ground that only trans-border relations with the United States were involved. There was a good deal of correspondence on this subject with London, which King handled mostly on his own, with some help from Lapointe. The department functioned mainly as a post office.

Independent signature of the treaty was an objective of sufficient importance to King that he was prepared to threaten opening a legation in Washington if he did not get his way. Since the latter possibility was considered by the British to be the greater evil, news of King's intention from the governor general, Lord Byng, produced a co-operative attitude in London on the treaty. Although empowered to use his own judgment, the British ambassador in Washington, Sir Auckland Geddes, was made aware of the implications of resisting King's wishes. Since he, too, wanted to avoid the opening of a legation, Geddes went along with the Canadian position on the treaty, and Lapointe signed alone for Canada on March 2.[7]

King and Skelton

The foreign policy issues that arose in quick succession after the election of 1921 gave King an understanding of both the limitations of the department and the need for better resources for policy making. If he were to advance Canada's exernal interests without undue distraction from his duties as prime minister, King needed a stable source of assistance in articulating his ideas and developing a strategy for giving them effect. For this he turned to Oscar Douglas Skelton, dean of arts at Queen's University. Thus began an association that led to Skelton's appointment as undersecretary of state for external affairs in 1925 and lasted until his death in early 1941.

Skelton was born in Orangeville, Ontario, in 1878, to parents of Anglo-Irish descent. After receiving a master's degree from Queen's, he went on to doctoral studies in political economy at the University of Chicago. In 1907 he returned to Queen's as a lecturer in economics. He became head of the department a year later, at the age of thirty, and dean of arts in 1919. A prolific writer on Canadian history and contemporary politics, he had an influence that spread well beyond the university.

The relationship with the prime minister went back to the days after King had joined Laurier's cabinet as minister of labour, in 1909. Skelton kept in touch during the years King was out of politics following his defeat that year. In 1919, King's election as party leader was the occasion for a complimentary letter from Skelton, which brought the reply that the latter's advice would be welcome. The two met at a convocation at Queen's in the autumn of 1919, when King was given an honorary doctorate, and correspondence on a variety of subjects followed. Skelton had much to say about the tariff and also about Sir Wilfrid Laurier, whose political biography he was soon to complete.[8]

Many of Skelton's views were a matter of public record. He had written the first extended economic history of Canada, in which he examined anti-imperial ideas, the development of Canadian representation abroad, and the position of the country in tariff wars. There was also a biography of Sir Alexander Tilloch Galt, whom he described as Canada's "first diplomat" in his role as high commissioner in London. Together with the biography of Laurier, these works demonstrated Skelton's understanding of Canada's interests in world affairs, from a perspective that was shared by King.

When Skelton went to Ottawa in mid-January 1922 to address the Canadian Club on "Canada and Foreign Policy," King was there to hear him. In his speech, Skelton gave a rebuttal to Lloyd George, who had claimed that the British Foreign Office was still the only acceptable channel for

93

the empire's foreign policy. That contention, Skelton argued, was contrary to precedents established during the Paris Peace Conference. As an alternative, he offered a rationale for control by Canada of its foreign affairs. Skelton pointed out that foreign policy "was an extension of domestic policy and that as we had gained control of the one so we must gain control of the other as to matters affecting ourselves, and by conference and discussion co-operate with other parts of the league of Britannic Nations on the things we have in common."[9] While issues affecting the empire as a whole should be the subject of round-table discussions, any decision to act must be approved by the parliament of each dominion. Canada must take its rightful place in the world as a member of the League or any other international body, but, instead of seeking influence and prestige through external commitments in the way Borden had done, Skelton wanted foreign involvement to flow from national unity and development. He reminded the Canadian Club that the government was developing the capacity to act on its own: "We have a Minister of External Affairs, and we are building up—it has not gone very far yet, but so far as it has gone it has been effective in its personnel—a Department to deal with those questions."

King left the room well pleased with what he had heard. Skelton's speech had given him a coherent and organized plan of action for imperial and international relations. Skelton had expressed ideas that King recognized as his own and had applied to the international sphere some of the concepts the prime minister had dealt with in his book on labour relations, *Industry and Humanity*. Noting that the speech could be used as a basis for a Canadian foreign policy, King wrote of Skelton that night: "He might make a very good Under-Secretary of State [for External Affairs] in succession to Sir Joseph Pope. He certainly has the knowledge and the right point of view."[10] Meanwhile, King was attracted by the possibility of using Skelton as an adviser when circumstances required, and he had so indicated to the speaker at the conclusion of his address.

It did not take long for King to start making use of Skelton's services: in the autumn of 1922 the prime minister sent him, along with the dominion archivist, Arthur Doughty, and the latter's assistant, Gustave Lanctot, to Rio de Janeiro to represent Canada at an international meeting of historians marking the centenary of the independence of Brazil. One result was that Skelton was not available for consultation during the Chanak crisis. He approved of the way it had been handled, however, and on his return to Queen's wrote to King to tell him so. The prime minister responded by inviting Skelton to discuss with him "the whole question of inter-imperial relations and Canada's foreign policy," in the light of his "splendid" address to the Canadian Club.[11] From this encounter flowed an invitation to be King's special adviser on the Canadian delegation to the Imperial Conference of 1923 and the Imperial Economic

Conference that followed it. The assignment was highly important in view of the effect of the Chanak crisis on the prime minister's approach to imperial relations. "I am determined," King noted in his diary, "to smash this secret diplomacy between diff[erent] parts of the Empire, if it is not smashed the Empire will be smashed. . . . I shall force the matter to the fore at the next conference of Prime Ministers."[12]

The Canadian party in London was made up of the usual complement of cabinet ministers and officials, plus J. W. Dafoe, editor of the *Manitoba Free Press*, who was invited to join in the hope that his nationalist position would offset the imperialist interpretation of other writers. In this group, it was Skelton more than all the rest who prepared King to resist centralizing forces in London. King arranged for Skelton to meet with Pope beforehand, and the under-secretary received thanks from the prime minister personally for his assistance with the preparations. Skelton, however, does not seem to have drawn heavily on the resources of the department in carrying out his part of the work. On his own, he prepared memoranda and briefs on constitutional questions, naturalization, extra-territoriality, defence, and tariffs, all of which King had the cabinet approve before the party left for London. On Skelton's brief on the control of foreign poliicy, King commented: "With every line . . . I am in hearty and entire accord. He has an unusually clear mind and brain, his work is excellent."[13]

At the conference, King and Skelton worked successfully to avoid committing Canada to policies and procedures with which they disagreed. As a result, Skelton's advice on imperial matters became well-nigh indispensable. King had always shown a profound respect for Ewart's opinions on this subject, but an entry in his diary after he had had dinner with him and Skelton indicated preference for the latter: "Ewart is very able and better informed than anyone in Canada on foreign affairs, but too extreme. Is for separation. I'm not, I believe in the Br. Empire as a 'Cooperative Commonwealth'. Skelton, I think has modified his views somewhat."[14] But Skelton's main responsibility was still to Queen's, and, while he remained in Kingston, he was not as readily available as Ewart, the prime minister's neighbour. Thus it was to Ewart's house that King went to get advice on the precise wording of the reply to the British on Canada's position regarding the treaty of Lausanne, both before and after cabinet considered it.[15]

League of Nations affairs

With Skelton in Kingston, King had to look elsewhere for help in dealing with issues that arose at the League of Nations. Although not as strong a supporter of the organization as Borden had been, King, without an alternative source of advice in Ottawa, accepted the former prime minister's recommendation that Canada support the reference to the League of a dispute between Italy and Greece over the former country's occupation of Corfu in 1923.[16]

After Christie's resignation, the government had to make new arrangements for responding to schemes arising at the League for the resolution of international disputes, mutual guarantees of security, and disarmament. Ewart, despite his experience of international law, was not an obvious replacement for Christie, for he was in his mid-seventies and was not in government service. Instead, King in January 1924 turned to O. M. Biggar, the chief electoral officer, who, as chairman of the Canadian Bar Association's committee on international law and chairman of the League of Nations Society's executive committee, had an acquaintance with the issues. He was directed "to prepare opinions upon the questions involving the external relations of Canada that may arise from time to time until an appointment has been made to the vacant office of Legal Adviser to the Department of External Affairs."[17]

Christie, when asked by Biggar for advice, commented sharply on the department's lack of resources for dealing with Canada's international interests. King apparently was not insensitive to the problem, for in a letter to the high commissioner in London he acknowledged the need for someone of Christie's calibre who could relieve the prime minister of the burden of drafting his own communications. "I am trying," he concluded, "to persuade Professor Skelton to enter the service, and am not without hope that he may do so."[18] Skelton, who was fond of teaching and loved Queen's, could not easily be torn away from there, but he did arrange a leave of absence. When the university term in 1924 ended, he left the campus for a trial run as counsellor in the Department of External Affairs. Skelton's arrival in Ottawa abruptly ended Biggar's role.

Skelton became involved in League of Nations work as adviser to the Canadian delegation to the assembly in 1924. The leaders of the delegation, Sen. Raoul Dandurand and the minister of national defence, E. M. Macdonald, were divided on one of the main issues for discussion there—the protocol for the pacific settlement of international disputes (the Geneva protocol), produced by a committee of the League, which proposed combining compulsory arbitration, security, and disarmament in a single package. Dandurand wanted to declare Canada's agreement, but Macdonald, suspecting that the protocol would give the organization the capacity to interfere in Canadian affairs, wanted no part of it. Skelton favoured Macdonald's position, for he was concerned that the protocol would involve Canada should the League of Nations ever decide on the application of sanctions against the United States.[19]

Unable to reach a common position, Dandurand and Macdonald had to refer to Ottawa for guidance. With Skelton in Geneva, King turned once again to Ewart, who, claiming inadequate knowledge of the subject, suggested asking the assembly to defer the issue to its next session. This advice was incorporated into the instructions issued by the prime minister.

A liberal interpretation of the instructions enabled Dandurand to make a statement of historic importance on Canada's international responsibilities when his turn came to speak in the assembly. "In this association of mutual insurance against fire the risks assumed by the different states are not equal," he observed. "We [Canadians] live in a fire-proof house, far from inflammable materials. A vast ocean separates us from Europe." Although this part of his speech was later interpreted as a statement of isolationism, Dandurand was not rejecting Canadian participation in an international fire brigade but rather re-emphasizing the conditions for participation. On that basis, he gave as much encouragement as his instructions allowed to Canadian acceptance of the protocol. "It is my firm conviction," he said, "that Canada, faithful to her past, will be prepared to accept compulsory arbitration and the compulsory jurisdiction of the Permanent Court of International Justice. . . . Our Governmnent and our Parliament will have to consider in what measure this Protocol will meet the conditions of our country, and decide whether it can undertake to subscribe to its obligations. . . . We can assure our colleagues that this study will be made with the fullest sympathy."[20]

Having made this commitment in Geneva, Dandurand, on his return to Ottawa, lost no time in urging upon King that Canada accept the protocol, assuring the prime minister that it would be possible to contract out of any automatic commitment to the application of sanctions. King listened but would not discuss Canada's position unless Skelton were present. When Skelton joined in, he raised the concern, which King shared, that despite what Dandurand had said Canada might have to apply sanctions against the United States if that country became involved in an international dispute. But Dandurand had already established close ties with Borden and the League of Nations Society, who were ready to espouse his cause. As a way of avoiding a public debate, King agreed to formation of an interdepartmental committee under Skelton's chairmanship to review the protocol.

Although it later became commonplace, the idea of an interdepartmental committee was at the time a novel means of arriving at external policy. In addition to senior spokesmen for the military, the members were an eclectic mixture of officials who had in some capacity gained an interest in or acquaintance with League affairs. The only outright supporter of the protocol was Biggar, who was concerned lest rejection by Canada hurt the League's prestige. Outspokenly opposed to him were the representatives of National Defence, the dominion statistician, and the undersecretary of state. On their side was a memorandum by Skelton which, by a technique he was to employ effectively over the years, outlined the advantages and disadvantages of the proposal in such a way as to lead the readers to the conclusion he wanted them to draw. In this instance, Skelton favoured a negative outcome. The memorandum, therefore, emphasized the disadvantages of accepting the protocol: the benefits were presented as being all in the realm of idealistic notions of arbitration and security for the world at large, while Canada would be saddled with formidable and precise obligations that could adversely affect the national interest.

Even before the committee reported, King had made his decision. Over dinner at King's home, Laurier House, on February 2, 1925, a group of cabinet ministers heard Dandurand's project criticized by Skelton and Ewart. Three days later the case against the protocol was clinched when the new Conservative prime minister of the United Kingdom, Stanley Baldwin, warned King that "there will be serious risk of grave trouble with the United States in the future if we ratify the Protocol."[21] King needed no more convincing. Skelton was instructed to draft a negative reply to the League that would at the same time show that distinctively Canadian thinking had led to this conclusion.

The Canadian reply, based on the report of the interdepartmental committee, rejected the protocol but took a softer position than that which the United Kingdom had urged upon the dominions. Perhaps encouraged by this positive tone, the secretary general of the League suggested that a bilingual Canadian such as Dandurand could be elected president of the next assembly. King agreed, supported by Skelton, who favoured the idea as a means of underlining the difference between the dominions and Britain. Since Dandurand had British and French backing and considerable standing of his own among the delegates at Geneva, his election was assured.

Dandurand's presidency of the assembly in 1925 was an indication of Canada's widening range of international concerns. The opening of a Canadian office in Geneva at the beginning of 1925, however, had very little to do with External Affairs, for it originated in the government's relationship with the International Labour Organisation (ILO). Although Christie had been on the Canadian delegation to the founding conference of the ILO in 1919, the Department of Labour had the leading role. The ILO's constitution, in fact, authorized it to deal with the ministers of labour of member governments without having to go through normal foreign office channels. When the Department of Justice suggested that items pertaining to the ILO be handled by various departments in Ottawa,

Rowell, president of the privy council and acting secretary of state for external affairs, told the minister of labour: "I think it is desirable that these Departments should make their recommendations as to the actions to be taken, rather than that the Department of External Affairs should take the matter up."[22] Thenceforth, the assistant deputy minister of labour co-ordinated the making of Canadian policy on the ILO and its extensive relations with the provinces.

Thanks to the minister of labour at the time, External Affairs was assigned a role in relations with the ILO by becoming responsible for all submissions to cabinet dealing with ratification of its conventions. Whenever this happened, External Affairs had to obtain the necessary background information from the labour department. Otherwise, External Affairs remained detached from all ILO activities in Canada and would have had little to do with the organization in Geneva had it not been for the difficulty of finding a Canadian representative to attend the quarterly meetings of the Governing Body. The official delegate was the minister of labour, but in practice he was always represented by a substitute. If the assembly of the League were meeting at the same time, one of the delegates did double duty. At other times the Department of Labour either sent someone to Geneva from Ottawa or asked the office of the high commissioner in London or the Canadian commissioner general in Paris to provide a representative. As the Department of Labour readily admitted, a more effective system of representation needed to be devised.[23] But the decisive impetus for a change came not so much from that department as from Dr Walter A. Riddell, a Canadian working for the ILO.

Riddell had attended the founding convention of the ILO as Ontario's deputy minister of labour. In 1920 he joined the permanent staff in Geneva, and from that perspective he came to appreciate the difficulties of Canada's representation on the Governing Body. The idea of a permanent office in Geneva to represent Canada at the organization was his brain-child, which he took to advocating in speeches before Canadian Clubs in March 1924. With the help of Dandurand, King was persuaded to broaden the mandate of the office proposed by Riddell to include assistance to all Canadian delegations to meetings of both the ILO and the League.

Commencing on January 1, 1925, Riddell, who left the staff of the ILO at that time, was appointed Dominion of Canada advisory officer, League of Nations. Since his main work was still with the ILO, Riddell himself having confessed ignorance of League matters, he was to report to the minister of labour, who for the remaining portion of the financial year also paid his salary and expenses. Thereafter, Riddell's office came under External Affairs. As his title implied, Riddell did not have diplomatic status, but, because of the nature of the activities going on in Geneva, he quickly became heavily engaged in League as well as ILO activities.

"There were years," he later reflected, "when I sat in League and International Labour Organization meetings more than two hundred days."[24]

Skelton becomes under-secretary

Issues such as those Riddell had to deal with in Geneva made it all the more necessary for the government to devise some means of keeping on top of events beyond the country's borders and outside its traditional concerns. That was to be Skelton's task. As a result of his role at the Imperial Conference of 1923, he had become the prime minister's chief adviser on the imperial relationship; his contribution to the decision on the Geneva protocol assured him a similar position on League matters and international affairs generally.

By the beginning of 1925, King had decided that he wanted Skelton to take over as under-secretary and that he did not want to wait for Pope, over a year hence, to complete his paid leave. He therefore decided, in lieu of granting the leave of absence, to ask Parliament for a special vote of $8,000 to be paid to Pope in monthly instalments over the year 1925, enabling him to give up his office altogether on March 31. Pope was not offended by this prospect but regarded the prime minister's conduct as kind and generous. He put in a good word for Walker as his successor, considering him to have been a "most efficient" assistant under-secretary who had "acceptably discharged" the duties of the permanent head when Pope was ill. But Pope recognized that King had already settled on Skelton and, although sorry that Walker did not get the promotion, acknowledged "the right of the Premier to make his own selection."[25]

Pope's long service earned him a room in the East Block for a while after his retirement and the offer of another if he needed it in the Dominion Archives. Insofar as his health permitted, he used his retirement to work on his memoirs, but he died in Ottawa on December 2, 1926, at the age of seventy-two, before they were completed. The Ottawa *Citizen* on December 2, 1926, remembered him as

> the Chesterfield of Canada, a sort of latter day Patronius [sic]. He could be called the arbiter elegantiarum—the ruling authority on official elegance and etiquette; on how to do things and do them properly. Of the functions of government, the deportment of officialdom, the procedure for great events, the drafting of official communiqués and diplomatic correspondence; the exchange of international amitiés . . . Sir Joseph was the recognized master, the court of last resort. He would view with pain any departure from long established customs, any variation of time honoured tradition. He was a stickler for form. A letter

must be written in just such language, and public correspondence carried on with the most exacting propriety.

Pope's achievement of course went well beyond this, for earlier in his career he had been an important negotiator, and, as the founding under-secretary, he had provided the department with sound procedures and a firm documentary basis for decision making. As the *Citizen*'s verdict indicates, however, Pope—and, indeed, the department as a whole—had toward the end of his life become identified much more with the style than with the substance of Canadian external policy.

The preoccupations of the department would be very different under Skelton, in view of his highly developed interest in policy and his determination that Canada move away from the dependent position in the empire favoured by Pope: unlike his predecessor, the new under-secretary was prepared to exploit the constitutional implications of the External Affairs Act, and he wanted sufficient resources in his department to enable him to do so effectively. "Sir Wilfrid would have been genuinely pleased with this relationship of Skelton and myself in our present positions," King recorded in his diary on the night of April 1, 1925.[26] Ewart, Biggar, and later on Dandurand all faded away as advisers on external policy. Henceforth King and Skelton set the course for Canada in foreign affairs and, because of their close relationship, in many other aspects of public life as well.

THE DEPARTMENT UNDER SKELTON

Personnel

"The machinery of government as regards external affairs," King noted at the end of 1925, "will largely depend on the end we are seeking to attain and the principles of imperial and international relationship which are being applied."[27] Since the objectives that he shared with Skelton assumed a high degree of autonomy, the implication was that resources should be expanded beyond those that had served Pope's purposes.

King had already taken some interest in the administrative side of the department, making inquiries during visits to London and Washington concerning the operations of the Foreign Office and the State Department. He and his government were also concerned about staffing, particularly francophone representation in the senior ranks. Ernest Lapointe, the prime minister's Quebec lieutenant, wanted to be kept informed of departmental appointments and promotions and over the years paid particular attention to the progress of francophones within the service. It was King's practice always to include a French Canadian in delegations to the League of Nations, and after taking office he named Lucien Pacaud parliamentary under-secretary of state for external affairs.[28]

By order-in-council in October 1922, Pacaud, having resigned from the Commons, became the first French-Canadian officer (other than the commissioner general in Paris, Philippe Roy) in the department. Soon afterward Pacaud was sent to London, where he remained until his resignation from the department in 1931. As assistant secretary and later as secretary in the high commissioner's office, Pacaud's primary function was to assist and advise his chief. When secretary, he also took charge of the office when the high commissioner was absent. Important among his duties was attendance at meetings of the League of Nations, the ILO, and other international gatherings in Europe, as either an adviser or a delegate, as circumstances required. A second francophone to enter the service at this time, destined for a much longer career with External Affairs than Pacaud, was Pierre Dupuy. In November 1922, he was appointed secretary in the office of the commissioner general in Paris.

The appointment of Pacaud and Dupuy, since they served abroad, did nothing to improve the personnel resources at headquarters. Rowell, who like King had studied the practice of the US and British governments, suggested the addition of four officers, to be charged with Far Eastern, North American, League, and imperial affairs. The prime minister, who as a result of the election of 1925 had fewer seats than the Conservatives and was able to retain power only with the precarious support of the Progressives and others, was worried about criticism for expanding his own department. He therefore was prepared to envisage at most only the addition of a single promising university graduate every year or two.[29] But he had little time to give to staffing questions of any kind, even the need to fill the counsellor's position that Skelton had vacated on his promotion to under-secretary.

The first claim on King's attention was the survival of his government. Much of his energy was devoted to problems in the Customs Department, which cost him control of the House of Commons in June 1926 and produced the celebrated constitutional dispute with the governor general, Lord Byng, when the latter refused King's request for dissolution and instead called on Meighen to form a government. With such preoccupations, politicians could not be expected to take much interest in the task of building a foreign service, which was left to Skelton. This activity was one for which the under-secretary was well prepared, for one of his concerns at Queen's had been the production of graduates educated to supply the contemporary needs of the state.[30]

Although Skelton inherited 101 employees, they could scarcely be called a foreign service. Twenty-one were in the Passport Office, and another fifteen served the prime minister's requirements. There were thirty-eight employees in London, Paris, and Geneva, and three more worked in Washington, although the funds appropriated by Parliament for full representation there had never been used. That left a total of but twenty-four at headquarters to handle matters connected with international affairs. Only three of the positions there were for officers, and the number included Skelton's own and the one he had vacated.

Thus, for major policy questions, Canada still had a one-man foreign office, but the burden had shifted from the prime minister to a departmental officer, who now, as in Pope's heyday before Christie's appearance, was the under-secretary. Times had changed a good deal, however, and Skelton found that he could not work effectively with only the meagre assistance that had been available to his predecessor. King very quickly made it clear that the new under-secretary would be given much more extensive duties than Pope. He was to take on greater responsibility for policy on international affairs and to advise the prime minister on a wide variety of domestic matters as well. These duties were increased by the requirements of the prime minister: the task of administering the department's accounts, for example, included purchasing his car and paying the chauffeur and a general servant at Laurier House. While Walker, as assistant under-secretary, could be counted on to supervise issuance of passports, consular matters, and preparation of confidential prints, Skelton was expected to fill the combined roles that Pope and Christie had played under Borden. As well, from the very outset he began functioning as a de facto deputy minister to the prime minister. He was called on to help to write throne speeches, and he became King's confidant during the constitutional dispute with Byng.

In view of all these responsibilities, the under-secretary's office became a livelier place with Skelton as its occupant. It was his practice to arrive early in the morning, and he frequently remained late into the evening. To assist him he brought from Queen's his secretary, Marjorie McKenzie. She was classified as a stenographer grade 3, a category introduced by the Civil Service Commission in 1919 when the clerical ranks were reorganized. In acknowledgment of the growing importance of female shorthand typists in its work, the department had begun to make use of this classification shortly before McKenzie's appointment.

With a master's degree from Queen's in French and German, Marjorie McKenzie, like Agnes McCloskey, exerted, on the basis of her particular talents, a good deal more influence on the department than her rank might have suggested. McKenzie's interest was not in the administrative process but in the substance of foreign policy and the quality of written expression. Responsible for overseeing the paper flow through the under-secretary's office, she was well placed to comment on ideas coming forward from the department. Enjoying Skelton's trust, which made her the keeper of his confidential records and the author of some correspondence for his signature, she could expect to receive an attentive hearing for her opinions. These she expressed, a colleague remembered, in "an intriguing blend of precise phrases, abrupt condemnations, and down-to-earth remarks," free of the "officialese" and "gobbledegook" that were her constant enemy.[31]

There were other administrative changes at this time as well. Joe Boyce, who had been transferred out of the prime minister's office in 1922 and had been working in External Affairs in fact as well as in name since then, was elevated to chief clerk in succession to Baker; at this time, the most important responsibility of this position was the departmental records. Agnes McCloskey, meanwhile, had established herself as the departmental accountant, earning praise as a "most capable, clever and energetic clerk," with "four [other] clerks assisting her in her work."[32] Together, McKenzie, Boyce, and McCloskey handled the routine of daily operations, but Skelton was never far from their work, signing and approving virtually everything they did.

Most pressing on Skelton's agenda for the officer ranks was filling the position of counsellor, since King wanted the under-secretary to be available for imperial and international meetings. For this position Skelton set high qualifications: a law degree or membership in a provincial bar association, two years of post-graduate studies in international affairs, practical experience in legal work, and a good knowledge of both English and French.[33]

Having been a successful exponent of the merit principle at Queen's, Skelton intended to hold a competition for the new position in External Affairs, but only one qualified candidate presented himself. The new counsellor was Jean Désy, a bilingual professor of international and constitutional law and political history at the University of Montreal and a former professor of history at the University of Paris. He also had the advantage of having been a "technical adviser" to the Canadian delegation to the League. Now for the first time External Affairs had a senior francophone at headquarters. Désy was given responsibility for legal matters, protocol, treaties, the League, and, when time permitted, commercial subjects. Skelton thus was free to focus on imperial affairs, as King desired, and on general administration.

More officers were needed if the department were to give the government sound advice and represent its interests abroad effectively. "It is absolutely impossible," Skelton told King after his first nine months in office, "even with 7-day weeks and 16-hour days to secure the independent and exact knowledge of external affairs which has now become desirable."[34] Without a lot of research, Skelton could usually provide King with an appropriate response to any thought of encroachment on Canadian autonomy, but he was aware that the advice he gave was often based on limited research and a non-Canadian perspective, since much of the department's information came from the British. Even in the analysis of this information, there was only so much that Skelton and Désy could do by themselves. King appreciated the problem but did nothing to alleviate it, since he did not want to risk being charged by the opposition in Parliament with unduly increasing his personnel resources. When Skelton asked for assistance, King complained about the inadequacy of staff to serve the other needs of the prime minister.

Offices outside Canada

The only way of justifying an increase in office staff at headquarters was to tie it to the opening of new posts abroad. These, it could be argued, would enhance Canada's international status. So far, as Rowell had pointed out, little had been done to secure this status by expanding the department's operations.

Rowell's criticism of Canadian representation abroad was least apposite when applied to London. After becoming prime minister, King replaced Sir George Perley, Borden's appointee as high commissioner, with Peter Larkin, president of the Salada Tea Co. and an important benefactor of the Liberal party. Larkin's personal wealth enabled him to consider it undignified to draw a salary, but even so his incumbency cost the government a good deal of money. The high commissioner's office was to be relocated from the dingy quarters that it had occupied since its establishment to a new building which would accommodate all the federal government's activities in London. After considering various possibilities, Larkin settled on a handsome neoclassical building in Trafalgar Square designed by Sir Robert Smirke, the architect of the British Museum, and occupied by the Union Club. At a cost, approved by Parliament, of $1,300,000 (including renovations), this became Canada House. Officially opened by King George V and Queen Mary on June 29, 1925, the building gave Canada an establishment in London judged equal to Australia's, in the Strand. It also formed the core of a larger Canadian presence in the vicinity of Trafalgar Square, including the representatives of several provinces and the offices of various transportation companies, banks, and other businesses associated with the country.

There was no counterpart to these changes in Washington, the other capital so important to Canadian interests. Merchant Mahoney, who continued to work in the British embassy as agent for Canada, was all but forgotten in Ottawa. In October 1922, the prime minister added to the Canadian presence by appointing Tom King, a veteran journalist, as part of what he called the department's "intelligence branch" in Washington. External Affairs paid Tom King's salary while he sent reports on legislative, administrative, and judicial developments to the prime minister. It was not unusual for foreign governments to employ journalists in this way; the British ambassador had two on his payroll. The usefulness of such an arrangement, however, was limited. Politicians in Washington were much less accessible to a Canadian journalist than were their counterparts in Ottawa. Certainly Skelton thought the Canadian presence inadequate and considered that reliance on Mahoney and Tom King simply accentuated the need for proper representation. But the prime minister and other members of the cabinet found Tom King's reports useful,[35] so Skelton had to make the best use he could of the resources available in Washington until more formal representation could be established.

The prime minister had long favoured appointment of a full-fledged Canadian representative but was somewhat ambivalent about the form the office should take. At first, he saw merit in the possibility of a non-diplomatic representative to handle trade and tariff questions,[36] but he changed his mind after the governor general criticized the tabling in Parliament of the correspondence on the halibut treaty without British consent. The prime minister then declared himself for full diplomatic representation, something easier to achieve after the Irish Free State established a minister in Washington in 1924 and the principal opponent of similar action by Canada, Fielding, became inactive as a result of a stroke in December of that year.

Partly because the high cost of moving in the social circles of Washington exceeded the stipend offered by the government, King had difficulty in filling the position,[37] but after some delay he found a suitable candidate, Vincent Massey. As president of the farm-implement manufacturer Massey-Harris, he had the necessary personal fortune. Although not a member of Parliament, he had been recruited to the cabinet by King as a minister without portfolio before the election of 1925 but had been defeated in his attempt to gain a seat in that contest. Before the final arrangements for both creating the new office and sending Massey to fill it were completed, however, King lost his argument with Byng and handed power over to Meighen, leaving the project once more in doubt.

The department in 1926

In practical terms, the department might seem to have made little progress by 1926. Canada still had no diplomatic missions abroad and at home only very slender resources for making foreign policy. In the volatile political environment of the early 1920s, a minority government had little time or energy for matters that were not of political urgency and every reason to proceed with caution when it contemplated innovation. All the same, foundations were laid during these years for future advance. Pope was succeeded by a vigorous and innovative under-secretary who was interested in an enlarged and more independent international role for Canada. The days of the one-man foreign office had come to an end, for with the engagement of Désy the department now had a full-time officer in Ottawa able to contribute substantially to the policy side.

More important still, King and his under-secretary had well-defined goals and a strategy for realizing them. They wanted to give effect to the autonomist implications of the External Affairs Act and to make the department an effective instrument both for that purpose and for subsequent international activity, through diplomatic representation abroad, especially in the United States, and also through a more elaborate headquarters organization. These were not the goals of Meighen, heir as he was to Borden's very different approach to Canadian external policy. The department's direction, therefore, would depend on the election of 1926; rapid progress would require a majority government.

Part Two

The Foreign Service: 1926–1939

Chapter Five
Creation of a Foreign Service:
1926–1930

THE VOTERS GAVE MACKENZIE KING a workable majority when they went to the polls on September 14, 1926: 128 Liberals to 91 Conservatives, 20 Progressives, and 6 others. The government, therefore, was in a much safer position to take initiatives intended to further its objectives in external affairs. It also had an incentive to do so, for the dispute with Lord Byng had left the prime minister determined to obtain relief from the remaining restrictions that the imperial relationship imposed on dominion autonomy.

The first legations

The government's first priority in its external activities was to complete arrangements for opening a legation in Washington. To underline the importance of this objective, King took Massey with him to the Imperial Conference in London in 1926. Ireland having set a precedent, the principle no longer had to be argued: the conference accepted the idea of representation abroad by the dominions, and the British foreign secretary asked only that the British ambassador in Washington be kept informed of the activities of the Canadian minister. The Foreign Office, however, was intent on preserving the diplomatic unity of the empire, and a note to the US State Department remarked that "matters which are of Imperial concern or which affect other Dominions in the Commonwealth in common with Canada will continue to be handled as heretofore by this [British] Embassy."[1] Although Skelton vigorously objected to this condition, King accepted it as the price of British co-operation and goodwill. So did Massey, who with King was receptive to the Foreign Office's suggestion that the British ambassador stand at the side of the minister for Canada when he presented his credentials to President Calvin Coolidge on February 18, 1927.[2]

The United States soon reciprocated, opening a legation in Ottawa under a vigorous and fast-rising career officer, William Phillips, who presented his credentials to the governor general on June 1, 1927. He received a good deal of publicity after his arrival: he was the first minister plenipotentiary to take up residence, had a forceful personality, and habitually appeared at public functions at King's side—perhaps appropriate given his rank but open to misinterpretation so long as he remained a one-man diplomatic corps.

The speech from the throne on January 26, 1928, let it be known that the government intended to expand Canada's diplomatic relations further, by converting the office of the commissioner general in Paris to a legation and appointing a minister to Japan. Priority was given to upgrading the office in Paris. The change, King observed in his diary, was bound to appeal to French Canadians, and it would be received as a "compliment" to them if it took place before an exchange of legations with Japan.[3] King wanted to inaugurate the legation while he was in Paris to sign the Briand-Kellogg pact on August 27, 1928. To the prime minister's annoyance, he was unable to do so because the British, concerned to preserve the concept of the diplomatic unity of the empire, had been slow to send official notification to the French government. In due course, the same formula was used as in Washington. Roy presented his credentials on September 29, 1928, accompanied by the British ambassador. "Our opening of Canadian Legation was the triumph of our policy, a policy Sir Wilfrid would not have believed could have been realized so soon," commented King.[4] The French reciprocated later in the year, their first minister in Ottawa, Jean Knight, presenting his credentials on November 16.

Plans for a legation in Tokyo were in part a response to renewed hostility in British Columbia to immigration from Japan. Demands in the province for exclusion of immigrants were bound to be resented in Japan. When the Conservative party supported exclusion, King noted in his diary that "our only effective way to deal with the Japanese question is to have our own Minister in Japan to visa passports." That, he concluded, would be "the way to meet the Tory policy of 'exclusion' which we can never consent to."[5]

In public, the proposed legation was presented as a means of expanding trade and acknowledging Canada's growing interest in the Pacific. Arthur

Meighen's successor as Conservative leader, R. B. Bennett, did not think diplomatic representation necessary to serve these purposes in Japan and predicted that the result would be "disaster." "What this country wants in Japan and all other foreign countries," he said, "are trade commissioners under the Minister of Trade and Commerce to carry forward Canada's trade . . . not our diplomatic skill and power."[6] Sir George Perley, now back in politics, warned of a "dangerous precedent." He suggested that, although trade might be Canada's responsibility, diplomacy should continue to be handled by the British Foreign Office. The latter, he argued, should be turned into a truly imperial agency, making it possible for Canadians to enter its service. To counter the opposition's arguments, King decided to publish a treatise on the opening of Canadian legations. Probably prepared by Skelton, the article, which argued that current developments had been foreshadowed by Sir John A. Macdonald and Sir Robert Borden, appeared in the *Canadian Nation* under the name of the prime minister.[7]

Notwithstanding this effort, over a year passed after the debate in Parliament before a legation was established in Tokyo, because of difficulty with the British over the "diplomatic unity of the empire." Until that issue was cleared up, the British were determined to delay the opening of the Canadian office and of four others being planned by the Irish Free State and South Africa. King's suggestions for a compromise formula were not acceptable to the British or the Irish, but eventually all agreed that diplomatic appointments should derive from the initiative of the dominion governments. The representative of a dominion would receive instructions from his own government, but the British ambassador would be the channel for making common imperial views known to the authorities in the host country. To the satisfaction of the Foreign Office, therefore, there was an implication that there should be consultative co-operation between the dominions and the mother country on matters of common imperial concern. The way was now clear for the opening of a Canadian legation in Tokyo in May 1929.[8] In the following month, Japan closed its consulate general in Ottawa, reopening it immediately as a legation, with the former consul general as chargé d'affaires. The minister, Iyemasa Tokugawa, arrived later in the year.

Relations with the United Kingdom

The considerations that led to the Canadian government's campaign for establishment of diplomatic missions of its own in foreign countries also changed the means of conducting business between Ottawa and London. The constitutional crisis involving Lord Byng contributed to King's determination, when he went to the Imperial Conference in 1926, to secure clarification and limitation of the governor general's role. He wanted agreement, in particular, that the governor general represented only the crown and not the British government. On this point there was little debate, for the British, who had established the Dominions Office separate from the Colonial Office in 1925, were prepared to agree, provided the governor general continued to see all intergovernmental correspondence and was kept informed of cabinet business and public affairs generally. As a result, the governor general ceased to be a channel of communication between the British and Canadian governments.

The new situation was described by Byng's successor, Lord Willingdon, just after the conference: "I feel strongly that while I'm here I represent in my official capacity the King alone, and must leave all administrative matters to be settled between the two Governments. In a word, I don't think that it's right for me in future to learn from you [the dominions secretary] what you want in order that I may try to put it in the mind of my Prime Minister. I must be outside all such matters and you must communicate direct with him. I'm afraid that my letters home to anyone but His Majesty must be of a very uninforming character."[9]

It was necessary, therefore, to find a substitute for the governor general as the link between London and Ottawa. The Dominions Office preferred a consultative council among the high commissioners in London, but King considered such an arrangement susceptible to manipulation by Downing Street. He suggested instead that the British government appoint high commissioners with "diplomatic and consular powers" to handle their direct and regular dealings with the dominions.[10] While the proposal brought forth considerable opposition in the British cabinet, it had some important supporters, including Willingdon. As a result, it was given further study, which led to a British high commissioner, Sir William Clark, being appointed to Canada in April 1928. In the words of the foreign secretary, Austen Chamberlain, the office was a means "of keeping the different Gov'ts of the Empire in step."[11] Canada was the first country to receive a British high commissioner, the next such appointments being to South Africa, in 1931, and to Australia, in 1936.

The change in the governor general's role enhanced the position of the Canadian high commissioner in London. In 1925, as a result of Peter Larkin's efforts, the high commissioners had been ranked in the order of precedence behind the lord chancellor, the prime minister, and six secretaries of state. Three years later they were given the right to wear uniforms as ambassadors, although diplomatic status, conferring the same immunities as those enjoyed by the envoy of a foreign power, was not awarded until 1952.[12]

PROVIDING THE RESOURCES FOR DIPLOMACY

Heads of post

As a result of the government's various initiatives from 1926 onward, Canada had diplomatic representation or its equivalent in the four capitals of most importance to it, London, Washington, Paris, and Tokyo, as well as in Geneva at the headquarters of the League of Nations and the ILO. All these offices came under the Department of External Affairs, but the choice of ministers and the high commissioner remained the prerogative of the prime minister. As the appointment of Vincent Massey to Washington indicated, private means and acceptable political connections were essential qualifications for the job.

To these requirements Massey added personal qualities that earned him a warm welcome in the United States: cultivation, urbanity, and an interest in the arts. He moved quickly into the upper levels of Washington society and became well known in the artistic and literary communities. According to Claude Bissell's biography, Massey represented Canada's political and commercial interests "competently," while in the cultural sphere he was an "extraordinary success."[13] The balance was perhaps not inappropriate for the time. The government in Ottawa, still cautious in its approach to international affairs and not yet caught up in the preoccupation with the economic side of the relationship with the United States, did not encourage the legation to be aggressive in its approach to political and economic work.

There was, however, a major task awaiting Massey in making Canada better known in the United States. Even the president was not very well informed, asking the new minister when he presented his credentials "whether Toronto was near the Lake and if this was the first Canadian diplomatic mission."[14] Massey, a longtime friend of such American thinkers as the jurist Felix Frankfurter and the journalists Walter Lippmann and Herbert Croly, was well placed to advance his country's reputation from the top down, and his work earned him praise from the *American Historical Review*, the New York *World* (edited by Lippmann), and the *New York Times*.

Despite such tributes, Massey's efforts were not always fully appreciated in Ottawa. His fondness for ceremony no doubt contributed to the success of a visit in December 1927 by the governor general and Lady Willingdon. Display in Washington, however, attracted unfavourable attention in the Canadian Parliament and, when combined with an inclination to give meticulous advice on the finer points of protocol, irritated Skelton. The latter's responses could be touched with irony and the suggestion of superior knowledge which Massey found less than congenial. "Herr

Doktor Skelton'' he called the under-secretary in his diary on one occasion. Thus the relationship between the two was rather cool, and Massey had little in common with the prime minister.

As a result, there was a certain wariness in Ottawa about the minister's judgment. His extensive program of public speaking, an effort to make Americans better aware of Canada and its constitutional position, attracted attention at home and worried the prime minister, although Massey secured assurance, after the two had a frank talk, that he might continue to use his own judgment. He was not so successful when it came to satisfying his own curiosity about the United States. When he proposed to attend the conventions of the Democratic and Republican parties in 1928, for example, he was instructed not to, after the idea was criticized as improper in the House of Commons.[15]

Stationed in a capital close to Ottawa which was the destination of many Canadian visitors, Massey attracted much more attention at home than his counterpart in Tokyo. The announcement that a legation would be opened there brought a number of unsolicited suggestions on who should be the first minister. King disregarded them, choosing George Stephens, a Montreal-born businessman who, after distinguished war service, had demonstrated diplomatic skill by mediating the conflicting claims of the French and the Germans on the Saar Commission, established under the League of Nations to govern that region pending a plebiscite on its future. Stephens's wife, however, persuaded him that they had had enough service outside their country. King's second choice was a wealthy notary from Montreal, Herbert Marler, who like Massey was a former cabinet minister defeated in the election of 1925.

Property abroad: the legation in Washington

Creation of a new office placed substantial administrative demands on the government. The first of these was acquisition of property for a chancery and an official residence. This was not a matter that the department or for that matter any other branch of government had the resources to handle. As had happened with Canada House in London, therefore, the choice was left to the minister and, with regard to the living quarters at least, his wife. The department and the government, however, had to grant approval before the transaction could be completed. As the experience with the Masseys in Washington was to show, the process could be a cause of strain between headquarters and the field, particularly when the new quarters attracted unfavourable attention in Parliament. Reaction in Canada was important, because the legation in Washington was a pilot project for the others.

The Masseys chose, as a combined office and residence, a mansion on Massachusetts Avenue, a prestigious address in central Washington in an area with a number of diplomatic missions. Attractively decorated and possessing a beautiful staircase and handsome drawing rooms and dining room, the house was well suited to the social side of the Masseys' mission in Washington. It was also expensive, carrying a price, with some furnishings included, of nearly $500,000. Skelton was opposed to the expenditure, and the issue was one cause of tension between him and Massey. There was also criticism from members of Parliament, including many Liberals who saw evidence that the Masseys were showing excessive concern for the social side of the legation. King none the less supported the purchase and secured its approval by Parliament.

Since the building was to remain the core of Canadian operations in Washington for many years, its suitability for the purpose intended is perhaps more pertinent than the purchase price in assessing the wisdom of the investment over the long term. Certainly the location was excellent, and its convenience increased over the years. As a model for other Canadian establishments, however, it was considered unsuitable, particularly in combining living quarters and working space. The minister's office, on the ground floor, was separated from the rest of the staff at the top by the family premises in between. "The whole atmosphere," observed a visitor interested in plans for the legation in Tokyo, "was intimate and social rather than professional and business-like. It impressed me as being impractical, inefficient, and somewhat daunting for visitors unacquainted with such baronial surroundings."[16]

Personnel

Notwithstanding his occasional unease with some of Massey's activities in Washington, King was pleased with his appointments. "With Massey, Marler and Roy," he believed, "we had the beginning of a diplomatic service which has not been surpassed by any country in the world."[17] If they were to be effective, however, the ministers and the high commissioner needed staff support and also a headquarters organization able to direct their efforts and make sure the results were put to good use for the Canadian government.

In Washington, Merchant Mahoney, representing Canadian interests in the British embassy, was transferred to the legation. To handle the workload, it was determined that Massey should have three additional officers to assist him. The cabinet then had to decide whether these officers should come under the Civil Service Act, be exempted as diplomats were in the United States, or simply be named as employees in the department's estimates. The last course was chosen, since it provided for easy transfer between posts, but that led to other administrative problems for the department and for the employees themselves. While officers appointed in this manner might be moved easily from one post to another outside Canada, there was no provision for service at headquarters: when they were stationed in Ottawa, therefore, their salaries had to be charged to the allotments for missions abroad. The appointments, moreover, were made by order-in-council and hence were at the pleasure of the government of the day. As a result, the incumbents did not have the customary benefits of position and rank within the public service.[18]

Despite Skelton's preference for the competitive principle, it was not applied to the recruitment of three new officers for the legation in Washington, because of the time constraints involved. Instead, Massey, in consultation with King and Skelton, was given a fairly free hand in recruiting. First to join was Thomas (Tommy) Stone, as third secretary and Massey's private secretary. Laurent Beaudry was enticed back into government service from the editorial offices of Le Soleil, as first secretary, and at the end of the university term he was joined by a young teacher of history at the University of Toronto, Hume Wrong.

With the legation in Washington in operation, the government could approach additional appointments in a more leisurely fashion. It had to decide whether to continue to rely on patronage, to develop a professional foreign service entirely by competition, or to combine the two systems. In the establishment of its first offices abroad, the government had followed the US example by staffing primarily by patronage at the senior levels. By the 1920s, this practice had been practically eliminated in the selection of support staff for the public service, but cabinet ministers and their deputies still had considerable latitude in deciding how they would handle administrative and professional positions. That latitude, however, was circumscribed by changing public attitudes: increasingly, patronage was seen as immoral and contrary to the "forces of decency, civic-mindedness, and efficiency."[19]

These attitudes favoured Skelton in his advocacy of appointment by competition. Starting in 1927, career officers were admitted by examination and promoted on the basis of achievement. The principle was not enforced with absolute rigidity: the officers already at posts abroad who were transferred into the service were not required to submit to examination, nor were the three recently sent to Washington. Similarly, positions with special requirements that a candidate was known to possess might be filled without examination. But for the mainstream of the foreign service the merit principle governed entry.

Although Skelton was committed to the idea of a career service, he had much to learn about how it could be established. In this regard, he found particularly helpful John Hickerson, a young officer in the US foreign service who had been posted to Ottawa shortly after Skelton's own arrival. Skelton was interested in the legislative background and administrative practices of the US foreign service, and Hickerson willingly supplied him with his own copies of the regulations. Together they spent many hours discussing the type of foreign service that Canada would need.[20]

The British also offered help. The governor general sent King a proposal that two or three young Canadian officers be sent each year for a three-year training period in the Foreign Office and its embassies.[21] Such a project, however, was not feasible, for the department needed new officers to relieve the workload at headquarters and to staff Canada's missions. Skelton therefore had to proceed with the recruiting of officers for immediate service in the department.

The Civil Service Commission had methods for selecting technicians and scientists but nothing comparable for foreign service officers. Skelton filled the gap. According to the requirements for the examination in 1927, candidates had to have university graduation or its equivalent, preferably with post-graduate training in political economy, political science, or international law. While age might be a determining factor in selection, no arbitrary limit was set. Only men were eligible to compete. Unless a veteran, a candidate had to pay two dollars to write the examination and have his curriculum vitae reviewed.

The examination questions, which were designed by Skelton, were aimed at assessing the candidate's general aptitudes rather than evaluating his technical or professional expertise. The written examination, spread over a couple of days, consisted of four parts. The first essay, which was usually on nationalism and internationalism, was designed to elicit the candidate's attitude toward Canada's role in the empire and enabled the department to determine whether he accepted the government's position as enunciated at recent imperial conferences. This was followed by questions on Canadian and international affairs, an essay of the candidate's choice from political economy, political science, or international law, and a précis. Skelton himself marked the examinations in the early years and then proceeded to grade the candidate's curriculum vitae.

Those candidates with an average of at least 70 per cent and a pass in all four sections were invited to an oral examination designed to gauge the best among them. Here the emphasis was on personality and deportment.[22] Usually Skelton, or on occasion Désy, was chairman of the oral committee, which was composed of colleagues from the department and a representative of the Civil Service Commission. The latter played a passive role, for, although recruitment was carried out under the nominal auspices of the commission, in effect the department had a free hand in setting standards and designing the means of selecting the successful candidates. In the earliest days recruitment might also involve an interview with the prime minister, perhaps because of reservations about Massey's selections for Washington, where some fairly sharp personality conflicts had arisen.

Skelton was not content to let the process run entirely on its own; he wanted to ensure that the most suitable Canadian graduates presented themselves. In addition to the normal circulation of competition notices by the Civil Service Commission, he had them sent to specific universities and often wrote to or met with professors to encourage them to have their best students try the examination. As well, he wanted to attract Canadians doing post-graduate studies abroad, to take advantage of their more varied education and their experience of living in an unfamiliar cultural setting; indeed as time went on he developed a marked preference for candidates with such background.[23] Since the Civil Service Commission could not run competitions outside the country, Skelton obtained permission in 1928 for heads of post to do so.

Discounting the examination held to recruit a counsellor in 1925, the first real competition reflecting Skelton's standards was in 1927. To the disappointment of the under-secretary, there were few candidates that time, but more than sixty presented themselves when the next examination, the first to be really nation-wide and extraterritorial in scope, was held a year later. In 1932 the number increased to more than 500. In interpreting the examination results, the department received some suggestions from politicians and other prominent citizens who favoured one candidate or another, but Skelton allowed the merit principle to rule. The department was obliged by statute to give veterans a preference, but Skelton did so only after the written examination.[24]

There were two successful candidates in 1927. One, E. D'Arcy McGreer, was slated for Geneva, because Canada as a member of the League of Nations Council had urgent business to attend to. The other, J. Scott Macdonald, formerly of the Tariff Section of the Department of Trade and Commerce, was needed for commercial matters which neither Skelton nor Désy had been able to give enough time to.

As a result of the next examination, six more officers were added in 1928-29: Keith F. Crowther, Hugh L. Keenleyside, Kenneth Kirkwood, Lester B. Pearson, Paul-Emile Renaud, and Norman Robertson. This competition was affected by veterans' preference: Pearson, for example, as a result of war service, had preference over Robertson. Skelton personally spent time persuading some of the candidates to write the examination, and he considered the group the most impressive of those recruited during his years as under-secretary. In view of Skelton's interest in this group, it may be assumed that it represented the qualities he most valued in members of the foreign service. Ranging in age from mid-twenties to early thirties, these men were more mature than the entrants to many occupations. All had previous work experience, and Kirkwood and Keenleyside, as well as Pearson, were veterans. Most important, all had strong academic backgrounds, with post-graduate degrees obtained (except for Crowther, who had an MA from Queen's) outside Canada. Five of the six had taught at the university level, and Crowther had taught in private schools. One, Robertson, had been a Rhodes scholar at Oxford, and Pearson was also a graduate of that university. The highest academic qualifications were possessed by Renaud, who had doctorates in law from the University of Paris and in economics from the London School of Economics. Keenleyside as well had a doctorate, in history from Clark University in the United States, and Kirkwood had an MA from Columbia. By virtue of their own attainments before entering the department, they might be regarded as members of the intellectual middle class, whose educational background had established associations with their peers outside as well as within Canada. Crowther, a partial exception to this last generalization, was the one member of the group to have only a short career in the department, which he left in 1932.

By 1930, 30 per cent of the officers were French Canadians, a fact that Skelton used to answer protests from two Franco-Ontarian associations.[25] These officers encountered some problems in the department. There was, according to a critical observer, "bitterness and jockeying, as well as one case, at least, of flat refusal on the part of an English Canadian to serve under a French Canadian, which bodes ill for the future of this Service. Perhaps, in course of time this acrimonious feeling may be toned down; otherwise we shall have Paris more or less stocked with French Canadians, London with English Canadians, and Washington probably with those belonging to the nationality of each minister appointed."[26] Skelton read French and, although not fluent, spoke it on occasion. King also read French and was able to deliver speeches written for him in the language but did not use it in conversation.[27] As in the rest of the public service in Ottawa at this time, the language of work in the department was almost exclusively English.

Advancement was another sore point.[28] In so far as the top positions were reserved for political appointees, the problem was shared by all members of the department, English as well as French speaking. But the language of work in Ottawa created an additional barrier for the latter. Since life abroad, especially in France, offered greater opportunity for French-language officers to work in their own language, it was highly attractive to remain on posting rather than return home. Headquarters, however, gave a young officer the best chance to attract favourable notice from superiors in the department—and from other senior public servants and ministers—and the best opportunities for advancement, so long as heads of post were chosen from outsiders. The most congenial working environment for a francophone, therefore, was not necessarily the one most likely to bring preferment.

While service abroad might not be the surest means of gaining recognition, it could none the less be demanding, for even a new officer might be given considerable responsibility in a service as small as Canada's. In 1929 Hugh Keenleyside, at the age of thirty, was sent to Tokyo in advance of the Marlers to open the legation. He was not entirely on his own, for the Department of Trade and Commerce had for some years maintained a trade commissioner in Kobe (now to be transferred to the legation as commercial attaché), and Keenleyside was accompanied by a secretary, but both the preliminary arrangements for the mission and the initial decisions in Tokyo were his responsibility. To guide him he had no instructions beyond Skelton's advice to use his head and, if difficulties arose, to consult with Ottawa by cable. Keenleyside therefore had some opportunity to act according to his inclinations, for example, seeking to establish rather greater distance from the British embassy at the start of operations than had been done in Washington or Paris.

Much of Keenleyside's activity was administrative, locating temporary accommodation, engaging a translator, establishing procedures for handling passport and immigration work, and so on. This was a side of the work for that he displayed particular aptitude: under his direction, the legation's accounts were considered by Agnes McCloskey to be a model for other Canadian offices to emulate, and the filing system that he devised was still in operation when the mission reopened after the Second World War. He also had a sense of occasion. The first public gathering at the legation took place on July 1, 1929, when all Canadians resident in the country were invited, for the first time, to come together as a community and witness the raising of the Canadian red ensign over the building. Despite these accomplishments, however, he could not escape the frustrations of serving abroad. Like Galt in London many years before, he was disappointed to discover, once he began sending reports to Ottawa, that they seldom elicited a response.[29]

In Ottawa the tone for the department was set by the under-secretary. By comparison with Pope, Skelton was little interested in the social life of the capital and of its diplomatic and consular corps. He was also much less concerned with the ceremonial side of diplomacy. On these subjects, Skelton's attitude was shared by others in the department, whether they had entered by competition or otherwise. For junior staff on posting, the preoccupation of some of their chiefs with diplomatic uniforms was a cause of particular irritation. While the right to wear them might have had transitory symbolic importance in London, Canada's lack of a tradition of civil uniforms made their habitual use seem artificial. Exasperation over this issue and other matters of ceremony was a major cause of tension between Hume Wrong and Vincent Massey in Washington. Keenleyside in Tokyo had a similar aversion to uniforms and was uncomfortable with the degree of ceremony favoured by the Marlers.[30]

While Skelton had tried to recruit candidates committed to the idea of dominion autonomy, there was otherwise no uniformity of opinion on political, social, and economic matters. These varied from radical to conservative; Skelton's method of recruiting had tested not so much the point of view as the ability to express and to defend it well. Diversity of opinion did not bother Skelton, who could encourage debate secure in the knowledge that his own views in the end were the only ones that would go before the prime minister.

Skelton created a congenial working environment. Intellectually stimulating, he knew how to challenge his officers to meet high and exacting standards, and he improved their writing skills by careful correction of the drafts they submitted to him. He was considerate of personal needs and democratic in dealing with his staff, those in support positions as well as officers. So far as the latter were concerned, he made certain above all that the department remained an attractive employer for men of talent and ambition. Although promotions were slow, there was the prospect of more new missions that would increase the opportunities for advancement and for interesting work. As well, Skelton was a staunch defender of the merit principle against those who would have made the foreign service a vehicle for training cadets of "manners and wealth" to head Canada's missions abroad. The results of Skelton's efforts were satisfactory to the prime minister. The department, King noted in his diary in August 1929, had expanded "into the most conspicuous and in some respects the most important department of government."[31]

While most of the new recruits who contributed to this development were generalists expected to develop into all-round members of the diplomatic service, a need was also recognized for specialists. One such was John Read, dean of law at Dalhousie University, who was named legal adviser in 1929. Read was given the post without submitting to a competitive examination. When questioned in the House of Commons about this method of appointment, King replied: "I fancy that after the discussion we have had on the *I'm Alone* [a Canadian rum-running vessel in difficulty with the US authorities] and the importance that has been ascribed to the necessity of having communications in external affairs very carefully considered from the legal point of view, hon. members will agree that it is wise to make this provision forthwith."[32] By contrast with the earlier period when Christie had occupied the position, the department now had enough legal work to keep Read employed exclusively in his area of specialization.

Another specialist engaged at this time was the first professional librarian, Grace Hart, who joined the staff in June 1928. She also functioned as the prime minister's personal librarian and purchasing agent.

Officers of the department had access to the Library of Parliament and other major collections in Ottawa, but, until Skelton became under-secretary, External Affairs had no well-organized facility of its own. There had been a library of sorts since the foundation of the department, but it had been very much Pope's fiefdom during his years as under-secretary. Much of it had been under his personal care, and his name had been inscribed in gold on many of the books. Although J. A. Leblanc had been designated librarian when he was brought into the service in 1910, his main responsibility was translation, and he apparently was not expected to do a great deal to organize the collection. The larger department under Skelton needed a serious reference facility of its own, where officers could find the books, newspapers, and periodicals necessary for their work. The appointment of Grace Hart reflected the under-secretary's desire to bring this change about.

A graduate of Queen's and of the library science program at McGill, Hart apparently entered the department at Skelton's personal initiative. Like his other recruits, she was widely read, cultured, and profoundly concerned with the world around her. Reporting to Skelton at first and working without an assistant until 1938, she consolidated and organized the collection and introduced the Library of Congress cataloguing system. She fought for space in the department's crowded quarters, reinforced the collection by the acquisition of current books and articles, and instituted a newspaper clipping service. The last depended on the co-operation of officers, each of whom was responsible for selecting items from a newspaper.

Grace Hart, like Agnes McCloskey and Marjorie McKenzie, had a special talent that contributed to the department's development. Hers, not for administration or policy but for research, helped the library to fulfil Skelton's expectations. Based at first in one small room on the top floor of the East Block, with the overflow in nearby offices, the library might look disorganized to outsiders, but Hart had every aspect of its operations at her disposal. She was, wrote Keenleyside, "prepared with the slightest encouragement to spend almost endless effort in the search for any material that might be requested. She always gave the applicant the impression that it was a great favour to her to be asked for help."[33]

Creation of new missions increased the demand not only for officers but also for support staff. Canada-based personnel had not normally been sent to the oldest post, the high commissioner's office in London, where British subjects could be recruited locally. Ministers destined for legations were usually accompanied by personal secretaries of their own choice, but other secretarial and clerical staff members were provided by Ottawa. Practice was not uniform from one place to another: in Tokyo, for example, one of the secretaries was British and another was American. As of 1929, however, an effort was made to be consistent in dealing with arrangements for Canada-based staff. Appointments were to be made from the Civil Service Commission's lists of qualified candidates, and those already outside Canada who had not taken the required examinations were to be enabled to do so at the post. In the following year, it was laid down that leave and other regulations should as far as possible be the same as those prevailing in Canada.[34]

Another activity for which support staff had to be provided in this period was communications. Since, as a result of the Imperial Conference of 1926, the channel between London and Ottawa had become government to government, departmental correspondence with the British capital began to be routed exclusively through Canada House. On July 1, 1927, the department took over from the governor general all responsibility and staff for cypher work. At the time, cryptography was done manually with dictionaries and one-time (numbered) pads. Cypher work, at the time, was an extremely laborious and time-consuming operation which necessitated an increase in clerical staff.

The department in 1929

The total number of departmental staff members in Ottawa increased from sixty-one in 1925 to eighty in 1929, but more than one-third of these continued to be shared with the prime minister and the Passport Office. The remainder of the support staff performed accounting, translating, secretarial, stenographic, and records work, and the new communications duties, with the last accounting for most of the increase of the previous four years.

At the senior levels, not all the inefficiencies of the department's early days had been removed. In particular, the overlap between the prime minister's staff and the department continued. At one point in 1927, King attempted to make a clearer distinction between the administration of domestic and that of external policy by asking Parliament to approve a new position of deputy ministerial rank in External Affairs to serve the needs of the prime minister.[35] Although the House of Commons finally authorized the position, there was considerable opposition, and King, after weighing up the arguments, decided not to hire anyone. Thus Skelton remained the prime minister's deputy for internal as well as external matters.

Problems of this kind might go unresolved, but in the department Skelton could now draw on sixteen generalist officers eligible for service at home and in five posts abroad under the department's jurisdiction. In addition, he had the support of the assistant under-secretrary, Walker, and the legal adviser. While the high commissioner in London and the ministers elsewhere were still political appointees, the other officers, whether or not they had undergone examination, were now considered members of a professional foreign service, recruited and promoted on the basis of demonstrated merit. With these resources in place, the department was better able than ever before to lead in the formulation of Canadian foreign policy.

WORK EXPANDS

Principal activities

Subjects dealt with by the department were divided between those involving governmental policy and those related to the protection of individual Canadians' interests.[36] In the first category, in order of importance as measured by the amount of time spent on them in 1929, came international arbitration, defence and disarmament, trade and tariff matters involving other governments (Trade and Commerce handled business and other non-governmental dealings), immigration, extradition, double nationality, territorial sovereignty, boundary waters disputes, wireless communication, and international aspects of taxation. Much of the work concerned US relations. The major issues in the second category were claims against foreign governments, deportation and immigration difficulties, imprisonment of Canadians abroad, seizure of Canadian vessels and goods, settlement of estates, and complaints of discrimination in trade or taxation.

Omitting minor and technical gatherings in which the department was only marginally involved, its officers handled policy issues arising at eight international conferences in 1929 in addition to the annual League of Nations meetings. These conferences dealt with such diverse subjects as commercial smuggling, the allocation of short-wave radio channels, and the safety of life at sea. There were also negotiations for seven bilateral conventions—dealing with such subjects as the preservation of Niagara Falls, Fraser River sockeye salmon fisheries, and civil aviation—and three multilateral agreements.

Much of this workload involved international law. While John Read led on these issues, the department also engaged outside experts for temporary assistance. John Ewart and Charles Burchell, an authority on maritime law from Halifax, worked with Read on imperial legislation. The department turned to Norman MacKenzie of the University of Toronto, Canada's foremost scholar in the field, when work began on codifying international law under the auspices of the League of Nations. Thus began a sustained relationship with the legal fraternity in Canada. While the department did not require a large legal staff full-time, it now needed some expert assistance from outside to deal effectively with all the problems of international jurisprudence coming before it.

To handle the workload in Ottawa there were in 1929 only three more officers than there had been four years earlier, for the majority of recruits had been sent to offices abroad. Even so, the increase was sufficient to permit a broad division of labour, which could be represented as follows:[37]

Under-secretary	O. D. Skelton	General
Assistant under-secretary	W. H. Walker	General, passports, consular appointments
Legal adviser	J. E. Read	Legal matters and International Joint Commission
Counsellor	L. Beaudry	United States, France, and the European continent; treaties
First secretary	L. B. Pearson	British Empire and League of Nations
Second or third secretary	H. L. Keenleyside (vacant after his posting to Tokyo)	United States and Asia
Second or third secretary	J. S. Macdonald	Commercial questions

In practice, duties were not so neatly defined or categorized. Pearson's work that year, for example, ranged over light-houses in the Red Sea, international tariffs on cement, the nationality of Anglo-Chinese children living in Canada, aviation licences in Canada and Switzerland, and the protection of young female artists travelling abroad. Other officers had similarly disparate portfolios, since Skelton often assigned tasks on the basis of an officer's availability. Except in rank and pay there was no clear hierarchy. Everyone was directly responsible to the under-secretary, who chaired or attended all meetings requiring a departmental representative. He corrected everyone's drafts for clarity, precision, and economy of prose. Every letter and telegram came in and went out over his desk, and he alone was responsible for every recommendation proceeding to the secretary of state for external affairs.

In the late 1920s, as earlier in the decade, the most important questions of external policy requiring the government's attention involved the empire and the League of Nations. Besides King, two members of the cabinet were seriously interested in these issues. One was the minister of justice,

Ernest Lapointe, who shared the limelight with the prime minister on imperial matters and did much of the important work on devising the formula for the new commonwealth. Lapointe also paid considerable attention to the League, joining forces with Sen. Raoul Dandurand, whose acquaintance with that body was well established. But on both these subjects the pre-eminent authority, as a result of his work before 1926, was Skelton, and there was never any question about his place as the prime minister's foremost and usually sole adviser on external policies and their implementation. This preoccupation, perhaps combined with the small number of officers at headquarters, no doubt helps explain the infrequency of departmental response that so disappointed Keenleyside.

From empire to commonwealth

Skelton's anti-imperial views made his closeness to the prime minister a cause of concern to the British and the subject of unfavourable comment after their high commissioner's office was established in Ottawa. Yet it was becoming evident by 1926 that the two held somewhat divergent if not incompatible opinions on the empire. As one who observed them at work that year at the Imperial Conference noted: "Mackenzie King was fully persuaded that some advance was necessary. . . . I think it was not clear in his mind as to what shape that advance to independence would take. Dr. Skelton was, if anything, more advanced than Mr. Mackenzie King. As he had a very logical clear mind, he became invaluable . . . to Mr. Mackenzie King suggesting ways and means by which his object should be attained."[38] Much as he valued the under-secretary's help, the prime minister was aware of the difference. "Skelton is at heart against the Br. Empire, while I am not," he noted in his diary in September 1929. "I believe in the larger whole, with the complete independence of the parts united by cooperation in all common ends."[39] For his part, Skelton recognized that King had limitations beyond which he was not prepared to go. The under-secretary was willing to work within the restrictions thus imposed.

King had Skelton make detailed preparations for a full and frank discussion of the future operation of the empire prior to the Imperial Conference. This preparation helped the Canadian delegation to perform effectively on the main issue, the declaration of a new imperial relationship confirming the autonomy of the dominions. According to D. B. MacRae, who covered the conference for the *Manitoba Free Press*, the delegation's work was handled mainly by Lapointe and Skelton, with King heavily engaged on the social side. Lapointe took a special interest in the issue of appeals to the Privy Council and in the consideration of the Locarno agreements, which guaranteed existing European boundaries and established arbitration procedures to resolve disputes, and he chaired the Treaty Procedure Sub-Committee. Skelton served on the secretariat and several committees and gave particular attention to organizing the Canadian delegation and to the critical job of drafting alternate texts.[40]

The idea of a commonwealth of fully independent dominions equal in status to but closely associated with the mother country, which emerged from the conference, was articulated in the Balfour report, produced by the Committee on Inter-Imperial Relations chaired by the former British prime minister. Representatives of the states affected met again in London in the autumn of 1929, at the Conference on the Operation of Dominion Legislation, to do the technical work necessary to give the change legal effect. Initially, King paid little attention to this conference, assuming that it was convened only to prepare advice for the next meeting of government leaders. Skelton, however, appreciated its importance and brought to King's attention plans by other dominions to be represented by their attorneys general. As a result, the prime minister was persuaded to send Lapointe as leader of the delegation and to begin more extensive preparations than ever before for an imperial conference. Next to Lapointe on the delegation was Skelton, followed by the assistant deputy minister of marine, E. Hawken, and the senior advisory counsel in the Department of Justice, C. P. Plaxton. Désy, who had been posted to Paris as counsellor of the legation in 1928, joined the secretariat of the conference. Lapointe took his secretary, and Marjorie McKenzie (who had been at the Imperial Conference of 1926 as stenographer to the delegation) served as delegation secretary.

The main Canadian position paper was written by John Read while still dean of law at Dalhousie, and Charles Burchell was contracted to produce a brief on merchant shipping. In preparing his paper, Read consulted Skelton a good deal and also had the services of Pearson and Ewart. After these and other preparations in Ottawa, the work was completed on the journey to London, with results that Burchell considered highly satisfactory. The extraordinary effort that had been mounted before the conference was sustained during the eight weeks of sessions, to enable Canada to help shape the final constitutional settlement on the basis of equality. This position, approved by the Imperial Conference of 1930 and enacted into law by the British Parliament in 1931 as the Statute of Westminster, suited King's conception of the relationship. While the word "empire" remained current for a long time, especially when the dependencies were included, the context for Canada was now the British Commonwealth of Nations (or simply "the Commonwealth," although "British" was not formally dropped until 1949). The success of the endeavour to achieve the constitutional change no doubt strengthened the prime minister's belief that "we in Canada had just as good material and brains for the Foreign Service as any other part of the Empire."[41]

The department and the League of Nations

The "material and brains" of the foreign service were also needed to support Canadian activity at the League of Nations. That was an organization about which there was less uniformity of opinion among the principal decision-makers in Canada, for Lapointe and Dandurand favoured a more active role than King.

On a few occasions, Lapointe and Dandurand were successful in directing policy away from the line favoured by King, the most noteworthy example being Canada's candidature for a non-permanent seat on the League of Nations Council in 1927. Reluctant to become involved in European affairs, King was unenthusiastic, but he eventually gave his approval as a result of pressure from Lapointe.[42] The Canadian bid, which succeeded by a single vote, carried consequences for the department that had to be taken seriously. "It will not be easy to carry out effectively the new duties we have assumed," Skeleton told King. "We will have to give a good deal more time and attention to League matters."[43]

Hitherto Canadian delegations had not usually been well prepared for meetings of the League. Delegates were chosen by the prime minister, but not far enough in advance to allow them time to become fully acquainted with the issues on the agenda. King preferred throughout the 1920s that delegates be given oral briefings. If circumstances permitted, they might have an evening with him at Laurier House, but this was not a regular practice. Only Dandurand could and did insist on a pre-departure meeting with the prime minister. At the time of embarkation, delegates received from the department a sheaf of League documents for reading en route, along with a reminder to ask for instructions should any important decision have to be made.

Preparing delegations for Geneva remained an unsolved problem throughout the 1920s. When the Meighen government in the summer of 1926 appointed, as delegates to the seventh assembly, Sir George Foster, Philippe Roy, and Sir Herbert Ames, an international public servant recently retired from the secretariat of the League, written instructions prepared by Skelton and approved by the cabinet were for the first time provided. This practice did not survive King's return to power that autumn. It was resumed regularly only after the change of government in 1930.[44]

Although Riddell was on hand in Geneva, ministerial delegates were not in the habit of calling on him for assistance.[45] They were willing to rely on Skelton when he attended but otherwise had substantial leeway. Dandurand in particular felt free to become involved in issues not immediately germane to Canadian interests. One of his pet projects was agreement by Canada to the optional clause of the charter of the International Court of Justice, making compulsory the jurisdiction of that body in international disputes. In his favour was parliamentary and public interest stimulated by the League of Nations Society in 1927. By the end of 1928, this interest was persuasive with Skelton. "Public opinion, so far as vocal," he advised King, appeared to support the movement in favour of the clause. "Not all who support it understand it," he continued, "and those actively in support are only a minority of the whole people, but of what popular movement could not the same be said?"[46] The following year, Dandurand was authorized to sign the agreement giving effect to the clause.

Co-ordination of foreign policy

The importance of the department was enhanced by King's success in keeping control of external relations largely in the hands of the executive. In 1926, King had the House of Commons adopt a resolution requiring parliamentary approval of "important treaties such as involve military or economic sanctions," categories that were broadened in 1928. King also accepted Meighen's position that the prime minister should place other foreign issues before Parliament if he deemed them important.

There was, however, one noteworthy exception, involving "matters of possible controversy . . . because of a desire to have agreement between all parties in this house as far as possible in connection with the questions which relate to our inter-imperial and international relations."[47] At this time and for many years to come, leading members of all parties believed strongly that any parliamentary division on foreign policy would weaken Canada's voice abroad. King used this notion to avoid parliamentary discussion of the Geneva protocol and the Locarno treaties and to justify his refusal to make a general statement on Canadian policy regarding the League or foreign policy generally.

King had little to fear from opposition challenges to his handling of external questions. Only 4.3 per cent of the questions asked in the House of Commons between 1920 and 1930 dealt with foreign affairs, and only a small fraction of these went beyond a request for information.[48] King was a skilful manager of the parliamentary agenda, and on all but two occasions in the 1920s the External Affairs estimates were introduced in late-evening debates at the end of the session, when there was little likelihood that members would pursue the issues. In 1923 the estimates were suddenly introduced without advance notice at a time when the government's most prominent critics, who had previously indicated their intention to speak, were out of Ottawa. In 1928, the estimates were presented before the end of the session, enabling King to benefit from his recent return from a successful session at the League's assembly. Similarly, the Briand-Kellogg pact, which was of special interest to King because of its similarity to the North American example of peaceful coexistence, was given two days' examination. The only other occasions for debate were one-day discussions before the imperial conferences of 1923 and 1926, which followed a precedent set by the previous government, and another on the treaty of Lausanne.

One reason that the House of Commons did not take more interest in external issues, no doubt, was that Meighen had little time for them. Although King made available to him copies of a protocol amending the covenant of the League several weeks in advance of asking for parliamentary approval, Meighen did not find time to read it. Annual reports of the delegations to the League were tabled but never discussed. The League's journals were sent to members' offices, but interest seems not to have been great. Another source of information was the Interparliamentary Union, which existed to promote personal relationships among legislators in different countries in order to advance international peace and unity. About half the members of the Canadian Parliament belonged to the union, but few could afford to travel to its annual meetings.

In 1924 the government had secured the establishment of a House of Commons standing committee on industrial and international relations, principally to sound out parliamentary and public opinion on accepting certain international labour conventions. After reporting that the Supreme Court should decide, the committee was inactive for the next four years and then came to life to discuss civil service councils and unemployment insurance. The committee never dealt with international affairs,[49] except perhaps in 1931, when a motion for establishment of university chairs in international relations was referred to it. Thereafter, the committee fell into disuse, except for a quick look at employment in the shipping industry in 1935–36.

International affairs were given a regular airing in the Senate, where there were special debates on minorities, disarmament, France and Belgium's occupation of the Ruhr after Germany had been declared in default on reparations payments, and the Geneva protocol. Dandurand, Foster (appointed to the upper chamber in 1921), and a small group of interested colleagues were the primary instigators. But debates in the Senate were not nearly as newsworthy as those in the Commons and did not much affect public awareness or government policies.

The prime minister's control of the House of Commons discouraged challenges to the line of policy he favoured, but the small amount of questioning is no doubt also a tribute to his political judgment, indicating that he had found a course acceptable to most Canadians. This lack of debate gave the department considerable freedom of action during the later 1920s and left it alone to help King formulate his policies and to carry out his wishes.

Even so, the department had to take account of the well-established interests of other branches of government in certain aspects of external relations. Skelton endeavoured to forestall competition by his definition of the department's mandate for the Standing Committee on Industrial and International Relations. "We have in the Department at Ottawa a central agency," he told the members, "whose duty it is to provide a permanent storehouse of information and a central directing force for the work in the legations abroad, and to facilitate participation in the Imperial Conferences, the League of Nations and the special conferences from time to time."[50]

The notion of External Affairs as a central agency first surfaced in Skelton's writing in 1927.[51] By that he did not mean exclusive control of external relations, for he acknowledged that other departments were also interested in "their special phases of this international work." Nor had King ever intended that External Affairs have the only voice in formulating foreign policy. Rather, he wanted all departments affected by an issue to work in co-operation, as they had in interdepartmental committees to study the Geneva protocol and navigable waters shared with the United States.[52] Skelton sought to give External Affairs co-ordinating and directing responsibiliity for such issues among departments. This was his conception of a central agency.

On many subjects, especially those of a specialized technical nature, the department remained by choice merely the conduit of information. Questions pertaining to radio wave-lengths went to the Department of Marine and Fisheries, the custody of enemy property to the Secretary of State, landing certificates for liquor shipments to National Revenue, questionable activities of foreign nationals to the RCMP, and so on. The minister of finance managed the negotiation of a commercial agreement with Cuba. The trade commissioners continued to report to Trade and Commerce about their activities abroad. Where there were international political implications in the activities of any branch of government, however, Skelton on his own or at King's request would intervene. Thus while the Department of Public Works was responsible for improvements in shipping facilities on the St Lawrence, Skelton gave advice to King on the impact of dredging projects on the future of proposals for a seaway. When the United Kingdom invited the dominions to be represented on a subcommittee of the Imperial Defence Committee, External Affairs took the lead in replying. A good example of the department's central co-ordinating role arose in connection with preparations for the Conference on the Operation of Dominion Legislation in 1929. When the Department of Justice inquired whether the question of merchant shipping should be referred to Marine and Fisheries, Skelton intervened to say: "Not at present; I am having a memo prepared in the Department first.''[53] Marine and Fisheries never did get to turn its hand to this subject, for the memorandum "Bases of Canadian Jurisdiction in Merchant Shipping Legislation," prepared by Charles Burchell for External Affairs, became the foundation of the government's policy.

Attempts were also made at this time to strengthen External Affairs' control over communication between posts abroad and other departments in Ottawa. When Wrong reported that there had been direct correspondence between the legation in Washington and the commissioner of immigration in Ottawa, Skelton, through Walker, replied that "it tends to confusion to have directions from the Government reaching the Legation through various channels, and that unless for some very strong reason of practical convenience official correspondence from Canada should pass to you through this Department."[54]

By 1930 the constitutional implications of the External Affairs Act of 1909 had been fulfilled. The department had contributed to that achievement. Now organized into a true if small foreign ministry, it was equipped also, as that legislation had intended, to serve as the focal point for the conduct of the government's external relations. The department and especially its under-secretary had been of service to the prime minister in other capacities as well, as the amendment of 1912 had made possible. But the department's position was still not entirely secure: could it continue to grow, or even survive, under another government? With the exception of Walker, and Mahoney in Washington, all the officers in the service had been appointed since King had come to power. Skelton was just as close as Christie had been to the prime minister who had hired him. How would they fare under a prime minister with a different view of how Canada's external relations ought to be conducted? Although not an election issue, these questions had yet to be settled when the voters went to the polls on July 28, 1930.

Chapter Six

The Foreign Service at Work: 1930–1935

MAINTAINING CREDIBILITY

A government with different objectives

THE ASSUMPTION OF OFFICE BY the Conservatives under R. B. Bennett, on August 7, 1930, was a major challenge to the department. There was now a foreign service of sufficient size and talent to be a valuable instrument of public administration, but the election had placed it at the disposal of a government sceptical of the objectives for which it had been created. In the tradition of Sir Robert Borden and Arthur Meighen, Bennett did not share the autonomist views that had animated the authors of the External Affairs Act of 1909 and were reflected in the examinations on which appointment to the foreign service was based. Indeed, the new prime minister was on record as being opposed to the establishment of diplomatic missions on the ground that they weakened imperial unity.[1]

Bennett and his party espoused policy objectives very different from those of their predecessors, and these suggested that international questions would be accorded less importance and looked at from another perspective. In support of Bennett's claim that he would "blast a way into the markets that . . . had been closed," the Conservative electoral platform had concentrated on economic issues, calling for higher tariffs, unemployment relief, increased imperial trade, and measures to protect agriculture, particularly dairy products, from outside competition. As well, the party was committed to economy in government and to administrative reform, goals that called into question both the continued growth of the department and provision for the distinctive requirements of its overseas operations. These priorities, too, had already been reflected in statements by Bennett, who had been critical of the department in parliamentary debates and had expressed a distinct preference for representation abroad by the trade commissioner service. Similar views had been expressed by other members of his party, who had complained that the costs of overseas legations were not commensurate with the benefits and suggested that the savings to be gained from abolishing them could be used to provide pensions for the elderly.[2]

The new government's priorities were reinforced by the deepening economic depression of the 1930s. The stock market crash of October 1929 was the most striking symbol of this calamity, but the problems for Canada had begun to appear earlier in the declining export demand for foodstuffs and raw materials in the late 1920s, and the causes lay deep in the worldwide economic malaise. The crisis permeated every area of government activity. The quest for solutions to massive unemployment (estimated at 25 per cent of the labour force in September 1932), to dwindling exports, and to rising poverty and consequent social unrest had to be the government's first priority. Even had Bennett wished otherwise, economic problems and trade, austerity, and administrative reform would have come to the fore. Exports, rather than status or autonomy, would have to be the main concern of external policy.[3]

The priorities were established soon after the new government took office. Within days the prime minister laid plans to summon a special session of Parliament in September 1930, to approve unemployment relief legislation and extensive tariff increases affecting most Canadian manufacturing and certain farming interests. The tariff increases, it was hoped, would create 25,000 new jobs.

Bennett's work habits as well as his policy objectives served to put distance between himself and the department. The problem was not dilatoriness; Bennett was a prodigious worker. From early morning, when he arose to review documents over breakfast in his suite at the Chateau Laurier Hotel, to late at night, he worked at a furious pace. Mornings were spent in meetings and dictation, afternoons and evenings in the House of Commons, where he spoke on every government measure and responded to virtually every challenge from the opposition. But the new prime minister was more intimidating and less subtle than his predecessor, and he was solitary by nature. As a result, he seemed disinclined to share responsibility or to delegate work to subordinates.[4] He became the final arbiter not just on matters within the portfolio that was his direct responsibility, external affairs, but on those in the charge of other ministers as well. Their frequent need to consult him meant that much of Bennett's time had to be spent in meetings with ministers. Under Bennett, some believed, government had become a continuous cabinet meeting, so that he had little time, compared with other prime ministers who also had had responsiblity for External Affairs, for the business of that department.

Nor was external affairs the only portfolio Bennett kept for himself. Determined to take the leading role in redressing Canada's economic ills, he was also until early 1932 minister of finance and receiver general as well as president of the privy council. The finance portfolio placed a heavy demand on him. The Depression made it more onerous than usual, at a time when the post of deputy minister was vacant. Consequently, the prime minister had to take on much of the responsibility that otherwise might have been assumed by the permanent head.[5]

Important as these pressures on the prime minister were for External Affairs, more was at stake than the amount of time he might have to give to foreign policy and the importance it might assume in his order of priorities. Since the department as Bennett inherited it was largely the creation of Mackenzie King's government, the new prime minister had reason to question its neutrality, in terms not only of party politics but also of policy objectives. Political appointees to diplomatic posts obviously were targets of suspicion, but so were senior headquarters personnel recruited under King, particularly the under-secretary, O. D. Skelton. When combined with the doubts about the department expressed earlier by Bennett and other Conservatives, this suspicion made its future seem decidedly precarious. Rumours abounded in Ottawa during the summer of 1930 that the prime minister might abolish the department altogether, or at the very least make some major changes in personnel and direction.[6] Nor was all the reason for the rumours on the government side. Skelton himself, he later confessed to King, would have left the public service to become principal of Queen's University had he foreseen Bennett's victory at the polls.

Bennett may never have contemplated the wholesale changes rumoured in 1930, but he did intend to replace Skelton. The prime minister did not move immediately, however, and the under-secretary therefore had the opportunity to give evidence of his usefulness. Bennett later told Lester Pearson: "I, of course, had every intention of . . . disposing of him [Skelton] at once. He was close to Mr. King and his views were so far removed from any I had, his ideas and so forth, but I made a great mistake. I didn't do it within the first 48 hours, and then I began to find that I couldn't get along without him. He knew everything," Bennett said, "I kept saying, I'll fire him next week."[7]

Adjustment begins

Although "next week" never came, Bennett and Skelton's relationship was not at the outset an easy one. The first confrontation arose when Bennett, once his economic measures had been dealt with by the special session of Parliament, began making plans for an impending imperial conference in London. When Skelton submitted a list of recommended advisers, which included himself and Pearson, his initiative was rejected. Bennett, John Read recalled later, informed the under-secretary: "I'm not going to have you monkeying with this business. It is for the Prime Minister's office and not for External Affairs to run these conferences."[8]

The only External Affairs official in the party was Read, whose grandfather had been an employee and a close friend of the prime minister's father. Bennett's main support was supposed to come from political associates: William Herridge, his lawyer and chief political adviser, and a group of cabinet ministers. Unfortunately, their knowledge of the issues being discussed was slight, with the result that the Canadians at first had little impact on the conference. Bennett then decided to try Read as a source of information and advice, thereby securing briefings that brought a marked improvement in the quality of the Canadian statements. According to Read, Bennett, having been shown that an official of the department could play a pertinent and useful role, began to revise his attitude.[9]

Bennett seems to have recognized early on that the department was a useful repository of constitutional expertise on the Commonwealth. He made Pearson secretary of the dominion-provincial conference that, to fulfil a promise by the prime minister, was summoned in April 1931 to approve the Statute of Westminster, which brought about legislative equality between the dominions and the United Kingdom. A long process of constitutional evolution was thus completed, but the final step had little effect on Canada's international position beyond a change in formalities. British ambassadors ceased to introduce Canadian ministers to host governments when credentials were presented. Canada could now be invited to join some international organizations, such as the Pan-American Postal Union, which did not recognize dependencies or colonies. The right to independent conduct of external relations and to separate representation abroad, however, had already been accepted by London and was merely confirmed by the Statute of Westminster.

Skelton, meanwhile, assumed a low profile while waiting for the prime minister to call for his services. Since Bennett was too busy on economic matters to see him regularly, the under-secretary instituted a systematic means of keeping him abreast of what was going on in the world. Each week a report of five to a dozen pages outlining major events was prepared by Skelton's secretary, Marjorie McKenzie, from Foreign Office prints,

Dominions Office dispatches, reports from Canadian posts, and foreign newspapers. In addition, correspondence with the posts was summarized in convenient form. As a result of these initiatives, Bennett, who unlike King did not wish to read everything himself, was able to keep informed of major developments. Skelton also made the department serve the government's economic policies: his first major memorandum for Bennett focused on outstanding economic problems.[10] Finally, and most important, Skelton knew what to put before the prime minister, and when. Thus Skelton's productivity, his breadth of knowledge, and his ability to give non-partisan advice gradually became apparent to Bennett.

Since Bennett, unlike King, kept no diary and Skelton's papers disappeared in a fire long ago, it is hard to say precisely how the relationship evolved initially. What is clear is that the establishment of confidence between the prime minister and the department took place only gradually. The rapprochement apparently was not complete by the time Bennett visited Washington in January 1931. Because the president, Herbert Hoover, was unpopular, Bennett wanted to attract as little attention as possible to this trip, even avoiding being photographed with his host; he was so successful that the enterprise was referred to in the press as the "mystery tour."[11] Bennett was accompanied only by Herridge, who, since he was not part of the public service, could not serve as a link between Bennett and the officials concerned with the results of the visit. To them as well it was a "mystery tour," for Bennett seems to have kept to himself what transpired.

Heads of post and officer personnel

Even more uneasy was the position of heads of post, hitherto recruited from outside the public service by the government of the day. When, after Bennett took office, the press reported rumours that the incumbents might be removed, the new prime minister received some countervailing advice from Newton Rowell, Sir Robert Borden's old associate in the Union government. The prime minister, Rowell hoped, would not opt for US practice, which left foreign service appointments open to the oscillations of politics, in preference to the British tradition of career appointees.[12]

Confronting Bennett were decisions about the two most important representatives, the high commissioner in London and the minister in Washington. Peter Larkin having died in London in February 1930, Vincent Massey had been named by King as his successor three weeks before the election. No replacement had been selected by the outgoing government for Massey in Washington.

If he wanted to substitute his own candidate for Massey in London, Bennett would have to cancel the appointment of a high commissioner, already announced, who had not yet proceeded to his post. A possible rationale was the argument that the office of high commissioner was one unlike that of other Canadian representatives abroad. This was not an approach that commended itself to Rowell, who favoured the position that this was a diplomatic appointment akin to that of Canadian ministers in other capitals and of foreign representatives in London. Having heard that Massey might be dealt with separately, Rowell wrote to Bennett: "It does not appear to mc that this distinction is sound. I look upon the position of the Canadian High Commissioner at London as the most important diplomatic post in the Canadian Government Service, and I am sure you do also." The high commissioner's office, Rowell argued, should be made more effective as a diplomatic mission. "I think," he said, "one of the weaknesses in the High Commissionership in recent years has been that the diplomatic side (by which I mean consultation with respect to imperial and foreign affairs) has not been developed as it should have been."[13]

Bennett did not follow Rowell's advice. When Massey visited him to seek instructions on August 13, Bennett explained that the post in London was, in his view, a political one and that Massey, who had once been in King's cabinet, could not accurately reflect the policies of the Conservative government. Nor was a return to Washington possible, since Massey's letter of recall had already been signed by the king. Massey gave Bennett his resignation orally and, contrary to advice he received from King,[14] left the foreign service the next day.

Massey's fate stimulated fears of a more widespread purge. In particular, the recently arrived minister in Tokyo, Herbert Marler, had reason for concern about his tenure. Not only had he also been in King's cabinet, but Bennett had criticized the establishment of the legation in Tokyo. Believing that letters addressed to the prime minister might be interpreted as asking for favours, Marler instead sent personal inquiries to Skelton.[15]

The under-secretary offered cautious reassurance that the intentions of the new government did not for the present seem to include changes in Tokyo or Paris. Still, rumours and uneasiness prevailed, and, when Parliament was called into special session in September, Bennett decided to explain the distinction the government made between the high commissioner in London and other Canadian representatives. For the latter, he was prepared to follow Rowell's advice. "I may say," Bennett stated, "that the conception of policy of this government is that the ministers to France, Japan and the United States are permanent and are not to be subject to changes of administration." London, however, was a special case. "With regard to the position of High Commissioner," he continued, "I can point out only that it is a statutory office. Provision is made for that office by a statute passed by this parliament in the days of Sir John A. Macdonald.

From that day to this the position has been of a political nature."[16]

The high commissioner's post was apparently first offered to Maj.-Gen. A. D. McRae, the Conservative party organizer and fund raiser in the election campaign of 1930, who turned it down for family reasons. Bennett then approached the Conservative premier of Ontario, Howard Ferguson, who accepted the appointment on November 28, 1930. At this time, the salary was raised from $10,000, the level maintained since the office had been created, to $12,000, the rate paid to Marler in Tokyo and to the minister in Paris, Philippe Roy. Because of the high rents and the cost of entertaining in London, Ferguson was given an allowance of $28,000, bringing his total remuneration to $40,000. This was less than half his original request of $100,000, but far more than was being paid to Marler or Roy, each of whom received living and representation allowances of $12,000, plus a car allowance of $3,000.

Ferguson's transition to diplomacy was not entirely smooth. "Now I am not going over there to sell wheat," he told one audience. "I am going to London with the hope that I may be able to do something to re-mould, to revise the contemporary spirit of the British people. In the Old Country patriotic fervour, British persistence, British traditions have to a large extent broken down." Ferguson's statements were questioned by the opposition in Parliament, and the British took the view that it was "undesirable and wholly contrary to accepted practice" for a high commissioner to "appear to take part in the domestic politics of the country in which he is stationed." The prime minister refused to be drawn into public debate about Ferguson's statements, but the controversy did give him an opportunity to reiterate the position that the high commissioner held an office distinct from that of other Canadian representatives. Unlike them, Ferguson was made a privy councillor, as his predecessor Larkin had been. In Bennett's view, "one who is charged with the responsibility for the conduct not of one but of several departments of the public service in London must occupy a position almost analogous to that of a member of the government, and he is so treated."[17]

Other heads of post, Bennett argued, did not have such duties, nor did they exercise any statutory oversight of other Canadian activities in the countries where they were stationed. They occupied diplomatic offices and were responsible solely to the secretary of state for external affairs, whereas the high commissioner held "a political office" and reported to the prime minister in such a manner as to indicate that he had the confidence of the government of the day.[18] The fact that the prime minister was also secretary of state for external affairs obscured the distinction, but nonetheless, so long as Bennett was in office, the high commissioner was not considered to be an integral part of the foreign service. The relationship with Ottawa inevitably was affected, for Ferguson could claim that he need defer only to the authority of the prime minister, not to that of the under-secretary or his department.

Although not singled out the way London had been, the legation in Washington, by virtue of Massey's departure, offered another opportunity for a political appointment. The choice this time was not controversial, for there was no designated incumbent to deal with. There was no argument to be made about special status, and the appointee himself from the first displayed a good understanding of the requirements of his position.

In March 1931, Bennett announced the appointment of William Herridge as Massey's successor in Washington. Already close to Bennett, the minister-designate, a widower of forty-two, became even closer the following month when he married Mildred Bennett, the prime minister's sister. Two months later the Herridges set off for Washington.

Herridge's appointment was well received. Retiring by nature, he was considered by the journalist Grant Dexter to be something of a mystery and "the most unlikely material for public life," but even Dexter acknowledged Herridge's "personal charm," his public spirit and "talent for friendship," and his effectiveness at the Imperial Conference of 1930.[19] Through his practice as a specialist in patent law, Herridge was well acquainted with the US business community, particularly those firms with interests in Canada.

Ferguson and Herridge were Bennett's only political appointments as Canadian representatives. As Skelton had foreseen, Marler and Roy were left in place; so was Riddell in Geneva. Except for London, therefore, Rowell's advice was followed. Practice in Canada was closer to that in Britain than in the United States: it was not assumed that heads of post would offer their resignations when the government changed. This course was supported not only by Rowell's argument but also by an analysis of the US diplomatic service by Hume Wrong of the legation in Washington. He reported a malaise among career officers in the US foreign service arising in part from the high percentage of non-career appointments at the chief of mission level. As a result, some of his informants advised against emulating the example of their own government.[20]

Not only were rumours of a purge thus disproved, but recruitment continued. The first competition of the Bennett years took place in 1930. As a result, two new officers, H. F. Feaver and Alfred Rive, joined the department. Tied for first place in the written examination was Skelton's secretary, Marjorie McKenzie, who, although ineligible as a woman to become a departmental officer, undertook the exercise to establish standing for promotion.[21] She became principal clerk on January 1, 1936.

The Imperial Economic Conference of 1932

Having been maintained and even modestly expanded by Bennett, the department had to adapt to the economic priorities of the day in order to serve the new government effectively. This it was well able to do at a time when, even in the Department of Finance, there were few professional economists in the public service. Skelton was the senior public servant best qualified for economic work, and as a result of recent recruitment he had strong support in the department: Scott Macdonald had had practical experience with the Department of Trade and Commerce, and Norman Robertson and Alfred Rive were both trained economists. Evidence of the department's capacity in the field appeared shortly after the election, when Macdonald produced a memorandum on commercial missions and Rive undertook a detailed analysis of the prospects for developing trade in South America.[22]

A major opportunity for the department to display its mettle in economics arose in 1932 when, as a result of an initiative taken by Bennett at the Imperial Conference of 1930, the Imperial Economic Conference met in Ottawa. While several colonies had come together in Ottawa for the meeting on Pacific trade in 1894, a full-scale imperial conference had never been held outside London, and Canada had never organized such a large international gathering. There were nine delegations (from the United Kingdom, Canada, Australia, New Zealand, South Africa, Ireland, India, Southern Rhodesia, and Newfoundland) with advisers and support staff totalling 280 people, to which were added some 200 representatives of business and industry. In addition there were 190 journalists. The Canadian government had both to prepare the agenda and develop its own position on the issues.

External Affairs played a key role in organizing the conference. Responsibility was assigned to an interdepartmental preparatory committee with Skelton as chairman and Macdonald as secretary. This group reported to the cabinet committee where policy decisions were made. In the department, Skelton and Macdonald were assisted by Pearson, who had useful recent experience as secretary of the dominion-provincial conference, and by Beaudry, Feaver, Read, Rive, Robertson, and Howard Measures, the last responsible for protocol in the prime minister's office. Wrong and Mahoney were recalled from Washington, and Keenleyside from Tokyo, to help. In a document prepared early in 1932, Skelton listed fifty-two subjects on which various departments were to write briefs dealing with specific questions. External Affairs was assigned responsibility for preparing twenty-four briefs, as against ten for the Dominion Bureau of Statistics and eight for Trade and Commerce. Within External Affairs,

Macdonald was responsible for eight, Robertson for seven, Rive for five, and Feaver for four.

Skelton mapped out the policy studies and worked along with Read and Pearson in preparing papers on organization and administration. Skelton also went outside the government to individual persons and institutions for additional position papers. Most notable was his friend and former student, Clifford Clark, professor of commerce and director of courses in commerce and administration at Queen's, who prepared papers on prices, exchange, and monetary reforms. Favourably impressed, Bennett later in the year appointed Clark deputy minister of finance.

Once the conference opened, on July 20, 1932, the entire administrative machinery of External Affairs was pressed into service, with an allotment of $350,000 in addition to its regular annual budget. Officials from the department were assigned mainly to secretarial activities, while the substantive work of the conference went to technical personnel from Agriculture, Finance, National Revenue, and Trade and Commerce. Bennett chaired the conference. Skelton was secretary, with Read as assistant secretary and Lt.-Col. H. J. Coghill of the House of Commons staff as administrative secretary. Feaver, Keenleyside, and Wrong were attached to the secretariat. Robertson was secretary of the Canadian delegation and of the Committee on Marketing and Financial Questions, chaired by the minister of trade and commerce, H. H. Stevens. Pearson was made responsible, under the minister of railways and canals, Robert Manion, for organizing and running a press office for the journalists, seventy-five of whom had come from other countries. The social program was largely the work of Measures.

As a result of delays in formulating positions both in Canada and in other participating countries, the final agenda emerged only eight days before the conference began. Problems continued after the delegates assembled, not least because Canada's efforts to protect local industry were an obstacle to reaching agreement with the British. In the Canadian official party, the protectionist position was most closely associated with the commissioner of customs, R. B. Breadner, who was Bennett's chief adviser.

When the prime minister decided to move away from this position, he turned to Hector McKinnon, the tariff commissioner. McKinnon, with Dana Wilgress, director of the Commercial Intelligence Service (as the trade commissioner service had been known since 1911), and Robertson of External Affairs, formed a team of negotiators instructed to prepare a list of concessions acceptable to the British. Stevens apparently worked with them in producing the compromise that formed the basis of a settlement between Canada and the United Kingdom. With this and a similar accord between the United Kingdom and Australia, the log-jam was broken, and a series of bilateral agreements followed that together constituted the system of imperial tariff preferences.

Despite the result, the problems both before and during the conference provoked considerable complaint about the arrangements. The criticism, Skelton was assured, did not apply to his department: it was suggested that better management would have resulted from giving more substantive responsibility to External Affairs. "We have all been wondering," the senior Australian official told Skelton when the conference was over, "why the firstclass Canadian officials have been employed in nominal secretarial positions while the substantial work of the committees has been entrusted to officials of obviously much lower grade."[23]

After the conference there could be no doubt that the department had the confidence of the prime minister. As a result, officers were assigned important responsibilities related to the government's economic policies and other new activities, while at the same time being expected to handle the work that was the mandate of their branch of government. To carry out these multifarious tasks effectively, they had to adapt to changes, not only in policy priorities, but also in administrative requirements, as a result of innovations introduced by Bennett's government and the pressures of the Depression.

MEETING NEW ADMINISTRATIVE REQUIREMENTS

The department and the comptroller general

The most important Bennett-era administrative change to the department was the centralization of financial control as a result of amendments to the Consolidated Revenue and Audit Act which came into force in 1932. The amendments were not a direct consequence of the Depression, for the Department of Finance had earlier begun preparations to correct the inefficiency of the old, decentralized system, said to have led to "wastefulness, laxity and dishonesty" in the government generally.[24] Reform was made even more necessary, however, by the economic pressures of the early 1930s and was a project to which Bennett was strongly committed.

As a result of the changes in the act, a new position, comptroller of the treasury, was created in the Department of Finance. This officer and his staff were to administer certain financial activities for all government departments. Thenceforth, all departmental expenditures had to be approved in advance by the comptroller, who could prevent over-spending by the threat of dismissal for any infraction. He also had the responsibility of ensuring that funds were used for the purposes authorized by Parliament, with any unexpended portion reverting to the receiver general at the end of the fiscal year (March 31). Ironically, this last provision could be a disincentive to economy, since departmental managers, including heads of post in External Affairs, tended to leave no funds unspent on March 31, both to avoid the lapse of appropriations and to justify their estimates for the following fiscal year.[25]

Under the old, decentralized system, External Affairs had had a much better record than most departments. In revenue accounting, thanks to Agnes McCloskey, it was judged by the auditor general to have "one of the most air-tight and satisfactory systems in the Government departments."[26] A good record, however, could not exempt a department from the new system for financial accountability. The results were disconcerting to Skelton in various ways.

The most immediate effect was on staffing, since the change was meant to strip departments of their own financial administrative officers. External Affairs was asked to transfer to the Office of the Comptroller General three members of its accounting staff, but in fact released only two, for Skelton would not give up McCloskey. Instead, she got a promotion within External Affairs: on July 16, 1935, she was reclassified to chief clerk (at an annual salary of $2,904, a modest raise from her previous level of $2,808) rather than departmental accountant, although there was no change in her duties or in her responsibility for finances.

More serious were the implications of centralized control over expenditures, which, if imposed too vigorously, would make it difficult to adapt to variations in conditions from one post to another. This was troubling to Skelton but less so to McCloskey, who assured him that "there is no use crying over all the trouble this Audit Act has got us into."[27]

Agnes McCloskey was determined to remain the focal point of the department's financial operations. Thus she wanted to deal herself with the auditor general, who performed the post-audit of departmental accounts and reported to Parliament on the government's financial management. When the auditor general, Georges Gonthier, proposed examining the accounts of the legation in Paris, she advised the post: "Understand Gonthier may ask some questions regarding Paris expenditure. Be as non-committal as possible suggesting that enquiry might be made through External Affairs." Paris replied: "Gonthier very tired now resting near Geneva, does not seem inquisitive. Shall be cautious."[28]

Minor flurries of this kind were a commonplace of departmental housekeeping during the 1930s. They were part of McCloskey's personal control system, which was designed to discourage curiosity on the part of the supervising agencies while maintaining her own and the department's reputation for probity and efficiency. Her effort seems to have been successful, for the auditor general found little in the department's financial operations to complain about, apart from the practice of charging against public funds some of the costs of travel to Canada by wives of "certain" heads of post.[29] Only one example of theft can be found in the existing records. This occurred in 1933 at the office of the high commissioner in London. Since the amount was insufficient to justify court proceedings, the matter was settled quietly.[30]

The department resisted undesired interference not only by being careful of its reputation but also by taking a suspicious view of innovations that might enhance the power of the supervisory agencies. When the comptroller general suggested in 1935 that he might make a preliminary examination of the department's estimates before their formal submission to Treasury Board through his office, Skelton replied: "If . . . the new procedure were to operate as the thin edge of the wedge for substituting the opinion of officers not familiar with the work or needs of a department for the judgement and responsibility of officials of a department who should be so informed, with regard to the relative necessity of various alternative departmental services, I consider it would be wholly inconsistent with administrative efficiency and the development of a competent Government Service."[31] Such vigilance ensured that the department retained the right to run its own affairs in the face of centralization elsewhere, because of the unique conditions it faced abroad. The achievement, however, may have been a mixed blessing, by depriving the department of the opportunity to educate the Treasury Board about the requirements of overseas operations.

McCloskey and financial administration

To meet the department's financial needs, Agnes McCloskey devised a simple system, but one effective for operations on a modest scale. She herself prepared the annual estimates of the cost of headquarters operations and also of the revenues earned by the department, mostly through the sale of passports. Each post was required to anticipate its own yearly financial requirements (not including salaries and allowances of Canada-based staff, which were paid from Ottawa). These figures then became the basis for the money voted by Parliament to support the department's operations.

Once the money was voted, McCloskey was strict in allocating it according to the budgets already prepared. Although the vote included provision for unforeseen contingencies, she was reluctant to draw upon this, and she also seems to have disliked requesting supplementary estimates. Posts therefore were expected to stay strictly within their budgets and, if they went over the limit on one type of expenditure, to find a counterbalancing saving elsewhere.

Posts were provided with advances at the beginning of each month, issued in Canadian funds and converted and banked locally. The posts themselves estimated the size of advance required and were expected to spend it all during the month; if anything were left over, it was allocated to the following month, and the advance for that month reduced accordingly. Thus every month tended to become a fiscal year in miniature, with posts endeavouring to spend the entire allocation without any carry-over. This the posts could do with reasonable security, since most of their costs (for example, for rents and the salaries of locally engaged staff) were constant. Miscalculation, however, could cause embarrassment. In 1936, the office of the high commissioner in London ran out of operating funds early in December. With the approval of the Treasury Board, the department had recourse to the highly unusual procedure of using a governor general's warrant to finance the post until the end of the fiscal year on March 31, 1937, there being no opportunity to submit a supplementary estimate in time to meet the need.[32]

Apart from occasional incidents of this kind, the system worked well from the point of view of headquarters. It certainly provided for accountability to Ottawa. Authority had to be secured in advance for all but small, run-of-the-mill expenditures, and all disbursements had to be supported by receipts, sent home with the monthly accounts by the fastest means available. The main complaint at posts was that the practice was too rigid, serving the interests of headquarters much better than those in the field. That of course was the intention. The department might want to keep its distance from agencies of central control in Ottawa, but in order to continue doing so it had to be certain that its financial affairs were conducted scrupulously, at home and abroad.

Austerity

Careful management could not offer the department the same defence against the other main feature of public administration in the Bennett years, austerity. The unique character of the department's operations, however, enabled it to withstand the full effect of financial cutbacks rather better than some branches of government.

Bennett's government came to office committed to solving the economic crisis by bolstering the economy and therefore did not at first resort to austerity. By 1932, however, when it had become evident that the strategy was failing, the government introduced cutbacks. Its first action was to abolish all vacant positions in the civil service and to order the dismissal of temporary employees. While the department had no vacancies, it did rely heavily on temporaries. It was thus liable to a severe pruning of staff, which would have required reallocation of personnel. Yet the effect turned out to be minimal, because of one of the department's special responsibilities. Heavily involved in the Imperial Economic Conference, External Affairs was eligible for extra funds to hire temporary personnel, some of whom were able to take on work formerly assigned to employees affected by across-the-board restraint.

Of more immediate import was Parliament's decision to reduce civil service salaries by 10 per cent as of April 1, 1932, with the object of producing economies of some $7.5-8 million in the fiscal year 1932–33. The result was to take salaries in External Affairs back to what they had been in 1927: for example, to a range of $2,520 to $3,000 for third secretaries and $3,840 to $4,000 for first secretaries. (There was no corresponding cut in allowances paid to those posted abroad, which ranged from $1,000 to $4,000, depending on location, rank, and marital status.)[33] Although the freeze was originally planned to last for only one year, it was not until 1937 that salaries were restored to the level prevailing before April 1932, with an additional lump sum to make up for the loss in the intervening years.

The hardship caused by the salary reduction was increased by the withdrawal of normal increments: the sum paid an individual employee, therefore, was frozen at the level produced by the cuts of 1932. As a result, promotions became the only means of achieving higher incomes. At home, however, promotions became virtually impossible, since attrition rates during the Depression were low and no new senior positions were being created.

The new rules, though stringent, could sometimes be circumvented. Robertson secured advancement after absenting himself temporarily from the department. Having received an offer to spend a year at Harvard University as a visiting lecturer in government, Robertson, apparently with the encouragement of Skelton, accepted in the hope that the distinction could be used to justify promotion on his return. When he got back to Ottawa, his position was reclassified from third to second secretary. At this time, however, promotion was not normally the result of a job well done. For Pearson, whose work was attracting favourable attention, the reward was to be made an officer of the Order of the British Empire. Observing to Bennett that "you can't raise a family on an OBE," Pearson offered to exchange the honour for upward reclassification of his position in the civil service.[34]

There were other means whereby employees of External Affairs could escape the full rigours of salary reductions. Postings abroad, eased by allowances, might result in promotion and in some instances were made with that objective in mind. The Imperial Economic Conference provided support staff with the opportunity to recoup losses through overtime work, and some officers assigned to it received bonuses that more than offset the cuts in their regular pay.

Not all the special advantages of service in the department survived the impact of the Depression and austerity. Hitherto, the financial benefit of posting abroad had been enhanced by the exemption from taxation not only of allowances but also of salaries and income on investments. The greatest gain from this arrangement obviously was enjoyed by wealthy heads of post with large private incomes. In Skelton's view, indeed, the exemption had been more than sufficient to compensate the former high commissioner in London, Peter Larkin, for forgoing his salary.[35] In 1933, a change in the Income Tax Act made taxable any investment income received by Canadian government employees abroad, although salaries remained exempt.

Financial problems of more general application to those abroad resulted from constant fluctuations in exchange rates and the instability of certain foreign currencies during the Depression. These conditions led to discrepancies that penalized employees at some posts and favoured others. For a long time adjustments were made piecemeal, because Skelton and the comptroller general, Watson Sellar, were unable to agree on a formula to recommend to Treasury Board for smoothing out fluctuations on a permanent basis. In 1938 such a formula was finally adopted: when depreciation went beyond 10 per cent, employees were allowed full compensation for exchange losses on salary up to $1,500, and half for any losses over that amount.[36]

Once the initial impact of austerity had been absorbed, most of the department's expenditures survived without further serious reduction. The minister of finance, E. N. Rhodes (who succeeded Bennett in February 1932), called for reduction in government expenditure by $14 million in 1933–34, distributing the burden equally, on a percentage basis, among all departments. External Affairs, with its small appropriation, accounted for only $15,000 of the total. The saving was made by cutting the budgets of posts, the practical result being reduction in local travel. Budgets for entertainment were not substantially affected, since much of that activity continued to be subsidized from the personal fortunes of heads of post. The posts, moreover, did not always expend their entire allocations, so that there was some room to report savings without affecting actual operations. In Tokyo, the tighter operation resulting from the reduced appropriation was considered to improve efficiency.[37]

Officer recruitment continues

Notwithstanding austerity, a second officer competition was authorized by the prime minister for 1932–33, and he took a personal interest in the results, interviewing those who passed the written examinations. This time the successful candidates included a Franco-Manitoban, Hector Allard, a francophone from Quebec, Léon Mayrand, and two anglophones, R. M. Macdonnell and Charles Ritchie. Although no further competitions were held until 1937, Skelton was well satisfied with the results thus far and thought that the department had established a standard of recruitment that should have more general application. "I think," he wrote in 1934, "we may fairly say that the endeavour of our Department to obtain men . . . through special examinations has started a number of other Departments in the right direction. . . . Their superiority in general to men obtained by other Departments through the ordinary Civil Service procedure, has been a matter of comment and envy, and I hope in time of emulation."[38]

Some appointments continued to be made without competitive examination. In 1928, Lt.-Col. Georges Vanier of the Canadian Army had been seconded to the staff of the Dominion of Canada advisory officer, League of Nations, to represent Canada on the League's Permanent Advisory Council for Military, Naval and Air Questions. In 1931, he was transferred to London to replace Lucien Pacaud as secretary to the high commissioner.

Another departure from the competitive principle resulted in the return to the department of Loring Christie. The decision to bring him back was taken sometime during the late spring or early summer of 1935. The circumstances are unclear, but the invitation seems to have come from Bennett, with the support of Skelton. Since there was no vacancy at an appropriate level, or funding for an additional position, on the headquarters staff, an allocation for Tokyo was used. Christie was nominally appointed counsellor of the legation there, although he was never posted to Tokyo, the assignment being strictly for bookkeeping purposes. His work was at headquarters, where he was given responsibility for defence, disarmament, and the British Empire, replacing Pearson, who was going to London as first secretary in the office of the high commissioner.[39]

The addition of eight officers between 1930 and 1935 was offset by the loss of four others. Lucien Pacaud left the service in 1931, having declined for personal reasons a transfer to Tokyo. Keith Crowther, posted to Washington as third secretary in 1929 and promoted to second secretary the following year, was judged by Hume Wrong, chargé d'affaires after Massey's departure, not to have adapted well to the "jumpy sort of life" that a diplomat had to expect. Persuaded by Wrong to seek a more predictable occupation, Crowther left in 1932 and moved on to a career in the private sector. Thomas Stone, sent to Paris as second secretary in 1932 after five years in Washington, resigned in 1935, to manage family property in the United States. Part of the cost of his departure was to the linguistic balance of the Paris legation. "We will miss him very much," wrote the minister, "for his good knowledge of the English language—none of us here, is thoroughly master of that language."[40]

The final vacancy occurred at the top, when the assistant under-secretary, W. H. Walker, died after a short illness on April 26, 1933, at the age of sixty-eight. Walker had been a contributor to the legislation whereby the department was established, and he had occupied the second-ranking position, under Sir Joseph Pope and O. D. Skelton, ever since. His death therefore removed an important element of continuity, partic-ularly with regard to the consular and administrative activities which were his specialty.

When Walker's post became vacant, Bennett was urged—by the solicitor general, Maurice Dupré; by French-Canadian members of Parliament; and by Maurice Duplessis, leader of the (Conservative) opposition in Quebec—to appoint Laurent Beaudry assistant under-secretary.[41] Although delayed for sixteen months, the response ultimately was positive. For the first time the top direction of the department included a francophone officer, one who would take over from the under-secretary when the latter was absent.

Deployment of resources

Although recruitment of officers continued on the basis of the principles favoured by Skelton, the new priorities and pressures of the Bennett years required reconsideration of the way in which they were developed. The period saw reassessment of departmental activities and of the resources needed to carry them out.

Early in the period, when the department's future was still in doubt, Skelton assigned Pearson the task of writing a defence of its functions and its establishment at home and abroad. Also at this time, studies were undertaken of the diplomatic establishments and foreign services main-tained by other governments. Wrong's report on US practice was one of these; another was prepared by Beaudry shortly after his return from Washington.

Beaudry argued that Canada needed greater representation abroad to keep pace with its growing international commitments and its trade and industrial position in the world. The time had come, he contended, to reduce reliance on the British diplomatic service. As a means of financing his proposals, he recommended taking over consular work from the British and using the fees to support a Canadian consular service, which would function in a quasi-diplomatic capacity pending expansion of the network of legations. Among the benefits would be relief from a problem that had long concerned Canadian trade commissioners and immigration agents abroad: the impairment of their status by the lack of a Canadian diplomatic presence in most of the places where they served.[42]

Trade promotion

Because of his commitment to promote exports, Bennett was interested in the problems of trade commissioners and hence in a proposal put forward by Marler, intended to serve Canada's commercial needs in Asia. Dissatisfied with the efforts of British consuls and commercial agents to develop Canadian trade with China, Marler persuaded Bennett in 1931 that he should be accredited to that country as well as to Japan, with a chargé d'affaires resident in Nanking (established as the capital in 1928 by the government of Generalissimo Chiang Kai-shek). The British, mistakenly believing that Skelton was the originator of the proposal, were concerned that his anti-imperial views might be influencing Bennett, and they had a number of substantive reasons as well for opposing the proposal. In particular, they expected that it would be difficult for the British Empire to speak with one voice in China if Canada had a legation in Nanking while the mother country was represented in Peking, where the established diplomatic colony remained in place. They also anticipated friction over precedence between the Canadian trade commissioner and the British consul general in Shanghai if the status of the former were elevated. They therefore made strong representations to Bennett that the diplomatic representation of Canadian interests in China should be left in British hands. Despite counterarguments from Skelton, Bennett acquiesced, and Marler's scheme was abandoned.[43]

Even though he did not go ahead with the project, Bennett's enthusiasm for opening a legation in China was at odds with the position he had taken on representation abroad before becoming prime minister. Shortly after the plans for China had been aborted, he took advantage of a House of Commons debate on supply for the department to clarify his position. Without retracting anything he had said earlier, he gave assurance that the existing legations would be maintained and that he was open to persuasion about their usefulness, particularly for the promotion of trade.[44] He therefore was attracted by another scheme of Marler's, that the legation in Tokyo should co-ordinate the work of all the trade commissioners in Japan and China.

In Canada, various proposals emerged for integration of the foreign services of External Affairs and Trade and Commerce into a single diplomatic service or for creation of a consular service (absorbing the trade commissioners) with a status midway between the two. These received a positive response in External Affairs but were resisted by the trade commissioners. Although the minister of trade and commerce at first gave some support to Marler's proposal, he did not favour altering the status of trade commissioners. "The primary object of a trade commissioner abroad is trade," Stevens told a questioner in the House of Commons, "and the danger is that if you make the trade commissioner a diplomatic officer he will become obsessed with a glorified idea of his position."[45] Such resistance prevented change, even though Bennett recognized that increasing government control of foreign economies was making it more difficult for trade commissioners without diplomatic status to work effectively.[46]

The posts in operation

The government's failure to act on the various proposals for change rendered the department, in its dealings with representatives of other governments, a non-specialist diplomatic service. This pattern was confirmed between 1930 and 1935, as the recently created network of five diplomatic missions became fully operational.

The most important mission was the high commissioner's office in London, not only the oldest but also the largest and the most generously financed. Notwithstanding changes in the imperial relationship during the 1920s, many of Canada's principal external interests were still in the British capital, which also served as a window on the international situation, especially in Europe. Briefings by British officials were a major source of information, and the staff of Canada House was a useful resource for participation in international meetings.

In the fiscal year 1933-34, External Affairs paid the salaries of thirty-nine staff members (a few of whom worked for only a portion of the period) at the high commissioner's office. Of these, only one, the secretary (Vanier), was a diplomatic officer. The rest of the staff consisted of the private secretary to the high commissioner, an assistant secretary, an accountant, a head clerk, twenty-seven more junior clerical and stenographic staff members, five office boys, and two chauffeurs. Only Ferguson and Vanier were qualified for more than routine work.[47] Practically all the staff members were locally engaged British citizens or Canadians long resident in London. Despite encouragement from Ottawa at this time to hire more Canadians, it was impossible to make many changes because there were few turnovers of staff. The office of the high commissioner in fact was, and long remained, a Canadian-directed operation run by a largely British staff.

The expenses and salaries of the high commissioner's office in 1933 amounted to $121,970.10. Another $90,813.81 was allocated for trade promotion. The high commissioner, like other heads of post, was expected to draw on his own financial resources to cover part of the cost of entertaining.

Unlike newer missions, such as the legation in Tokyo, the office in London was not called on to submit regular political and economic reports. In fact, Ferguson did not realize until he had been in office for some weeks that he was expected to make reports to Ottawa. That he was unaware of this function no doubt was a reflection on his briefing before he left Canada and also perhaps on the guidance he received at the post. At any rate, it was from British rather than Canadian sources that Ferguson learned of the requirement. Skelton considered that Canada House, except for Vanier, was "much under-staffed in senior posts,"[48] and the opinion was shared by the Dominions Office. "Canada House as at present organized," it was noted there in 1935, "is not really equipped for sending to Ottawa accounts of the kind suggested by the Foreign Office."[49]

While Ferguson was numbered among Bennett's principal associates on foreign policy, he was not relied on heavily for advice. Instead, his main function was maintenance of liaison between the Canadian and British governments, an important task: after 1926, the dominions secretary communicated with the Canadian government via the secretary of state for external affairs rather than the governor general. Direct dealings also continued between prime ministers, other ministers, and, occasionally, officials.[50] The usual route, however, was through the Canadian high commissioner in London or his British counterpart in Ottawa. The British also consulted with the dominion high commissioners in London on the international situation and provided them with copies of reports from the diplomatic service abroad (the Foreign Office print).

The posting to London of effective younger diplomats helped to strengthen liaison, as they established fruitful associations with British officials and with colleagues in the offices maintained by other dominions. Relationships at this level tended to be rather less formal than among the senior ranks. Thus, observed a member of the Dominions Office of the same generation, there emerged something of "a new style of diplomacy." The "new breed . . . tended to be young, intelligent, serious, to feel completely at home in their new surroundings which they did not regard as foreign and where they made the widest possible contacts. They were frank and outspoken and made a break with 'old-school' diplomacy." Australia, he noted, was the pioneer in this development, but Canada followed suit in 1935 when Pearson was posted to London.[51]

Throughout the period, there was a heavy emphasis on economic issues in the work in London. Some of this arose from various continuing committees established over the years to deal with special aspects of the Commonwealth relationship, such as shipping and trade in agricultural products. Canada was represented on these bodies through the office of the high commissioner, and the office's staff assisted and advised delegations from Canada attending the many international and imperial meetings held in London.

Also requiring careful attention was the bilateral trading relationship with the mother country, still the most important market for Canadian exports, accounting for $184.4 million worth in 1933, or 39.3 per cent of the total. (By comparison, $141.1 million worth, or 33.6 per cent, went to the United States.) Ferguson took a strong interest in these activities and personally supervised all Canadian trade publicity in Britain. His efforts seem to have pleased the under-secretary. The high commissioner, Skelton observed after visiting Canada House in 1933, "keeps busy and seems to know everyone who counts in London."[52]

As well as taking on responsibilities related to the needs of the day, the high commissioner's office had to keep up various activities that went back to its foundation. A good deal of time was devoted to financial transactions affecting Canada, because London was a major source of investment capital. British businessmen and others requiring information about Canada had recourse to Canada House, as did Canadian government departments dealing with the authorities in London. A total of 5,874 Canadian visitors called at Canada House during 1933. The office provided assistance in obtaining admission tickets to sittings of Parliament and might be asked to help obtain invitations to royal garden parties and levées, to secure entrance to the royal enclosure at the Ascot race meeting, and, for a few, to arrange for presentation at court. The high commissioner and his wife represented Canada at numerous official social functions, which numbered slightly over 100 in 1933.

The provinces had to rely more heavily on the high commissioner's office than formerly for the representation of their interests in the United Kingdom. The offices of the agents general of New Brunswick and Nova Scotia had been closed in the 1920s, and those of Ontario, Alberta (revived in 1927 after having been inactive since 1918), and Quebec suffered the same fate in 1931, 1934, and 1936 respectively. Thereafter only British Columbia maintained an office in the British capital, but much reduced in scale, being run by an acting agent general on an appropriation less than one-tenth that provided in 1922-23.

The high commissioner's office was judged toward the end of Ferguson's tenure to be "well organized,"[53] yet there was one major disappointment. An effort to improve the co-ordination of the activities of various Canadian government departments in London, to which Ferguson attached considerable importance, proved largely unsuccessful.

Although sharing premises with them, the External Affairs staff of the high commmissioner's office did not involve itself in the work of officials from other departments represented in London: the chief Canadian government trade commissioner, the director of European emigration, the animal products trade commissioner, the overseas representative of the Department of Pensions and National Health, and a customs investigation officer. The centralization of all activity under the high commissioner, insisted on by Lord Strathcona, had long since disappeared. Ferguson wished to re-establish the high commissioner's control and, to that end, arranged for Bennett to remind ministers of other departments that, according to order-in-council PC 330, of February 10, 1922, "the High Commissioner is the head of Canadian activities in Great Britain."[54] Ministers were asked to correspond with the high commissioner on non-policy matters and through Bennett, as secretary of state for external affairs, when policy decisions were involved.

Ferguson did succeed in consolidating the public relations activities of the various departments by having their work and budgets transferred to External Affairs. Otherwise, however, he failed to bring about centralized control. The representatives of individual departments had become accustomed to conducting their activities without much local supervision, responsible only to their headquarters in Ottawa, and Ferguson's effort was insufficient to make them change. Despite his initiative, therefore, the old unco-ordinated approach continued.

With a much shorter history, the second most important Canadian diplomatic mission, the legation in Washington, easily adapted to new requirements as Bennett's and Herridge's priorities supplanted Massey's. Whereas the former minister had concentrated on promoting an understanding of Canada as an independent nation among the US cultural and political élite, the primary objective now was to ensure that the legation serve the requirements of the economy.

As chargé d'affaires between Massey's departure in July 1930 and Herridge's arrival in June 1931, Wrong had not been entirely happy, at least in the financial sense. Notwithstanding Skelton's resistance to considering personal means as one of the criteria for recruitment to the Canadian foreign service, Wrong had found that, even as second-in-command, his salary and allowances had been inadequate, and he had had to draw on his own resources to cover costs. As chargé he expected the drain to be greater, at a time when his small private income was falling. Unlike Massey, moreover, Wrong was not compensated for the cost of running the legation car and hiring a chauffeur, even though he based his claim on representational considerations.[55]

Prior to Herridge's arrival in Washington, Wrong prepared a detailed account of the work of the legation. After pointing out that the operation of the office had caused no friction with the British embassy, Wrong went on to describe the work as serving four main functions. First, said Wrong, the legation, along with its counterpart in Ottawa, acted as "a medium of official intercourse between the Governments of Canada and the United States." The second task, accounting for considerably more than half the correspondence with headquarters, was to supply Ottawa with "information concerning the activities and policies of the Government of the United States." Third was the protection of the rights of individual Canadians in the United States, a duty performed in conjunction with the British consular service. The presence of a legation of their own in Washington seems to have given Canadians in the United States heightened expectations, not all of them realistic. "I received a few days ago," Wrong reported, "a heated request for diplomatic assistance from a Canadian resident in a Chicago suburb, who was infuriated because the local water company would not connect its main with his house." Finally, the legation was called on to supply information to Americans interested in Canada. To do so effectively, it was essential "that comprehensive and recent information . . . be available and that the staff . . . know how to find their way through the Canadian statutes, year books, departmental reports, and so on."

In addition to the various work-day activities he had described, there was, said Wrong, another function, equally important but "scarcely definable . . . , which may be loosely described as helping to maintain the prestige of Canada in the capital of the United States." A person of high rank such as the Canadian minister, Wrong maintained, had to live up to the expectations created by his position; if he did not, his country's reputation would suffer. Social life was not intended "to pamper the vanity of diplomats," and it was related to more than "considerations of prestige and common politeness": "One would cut oneself off, if one were to attempt to carry out this precept, from most valuable personal acquaintanceships and essential sources of information. A familarity with important officials of the country to which he is accredited, easy enough to permit frank and free discussion, is the aim of a good chief of mission, and this he cannot attain by shutting himself inside the Legation and seeing only those who come to visit him. To a lesser degree the same considerations apply to the entire diplomatic staff as well as to its chief."

Wrong went on to look at the legation's problems. The chief difficulty was one that had troubled Canadian representatives elsewhere: insufficient outward communication by Ottawa. A problem peculiar to Washington was the inflexibility of instructions, a carry-over from the department's long experience of working through the British embassy. Less serious but still worthy of comment was lack of co-ordination with other departments that had direct dealings with their US counterparts. Difficulty could also arise from the activity of the few representatives of other departments resident in the United States: trade commissioners in New York, Chicago, and San Francisco, several immigration offices (recently reduced in number), and two or three offices for customs valuation.

In the final section of his memorandum, Wrong dealt with staff problems. Uppermost in his mind was the cost of living and of entertaining, which he claimed required the minister and his staff to subsidize the operation by at least 50 per cent over the annual appropriation of $100,000. Canadian practice, he asserted, compared unfavourably with that of the United States and the United Kingdom. It also played havoc with the merit principle: unless remuneration were more generous, he recommended that no officer (at least if married) be posted to Washington if he did not have a private income. Clerical employees, too, were inadequately compensated, making it difficult to staff the legation entirely by Canadians, who, moreover, had to be of a calibre to be trusted with work "of a confidential character requiring skill and discretion."[56]

Like Wrong, the new minister, Herridge, was interested in the effectiveness of the legation. He had ideas of his own on Canada's external relations and valued the means to put them into practice.

Herridge's influence with Bennett continued after his posting to Washington and was reinforced on frequent trips back to Ottawa. Thus it was via Herridge that Bennett later took over some of the ideas embodied in Franklin Roosevelt's New Deal. Yet the relationship was not without strain, for Herridge tended to act as though he were equal rather than subordinate to the prime minister. He also was critical of the government behind Bennett's back. Therefore his persuasiveness, although substantial, was limited, and he never converted Bennett to all his views. They had different perceptions of Herridge's position in Washington. Bennett saw the minister's role, rather like that of Ferguson in London, as handling liaison between the two governments. Herridge had a broader view and wanted to use the legation as "an agency for the continuing development of North American economic, political and social ties."[57]

Herridge quickly established good relations with leading members of the US administration, aided by a dinner given soon after his arrival by the US minister to Canada, Hanford MacNider, which included among the guests the secretary of war, the secretary of the treasury, and the chairman of the tariff commission. As time went on, Herridge became a close friend of Herbert Hoover's secretary of state, Henry L. Stimson. He was not as intimate with Stimson's successor under Franklin Roosevelt, Cordell Hull, but he was friendly with Dean Acheson, who served briefly in 1933 as under-secretary of the treasury, with Raymond Moley, assistant secretary of state and a longtime adviser of the president, and with some of Roosevelt's other New Deal advisers. He paid attention to Congress, reporting in 1933 on a long session with Moley and Key Pittman, chairman of the Senate Foreign Relations Committee, in which they "talked over their own problems with no more reserve than if I had been of their own party."[58] As well, Herridge was much interested in "officials and others who normally but infrequently appear along the diplomatic horizon"; that is, "the fellows behind the scenes." Introduced to this side of life in Washington by MacNider, Herridge immediately appreciated its importance[59] and established a network of relationships that he put to effective use during his tenure of the legation.

"Bill Herridge," wrote his friend Acheson in an assessment supported by Skelton and by comments in the press in Canada, "was one of the ablest diplomats this country has received and in the early nineteen-thirties one of the best-known and liked men in official Washington." In part this was a result of Herridge's success with "the fellows behind the scenes," especially important because the New Deal led to a proliferation of agencies whose activities were of interest to Canada.

Herridge's social life was tailored, to a considerable degree, to serve this objective. One function that he used effectively, according to Acheson, was "the luncheon for men." As well, Herridge took advantage of opportunities to get to know public servants through participation in outings organized by the various departments and agencies, frequent and popular activities at the time. He was, said Acheson, a welcome guest at these functions and benefited from being "particularly successful as a soft-ball relief pitcher for the civil servants against the political officers."[60]

Herridge's approach gave the legation's entertaining a different and a more modest character than that maintained by the Masseys. Even so, the position occupied by the minister and his wife meant that they could not escape a good deal of formal and conspicuous social life. The pace was such that Mildred Herridge, herself a popular figure in Washington, had to engage a private secretary of her own before the end of 1931. The social highlight of the Herridges' sojourn in Washington undoubtedly was the second visit there by Bennett, in April 1933. This was a much more attractive exercise for the prime minister than his earlier visit to Hoover, because of the popularity of the new president: far from avoiding photographers, Bennett took advantage of every opportunity to have his picture taken with Roosevelt. As part of the festivities, there was a dinner at the legation with a distinguished guest list including the secretary and the under-secretary of state.[61]

The changes introduced by Herridge went well beyond the social life of the legation. "I have conceived the purpose of this legation," he told Skelton at the end of 1933, "to be, primarily, not a liaison between the government here and at home, but an agency vested with certain independent powers; sufficient, at any rate, to enable it to act promptly and without the need of consultation, in any new-arising and unfavourable situation. Whether I am right or wrong in my conception of the present purpose of the Legation, I have, at any rate, acted in pursuance of my own definite views of what should be done. For it is imperative in this quickly changing situation that we move with speed and decisiveness; and we have tried to do so."

Herridge acknowledged that this approach had added to the work of the legation and that it became more onerous after the start of the New Deal, because of his concern that all his officers keep in touch with the new US government agencies. To keep up, he concluded that the staff must be expanded. In June 1931, the total of Canada-based and locally engaged personnel had been seventeen. The former included the counsellor (Wrong), the commercial secretary (Mahoney), two second secretaries (Stone and Crowther), a principal clerk/bookkeeper, a librarian/file clerk, three stenographers, and a doorkeeper. The latter included a telephone operator, a janitor, an outside messenger, an inside messenger, a night watchman, and two cleaners. Herridge requested three more officers, "not of too tender years, with some instinct for business and, as we say down here, good mixers." Pending thorough-going reorganization of the mission, which he considered necessary as a longer-term objective, he suggested seconding officers of other departments, particularly Agriculture and Trade and Commerce, as attachés.[62]

Skelton's response was not encouraging. Because of the Depression and consequent restrictions on government hiring, he pointed out, personnel resources in External Affairs were very strained. He did not favour secondments because of the adverse effect on promotional opportunities in External Affairs and, though willing to waive his objection if doing so would be of help to Herridge, did not think that men of the required calibre could be found in other departments. The best he could offer was the prospect of additional help from new officers recruited through the competition then under way,[63] but even this did not materialize during the remainder of Herridge's tenure as minister. Even so, the legation performed well. A cryptic report expressed ample satisfaction with the performance of the office in the latter part of the period: "Office in good shape; in close touch with United States authorities and actively on job; model despatches; Wrong and Mahoney first class."[64]

The legation in Paris had the same number of officers as that in Washington: in addition to the minister, Roy, there were a counsellor, Jean Désy, and two second secretaries, Pierre Dupuy and E. D. McGreer (appointed in 1929); the latter was replaced by Stone in 1932. The total staff of the mission in the fiscal year 1933–34 was twelve, and the cost of operation approximately $75,500.

The story of this legation's operations during the early 1930s is sketchy, for Roy did not submit annual reports and the mission's records were destroyed during the Second World War. The annual reports of the department enumerate the usual consular, representational, reporting, and economic functions, together with some activities arising from Canada's historic relationship with France. Canadian visitors, students, and permanent residents were of continuing interest, and the four hundredth anniversary in 1934 of the landing of Jacques Cartier in Canada was a symbolic event of much importance. As well, Roy and his officers participated regularly in sessions of the League of Nations Assembly and other international gatherings in Europe. This last activity was one for which Roy considered his mission to be particularly well placed: Paris was the headquarters for international meetings and for preparatory work in connection with various League conferences.

Roy thought Canada's standing in Paris would be enhanced if the government owned its residence and office quarters. He was unhappy with the attitude toward some of his material requirements, complaining particularly about having to use his own furniture and personal effects in the official residence and to pay the rent out of his salary and allowances. An increase of $5,000 in the legation's appropriation, he suggested, would enable the government to take over these responsibilities. He also contended that he had insufficient office staff, and he warned Skelton in 1934 that the strains "cannot be allowed to exist for very long."[65]

The government assumed direct responsibility for the rent on Roy's residence, but otherwise the minister's requests produced no results. Concerning staff, Skelton thought the legation had "enough for what it is doing," but he was interested in bringing its work more into line with current requirements by posting to Paris a new trade commissioner, who could be given diplomatic status as commercial secretary. The performance of the office was assessed by headquarters to be only "fair" but "improving distinctly in contact with French and general European questions and in value of despatches." What was needed, in addition to a commercial specialist, was better "general administration and more English-speaking representation."[66] Despite this assessment, another English-speaking officer was not sent to Paris until 1939, and commercial interests were left to trade commissioners without diplomatic status.

The legation in Tokyo, as Marler's interest in the representation of Canadian commercial interests indicated, was sensitive to the priorities of Bennett's government. Political and commercial activities were more closely integrated in Tokyo, in fact, than at any other Canadian post.

Under the minister in Tokyo, there functioned a staff of nine Canadians: two first secretaries (Keenleyside and the senior trade commissioner, James Langley), a second secretary (Kenneth Kirkwood, posted to Tokyo as third secretary in 1929 and promoted the following year), two assistant trade commissioners, a general attaché,and three stenographers. The legation also had five locally engaged Japanese citizens: two translators, an office boy, a telephone operator, and a janitor.

The requirement for translators was unique for External Affairs at this time: Japan was the only country in which Canada had diplomatic representation where neither English nor French was the national language. The circumstance was not one to which the department adapted well, and many years elapsed before it undertook to develop facilities for language training. Despite the employment of translators, therefore, the legation in Tokyo, like others established later in countries whose languages were difficult and unfamiliar, laboured under a severe disability. There was no Canadian on the staff proficient enough in Japanese to check the work of the locally engaged translators, and the latter did not understand English very well. As a result, the legation was handicapped in following events in the Japanese Diet and in carrying out confidential discussions with local officials who spoke only Japanese.[67] In the circumstances, External Affairs had to rely on Foreign Office prints for much of its information about Japan.

The cost of operating the legation in Tokyo in the fiscal year 1933-34 was $65,168.47. Of this the largest portion, 44 per cent, was for rent. The remainder was distributed as follows: travel, 18 per cent; cables, 9 per cent; office supplies, 6 per cent; telephone, 4 per cent; salaries for locally engaged personnel, 2 per cent; postage, 1 per cent; office furnishings, 1 per cent; and miscellaneous, 11 per cent.[68]

In addition to commercial work, the legation continued to spend a good deal of time on immigration, even though the effects of the Depression reduced the number of immigrants to fifty-five in 1934, well below the Canadian quota. Political reporting was also an important task because a number of developments in Japan in the early 1930s had serious implications for international stability. Among the subjects on which the legation reported during 1934 were the attempted assassination of the cabinet of Premier Keisuke Okada, the organization of the puppet state of Manchukuo (Manchuria), friction over the situation there between Japan and the Soviet Union, the sale of the Chinese Eastern Railway, in which the Soviet Union claimed ownership, and Japanese preparations for a conference on naval disarmament that opened in London in December 1935.

Important though such matters were, Marler's favourite project, during his early years in Tokyo, was the construction, in a prestigious location not far from the imperial palace, of buildings to house the legation residence and chancery. The government being unwilling to underwrite the cost, Marler contributed $25,000 out of his own pocket and arranged the rest of the financing (assumed by the government in due course) himself. He also supervised every detail of construction and chose the furnishings. As a result of the devaluation of the Japanese yen and Marler's good business sense, the project, completed in 1934, proved to be a good investment. The problem of combining office and residence functions in a single structure, as had been done in Washington, was avoided, and the residence, an elegant house set among beautiful gardens, provided an impressive setting for the Canadian presence in Tokyo.

Quartered in a handsome building, well staffed by comparison with other Canadian offices abroad, and comfortably adjusted to the requirements of Bennett's government, the legation in Tokyo was established on a sound footing during the early 1930s. "Office in good shape," was the judgment of headquarters toward the end of the period, "no changes essential."[69] The government too seems to have been well pleased, for Marler received a knighthood in 1935.

The fifth overseas mission, that of the Dominion of Canada advisory officer, League of Nations, in Geneva, was less favoured. There was in Ottawa, Skelton told Walter Riddell in 1934, a "mood of reaction against all Geneva activities."[70] Partly for that reason, this post, the smallest and least expensive, did not receive the increase in resources that Riddell considered necessary in the interests of efficiency and fairness to the staff.

In 1930 Riddell had two officers on his staff, Vanier and Paul Renaud, the latter having been sent to Geneva the previous year as third secretary. Vanier was not replaced when he was posted to London in 1931, and Riddell felt handicapped by the reduction in officer staff. Some help finally came when J. S. Macdonald was sent to Geneva on temporary duty as second secretary in 1934-35, and another third secretary, Alfred Rive, was assigned permanently to the mission in 1935. There was also a shortage of support staff, which, although it sometimes reached four in number, normally stood at three and, at one point in 1934, was reduced to two.

In the fiscal year 1933-34, when there was a staff of four in addition to the advisory officer, expenditure on local operations was $22,295.94, plus $5,319.77 for the "Expenses of the Canadian Delegate to the Assembly, Council and Commission of the League of Nations." Such a situation was not satisfactory to Riddell, who had requested substantially increased expenditures as early as 1930-31. At that time, Riddell pointed out, he had been in Geneva for almost five years, during which his salary of $6,000 had remained unchanged but his responsibilities and experience had grown. This rate compared unfavourably with that paid other officials with comparable duties, who earned $10,000 or more. The same was true of his allowances ($2,500 in 1929-30, raised to $3,500 the following year). His representations, however, brought no improvement in salary, nor did the government accede to his request to acquire an official residence by lease or purchase.

The third secretary received allowances of $1,250 per year, but nothing was done to supplement the salaries of Canada-based support staff until

1931–32, when annual allowances of $250 were provided. Riddell contended that the salaries of the support staff (the highest during the period was $1,620 annually) were inadequate for Geneva, which he claimed was the most expensive city in Europe, with a cost of living 30 per cent higher for women employees than in Canada. It was "unfair to Canadians to ask them to live abroad on the wages paid to Canadians at home."[71]

Inadequately funded and understaffed though Riddell might consider it, the office in Geneva none the less took on a broad range of activities. The work was different in many ways from that of other Canadian diplomats posted abroad, since the setting was the world security organization and ancillary bodies, not a national capital. In his own summation, Riddell's duties were "to act as permanent Canadian representative in Geneva accredited to the League of Nations; to maintain as close relations as possible with the secretariat of the League and of the International Labour Office; to communicate with the Canadian Government on all matters requiring its consideration; to act in an advisory capacity to the Government on the League of Nations and International Labour Office Conferences and to serve as substitute representative at such conferences and committees as directed."[72]

Notwithstanding the government's lack of enthusiasm for the work in Geneva, Riddell's activities were appreciated by the department and his problems were regarded sympathetically. "Busy office, understaffed," was the judgment; "Riddell has done a good job in spite of certain limitations."[73] Slowness to respond to requests for funds and staff was not an indication that his work was undervalued by senior officials at home. Nor were the reservations of ministers the cause. At bottom, the problem was the lack of resources, especially officer personnel. Headquarters itself was under severe strain, and the office in Geneva, like those elsewhere, would have to accept the reality that it would not be able to respond to all "the opportunities that larger staffs would make possible."[74]

The circumstances of the time also created problems for the families of officers posted abroad. Since these were the years during which the department first began to staff missions outside the country on a regular basis, there was little in the way of regulation or precedent on which to base departmental support for family life. For dependants as well as for employees, therefore, service abroad was something of a venture into the unknown, including unforeseen difficulties as well as opportunities. The sense of isolation, in a world where air travel was still rare, was strong. The Canadian community in a foreign land was likely to be small and scattered; regular travel home was not the well-established principle and right that it later became; and tours of duty, for which there was no fixed duration, were usually long. Children were much affected by these circumstances, especially if schooling were different from that in Canada or the local culture made friendships hard to form. For the parents, shortage of money could be a serious problem, made more difficult by the government's financial restraint during the Depression.

However, families abroad had rare opportunities, especially valuable during a period when few Canadians could afford to travel or live outside their country.[75] For young men from far away and for their families, first encounters with the international political and diplomatic world were exciting. "I loved the social side of [the London] Naval Conference in the thirties," Pearson wrote in his memoirs, "the more so, I suppose, because I had little worry and not too much work."[76] There was also exposure to new ideas, cultures, and languages and to exotic surroundings. Keenleyside, for example, reminisced warmly about summer at Lake Chuzenji, an idyllic refuge from humid Tokyo.

With representation in the countries of major interest, the department had the means of dealing with the appropriate foreign and British authorities on the issues of most importance to Canada. It also had independent sources of information, although, as the reporting from Tokyo showed, these could still not supply all departmental needs. Access to British resources therefore continued to be important. These, too, had been enhanced as a result of the creation in 1926 of the Dominions Information Department in the Foreign Office, which, according to an authority who had experience of its operation, provided "a regular, comprehensive and authoritative survey of the international situation that could readily be obtained in no other way."[77]

The diplomatic corps in Ottawa

Complementing the expansion of Canadian representation overseas was the presence of the small diplomatic corps in the Canadian capital, made up of the ministers of France, Japan, and the United States and the British high commissioner. These representatives were beginning to have an effect on the physical appearance of Ottawa. In 1930, the British high commissioner acquired the Victorian stone house Earnscliffe, on Sussex Drive, Sir John A. Macdonald's last home, for use as both residence and office. For more than thirty years, until the latter function was transferred to new quarters on Elgin Street, "Earnscliffe" was common departmental shorthand for the office of the British high commissioner. The US legation, in contrast, never had a distinctive name, but it did have an even more prominent location. In 1932, a handsome new chancery in the Palladian style opened on Wellington Street opposite the main gate to Parliament Hill and adjacent to the Rideau Club (destroyed by fire in October 1979), which it complemented in design.

Centralization at headquarters

The resources at the disposal of departmental headquarters to deal with its expanded responsibilities were by no means extravagant. With a staff of seventy-one in the fiscal year 1933–34, operations at Ottawa consumed only $133,859.20, or 14.5 per cent of the departmental budget. Activity at home, of course, was less expensive than abroad because there was no need to provide for the removal, travel, representational, and other costs associated with service outside Canada.

Even so, Skelton found the provision for his needs inadequate: like Canadian diplomats abroad, he complained of understaffing in the officer ranks. In 1935, the number in service in Ottawa, in addition to the under-secretary, was eight (compared with six at the beginning of the decade), and the way the work was organized, as the following list indicates, had not changed substantially:[78]

Under-secretary	O. D. Skelton	General
Assistant under-secretary	L. Beaudry	Consular, passport, treaty procedure, United States and France (except trade)
Counsellor	L. Christie	British Empire, defence, and disarmament
Legal adviser	J. E. Read	Legal and constitutional questions, International Joint Commission
Second secretary	J. S. Macdonald	Trade questions, League of Nations
Second secretary	N. A. Robertson	General economic questions, League of Nations
Third secretaries	H. Allard L. Mayrand C. S. A. Ritchie	Assistance to senior officers on specified assignments

While insufficiency of officer staff may well, as Skelton apparently believed, have been the major administrative problem confronting the department during this period, the expanded activity of the early 1930s exposed others as well, arising from the way the under-secretary approached his work. Skelton had no experience of diplomatic service abroad and therefore was not well equipped to give training on how to set up or manage a post or to guide a politically appointed head of mission unfamiliar with the requirements of diplomatic life. Skelton's success in recruiting helped to offset this weakness, but it did not deal with another, also the result of his service exclusively in Ottawa. That was a tendency to view the department's operations very much from the perspective of the capital and to overlook the importance, noted for example by Wrong and Keenleyside, of communication outward to the posts. One result was a sense of isolation at the latter. Another was a tendency, on the part of both diplomats on posting and delegates to international gatherings, not to expect detailed instructions and therefore to act with a greater degree of independence than Ottawa may have anticipated.

A second group of difficulties was related to Skelton's approach to head-quarters management. He continued to assign work pretty much on an ad hoc basis, at times producing lack of continuity and compounding the problem of spotty and slow communication with the posts. Equally serious were delays in communication in Ottawa resulting from the centralization of all control in the under-secretary. Skelton delegated work readily enough, but the documents produced had to pass through him on their way to the prime minister or out to the posts. The result was a bottleneck in the under-secretary's office. Also, all communication from heads of post had to be directed to the secretary of state for external affairs, via the under-secretary.

Walker had not provided relief from this problem, but when he died some hoped that his replacement would do so. In some ways, Beaudry seemed more suited to share the burden of decision making, for he had broader experience than Walker. But Beaudry, friendly, quiet, and courtly in manner, was not ideally suited to take on this task; in personality, indeed, he was rather similar to Walker, and he was assigned some of the same responsibilities: that is, consular and passport work and preparation of confidential prints. Skelton therefore remained the fount of all authority, and his office an obstacle to the movement of paper.

Notwithstanding these administrative weaknesses, External Affairs was relatively strong as compared with other departments in Ottawa in the early 1930s. Skelton, as Bennett recognized, had outstanding qualities as a policy adviser and a range of knowledge of governmental requirements extending well beyond the confines of his own department. His success as a recruiter, moreover, had brought to his staff a number of younger men of high ability who provided the government with a valuable resource not readily available elsewhere. As a result, the department was a major contributor to government policy during the Bennett years.

BENNETT'S SECRETARIAT

The world economic crisis

As a result of the favourable impression created at the Imperial Economic Conference, the department became to a considerable degree the prime minister's secretariat for handling economic problems. Some of the work resulted from the ongoing process of Commonwealth consultation stimulated by the conference, but numerous other needs had to be met as well.

There were various international wheat conferences in which Canada had a predominant interest. When it came to choosing and instructing delegates to a conference in Rome in March 1931 to discuss the disastrous state of the world's wheat trade, Trade and Commerce informed Skelton that this was "a matter of policy and not within the purview of this department, though we weigh and inspect grain."[79] The task therefore fell to External Affairs, with technical help from Agriculture. Ferguson led the Canadian delegation in Rome, on the basis of instructions drafted by Robertson and Skelton. On this occasion, Ferguson went against Bennett's preference by issuing invitations to a conference at Canada House to discuss the international control of exports.[80] Partly because of the difference between Ferguson and Bennett, that conference was not an outstanding success, but the high commissioner none the less remained a major participant in wheat negotiations until 1935.

Although Clark at Finance took the lead in preparing Bennett to head the Canadian delegation to the World Monetary and Economic Conference in London in 1933, Ferguson and Robertson figured prominently as well. At this conference, the grain trade was again a subject of foremost importance to the Canadians. Ferguson and Robertson were closely involved in formulating policy and in the exporters' conference held afterward at Bennett's instigation and under his chairmanship. Out of the latter emerged an international wheat agreement—stocks and acreage were to be reduced without sacrificing prices or allowing importing countries to take advantage of the exporters' voluntary reductions—and the Wheat Advisory Committee to monitor it. The ongoing work involved Vanier and the department in continuing discussions with the committee. In this activity, the chief collaborator was not the Department of Agriculture but, on Bennett's insistence, John McFarland, general manager of the Canadian Cooperative Wheat Producers. Although a highly regarded expert on the wheat trade, McFarland deferred to Vanier in deciding on the negotiating practices to be followed in the committee. Together they represented Canada's interest in promoting its wheat sales at a meeting of the committee in Rome in 1934.

External Affairs was also represented in more general attempts to advance Canada's economic interests through international action, Robertson in particular emerging as a leading participant.[81] The most important project of the later Bennett years, inaugurated when the prime minister paid his visit to President Roosevelt in the summer of 1933, was for a commercial agreement with the United States. Talks were held rather spasmodically during the summer and autumn of 1934, and in August 1935 the negotiations really got under way. Herridge, with the best contacts in Washington and the closest relations with the prime minister, led the Canadian team, assisted by McKinnon, Robertson, and Wilgress. Although not completed while Bennett was prime minister, these were the first step toward Anglo-American-Canadian economic rapprochement in the later 1930s.

Bennett used External Affairs for handling domestic economic difficulties as well. Some of the most serious of these were in the agricultural sector, especially grain growing in western Canada. To the problem of drastically falling export prices, as a result of world oversupply, was added that of drought in the spring of 1931, which meant that in some areas there was no crop at all. In 1932 Pearson was made secretary of a royal commission on grain futures and Rive of an interdepartmental committee on agrarian credits. Rive also studied US monetary policy for a committee on farm indebtedness.

Non-agricultural aspects of the domestic economy also created a good deal of work for officers from External Affairs. In 1934, Read was appointed a commissioner to deal with pension overpayments; Robertson became secretary of a federal-provincial conference on unemployment and relief measures; and Pearson served as secretary of a royal commission that investigated the spread between wholesale and retail prices, a cause of much discontent among workers, small businessmen, and farmers.

All this activity placed an additional strain on the department's manpower resources. From Geneva, Riddell commented to Skelton: "I quite understand the load your Department must be carrying when practically half your staff is either working with the Price Spreads Commission or for the offices abroad."[82] At the same time, the department, as a result of its usefulness on economic matters, protected its position with the prime minister and indeed won his praise. Pearson's work earned him his OBE. Bennett wanted to recommend a knighthood for Skelton, but the undersecretary declined. In the summer of 1935, the prime minister had Treasury Board approve bonuses of $2,000 for Skelton, $1,800 for Pearson, and $500 for Rive.[83] For the last two, the reward was for their assistance to the Royal Commission on Price Spreads.

International law

A second area of activity in which the department achieved greater prominence during this period was international law. The reason was increasing involvement in legal disputes with the United States.

One of the most time-consuming aspects of Canadian relations with the United States was smuggling, which, as a result of prohibition south of the border between 1918 and 1933, became big business. Both immediately before and after the opening of the Canadian legation in Washington, this was the subject of the most voluminous correspondence between the two countries. In June 1924, the minister of justice, Ernest Lapointe, signed a treaty in Washington laying down the basic tenets for dealing with the issue. The department was not much involved and in fact had relatively little to do with the smuggling problem, which was the concern mainly of the Royal Canadian Mounted Police, National Revenue (Customs), and Justice. Nevertheless, important international legal questions arose, the prime examples involving two Canadian vessels enaged in rum-running, the *I'm Alone* and the *Josephine K*. These were dealt with in the department by the legal adviser, Read.

While the repeal of prohibition brought the end of one type of legal dispute, another long-standing difficulty with the United States remained to be dealt with. Since 1918, periodic claims had arisen that fumes from the lead-zinc smelter of the Consolidated Mining and Smelting Co. in Trail, British Columbia, were damaging vegetable growth in the state of Washington. Because there were no settled procedures between the United States and Canada, it took many years to resolve the matter. In 1929, the Canadian government established the Trail Smelter Smoke Committee under the chairmanship of the president of the National Research Council, Dr H. M. Tory, to assess the sulphur dioxide content of the atmosphere and the extent of damage. The only lawyer on the committee was Read, who handled the international legal work and relations with the company. An arbitration agreement was signed on April 15, 1935, and an award to the aggrieved American farmers emerged three years later. The case involved the first transnational air pollution dispute to go to arbitration and signified the growing role of the legal profession in the department's work.

The department as a co-ordinating agency

Although Skelton had spoken vaguely at the beginning of the decade about the department as a central agency, the nature and success of this function depended on other departments. Once Canadian posts were functioning abroad, they seemed more willing to use External Affairs' services.

Nowhere is this seen better than in fisheries policy. In earlier times, under aggressive ministers such as Douglas Hazen, from 1911 to 1917, Marine and Fisheries (divided in two in 1930) had managed many of its own international activities. By the 1930s the situation was much changed. On July 20, 1931, the deputy minister of fisheries wrote to Skelton about the imposition of duties on Canadian halibut destined for US markets and the use of Canadian west coast ports by US salmon trawlers:

Fishery questions in their nature are always apt to result in international difficulties. It is surely desirable that the causes of such between Canada and the United States should be removed. . . . In all the circumstances, my Minister is of opinion that the most hopeful method of finding a solution of these questions would be a conference between fully accredited representatives of the two Governments. Hence before taking any action in connection with them from a strictly Canadian standpoint, he directs me to request that you will be good enough to ascertain if in the light of the above facts the United States Government is agreeable to holding such a conference.[84]

There continued to be many issues on which External Affairs acted as a post office between domestic and British authorities who handled relations with third countries where there was no Canadian diplomatic representation. With several posts in operation, however, External Affairs was now increasingly able to conduct Canadian business abroad. Despite the declared preferences of some Conservatives before they came to office in 1930 and the need to promote exports because of the Depression, the department had not been supplanted by Trade and Commerce. External Affairs in fact was well placed to lead in some areas of commercial activity, as a result of Bennett's personal involvement in wheat policy and the negotiation of trade agreements. There was also a determined effort in the department to look out for and deal with questions having international implications. "I do not wish to interfere in the affairs of another department," Skelton wrote to Bennett at the time of the Pan-American Postal Conference in 1931, "but . . . the international aspect of these postal arrangements makes them a subject of interest to External Affairs."[85]

Counterbalancing growing acceptance of the department as a coordinating agency was a decline of interest in subjects that had occupied it in the past. Tariffs, trade policy, and the world wheat supply, according to Skelton, had stolen the limelight from political issues in international affairs.[86] The latter continued to need attention but received less than formerly.

Disarmament

The best handled of these political subjects was disarmament. When the London Naval Conference met in 1930 to broaden the agreement previously reached by the Washington Conference on the Limitation of Naval Armament in 1922, the Canadian delegate was the minister of national defence, with the advisory assistance of Pearson, Vanier, and Cmdre Walter Hose, chief of naval staff.

A larger effort was required for the World Disarmament Conference scheduled for 1932. The Canadian position was prepared by an interdepartmental committee made up of Skelton, Hose, and the chief of the general staff, Maj.-Gen. A. G. L. McNaughton, who had considerable influence with Bennett on foreign policy questions with defence implications. Since the conference was under the auspices of the League of Nations, and External Affairs was the focal point for communications from Geneva and the Dominions Office on the subject, Skelton came to summon and direct the group and guide its deliberations. Pearson chaired a working subcommittee composed of four armed forces representatives and two from External Affairs, Robertson and Rive, the latter as secretary. Pearson did most of the drafting of policy documents, on the basis of technical information provided by the military. Liaison with the British was handled primarily by Vanier, although Hose, who was in the United Kingdom from July until November 1931, consulted with the Admiralty on naval questions. There was assistance as well from Riddell at Geneva, and Roy and Désy reported from Paris on French attitudes and policy vis-à-vis Germany.

The result of the preparatory work done in Ottawa was, in Pearson's estimation, a very well briefed Canadian delegation to the conference in Geneva. The leader was Sir George Perley, minister without portfolio, assisted by the solicitor general, Maurice Dupré, and the president of the National Council of Women, Winnifred Kydd. Riddell was senior adviser, McNaughton and Lt.-Col. H. D. G. Crerar of the Militia Service, a member of Pearson's subcommittee, were military advisers, and Pearson was secretary. Because of the extraordinary length of the conference (the last meeting was held on June 1, 1934), the delegates named in 1932 were present only for the early sessions. After they left their places were taken by officials.[87]

Guidance to delegations abroad

Not all Canadian participation in multilateral diplomacy in the early 1930s went as smoothly as that involving disarmament. The most serious cause of difficulty was insufficient support from Ottawa for delegations temporarily abroad. Increasingly preoccupied as he was with domestic problems, Bennett's attention to their activities was at best intermittent, and Skelton did not put in train means to ensure thorough briefing. Shortage of personnel, aggravated by diversion to serve the prime minister's domestic requirements, undoubtedly compounded the problem, by making it difficult to maintain constant communication with delegates and provide advisory teams as strong as those dealing with disarmament and major economic issues.

The danger inherent in these weaknesses became evident in 1932, when the League was considering the Sino-Japanese conflict over Manchuria.

The Canadian delegate, C. H. Cahan (the secretary of state), took a position favourable to the invader, thereby placing himself at odds with Ottawa, where the preference was to avoid controversy and "to act with the Assembly as a whole."[88]

Several key points about instructions emerged in a subsequent exchange of correspondence between Riddell and Skelton. Riddell pointed out that he did not see how Cahan "could overlook his instructions and that sometimes one had to suppress his own personal views."[89] Skelton's reply absolved Riddell from blame, but gave him "information" for his "future guidance." "I think," Skelton wrote on December 24, 1932, "it should always be made perfectly clear to Canadian delegates to the League and to other international conferences that they are in a purely representative capacity, that the views they express will be inevitably ascribed to their Government and should, therefore, be confined to the presentation of the policies which have commended themselves to the Government. . . . A casual opinion of this kind, expressed by a representative of a Government in the circumstances in which the Special Assembly were met, may acquire a peculiar and unfortunate significance."

Skelton then showed how and where Cahan's speech misrepresented or varied from the views of the Canadian government. He also pointed out that instructions sent to delegates were often not in a form that should be explicitly incorporated into a public speech. As the department's permanent representative in Geneva, Riddell had the responsibility "to interpret summary instructions in a sense consistent with the general policies of the Government," since representatives who lacked continuity in handling League issues could not always be expected to do so. Since Riddell had long complained about the inadequacy of his own instructions, Skelton ended his letter by promising that Ottawa in future would try to do better.[90]

The risks resulting from failure to develop a well-regulated system of departmental guidance became apparent once more during the crisis over the Italian invasion of Ethiopia in 1935. The problem began to reveal itself during Bennett's last days in office, although it was obscured at home by preoccupation with the federal election campaign, which began on July 5. Once again there was a difference of opinion between Ottawa and Geneva: Skelton enjoined a non-committal position, whereas the leader of the delegation, Ferguson, wanted to take a strong line against Italy. Instructions from the department were slow to come and were undermined by Bennett, who gave Ferguson a free hand when consulted by telephone. Ferguson, therefore, maintained an anti-Italian position until he received news of Bennett's defeat on October 14. He thereupon resigned, leaving Riddell in charge of the delegation. The need for guidance from headquarters did not diminish with the change, in view of Riddell's long absence abroad and consequent lack of familiarity with Ottawa during his years in the foreign service.[91]

The change of government, then, came at an awkward moment in the conduct of Canadian external relations. It also happened at a difficult stage in the evolution of the department. Despite austerity and the comparative lack of interest of Bennett's government in the early achievements of Canadian diplomacy, the department, with a total staff (exclusive of heads of post in London, Washington, Paris, and Tokyo) of 138, had, despite the Depression and austerity, maintained its personnel resources almost at the level (142) reached in 1930. It had been given so many new responsibilities, however, that a severe strain on resources had resulted.

Shortage of staff may have slowed the department's response to developments in Geneva during the Ethiopian crisis, but more important was failure to provide regular and steady guidance. Ferguson, it is true, was not amenable to such guidance and used his association with the prime minister to get around it, but no determined effort was made to instruct him effectively. The department, in short, was in need of more than an increase in resources. Reorganization of structure, accompanied by stabilization of functions, better communications, and a broader decision-making process, was also required. Officers such as Keenleyside, Pearson, and Wrong were beginning to experience the effects of these problems abroad. Others besides Skelton, therefore, would take an interest in shaping the department, as they assumed growing responsibility during the next few years.

Chapter Seven

The Foreign Service on the Rise: 1935–1939

The new government and the department

THE POLITICAL ENVIRONMENT IN WHICH departmental officers responded to an increasingly tense and complex international situation was determined by the requirements of William Lyon Mackenzie King, who returned to office in 1935 with the largest parliamentary majority (a margin of 113 seats) recorded up to that time. King's view of international relations remained firmly rooted in his concern for the domestic situation, especially the need to preserve national unity, which he believed would be threatened by public controversy over foreign policy. Thus he was reluctant to have Canada assume an active role in the Commonwealth and the League of Nations and was cautious about drawing attention to the department by substantially increasing expenditure on it or opening new posts abroad. The members of the foreign service could expect to assume greater responsibilities, commensurate with their growing expertise. They would have to do so, however, within the confines of a cautious foreign policy and a carefully limited budget.

Notwithstanding King's position during the election campaign that issues of foreign policy were for Parliament to decide, there was no relaxation of the long-established centralized executive control over this area of activity. Although the Senate created a standing committee on external relations in 1938, discussion of the subject in Parliament was not encouraged. At the executive level, the dominance of the prime minister was reconfirmed. Ernest Lapointe, King's senior colleague, would have liked to be named secretary of state for external affairs, but the prime minister demurred, arguing that the European situation made it necessary for him to retain the portfolio.[1] Lapointe resumed his former position of minister of justice, and, although King often consulted him on foreign policy, his influence on this subject was essentially that of Quebec lieutenant and longtime associate of the prime minister.

By retaining the external affairs portfolio, King was able to continue using the resources of the department to supplement the staff of his own office. When he took over from Bennett, he had at his disposal a private secretary, H. R. L. Henry, and an assistant private secretary, E. A. Pickering, plus a number of clerks, stenographers, and messengers. To these were added another private secretary, Edouard Handy, from the Franchise Office, and Walter Turnbull, from the Post Office, one of whose principal duties was to deal with visitors.

Assignments from External Affairs were usually of short duration, but some officers never returned to the department. One such was a new officer, J. W. Pickersgill. After Pickering's resignation in 1938, he became a key member of the prime minister's staff, contributing a wide variety of memoranda and speech drafts and assisting King to prepare for meetings, conferences, and debates in the House of Commons. Even with such help, however, King had only slender resources to deal with the multifarious problems requiring his attention as prime minister. Having left the post of principal secretary vacant, he had no one to co-ordinate the activity of the staff. His own work habits, moreover, were unpredictable. Alternating between "periods of procrastination and spurts of feverish activity," he tended to be unpunctual, he kept no regular office hours, and he worked out of a variety of quarters, including Parliament Hill, Laurier House, and his estate at Kingsmere.[2]

For a full range of policy advice and the execution of his government's decisions, the prime minister continued to rely on the public service. These functions were being performed with increasing professionalism, as a result of improvements in recruitment to the senior ranks, which had begun in the 1920s when Skelton had been brought to Ottawa. Partly because Skelton was under-secretary, partly because it was the prime minister's department, and partly because of the calibre of its officers, External Affairs played a leading role in the change.[3]

The usefulness of the department was enhanced by a smooth transition from the old government to the new. King evidently accepted without question that the under-secretary must demonstrate impartiality between the political parties, for he expressed no concern about Skelton's record of loyal service to Bennett. Skelton did not communicate with the prime minister until after the cabinet had been sworn in, but in the interim he did anticipate his needs. His first memorandum, after expressing "great pleasure in being able to work with you again,"[4] brought various matters to King's attention, placing particular emphasis on the situation in Ethiopia, and the prime minister responded in kind. The two welcomed the resumption of their old relationship. "It was a great delight to me to be again in association with Skelton, and he spoke of our relationship in similar terms," King wrote in his diary after their first meeting, on October 25, 1935.

There was no question now of Skelton accepting another offer of the post of principal of Queen's University, although the salary of $15,000 per year was nearly double his public service pay of $8,000 and the university provided a free residence. Clearly Skelton liked his work and the opportunities it afforded him. Certainly Queen's could not compete with the federal government in one of the benefits deriving from Skelton's standing in the public service and his closeness to the prime minister. "He has," King noted, "great power where he is."[5]

That power undoubtedly was enhanced by the close harmony between King and Skelton, especially in the early part of the government's mandate. Even so, their approaches to the international situation were never fully aligned. King, viewing external affairs in terms of national unity, approached overseas commitments with extreme caution. Skelton, too, favoured such a course, but for different reasons. He addressed events abroad from a background of determination to stand apart from Whitehall. Although this stance arose, it has been argued, not from anti-British prejudice but from a conviction that the foreign policies of all countries must be dictated by national interest, the result none the less was to make him increasingly isolationist and neutralist as the decade advanced. King did not share this position, for he was susceptible to the pro-British sentiments of English Canadians, and he recognized the political imperative of respecting them if the mother country should be in danger.[6]

The two men's working relationship remained effective in spite of these differences because of Skelton's view of his position as a public servant. The under-secretary "had a clear perception of the subordinate role of a civil servant; he expressed his own opinions to his Minister with great frankness but he accepted his instructions loyally even when he disagreed with them."[7] Thus throughout the period after 1935 he retained the confidence of the prime minister.

The Ethiopian crisis

To influence policy in Ottawa in these circumstances, rising members of the foreign service had to work through the established departmental structure, whereby the under-secretary controlled communication with the prime minister and cabinet. There was more scope for initiative abroad: lines of communication and mechanisms of control were rudimentary, and one had on occasion to respond promptly to rapidly evolving situations. During the Bennett years, the Manchurian and Ethiopian crises had shown that difficulties could arise for the department when it was at odds with a spokesman overseas. Howard Ferguson's resignation removed that challenge to the department's authority regarding Ethiopia, but the problem remained in a different shape. Walter Riddell, who took over leadership of the delegation, like Ferguson favoured the use of sanctions against Italy, a policy far removed from the department's and from that developed by the King government. With the fragile lines of control from Ottawa further impaired by the process of transition to the new regime, Riddell at first continued the course that he and Ferguson favoured, to the embarrassment and irritation of the authorities at home.

Once the new government had taken office, it was apparent in Ottawa that, as a result of King's sensitivity to the domestic implications of foreign policy, the possibility of initiative in Geneva that had existed under Bennett was a thing of the past. Riddell, after long residence away from the capital, may not have realized the extent of the change, and he was not kept abreast of developments at home by the department, which was slow to provide him with instructions. When the occasion arrived for him to state the Canadian position on sanctions against Italy, he proposed, without authorization from Ottawa, that petroleum, coal, iron, and steel be added to the list of embargoed materials. This was a position that he believed would have British and French support. The suggested prohibition on the export of oil to Italy was especially important, because without it Mussolini's war machine would be paralysed. Riddell's action, closely identified in press headlines with Canada, therefore attracted wide public notice.

Riddell's action caused consternation in Ottawa. His three-line telegram describing what he had done brought an expression of "much surprise" and a reminder of the importance of instructions. "When you desire instructions on any proposal," he was told, "you should communicate sufficiently in advance to give time for consideration here. Every effort will be made to give prompt instructions but in any case you should not take action on any question of importance . . . without definite and positive instructions."

Displeasure in Ottawa was sufficient that Riddell's subsequent explanations brought a sharp rejoinder: "I have noted your explanation but must insist that position which you took was not in my judgement in conformity with important factors in Canadian situation and not within scope of your authority. As I have already indicated no position on any question of importance shall be taken without positive and definitive instructions.''[8]

"Riddell's action is interesting," it has been observed, "as an example of what a strong-minded delegation could do to commit an unwilling and unwitting government to a course of action of which it fundamentally disapproved."[9] But Riddell, as a civil servant, could not go over Skelton's head to the prime minister and hence did not have the luxury of speaking first and informing Ottawa later, as some political appointees had been able to do. In fact, King's displeasure was sufficient that he was in favour of dismissing Riddell, but Skelton dissuaded him from doing so and later convinced the prime minister not to reprimand him. Some of the blame, King concluded, rested with Skelton himself, as a result, he suspected, of becoming accustomed to slack practices during the Bennett years. "Even Skelton had not seen how far Canada was going in taking the lead at Geneva," King observed in his diary. "I can notice that the five years' association with Bennett has made Skelton less sensitive to these dangers, and more inclined to protect officials, etc., than he would have been many years ago."[10]

The Ethiopian crisis strengthened King's concern, already evident in the 1920s, to restrict the independence of heads of post, who were the principal object of his effort to ensure the orderly conduct of external relations. They were kept on a tighter rein than had been the case under Bennett, especially during King's first years back in office. As well, the development of a close personal relationship with President Roosevelt, which was to be so important a determinant of Canadian–US relations during the next decade, indicated that this prime minister would play a more direct role in external affairs than his predecessor had done. The change from the previous regime was evident at the League of Nations Assembly in 1936, when King, accompanied by Skelton, led the Canadian delegation and assumed a much higher profile than Bennett had done in the same capacity.

The trade agreement with the United States

Offsetting the impression created by the Ethiopian crisis was successful conclusion of the other major international project left over from the previous government, the trade negotiations with the United States. Here King took the initiative, having made a commitment during the election campaign to complete the process by the end of the year. He handled relations with Franklin Roosevelt himself, assuring him that he appreciated the political difficulties arising from the matter in the US. He did not deal with matters of detail, relying instead on Skelton and the Canadian negotiating team for briefing on key points.

On the day after his government was sworn to office, King indicated to the US minister in Ottawa, Norman Armour, that he was ready to go to Washington for early talks with Roosevelt about the trade agreement. Roosevelt agreed, and they met on November 8, King staying at the White House, where he was warmly received by the president. William Herridge, Bennett's appointee as minister to the United States, had, like Ferguson, resigned immediately after the election, but the rest of the negotiating team (Norman Robertson of External Affairs, Hector McKinnon of the Tariff Board, and Dana Wilgress of Trade and Commerce) had resumed their work. On the basis of the continuity thus provided and advice that King secured from the US secretary of state, Cordell Hull, on dealing with the president, events moved rapidly to a conclusion. Hull and King initialled an agreement on November 9 which was formally signed six days later, after being submitted to the Canadian cabinet for approval. Each country was to afford most-favoured-nation treatment to exports from the other, but Canada's imperial preferences were an exception to the rule.[11]

As the first general trade agreement to be concluded between Canada and the United States since the lapse in 1866 of reciprocity, this accord was a considerable triumph for King's foreign policy early in the life of his new government. It also provided the prime minister with an opportunity to see departmental officials, other than Skelton and heads of post, at work abroad and to form opinions of such officers as Hume Wrong at the legation in Washington and Norman Robertson from headquarters in Ottawa. The latter in particular impressed King favourably.[12]

IMPROVING CONDITIONS FOR THE CAREER SERVICE

Although King may not have paid much attention to the problem, the need for better procedures and fuller and clearer guidance to posts was not lost on the department. Another concern was strengthening senior ranks in Ottawa, in order to relieve over-concentration in the under-secretary's office. Efforts to improve these aspects of administration were important features of the latter part of the 1930s. Senior officers besides Skelton contributed to the process, on the basis of their experience in the service.

The problems identified

The first proposal for reform came forward even before the new government had assumed office. In the hope that King would look more favourably on change if he were assured that the new leader of the opposition would raise no objection, Hume Wrong sought to reach Bennett through his secretary, R. K. Finlayson, to whom he suggested that the outgoing prime minister leave King a memorandum on the department's problems. Finlayson did not co-operate, but Wrong's submission is an interesting analysis of the problems affecting the department at the time.

The department, Wrong argued, needed to be expanded and to recruit the "best brains" that could be found. He suggested a more effective organization, to provide clear lines of authority and a rational grouping of the tasks assigned to each officer; legislation to create a specialized diplomatic service, able to move its officers about without the encumbrance of the Civil Service Commission's regulations; and a much higher salary scale. As well, he complained that gifted departmental officers did not have sufficient career opportunities, since heads of post were always political appointees.[13]

Skelton, too, disliked undue reliance on political appointees and urged King gradually to begin choosing heads of post from the career service. "There is no hope of securing united national confidence in our diplomatic experiment," he told King early in 1936,

> if appointments to the Service continue to be confined to party figures. . . . I fully recognize that it is desirable for many years to come that a large proportion of Ministerial appointments should be drawn from men in public life, and if so, that it will be inevitable that in a majority of the cases, these men would be of the same faith as the party in power. But gradually some appointments should be made from the Permanent Service . . . and it would also be helpful if an occasional appointment could be made of some man . . . with no political leanings or even with leanings against the Government of the day.[14]

Choosing heads of post

An opportunity to act on these precepts had occurred earlier, with the resignations of Ferguson and Herridge, but King did not do so, looking instead to supporters of his own party. The first choice for Washington was John W. Dafoe, editor of the *Winnipeg Free Press*, but he declined rather than agree to represent views possibly contrary to his own, which he believed he would find an intolerable difficulty.[15] King then turned to Sir Herbert Marler, who was transferred from Tokyo to Washington in 1936. To succeed Marler in Japan, King selected another prominent Liberal, Robert Randolph Bruce, lieutenant-governor of British Columbia from 1926 until 1931 and an unsuccessful candidate in the federal election of 1935. To London the prime minister sent Vincent Massey, who resigned as party president on the day of his appointment (October 31, 1935).

Although Skelton was still no admirer of Massey, there was no question about the new high commissioner's capacity for the job. The other choices were less well received. According to King, there were reservations about Marler both in cabinet and in the US State Department, the feeling in the latter apparently being that he lacked a common touch considered important to success in Washington. Bruce, seventy-three in 1936, had lost his eyesight, and his ability to represent Canada effectively was questioned by Bennett on that ground. An important reason for choosing Bruce, King indicated, was his understanding of opinion in British Columbia, useful in view of the sensitivity of attitudes there toward Japan, especially concerning immigration.[16]

The claims of the career service received some recognition in October 1937, when Wrong was sent to Geneva, exchanging places with Riddell. The choice confirmed that this post was to be headed by a public servant rather than a political appointee. Wrong was the first career officer in the Canadian diplomatic service to be given charge of a mission abroad, Riddell not having been a member of the department before his appointment. In April 1938 the title was changed to permanent representative.

Seasoned by over ten years of diplomatic experience abroad by the time he went to Geneva, Wrong could be relied on to administer his mission responsibly and, as a career public servant, to respect the limitations on his authority. He also was well aware that heavy emphasis on protocol and the social side of diplomacy could have unfavourable political repercussions at home. The same could not be said on the last point for the political appointees, and King soon began to show annoyance at what he regarded as status-seeking on their part.

Another problem was that Bruce, Marler, and Philippe Roy, in Paris, were all somewhat impaired in their ability to give vigorous direction to their missions. Bruce was the eldest and the most seriously handicapped, followed by Roy, who was sixty-eight in 1936 and hard of hearing. Marler, sixty when he went to Washington, was considerably younger but required surgery ("under cover of a rest and holiday") before taking up his post.[17] As a result, more reliance was placed on the members of the career foreign service on the staffs of Canada's three legations. That diplomatic officers were able to take on these added responsibilities was a tribute to their calibre. The effectiveness of the missions none the less was affected, for junior staff members lacked the local prestige conferred by the rank of minister. They also had less autonomy vis-à-vis the department than their chiefs, since they did not have direct access to the prime minister.

Controlling the posts

Despite this access, heads of post had to be a good deal more careful about acting on their own than had been the case under Bennett. Particularly subject to control were relations with the British, lest there be any erosion of the diplomatic autonomy confirmed by the Statute of Westminster. In Washington, Marler was reluctant to collaborate with the British embassy on even a matter of small importance without first obtaining clearance from Ottawa.[18]

Most affected by this attitude was the high commissioner in London. Forty-eight years of age when he assumed the position, Massey was the most effective of King's political appointments, but his scope was limited as a result of the reserve in Ottawa toward the United Kingdom. King had his own version of the special character of the office of high commissioner. There was, he pointed out, "no diplomatic service within the Empire." The high commissioner was merely "the agent of the [Canadian] Government in London," with no right to raise issues of foreign policy with the British prime minister or to make statements about them in public.[19] The most important reason for this attitude seems to have been the example of Riddell. His "action at Geneva," Massey was told soon after his arrival in London, "shows how great a need there is for no member of the Public Sevice taking action, except under the authority of those who, throughout, are responsible."[20]

This doctrine applied to all Canadian representatives abroad, but in Massey's case it was especially easy to enforce, because of the position of the prime minister and secretary of state for external affairs in the relationship with the United Kingdom. Massey was told by cable early in 1936,

My colleagues and I very strongly of opinion that any important communication between British Government and Canadian Government should be direct in form of communication from Prime Minister to Prime Minister or between Secretary of State for Dominions and Secretary of State for External Affairs as has been customary in past and should not be through High Commissioner. This is the only way in and which we can possibly have opportunity required collectively to consider and state attitude and policy and which will ensure full responsibility of British as well as Canadian Government with respect to any statements of policy or position and avoid all possibility of misunderstanding as to what has been said or meant in any verbal discussions.[21]

Massey, like Peter Larkin before him, was not permitted to participate in meetings between the dominions secretary or other British ministers and representatives of the dominions. Although this restriction was relaxed in 1938 as a result of the deteriorating international situation, it could not be assumed that there had been any fundamental change of policy. Thus when he attended the meetings, Massey was careful to arrive and depart inconspicuously, so as not to attract the attention of the press.[22]

Not just Massey but the officers on his staff were affected by the attitude of headquarters. The position was made clear to Pearson by Skelton in 1935. In particular, Pearson was to beware of being used as a channel for communication of "anything . . . that the British might want us to know merely for their own purposes." Close relations with British officials, Pearson felt, were a cause of some concern to the under-secretary: "My independent sturdy Canadian attitude could be weakened, presumably, and I might be lured into the Whitehall net."[23] By the time Charles Ritchie joined the staff in 1939, the mood of caution was pervasive and its ultimate source clearly identified. The estrangement between Massey and King, Ritchie recalled, "put the staff of Canada House in a difficult position. The disembodied presence of the Prime Minister brooded over us. It was not a benevolent influence. In the flesh he was thousands of miles away, but he needed no modern bugging devices to detect the slightest quaver of disloyalty to his person or his policies."[24]

While Massey hoped to make a greater contribution than his predecessors to the formulation of policy on the great international issues of the day, King and Skelton preferred that he and his staff concentrate on the work that traditionally occupied Canada House, particularly promotion of trade and dissemination of information.[25] Massey was not as enthusiastic about trade promotion as Ferguson had been but recognized that it was an important responsibility of his office. He gave particular attention to a revamped advertising program, supported by the senior trade commissioner, Frederic Hudd. An Englishman in the Canadian service, Hudd had been posted to Canada House in 1934, after service in New York, and he was a mainstay of the high commissioner's office until his retirement in 1956.

Massey was well pleased with the results of the publicity program, but a report by a committee of the Department of Agriculture suggested that it had not been as successful as earlier campaigns. In his memoirs, Massey complained that rivalry between Agriculture and Trade and Commerce hampered a co-ordinated effort abroad. The problem, he made clear, was at home, not in London. Although the effects were inevitably felt in the field, he was less concerned than Ferguson had been about the need to control local representatives. In London, he noted, "they suddenly found their problems exceeded departmental dimensions, and cooperation between departments was more common abroad than at home." Massey was also co-operative with the provincial offices, so long as they remained active, avoiding the rivalry that had sometimes marred the relationship in the past.[26]

If Massey was dutiful in the promotion of trade, he was an enthusiast in the more general dissemination of information about Canada. This was an activity that he and his wife had pioneered in Washington. The objective in London was the same: to create a better understanding of Canada as an independent and culturally maturing nation within the Commonwealth. Both Masseys worked hard at this activity, and, as in Washington, their favourite means were the arts, especially music and painting. The latter was used to particularly good effect. Massey's connections gave him numerous opportunities to promote the work of Canadian artists, and his own fine collection (featured in an illustrated story in the *Sunday Times*) made his home a showplace used to advantage with British critics and connoisseurs. The crowning achievement was a comprehensive exhibition of Canadian paintings (thirty of them Massey's own) at the Tate Gallery, opened by the king's brother, the Duke of Kent, in the autumn of 1938.[27]

In the furtherance of Canadian interests in London, Massey, with the approval of King, was scrupulous in avoiding discrimination against Canadian clients based on party affiliation at home. Even so, from time to time he was accused of favouritism. Such complaints were for the most part trivial. He was hurt, however, by the unjustified suggestion that some of the funds intended for trade promotion had been diverted to entertaining. King was always quick to defend him in public against such charges. Although control of the funds for trade publicity in the United Kingdom was shifted from the high commissioner to Trade and Commerce, King made it clear in Parliament that there had been no question of misdirection to social purposes, that Massey fully agreed with the change, and that he remained ultimately in charge of public relations at his post. This action seems to have been based on genuine satisfaction with Massey's work, within the limitations imposed by Ottawa. Massey's representational activities received particularly warm praise, expressed after the prime minister visited London in 1936.[28]

Since neither Roy nor Marler aspired to as active a role as Massey, closer control from home was not a cause of friction with them. Marler did not emulate Herridge in getting to know "the fellows behind the scenes." Rather, he proposed to work through social relationships with the men at the top. There was at this time perhaps less need for the minister to be deeply involved in the day-to-day business of Canadian-American relations, in view of the close attention paid to the subject in Ottawa. As a result of his developing rapport with President Roosevelt and some of his advisers, King was establishing a dominant position in dealing with the larger issues, and the details could be handled by specialists reporting to him and his cabinet colleagues.[29]

As a result of Japan's military action in China, the post in Tokyo, occupied by the only novice appointed by King, had the most pitfalls for an unwary and inexperienced minister. Bruce fell into one of these when he was in Canada in the summer of 1937 and was reported in the Toronto *Star* to hold opinions highly favourable to the invader. In response there was widespread criticism in Canada, combined with expressions of concern by the Chinese government. The embarrassment was compounded when the Japanese legation in Ottawa used the statements attributed to Bruce to defend its government's actions in China.[30]

King, although letting it be known that he "would have preferred if no interview at all had been given or any opinions expressed on such highly controversial matters," considered it "out of the question" to accept Bruce's offer to resign. Nor did the prime minister act on Skelton's advice that he "set a terminus to the appointment." That, the under-secretary acknowledged, would be difficult to do, since Bruce had "fine personal qualities" and, with the assistance of his wife, had made "a first-rate impression in Japan."[31]

In Tokyo, the incident did Bruce no harm. "His popularity and that of Mrs. Bruce," reported a member of his staff, "continue to be undiminished." The minister gave the impression of taking his discomfiture very well and insisted that "every item of criticism in Hansard" be read to him, a task his staff found "most embarrassing." Despite appearances, however, Bruce had in fact been deeply wounded.[32] Indeed, he seems never to have been very happy in his post. "Mr. Bruce," Hugh Keenleyside learned some time in 1938, "has been waiting and wanting to go home since last June; it is rather pathetic to see him, tired but patient, waiting hopefully but silently for every mail, to see if there is any word for him. Meanwhile he just sits and waits to be read to; has a few friends in to lunch or tea, and listens to his radio in the evenings." In such a frame of mind, Bruce was not inclined to be innovative. "He prefers," Keenleyside's informant reported, "to take most of his cues from the British Embassy, and believes that you get all the essential Far East news from London." As a result, the staff was able to do little in the way of reporting and was confined mainly to forwarding "batches" of press clippings to Ottawa.[33]

Notwithstanding Bruce's unhappiness and its effect on the work of the legation, King did not suggest his return to Canada until October 1938, when a number of decisions about changes in representation provided the occasion for a dignified removal. The prime minister conveyed the news in a tactful and appreciative letter, which made warm reference to the special importance, because of his impaired eyesight, of the work of Edith Bruce. "We all," said King, "know what her companionship and co-operation has meant to you, and are deeply grateful for what, together, your services at the Legation have meant to our country."[34]

Proposals for new posts

The changes in representation were part of Skelton's larger effort to over-come the Depression-era restrictions imposed on the department and to develop further the professional foreign service. He began early in 1936, by initiating a round of correspondence to find out the effect of six years of depression financing on working conditions at each mission. On the basis of the data accumulated in response, he put forth proposals for improvements and for a new period of growth in the department and the foreign service. Interrupted when Skelton fell ill, the completed report went to King in the autumn of 1937.

At the core of Skelton's paper was the contention that an expanded service would be an expression of Canada's international personality. This idea was advanced in terms of a need not only to respond to the imme-diate world situation but also to meet the long-term political and economic requirements of the country. As well, Skelton wanted to provide better salaries and allowances for his staff. As a result of the rollback in 1932, the External Affairs salary scale was what it had been in 1927, when he had first started recruiting in earnest. Canadian levels of pay were much lower than those of the US State Department, which Skelton wanted to match, and compared unfavourably with those of the British diplomatic service.[35]

By the time he formulated his proposals, Skelton's freedom of action in directing expansion had been limited by the government's agreement to Belgium's establishment of a legation in Ottawa. Although Canada made it clear that reciprocal action (not requested) could not follow imme-diately, an appointment to Brussels had to be taken account of in plan-ning for new posts.[36]

Belgium was not Skelton's top priority. Rather, he recommended to King, expansion should begin by exchanging high commissioners with the other dominions, partly to emphasize the recent constitutional changes. Considerations of trade with Australia, New Zealand, and South Africa also suggested moving in this direction. Commercial possibilities pointed as well to other countries, such as Denmark and Argentina, whose highly regulated economies required a diplomatic presence in order to secure access for Canadian products. In such countries, Skelton pointed out, Canadian exports were often in competition with British in such matters as the allocation of foreign exchange. Canada therefore was bound to be at a disadvantage if it relied on British representatives to promote its interests.[37]

Loring Christie had a different set of priorities, based on the deteriorat-ing international situation. He disagreed with the focus on smaller states such as Belgium, South Africa, and the Scandinavian countries. Observing that Canada already had missions in four of the seven great powers, Christie suggested rounding out the picture with Germany, Italy, and the Soviet Union. He considered it inappropriate, without covering the major capitals, to establish high commissioners' offices in the dominions, since he expected political exchanges with their governments to be minimal, although their markets were worth cultivating. If diplomatic representation in small countries were needed for the latter purpose, he suggested converting the trade commissioner service to a consular service under the control of External Affairs.[38]

Neither Skelton's priorities nor Christie's found favour with King. After considering the question of expansion during a wakeful night, the prime minister wrote: "Representation in any foreign country is almost certain to draw us into situations involving religious or other questions."[39] As a result, plans for expansion were rebuffed for the time being.

Skelton returned to the charge early in 1938. Canada, he pointed out to King, although priding itself on dominion status, had not done very much to manifest its independence through a diplomatic presence abroad— it had been outstripped by South Africa, with eight missions, and Ireland, with seven. South Africa and Ireland, moreover, had suggested exchanging representatives with Canada. Even more important were rising international tensions and the need to deal with various foreign governments over controls they had imposed on international trade. Now willing to accept that the first new mission in Europe should be in Belgium, Skelton suggested that the other posts should be in South Africa, Australia, Ireland, and Argentina.[40]

Skelton's proposal encountered a good deal of opposition when it went before cabinet in late January 1938. Some ministers were unenthusiastic about any expansion. Lapointe responded more favourably, supporting appointment of a minister to Belgium with dual accreditation to the Netherlands, but he wanted to delay a decision on high commissioners pending further study. King sided with Lapointe and agreed also that, pending a decision on representation in the dominions, the Canadian government should receive, without reciprocation, an envoy from South Africa, to be known, at that country's request, not as high commissioner but as "accredited representative."[41]

Having secured approval for expansion in Europe, Skelton turned his attention to Latin America when preparing his budget estimates for 1939– 40. Instead of one post, as he had suggested earlier, he now proposed two, in Brazil and Argentina. The former country had already asked to send a minister to Canada, thereby raising the question of reciprocity, and Skelton thought that Argentina as well as Brazil would have to be considered. He hoped that a presence in Latin America would appeal to opinion in Quebec, thereby making it easier politically to carry out his project of expanded relations with the dominions. "Coupling the establishment of Legations in Latin America and High Commissionerships in the other British Dominions," Skelton contended, "would be a balanced ratio likely to appeal to the country as a whole."[42] This time again the gain was only modest. About the time Skelton's new proposals were laid before cabinet, the Irish initiative to exchange high commissioners was revived. This the cabinet was prepared to accept, but it would wait for other Commonwealth countries to take the initiative before entertaining further requests.[43]

Skelton hoped that overtures from Brazil, Haiti, and Norway might produce further action, but none was taken apart from agreement to accept a minister from Brazil, without reciprocity. When Wrong, dissatisfied with the continued need to rely on the British, sent the under-secretary another plan for opening new missions, reorganizing the department, and taking over duties performed for Canadians by British consuls, he received a weary reply. "As to Canadian equipment for the conduct of External Affairs, I entirely agree with what you say," Skelton told him. "Not a month has passed for some years without this argument being urged but I hope that now the ice has been broken for the second time there will be development along the lines of new Legations, representation in the Dominions and the establishment of a consular service but I am not optimistic in making any forecast as to when the next steps will be."[44]

New opportunities for the career service

While the slow pace of expansion was frustrating, the opportunities for departmental officers had none the less improved modestly, and they were further enhanced by the prospective retirements of Bruce and Roy. "To attract competent men . . . ," Skelton reminded King, "it will be necessary to afford them a chance for advancement to the highest ranks."[45] The chances of the career men were helped by discussion in Parliament. When the department's estimates came before the House of Commons, Bennett made a strong defence of career appointments. "It should be understood," he declared, "that those positions are not reserved for those who have rendered services, politically or otherwise, but that they would be the meritorious right of those who have really rendered service in the department. Such promotion I believe will ensure a better service, and certainly a more contented one."[46] King moved strongly in the direction of such candidates as heads of post. Before the end of 1938, Georges Vanier became minister to France and Jean Désy minister to Belgium and the Netherlands. King seems to have had a similar change in mind for Tokyo,[47] but, as a result of the unsettled situation in Japan, no successor to Bruce was appointed. Instead, the post remained under a career officer, D'Arcy McGreer, as chargé d'affaires. Another member of the foreign service, Kenneth Kirkwood, was named resident chargé in The Hague.

As a result of the changes in 1939, all Canadian posts except London and Washington were under the direction of career members of the foreign service. They were brought about, King told Bruce, "with a view, amongst other things, of bringing our diplomatic service more into accord with that of other countries, and, in particular, the diplomatic service of the United Kingdom." The prime minister was not entirely pleased: "I am convinced that a policy of filling a proportion of the ministerial posts by promotion from the ranks is essential," he confided to Massey, "but it is one that will inevitably bring difficulty in some quarters."[48]

Modest post-1935 expansion and appointment of more departmental officers as heads of post created opportunities for advancement in the service, thereby relieving the frustrating Depression-era freeze on promotions. These opportunities were necessary to fulfil Skelton's objectives for the foreign service. Even during the depression, other employers sought the services of departmental officers with demonstrated capability. In 1936, for example, the possibility arose of Pearson going to the Canadian Broadcasting Corporation as director of public relations, and he subsequently had several attractive offers from the private sector.[49]

Expansion of the service

The opening of new posts made it possible to continue the recruitment of new officers. Six entered the department as a result of competitions held during these years: Jean Chapdelaine, J. W. Pickersgill, and Max Wershof in 1937, James Gibson and Benjamin Rogers in 1938, and Frederick Fraser (who left after a brief period) in 1939. Two others joined in 1939, by a somewhat different route. Escott Reid, national secretary of the Canadian Institute of International Affairs from 1932 until 1938, was named second secretary by order-in-council, Skelton considering him too senior to be required to take the examination for third secretaries. He was posted almost immediately to Washington.[50] Herbert Norman, an authority on Japan, was designated "language officer"; he was promoted to third secretary in December 1941.

These recruits reinforced the department's character, but certain features are worthy of notice. Only one, Chapdelaine, was a francophone. Another, Wershof, was the first Jewish officer and the first of neither British nor French origin. There was at the time, Wershof later recalled, a suspicion that the department was likely to discriminate against Jews. This suspicion, according to Wershof, was "completely unfounded."[51]

Norman was the first officer to be recruited for his knowledge of a foreign language. The son of Canadian missionaries in Japan, Norman was as well the first of a number of "mish kids," as they came to be called,

191

who contributed to the department's ability to function in Asia. Also note-worthy in Norman's case was his position on the intellectual left. The department had always absorbed a broad spectrum of political views, and other recruits had supported left-wing causes. Norman, however, partly as a result of his reaction to the Depression, had become a communist while at Cambridge. This was not known to the department, which, like the United States and the United Kingdom, had no regular system of security checks at the time. Later, during the Cold War of the 1950s, this association cast a dark shadow over Norman's career. The department as well paid a price then for its lack of means, in the early years of its growth, to protect itself against embarrassment by unexpected revelations about its employees.[52]

Salaries and conditions of service

In order to attract and hold high-quality personnel, the department had to offer salaries and conditions of service competitive with those of alternative employers. Relief from the freeze on salaries was finally completed when an improved scale went into effect on January 1, 1938.[53] As a result, officers on recruitment were paid at a yearly rate of $2,280 for a probationary period lasting six to twelve months. When appointment as third secretary was confirmed, the range was $2,520 to $3,000, an increase of $120 over the previous level. Second and first secretaries began at $3,300 and $4,400 respectively. Counsellors, the legal adviser, the assistant under-secretary, the representative in Geneva, and the secretary to the high commissioner in London received raises of $240, bringing their salaries into the range of $5,760 to $7,200. Skelton's salary remained unchanged at $8,000, as did those of the politically appointed heads of post, ranging from $9,000 to $12,000. Désy and Vanier received the same salary as Skelton, $8,000, on their appointments to Brussels and Paris, plus allowances of $13,000. For those abroad, there was further relief in the form of a new, flexible scale of allowances. Intended to cover extra living, representation, and housing costs, these varied according to the cost of living at the post and the rank and marital status of the officer.[54]

One other development assisted employees of the department: codification of leave regulations for those posted abroad. The provisions generally affecting the public service, which had usually been followed, were not entirely adequate for the department, since they did not provide for assisted home leave. Without an entitlement to such leave, employees could become out of touch with Canada, especially since there was no established rotation of appointments between the posts and Ottawa. The consequences, Wrong pointed out, were hard on staff and disadvantageous to the department.[55] In the summer of 1939, a new regulation authorized paid home leave for officers after three and one-half years of continuous service abroad. For support staff, home leave was provided every fourth year. Another new regulation extended to personnel abroad the requirement to sign attendance registers, as a basis for calculating superannuation benefits. This was not so welcome, since it was perceived as an attempt by Ottawa to control working hours and hence as interference with local management of the mission.[56]

Administrative problems

Offsetting the benefits gained from expansion and more consistent regulation were administrative problems arising from the under-secretary's domination of the department. The British high commissioner, Sir Francis Floud, though he liked Skelton, considered him "not a good administrator and his office . . . badly organized."[57] Bennett commented to Clifford Clark that Skelton "had the unfortunate habit of leaving much of the day's work for tomorrow, which militated against his successful administration, [although] not against his usefulness."[58]

When Pearson in London grew impatient over lack of response from headquarters, Robertson advised: "It might help to clear up the general mess if Canada House could collate the various unanswered despatches . . . and present us with an ultimatum."[59] Pearson admired Skelton but was deeply frustrated by his chief's neglect of personnel and organizational problems. "Lord knows how I would like to be given the job of pulling External Affairs and the Foreign Service apart and putting it together again with a few of the pieces left out," he wrote at the beginning of 1936. "Unfortunately the Head, ODS has apparently no inclination to do that. He is not ruthless enough; won't hurt people, won't fight for his subordinates."[60]

Skelton was unwilling to delegate. The result was overburden at the top, especially for the under-secretary, and underemployment below. On arrival, most new officers were assigned to the code room to encypher and decypher telegrams. This activity, which gave an overall view of the department's work, was supposed to contribute to training but, being routine in nature, was instead a source of dissatisfaction. Most of the other work assigned to low-ranking officers was likewise of little substantive interest. Supervisors, meanwhile, were becoming increasingly preoccupied with their own duties, with the result that nothing was done to formalize training or adapt it to the needs of the time. At headquarters, only Keenleyside and to some extent Christie provided new officers with basic guidance and training or sought interesting work for them to do.

The leisurely pace for new officers was recalled by Pickersgill:

> There wasn't all that amount of work . . . before the war started. . . .
> When I went into External Affairs—went up into the attic of the East
> Block in October of 1937, after I had read the *New York Times* through
> in the morning, and de-coded a couple of telegrams . . . I wondered
> what to do next. I gathered that there was a sort of ripening process
> that went on, . . . but you didn't ripen much if you never saw any-
> body. . . . I was rescued from this by Loring Christie who found various
> little jobs for me to do and then, . . . after two months, when I might
> just have begun to get people to take a little notice of me, I was told
> one day that I was to go to the Prime Minister's office the next day.[61]

The imbalance was not only frustrating for juniors, it was dangerous for
the under-secretary: he collapsed from overwork in mid-September 1937
and, as a result of heart strain, had to remain away from the office until
mid-January 1938.

Assisting the prime minister

The prime minister recognized Skelton's problem. "He has attempted far
too much," King wrote at the time of the under-secretary's illness, "is
overconscientious in all things."[62] Yet the demands of the prime minister
added to the burden, and evidence of frailty did not produce relief. Rather,
King's thoughts turned to what might happen to his own requirements
if Skelton were not around. "How I wish," he reflected, "I could find
such a man for the Prime Minister's Office."

King's effort to find "such a man" reduced the resources of External
Affairs for work within its own mandate. Keenleyside had been assigned
to his office for a few months early in 1936. Now several other senior
officers were considered, but rejected: John Read (thought too narrowly
interested in legal issues), Christie (absent from the capital), and Scott
Macdonald (not selected despite being favoured by Skelton). The choice
instead was Norman Robertson, whom King had recently heard the British
high commissioner praise "as the ablest brain he had met within Canada."
Robertson, who was deeply involved in trade negotiations with the United
States, did not want the assignment, and Skelton was reluctant to lose
his services. On a visit to the under-secretary's sickbed, however, the prime
minister extracted agreement that he "should have the call on any man
in the service."[63]

When he recovered from his illness, Skelton, on vacation in Florida with
King, convinced the prime minister that Robertson, who was unhappy in
his new assignment, was essential to the success of the negotiations in

Washington. In December 1937 Skelton substituted Pickersgill, who had topped the recent competition for entrance into External Affairs. Still King was not satisfied. "I told Dr. Skelton," he observed when the prospect of new posts was under discussion later in 1937, "my feeling was that instead of expanding the work of the Department of External Affairs, we should seek to properly organize the Prime Minister's office."[64] No provision was made to replace Pickersgill when the next officer competition was held for External Affairs: the purpose of that exercise was only to fill gaps resulting from postings. One of the successful candidates, James Gibson, moreover, went to the prime minister's staff, where he remained.

Apart from these assignments, the department's association with the prime minister was becoming less intimate. In 1938 King named Arnold Heeney, a Montreal lawyer and the son of a longtime friend, as his principal secretary. Organization was Heeney's métier, and he has been credited with bringing "a semblance of order to the Prime Minister's Office," insofar as possible, given King's variable approach to his work.[65]

Heeney co-operated with departmental officers on speeches and had some involvement in King's travels outside Canada, but his appointment marked the beginning of a clear separation between the prime minister and the department. Heeney took over domestic duties formerly borne by the under-secretary, and he entered the public service in 1940 as clerk of the privy council, not as a member of the department. While Pickersgill and Gibson retained their foreign service designations for purposes of pay and promotion, their direct links with External Affairs became tenuous. Gradually the prime minister's staff began to run its own affairs, with only the administrative back-up, at the clerical level, that External Affairs provided so long as the prime minister retained the portfolio.

The department in 1939

By 1939, in other words, External Affairs was on the way to assuming a distinct and specialized character similar to that possessed by other departments. No longer required to deal with so many of the prime minister's domestic responsibilities, it had more time for its own mandate, and its capacity for dealing with that mandate had improved. Control from headquarters over heads of post had become more effective, and the regulatory system more sophisticated. The most serious constraints on resources imposed by the Depression had been left behind, and the department had continued its careful growth. Canadian representation abroad had increased from five posts to seven, plus a commitment to open in Dublin. Five foreign countries (the United States, France, Japan, Belgium, and the Netherlands) maintained legations in Ottawa, compared with three in 1935, and the Commonwealth was represented by the accredited representative of South Africa and the British and Irish high commissioners. In addition, a number of consular offices in the capital, particularly those of Germany and Italy, carried out a broad range of activities approximating those of full-fledged diplomatic missions. The total staff of the department, at home and abroad, had risen from 178 in 1935-36 to 225 in 1939-40. The budget, too, was larger, having grown from approximately $1,032,000 (not including the cost of advertising in the United Kingdom) to $1,242,000.

Despite these changes, the department still possessed only slender resources for dealing with Canada's external interests and with the tense international situation. In the circumstances, the calibre of officer personnel was crucial. Skelton doubtless was gratified to be able to place departmental officers in charge of five of the seven posts by 1939 and to receive evidence that juniors, too, met a high standard. Léon Mayrand and Charles Ritchie, Massey reported after their posting to London as third secretaries in 1939, "promise to do very well. . . . They both have the combination of qualities which are so important in diplomatic work—good brains and pleasing personalities. If we continue to take men like this into the Department of External Affairs our little service will be a very efficient body."[66]

For the time being, the opportunity to develop efficiency was perhaps greater abroad than at home. In 1937, there were eleven officers at headquarters, only four more than in 1929. Of those available in Ottawa in 1937, moreover, one, Howard Measures, was in the prime minister's office and another, Pickersgill, was shortly to join him there, without being replaced in the department.

All the officers in Ottawa in 1937 were assigned specific duties:[67]

Under-secretary	O. D. Skelton	General direction
Assistant under-secretary	L. Beaudry	Consular, treaty publication (with assistance of Feaver and Pickersgill), passport, and radio questions; western Europe
Legal adviser	J. Read	Legal questions; International Joint Commission and Boundary Waters; navigation and shipping
Counsellor	L. Christie	British Empire, except commercial relations; defence; aviation

First secretary	H. L. Keenleyside	Far East, Latin America, and United States other than commercial; central and eastern Europe
First secretary	J. S. Macdonald	Commercial relations with all countries except United Kingdom and United States; League of Nations questions
First secretary	N. A. Robertson	General economic and financial questions; commercial relations with United Kingdom and United States
Third secretary (temporary)	H. F. Feaver	Immigration, deportation; general assistance to Beaudry and Read
Third secretary (temporary)	L. Mayrand	Assistance to Read in law and to Macdonald and Robertson in commercial questions
Acting assistant private secretary (to the prime minister)	W. H. Measures	Protocol, official visits, press clipping
—	J. Pickersgill	At first to concentrate on complete mastery of coding; also assigned considerable clipping

This distribution ignored an essential problem in the work of a foreign office, the tension between geographical and functional responsibilities. Except for Keenleyside, all officers had some of the latter, sometimes in combination with duties related to a particular region of the world. Relationships with particular countries tended to be treated according to subject, rather than being assigned to a single officer.

In practice, the lack of co-ordination was even greater than the list implies. Formal assignment of duties bore little relationship to tasks performed, since Skelton passed work to whichever officer was available. Nor were there hierarchical reporting relationships or groupings of officers based on links among specialized responsibilities. Rather, all officers in Ottawa came directly under Skelton. Except for the Passport Office, which reported through the assistant under-secretary, all administrative units also were responsible to the under-secretary, although, within each, support staff was supervised by the head of the unit. Posts as well were in a direct line of authority to the under-secretary and, via him, to the secretary of state for external affairs and prime minister. The under-secretary's span of control, therefore, was very broad, leading to imbalance in the distribution of the work.

So much did Skelton dominate the conduct of external relations through this organizational structure that King in 1936 found his own position somewhat obscure. "I had to impress on Marler once or twice," he noted, "that I was the responsible Minister, and had some say as well as Skelton in the affairs of the Department."[68] The prime minister's insistence on his own authority, of course, was not incompatible with Skelton's view of the role of the civil servant, but the under-secretary was not inclined to share the responsibility of providing ministers with advice on foreign policy. There was nothing collegial about the performance of this task in the department. The officer corps was growing in its capacity to contribute to the formulation of policy advice, and individual members might on occasion deal with the minister. They could do so, however, only as agents of the under-secretary, and their recommendations on policy could have effect only if they had his confidence.

THE DEPARTMENT AND THE ISSUES

The pressure on the department's policy-making machinery between 1935 and 1939 was heavy: the accelerating pace of international activity affected all the fronts of principal concern to Canada. The death of King George V in January 1936 began a chain of crucial events for the Commonwealth. The Depression gave continuing urgency to economic relations with the United States. The deterioration of great power relationships in Europe and the Far East affected all of Canada's major interests outside the North Atlantic triangle and raised major questions of immigration and defence.

Any of these subjects could cause controversy at home, and therefore they were followed closely by the prime minister. In cabinet he consulted Lapointe, when an issue had implications for Quebec, and occasionally Sen. Raoul Dandurand (minister without portfolio), when his experience at the League of Nations was relevant. Others, such as the minister of mines and resources, T. A. Crerar, who oversaw immigration, and the minister of trade and commerce, W. D. Euler, were involved in issues affecting their portfolios.

In the public service, the chief source of advice was Skelton, whose range extended to most issues with external implications. Staff work on a similar variety of subjects was performed by members of Skelton's department, and the pressures of the period sometimes allowed them to enjoy considerable independence, within the confines imposed by the policies favoured by the prime minister and communicated to them by the under-secretary. The effective performance of these assignments indicated the department's growing capability, particularly at headquarters. The posts continued to play a supporting role—useful sources of independent information and evidence of Canada's independence under the crown.

The monarchy and Commonwealth relations

The various dimensions of departmental activity all came into play on the death of King George V. The Canadian government was able to prepare for the formal observances without recourse to British assistance, because of careful study by External Affairs of the precedents established on the death of Edward VII in 1910 and the legal and constitutional implications. Massey was designated to represent Canada at the funeral, as Lord Strathcona had done in 1910. Arrangements for a memorial service in Ottawa were handled by Beaudry and Measures, with close involvement by King, who was much concerned with the details of all major events affecting the monarchy.

The observances in foreign countries provided an opportunity for evaluating the impact of Canadian missions abroad as evidence of the country's autonomy. Those in Tokyo were watched with particular care, in view of difficulties that had developed with the British embassy over the status of the Canadian legation when preparations were being made to celebrate the late king's silver jubilee in 1935. Skelton was disappointed to learn that imperial messengers had called only at the British embassy and not at the Canadian legation. "It will probably take some little time still," he observed, "for some representatives of His Majesty in respect of the United Kingdom clearly and fully to understand the status of equality between members of the British Commonwealth of Nations. Nor is the education of the Governments of certain Foreign Powers, I think, quite complete yet in this regard. It is, therefore, the duty of Representatives of His Majesty in respect of Canada to see to it that the diplomatic requirements of this status of equality be observed."[69]

The "status of equality" of the dominions soon provided a more urgent problem for the Canadian government: the abdication in December of the new king, Edward VIII, as a result of his decision to marry a divorcée, Wallis Simpson, a matter that King considered to require the direct application of his own political skills. The department served mainly as a means of communication with the British prime minister, Stanley Baldwin. Such priority was the subject assigned that some communication was by overseas telephone, a business method not favoured at the time in Ottawa.[70]

More typical of the balance between prime ministerial and departmental involvement were preparations for Canadian participation in the coronation of King George VI, on May 12, 1937. In Ottawa, Beaudry, Feaver, and Measures handled most of the work, but, owing to King's interest, Skelton had to spend a good deal of time on the subject, even though most questions involved administration or protocol. King had Christie draft a coronation address from the Canadian Parliament to the new monarch.

Requests for seats at coronation occasions and for other assistance to Canadians interested in the event were dealt with by Canada House. Since the interest of Canadians outstripped the space available for them in Westminster Abbey and along the parade route, Massey had to endure some unfair complaints of favouritism, against which he was defended by the prime minister. "My understanding was that they did a wonderful job," King told the House of Commons. "They were under great pressure at Canada House during the Coronation and I thought they handled the situation remarkably well."[71]

As well as being responsible for the reception of Canadian visitors, Massey participated in the preparations for the ceremony itself. A disappointment for him was Skelton's insistence on a relaxation of the requirement that court dress be worn. "Some of our Canadian party," Massey recalled, "held views that savoured of Jacksonian democracy rather than the tradition we are supposed to have inherited." Most of the Jacksonian democrats succumbed to the high commissioner's arguments in favour of court dress, but there was one important holdout: Skelton "refused point-blank" to appear in uniform.[72] Those who complied and rented their attire may have presented an appearance of dubious authenticity. When Pearson, an usher at the ceremony, sought to obtain a uniform suitable for a member of the Canadian diplomatic service, he found that Moss Brothers "had never heard of this branch of His Majesty's Service and had no idea what its uniform was." What was supplied, he learned from a friend in the Foreign Office, might be partly correct, but "I was wearing a coat which had enough gold braid on it for an ambassador and my cocked hat was certainly that of an admiral."[73]

The coronation was followed immediately by the Imperial Conference of 1937. Headed by King, the Canadian delegation included the ministers of justice (Lapointe), finance (C. A. Dunning), mines and resources (T. A. Crerar), and national defence (Ian Mackenzie).

Of the seven women listed among the more than two hundred names in the official directory of the conference, only Agnes McCloskey and Marjorie McKenzie of the Canadian party had positions of responsibility. The former was in effect the administrative officer of the delegation. It was her task to keep track of the expenses of the members of the party, their transportation arrangements, the hospitality they offered, and their lodging requirements. She also had to arrange for office equipment, suitable space for briefings and meetings, telephone, cable and mailing facilities, newspaper distribution, and so on. McKenzie provided liaison with the conference secretariat, circulated schedules and reminders to delegates about meetings, organized and supervised stenographic work, ensured that documents for Canadian use were on hand regularly and in sufficient quantity, and otherwise ensured effective Canadian participation. She kept a complete set of all records, which she organized for future reference on her return to Ottawa.[74]

The advisers from Ottawa included the service chiefs, Christie, Read, Robertson, and Skelton. Massey and Pearson were present but do not seem to have been much engaged in the proceedings. Massey took precedence over Skelton, but the under-secretary was pre-eminent among the advisers. With King, he attended virtually all meetings of the principal delegates, and he was the main source of instructions and guidance.

Skelton and Christie concentrated, with King, on defence and foreign policy, and with Read they assisted Lapointe on constitutional questions. Christie accompanied Crerar and Dunning to meetings on civil aviation and shipping. Dunning had the support of Robertson on the work of the Imperial Economic Committee. Robertson also assisted Crerar in discussions of British claims to sovereignty in the Antarctic. The delegation was anxious that the principles cited by the British not undercut the Canadian position in the Arctic.

Foreign and defence policies were of much interest to the Canadians, because of King's determination to avoid advance commitments to the empire. Canadian activity was orchestrated by Skelton, who even instructed the senior service officers to avoid the subject of military commitments in any discussions with their British counterparts. On one important issue, support for the policy of appeasement favoured by Neville Chamberlain, who succeeded Baldwin as prime minister during the conference, King had no difficulty agreeing to a common position. On defence and foreign policy, he fulfilled his objective of avoiding binding obligations.[75]

The department was also heavily involved in the tour of Canada by King George VI and Queen Elizabeth in the spring of 1939. Some issues, notably the governor general's role and King's desire to serve as minister in attendance while the royal party was in the United States, were handled by the prime minister himself, in communication with the monarch's secretaries, Sir Alexander Hardinge and Alan Lascelles, or other appropriate officials. Most of the planning, however, was the work of special committees established for the purpose. As soon as the king's decision became known, a special body, the Organization to Arrange for the Royal Visit, was established in Ottawa. Under King's direct supervision, this consisted of two committees. One, at the cabinet level, had overall responsibility for the tour; the other, made up of deputy ministers, was charged with planning, programming, and financing events. The latter committee was chaired by the under-secretary of state, Dr. E. H. Coleman. Skelton was a member, and Keenleyside was secretary. Keenleyside's skill as an administrator served him in good stead: he started work well before the group had its first meeting, and so it was able to provide the cabinet committee with recommendations on basic policy on three days' notice, as requested by King. Once the policy had been decided, Keenleyside provided liaison with provincial and municipal governments. As well, he had to keep in close touch with King, to whom he had direct access about anything connected with the tour and who followed the preparations on a daily basis.

King's interest required that Skelton be closely involved in the preparations, even with respect to quite small matters. Work on the tour also involved Chapdelaine and a number of support staff assigned to the secretariat of the interdepartmental committee. Drafts for King's many speeches were the work of Christie, in association with Heeney.

Probably the most deeply engaged after Keenleyside was Agnes McCloskey. She kept track of employees' hours, overtime, and meal entitlements resulting from extra work and paid hundreds of bills arising from the visit. In addition, she arranged for travel advances, some on very short notice, for officials' trips to work out attractive local programs. Finally, she had to ensure that funds were available in good time and were properly accounted for, in conformity with government regulations.[76]

Commercial relations with the United States and the United Kingdom

Closer to the mainstream of the department's work was the completion of triangular negotiations in Washington about US trade with the United Kingdom and Canada. For this purpose, the triumvirate of McKinnon, Robertson, and Wilgress was revived. It was subsequently strengthened by the addition of a member of McKinnon's staff, Arthur Annis, who remained behind the scenes, supplying information and "keeping the score."[77]

The negotiations started in Washington in October 1937 but really got under way only in March 1938. They were long, complex, and arduous, proceeding with hardly a break until they were successfully concluded on November 17. McKinnon and Wilgress were responsible for day-to-day aspects—working out the precise tariff concessions to be sought and those to be offered, under guidelines approved by the cabinet. Robertson held a watching brief on the entire negotiating process and was also charged with keeping Ottawa informed of developments. Within the cabinet's guidelines, to which Robertson had contributed, the team had a good deal of leeway.

Because of the complexity of the negotiations and pressing parliamentary business in Ottawa, King was unable to attend to them in any detail. He was kept informed by Skelton, who had recovered from his illness by the time the talks were seriously launched in 1938, and to whom Robertson reported regularly from Washington. In turn, Skelton was the channel to Robertson for instructions from Ottawa. On important issues, the ultimate source of these was King himself, who preferred to deal with the matter on his own rather than involving the cabinet, because conflicts among ministerial interests might impede progress.

The negotiations resulted in modification of the imperial preference between the United Kingdom and Canada, easier access to the United States for some Canadian exports, and an exchange of trade concessions between Britain and the United States. The agreements were signed at the White House by the secretary of state, Cordell Hull, King, and the British ambassador in Washington, Sir Ronald Lindsay. In the House of Commons on February 14, 1939, the prime minister praised the Canadian negotiators for their "efficient and highly skilled service," which, he declared, he did not "think it possible to commend . . . too highly."[78] As one of the three participating departments, External Affairs shared in this tribute. Its value as a contributor to economic decision making was confirmed, and, because such issues were important to national well-being, its credibility in government policy-making generally was enhanced. More particularly, of course, the compliment applied to Robertson. Although still the most junior member of the team, he was clearly a rising force in the public service, and his abilities were becoming increasingly evident to the prime minister.

The crisis overseas

Notwithstanding the increasing confidence placed in him, Robertson's responsibilities remained limited. Neither he nor other experienced officers were given authority to deal on their own with the deteriorating situation overseas. This was the preserve of the prime minister, alert as ever to domestic political implications. Skelton remained the source of departmental advice on matters in this area. All recommendations were subject to his close scrutiny before they reached the prime minister.

Most closely associated with the under-secretary in formulating departmental response to international events was Christie. Others involved in a more limited way, when their specialized responsibilities were affected, were Beaudry, Keenleyside, and Read. Junior officers might on occasion be asked for assistance, but they had little opportunity to contribute to policy. Not surprisingly, therefore, the growing urgency of the international situation did not relieve the sense of aimlessness in the lower grades.

As Massey's experience in London made plain, posts abroad were not closely involved in policy-making. They provided information, of which King took careful note. Unlike Bennett, he regularly read telegrams and dispatches, especially during the early years after his return to power, making marginal comments. Unfortunately, Ottawa was not systematic in responding to these reports, and so the offices in London, Washington, and Geneva, the last especially after Wrong's arrival in 1937, asked regularly if their reporting was timely and appropriate. They also complained about the failure of headquarters to keep them posted about events in Canada. Normally, Skelton responded to such comments with an individual letter, and on two occasions, one in early 1937 and the other in 1939, circulars of guidance went out about the type of report Ottawa found most useful. The letter sent in 1939, drafted by Skelton himself, described an imposing array of topics of interest to the department, including "the outstanding developments in the foreign relations of the Government of the country in which you are stationed; the trend of public opinion in the same field"; domestic political, social, and economic developments; and events in adjacent countries.[79]

Since there were insufficient resources to meet the needs thus identified, the circulars did not produce a lasting improvement in reporting. Ottawa therefore remained heavily reliant on information provided by the British, through such means as the Foreign Office print and circular telegrams from the Dominions Office. King and his colleagues, however, came to their own conclusions about the international situation. Decisions about Canadian policy, and the way they were expressed, were based on the national interest and on domestic political requirements, as understood by the Canadian government.

Keenly aware of the strains that would be imposed on national unity by the dispatch of Canadian forces overseas, King consistently encouraged efforts to avoid war and resisted pressures to make advance commitments. At the same time, he was increasingly conscious of the unlikelihood that peace could be preserved and of the inevitability of Canadian participation in a conflict between the United Kingdom and the European dictators. Because of his understanding of domestic opinion, these were not conclusions that King considered it prudent to make public, and, undoubtedly for the same reason, he found it preferable to retain as much flexibility as possible about the extent and nature of Canadian involvement if war should come. The avoidance of commitments, therefore, continued to be an important principle in relations with friendly governments and in the presentation of the Canadian position to the public.

In the department, Skelton was in agreement with the effort to avoid commitments but not with the underlying changes in King's thinking. Suspicious of Whitehall's intentions and convinced that Canada's best chance to prosper was by accepting, as the United States had done, its destiny as a North American nation, he wanted to keep out of overseas wars and entanglements. The senior officers most concerned with the international situation generally, Christie and Keenleyside, supported Skelton's objectives, as did Read, with his narrower but influential mandate as legal adviser. A number of others at headquarters, including Beaudry, Macdonald, and Robertson, wanted a stronger stand against the dictatorships, but they had little impact on the broad direction of policy. Overseas, Vanier throughout favoured greater Canadian engagement, and others more slowly reached the same conclusion. Massey, Pearson, and Wrong for a while saw merit in Chamberlain's policy of appeasement but in due course abandoned it, as did the British government.[80] The views of these officers, however, were not a serious challenge to Skelton, since the posts had little effect on decision-making in Ottawa.

As a result of Skelton's control, the department was a source of coherent advice on the Canadian response to international crises of the day, leading to the conclusion that overseas commitments should be avoided. Since this advice accorded with one of the prime minister's objectives, it received serious attention. The final word, however, remained with King, who was well aware of the differences as well as the similarities between himself and Skelton and who always weighed departmental recommendations against other considerations. Those other considerations often won the day: King was realizing that Canada could not much longer remain aloof from events in Europe.

The pattern of departmental involvement in Canada's response to the situation overseas was established with the first major crisis to emerge after King's return to power, on which he and Skelton were in substantial agreement. This was the civil war that broke out in Spain in July 1936, when the armed forces rose against the republican government in Madrid. On this issue, which soon became a subject of controversy in Canada, King controlled policy and consulted closely with a few cabinet colleagues, notably Lapointe, because of the sensitivity of the subject in Quebec. The principal source of information was the Dominions Office, supplemented by Canadian posts. Departmental officers were not expected to take initiatives; they were to receive instructions from above and deal with day-to-day aspects of the crisis as it evolved.

Skelton was consulted in the preparation of the Foreign Enlistment Act of 1937, which made it an offence to serve on either side in Spain, but the legislation was mainly the work of the Department of Justice. The department concentrated on day-to-day consular ramifications of the war, which were considerable, especially with regard to passport and repatriation requirements arising from the activities of volunteers in the Mackenzie-Papineau Battalion of the International Brigade, organized to fight in the cause of the republic. This consular work was dealt with mainly by Beaudry and Read, with help from Rogers after he joined the service. Posts abroad, especially London and Paris, were similarly involved in passport and other consular work, particularly repatriation of volunteers, in co-operation with major Canadian shipping companies.

In Ottawa, there was a good deal of liaison with the Royal Canadian Mounted Police, handled by Keenleyside, because of the Communist party's involvement with volunteers going to fight for the republic. A voluminous correspondence from the public also developed as hostilities mounted. Almost entirely from English-speaking persons and groups, these letters were answered at first by Christie but were taken over later by Skelton, whose approach tended to be more soothing.[81]

The Spanish Civil War dragged on until March 28, 1939, but long before then the department's attention had been diverted by other events in Europe; comparatively little attention was paid to the crisis developing in the Far East. The government's main interest in Japan continued to be immigration, followed by trade. The consequences of the Japanese invasion of China also required a response from time to time, because of their effect on Canadian missionaries.

As with the Spanish Civil War, the main source of information on Germany and Europe was the Dominions Office, supplemented by reports from Canadian posts. In Ottawa, résumés were prepared every now and then—on the basis chiefly of Dominions Office telegrams—of the positions of the various countries concerned with or affected by developments in Europe. These, sometimes drafted by Christie, were sent to the posts as circulars. Some indicated the Canadian position on the subject at hand.

As time went on, there was less harmony in the responses of King and Skelton to developments in Europe, and such disagreement could exclude the department from an activity that fell within its mandate. Thus, despite Skelton's prominence at the Imperial Conference, the department had little to do with the event that followed it, King's visit to Berlin, since the undersecretary saw no utility in dealing with Hitler.[82]

The department had little influence on policies for which the main responsibility lay elsewhere, as with refugees resulting from spreading instability in Europe. Because there was much opposition in Canada to increased immigration, ministers kept close watch on the subject, especially King, Crerar, the minister responsible for immigration, and Lapointe, because of the importance attached to opinion in Quebec. The public servant with primary responsibility was F. C. Blair, director of the Immigration Branch in Crerar's department. Considered especially sensitive by the government were requests to help deal with the effects of Nazi moves, beginning in 1933, against the Jewish population in Germany. Throughout, the policy favoured by the government and strictly enforced by Blair was restrictive.

External Affairs contributed to implementation of the policy in a number of ways. It was the point of contact for diplomatic missions whose governments wished help from Canada in relieving the pressure of refugees. Posts had to be given guidance on dealing with appeals by persons seeking, individually and in groups, to migrate to Canada and with governments urging this country to accept greater numbers. There were also international meetings to attend, primarily those of the Intergovernmental Committee on Refugees, which emerged from a conference held at Evian in France between July 5 and 20, 1938, under US sponsorship. In Ottawa, King used Skelton as a channel for dealing with Crerar and Blair and with public interest groups and others concerned about the refugee problem. The department also helped to draft policy statements and studies of the issue.

London was the source of much of the pressure on Canada for a more generous approach and was the headquarters of the intergovernmental committee. The meetings of the committee were attended by the representative of the Department of Mines and Resources, W. R. Little. Massey and Pearson were also involved in its work. Massey worked within the limitations of the government's policy. Approached in 1936 with a modest request to help Jewish refugees from Germany, he did not make a recommendation, but he did conclude with the observation: "I understand that among the German refugees in Great Britain there are persons with very high academic qualifications as well as others with valuable experience as scientists in different branches of industry."[83] Later the government's policies provided the context for an argument in favour of admitting refugees from another community, the Sudeten Germans. These, Massey said, "appear to be more desirable than any other refugees and if we could take a substantial number of them it would put us in a much stronger position in relation to later appeals from and on behalf of non Aryans."[84]

Some officers questioned the government's refugee policy. In a review of the subject in November 1938, Robertson observed that, "while this country's capacity to absorb immigrants is grossly exaggerated by Mercator's map, it undoubtedly can take in, in normal times, a good many more immigrants than it has in the last five or six years."[85] "The files of the Department of Immigration and of this Department," he concluded in another memorandum, "contain many applications for temporary admission to Canada from persons who profess to be able to meet any financial conditions the Government choose to set. It is true that a policy of selective admission, based primarily on the financial position of the applicant, might be open to criticism. Whether such criticism would be better directed than that to which a policy of total refusal of temporary admission is subject is another question."[86]

Obstacles to a change of direction, even on this basis, were formidable, in view of public support for the government's position. With ministers fully committed to a restrictive approach and the lead in another department, opinion in External Affairs sympathetic to change did not influence the Canadian attitude. The sense of hopelessness was caught by Massey early in 1939, following a meeting of the intergovernmental committee at which there had appeared to be "a possibility of organizing with the German authorities a controlled and orderly emigration of Jews from Germany." For this to come about, the high commissioner emphasized, the German government would have to be satisfied that "the countries of immigration are actually ready to carry on their part." About the intentions of those countries Massey was sceptical. "The question . . . arises," he observed, "What are the countries of immigration actually ready to do?"[87]

Another subject that the deteriorating international situation highlighted was defence policy, to which King paid close attention. The politicians he consulted were Lapointe and, on occasion, Dandurand. He seldom dealt with the deputy minister of national defence, Lt.-Col. L. R. Laflèche, or with the senior armed services establishment, instead using Skelton as his intermediary.[88]

In the department, Skelton was assisted on defence questions by Christie, who like the under-secretary wanted to avoid a commitment to the United Kingdom. Christie was normally the first point of contact with the armed forces establishment, and, since he resisted its efforts to prepare for engagement overseas and possessed a rather sharply etched temperament, the relationship became somewhat wintry.[89] No other officers in the department appear to have been involved on a regular basis. In the prime minister's office, Pickersgill's services were enlisted from time to time to help with collation and analysis of material for use in debates in the House of Commons.

When policy statements, recommendations, or analyses were necessary, or when comments had to be made on papers produced by the defence establishment, Christie generally prepared the first drafts. Nothing reached the prime minister, however, without the under-secretary's approval. Skelton often did the drafting himself on major policy positions or for important statements.

Christie worked with the Canadian Defence Committee, an organ of the cabinet created in August 1936. He was its first secretary but was replaced by Heeney when the latter joined the prime minister's staff in 1938. Chaired by the prime minister, the committee included the ministers of finance, justice, and national defence. Skelton attended its meetings, as did the senior service officers. This forum little affected policy. Intended to deal with questions of peace and security more expeditiously than the full cabinet, the committee met only infrequently.[90] The department's influence, therefore, depended on the credibility of advice going to the prime minister via the under-secretary.

That influence was greatest at the time of the Imperial Conference of 1937. During preparations, King became concerned about two British papers, which seemed to imply Canadian commitments in defence, munitions, and supply. These subjects, he further learned, had been dealt with in the "liaison letters," whereby the chief of the Imperial General Staff corresponded with his counterparts in the dominions and India. Christie had been aware of these letters for some time and had become troubled by them. As a result of representations from him and Skelton, King instructed the minister of national defence, Ian Mackenzie, to investigate the practice. The minister recommended that the correspondence be continued, because of the value of the information received, but that in future Canadian communications be "forwarded through External Affairs to the British authorities."[91] Cabinet approved Mackenzie's report, and thenceforth External Affairs transmitted the letters and also on occasion discussed their contents with National Defence. Only on minor issues of liaison was the latter department to deal with the British.[92]

One of the British papers recommended actions to be taken by the dominions in the event of hostilities. With King's approval, Skelton drafted a rebuttal which, after acceptance by the cabinet, became the basis of the Canadian position at the Imperial Conference. Therein lay the source of Skelton's dominance of this issue during the meetings and the core of his ideas on the subject: rejection of advance commitments overseas and concentration on home and North American defence.

Because Skelton remained committed to this position while King's approach evolved, the under-secretary's dominance of the defence issue did not long outlast the Imperial Conference. Convinced that the armed forces establishment was determined on sending an expeditionary force overseas in the event of war, as had happened in 1914, Skelton favoured holding defence expenditures at a time when King's reading of the situation in Europe and its implications for Canada disposed him toward an increase. Between 1934–35 and 1938–39, National Defence's expenditures went up from a little over $14 million to almost $34.5 million. It did not always get all it wanted, not because of Skelton's objections but because of the government's financial position and political considerations.[93]

King and Skelton worked in harmony during the crisis arising from German pressure on Czechoslovakia in the summer and early autumn of 1938 and shared in the relief at the news on September 29 of Chamberlain and Hitler's agreement at Munich. They still parted company, however, on the extent of Canadian commitment in the event of conflict. After an argument on the subject during a Caribbean cruise they took together in October, King reminded Skelton that he, as prime minister, was responsible for making political decisions, and he resolved to be wary of the under-secretary's influence. "He seeks to dominate one's thought, is intellectually arrogant in some respects," the prime minister reflected. He did not intend to do without the help of the under-secretary, still "the best counsellor and guide," but he was conscious of the need "to lead and not be controlled."[94]

Skelton's position was not held unanimously within the department. At the end of 1938 and during 1939 there was a serious internal debate, during which the arguments for and against participation in a potential conflict received an airing, by Wrong and Christie respectively. Even Skelton eventually acknowledged the likelihood of Canadian involvement if the United Kingdom were at war and the need to put the country's defences in order. He made these concessions only grudgingly, however, and the character of recommendations coming from the department did not change markedly. The result was further erosion of the department's influence on defence policy.

After the British announced, on March 17, 1939, the end of their policy of appeasement, and reinforced the decision by guarantees to Poland on March 31 and to Romania and Greece on April 13, King had more doubts about the advice coming to him from the department via Skelton. "I feel more and more," he noted in his diary on April 28, "that I have at this time made a mistake in letting myself be too controlled by the isolationist attitude of External Affairs."[95]

The department, meanwhile, was not preparing itself to meet the administrative requirements of war. Skelton, concerned with Canada's constitutional rights, was immersed in writing a paper on "Canadian War Policy," a blueprint for limited Canadian participation which set priorities for military and economic activities and closer consultation with allied nations. Christie was similarly engaged with the constitutional issue.[96] Junior officers were just about all working in the code room, which was being swamped by the increased flow of telegrams to and from the Dominions Office and the posts and from travellers and other concerned private citizens seeking advice about conditions in Europe. The situation in the code room during the last weeks of peace was chaotic, leaving little time for preparatory work on other matters.

Compounding these distractions was realization that preparation for full-scale Canadian commitment represented abandonment of Skelton and Christie's most cherished objectives. Lacking sympathy for participation in a war overseas and no longer seeing a place for his views in the public service, Christie told Pearson that he was contemplating resigning if he were not discharged beforehand. Skelton was deeply discouraged by the course of events, which he saw as a repudiation of his and his department's autonomist objectives. "The first casualty in this war," he wrote in a personal note, reflecting on the consequences of the British guarantees in eastern Europe, "has been Canada's claim to an independent control of her own destinies. In spite of a quarter century of proclamation and achievement of equal and independent status, we have thus far been relegated to the role of a Crown colony. We are drifting into a war resulting, so far as the United Kingdom's part is concerned, from policies and diplomatic actions initiated months ago without our knowledge or expectation."[97]

Even so, the department was by no means excluded from the government's preparations. Read was involved in such matters as emergency legislation, censorship, and the internment of enemy aliens. Reports were prepared on the steps being taken in the United Kingdom and the United States and on the organization of the Canadian government during the First World War. On August 30, the cabinet approved the replacement of the Canadian Defence Committee by a supervisory body, the Emergency Council (or Committee on General Policy), to review the war effort as a whole. Other cabinet subcommittees dealt with supply, legislation, public information, finance, and internal security.[98]

Despite the rush of events, the department still received a respectful hearing on defence planning. Five days after Skelton's memorandum on war policy was discussed by the cabinet, the chiefs of staff submitted a paper entitled "Canada's National Effort (Armed Forces) in the Early Stages of a Major War." It outlined the forms a Canadian effort might take, including the raising of an army corps of 60,000 men for immediate dispatch abroad. This proposal was sharply attacked by Christie in a paper he gave to King just before the cabinet considered the subject. The chiefs of staff were told by the prime minister that nothing should be done and no plans made before Parliament met on September 7.[99]

The decision to summon Parliament had been taken on September 1, the day Hitler began the invasion of Poland. Thus when the United Kingdom declared war on September 3 Canada did not follow suit but awaited the decision of its own Parliament. This was not an achievement that gave the under-secretary much consolation. As the cabinet deliberated on September 1, the press corps mingled in the antechamber and Skelton sat slumped in a chair in an adjoining office. Showing the strain of long hours of difficult work, he waited in what one observer called "courageous despair."[100]

The decision to act independently in the declaration of war left Canada technically neutral for a brief period, but early entry into the conflict was never in doubt. Many of the actions that followed, therefore, were more appropriate to the status of a belligerent. As soon as the British decision had been announced, Lt.-Col. Maurice Pope, secretary of the Chiefs of Staff Committee, informed Christie that censorship was in effect on all cables, mail, and transatlantic telephone calls. While the German consul general claimed all the rights available in a neutral country, the treatment accorded him was closer to that of a representative of a hostile belligerent, since his mail was opened and his luggage searched.[101]

Decisions taken during this period expanded the department's activities overseas. The prospect of entry into the war gave added urgency to the need for better means of communication with the other dominions. The prime minister therefore allowed the under-secretary to dispatch requests for the exchange of high commissioners with Australia and New Zealand. Australia agreed immediately, and New Zealand stated its willingness to accept a Canadian representative, although it was unable for financial reasons to reciprocate right away. South Africa and Ireland were informed that Canada would soon send high commissioners to their capitals, completing the exchanges begun when they had opened offices in Ottawa.

The debate in Parliament concluded on September 9, and External Affairs channels were then used to obtain the king's signature on the declaration of war. This was secured the following day. The department thought the process had been too slow, but Pearson considered the judgment unfair. In fact, he pointed out in his memoirs, a draft prepared in Canada House during the week of neutrality and submitted to Buckingham Palace for comment had not only been approved by the king but had been signed by him before Parliament reached its decision in Ottawa.[102]

Once Canada was in the war, the department had to help make up for lost time, for the cautious approach to the great international issues of the later 1930s left the country ill-prepared. On the policy side the department had remained preoccupied with imperial relationships at the expense of the matters at issue in the war. Structurally it remained weak. After a visit to Ottawa in July 1939, Pearson reported to Massey that the department was, "in one crude phrase, . . . in a mess." There were, he noted, "lots of people around to do things—but everything, at least everything of importance to us, is done by two or three. That is due to three things. First, the fact that the Prime Minister is our Minister. With the best departmental organization in the world this would make for confusion and delay. Second, instead of the best, there must be almost the worst departmental organization. A harried and harrassed Deputy relies entirely on one or two people. Three, the younger men are, as ever, not being trained to take an increasing share of the work."[103]

Yet the means were there for improvement, for the department had become more than an extension of the under-secretary and his political chief. The senior ranks now had a number of experienced men who were fully conversant with the government's priorities and could be relied on to be guided by them. Gradually, within these constraints, they were carrying out more of the government's international obligations. While more sophisticated organizational support would have helped them, their talent was such that they were not unduly inhibited by conditions as they were. War was bound to increase greatly the pressures on the departmental infrastructure while leaving little opportunity to deal with them. The pool of talent developed in the foreign service by 1939, therefore, would be vital to the department's support of Canadian participation in the conflict.

Part Three

**War and Transition:
1939–1946**

Chapter Eight
At War under Skelton: 1939–1941

CANADA'S BELLIGERENT STATUS INTENSIFIED PRESSURES on the department already apparent as the country moved toward war. For a time, however, the policy positions and the organizational principles that governed the department during O. D. Skelton's tenure as under-secretary could be sustained. Although it was announced on September 19 that the government had decided to send a force overseas, the commitment, for financial reasons, was less than the service chiefs had recommended. During the period of "phony war" which lasted until Germany began its successful invasion of western Europe in the spring of 1940, Canadians anticipated that the conflict would be "a war of limited liability," to which their most important contribution would be economic rather than military.[1] Such expectations suited Prime Minister King, who was concerned about the effect on national unity of the heavy employment of Canadian forces overseas. They also accorded with the objectives of Skelton, reserved as ever about making open-ended commitments to the United Kingdom. That the government had read the national mood aright was confirmed in the election of March 26, 1940: the Liberals were returned to power with an increased majority in the House of Commons.

As a result of the disasters that befell the allies soon after the election, culminating in the fall of France in June 1940, Canada became the second most important of Germany's enemies, after Britain. The demands on the department therefore increased, as did pressure to reassess policies based on the assumption of limited armed engagement. The department, like all agencies on the home front, responded willingly to the challenge. The under-secretary continued to provide invaluable support for the government's objectives, and his officers helped to articulate and execute policy. Yet the under-secretary's settled convictions about Canada's place in the world, particularly its North American destiny and the need for vigilance about British intentions, did not change, and he remained the unquestioned arbiter of advice prepared in the department. Nor, since he thought the department's resources were sufficient for a limited war, did the growing burden of work interest him in administrative innovation. As a result, the organizational structure remained substantially unaltered.

THE PHONY WAR

The Cabinet War Committee

While departmental organization might remain largely unaffected by war, the new circumstances would impinge on the department's place within the government. The centrepiece of the changes was the cabinet, for, although King made use of Parliament to endorse his government's actions, he did not favour frequent discussion there of the war effort any more than he had of international relations in peacetime.

The ministers responsible for the war effort continued to meet in the Emergency Council until a reorganization of cabinet committees was completed on December 5, 1939. The Emergency Council was then replaced by the Cabinet War Committee, whose "field of operation," it has been observed, "was as wide as Canada and the Canadian war effort."[2] Participation in its activities, therefore, allowed those involved, public servants as well as ministers, to shape the most important government activities of the day. From the first, the under-secretary was in regular attendance. The same was not true of senior officers of the armed forces until close to the end of the third year of the war.

The war and headquarters operations

Skelton's role as a key adviser to the government on war policy, exemplified by his involvement in the War Committee, kept his workload very heavy. His senior colleagues were similarly affected, but, because of his highly centralized mode of operation, the distribution of the burden was uneven. At the lower levels, not all areas of activity were immediately affected by the new situation, particularly before the war began in earnest overseas.

The code room, in contrast, had to respond to sharply increased pressures as soon as Canada became a belligerent. The code room had already had to deal with a greatly increased flow of telegrams during the summer. Now it had to transmit information and instructions to posts on such matters as enlistment in the armed forces and availability of transportation to repatriate Canadians stranded in Europe by the war. As well, headquarters needed more information from the posts, on a broad variety of subjects related to the conflict. Accordingly, Skelton cancelled all leave and holidays, introduced round-the-clock shifts, and reassigned clerks from other parts of the department. Even so the bottleneck remained: experienced staff lacked the time to teach newcomers how to encode and decode messages, and the operation needed reorganization to meet wartime needs. T. A. Stone returned to the department in September 1939 and spent six months in the code room adapting the service to the new level of demand.

The war and diplomatic representation

Canadian posts in Europe also had to take on new tasks as a result of the war, particularly vis-à-vis Canadians within their areas of representation. Before the conflict began, in fact, the posts had begun providing information, identity papers, and even gasmasks to expatriates.[3]

The war as well required the government to reach some early decisions about representation. The most urgent situation was in Washington, where Sir Herbert Marler had been seriously ill throughout the summer. On September 4, Beatrice Marler informed Skelton that her husband in all likelihood would not be able to resume his post. While Skelton had intended to leave the office for the time being in the hands of a chargé d'affaires, with Marler still the nominal minister, it now was impossible to do so, especially in light of Canada's imminent entry into the war.

King and Skelton were agreed that Marler's successor should be Loring Christie, the first career member of the foreign service to be named to the post. Christie had demonstrated capacity and extensive connections with influential US circles, established during his early professional life there, and longstanding association with the new British ambassador in Washington, Lord Lothian. Despite his earlier resistance to unrestricted commitments to the United Kingdom, Christie never doubted the necessity of Canadian involvement once war broke out. Thus he went to Washington fully committed to supporting the government's policies. At the same time, he was predisposed to be on guard against British attempts to present the imperial relationship to Americans in a manner not favoured by the Canadian government. This was a possibility anticipated with some apprehension in Ottawa, since Lothian was a well-known exponent of imperial solidarity, and Christie was well equipped to deal with it, on the basis of his friendship with the British ambassador.

Christie's work in Washington was interrupted twice by illness. The first lasted from mid-May until early July 1940. The second, which began on November 23 of that year, forced him to give up his post in February 1941 and caused his death in April. Partly because of these interruptions and partly because of dissatisfaction with the low profile of the Canadian legation, in contrast to Lothian's vigorous campaign to get US publicity for the British war effort, Christie came in for a good deal of public criticism at home. An unfavourable comparison was made with Marler, who, it was observed, had been a former cabinet minister as well as an experienced diplomat, and the wisdom of appointing a minister who had occupied "a subordinate position in the Department of External Affairs" was questioned.[4] In Christie's defence, it has been pointed out that the results of Lothian's publicity campaign were at best mixed and that the Canadian minister had a good record where it mattered most, in the conduct of business with officials and politicians of the host country. In so doing, he succeeded in keeping Canada's identity separate from that of the United Kingdom and thus contributed to the government's objective of avoiding a recurrence, under the pressure of war, of problems in relations with the United States arising from confusion about the imperial connection. He also gave considerable attention to the wartime needs of the legation, his principal achievement being the appointment between February and September 1940 of attachés for each of the three branches of the armed forces.[5]

Also considered important to effective prosecution of the war effort were the newly created positions of high commissioner to Australia, New Zealand, South Africa, and Ireland. All were filled by the end of 1939. Since three of the four nominees were from outside the department, they did not further Skelton's aim of using new posts to advance the prospects of the career foreign service, but he had never intended that all should be supplied from within the department.[6] In view of wartime demands on the senior public service, moreover, there was greater need than before to look to non-professionals to take charge of newly opened offices overseas.

For Canberra, the government chose Charles J. Burchell of Halifax, a former law partner of the minister of finance, J. L. Ralston. Burchell had an established interest in international affairs, especially regarding the Commonwealth and the Pacific, and he had attended the second British Commonwealth Relations Conference, organized by the Australian Institute of International Affairs, in Sydney in 1938. Australia reciprocated at this time with the appointment to Ottawa of Maj.-Gen. Sir William Glasgow, who had occupied several cabinet positions in the 1920s and who was considered to be the best of the high commissioners sent by the dominions to Canada during the war.[7] The Canadian appointment to South Africa went to Dr Henry Laureys, formerly dean of l'Ecole des Hautes

Etudes commerciales in Montreal. John Hall Kelly, a lawyer and provincial politician from Quebec City, became high commissioner to Ireland.

A career officer, Walter Riddell, counsellor in Washington, was made high commissioner to New Zealand. Having been chargé d'affaires in the US capital during Marler's illness, Riddell had been passed over in the appointment of a new minister, at least partly it seems because of the lingering effects of his handling of sanctions during the Ethiopian crisis. While Christie got along with Riddell, he was not comfortable with a possibly disappointed candidate for his own job on the staff. As well, apparently with the Ethiopian episode on his mind, Christie doubted that Riddell would be an effective member of the kind of team he wanted working for him. The minister therefore recommended a transfer, which he believed Riddell wanted. The posting to Wellington followed.[8]

While the war increased activity abroad, the situation in Geneva was the reverse, since there was little work for the League of Nations. Hume Wrong, therefore, was transferred to London as special economic adviser, to deal with matters involving trade with neutral European countries, while retaining his status as permament delegate to the League. Alfred Rive assumed charge of the mission as acting permanent representative, Wrong returning for a time in December for the assembly and other business of the League arising from the war.

Two byproducts of this round of post expansion affected the administrative procedures of the department. Both originated with Benjamin Rogers, posted to Canberra as third secretary to help open the high commissioner's office at the end of 1939. One was the cable address DOMCAN, selected in consultation with the Australian post office and later used generally for External Affairs offices abroad. (DOMINION, the cable address of the high commissioner's office in London, had already been claimed by someone else in Australia.) The other innovation was an addition (in due course required of all posts) to the monthly financial report to ensure that the accounts were properly reconciled.[9]

The war necessitated arrangements for protection of Canadian interests in enemy territory and of German interests in Canada. The United States undertook the task for Canada, as it did for the United Kingdom. The protecting power for Germany in Canada was Switzerland, which maintained a consulate general in Montreal.

Staff for the new missions abroad had to be found within the existing personnel resources of the department. Apart from accepting Stone's offer to return, Skelton took no immediate steps to augment his senior staff. Thus the department went through the build-up of activity during the phony war with only six officers, including Skelton, and forty-three support staff members at headquarters. Five heads of post, seventeen officers, and forty-seven Canada-based members of support staff served abroad.

221

Relations with the United Kingdom

Much as the government might hope to limit Canadian involvement in combat, the commitment to send troops to the United Kingdom necessitated sorting out the channels of communication. While some preliminary arrangements were made between the armed forces of the two countries, the Canadian government acted quickly to ensure civilian control over policy and avoid the dispersed authority that had characterized the Canadian presence in London in the First World War. This was achieved by greater reliance on communications through External Affairs. Communications at the service level were to be confined to "matters of detail not involving policy exchanges."[10]

Throughout the war, King and the department continued to use the arrangements for direct communication with the Dominions Office and the prime minister in London, even on trivial matters. Although this caused dissatisfaction in Canada House, especially early in the war, the high commissioners' offices were increasingly taking over the substantive traffic. Certainly the need to respond to the demands of war brought an end to many of the restrictions that Ottawa had imposed on Massey's activities in London.[11] There was now no question, for example, about his participation in meetings between the British and the representatives of the other dominions. The high commissioner, moreover, took more risks in his dealings with Ottawa than he would have assumed earlier. This was clear from his handling of one of Canada's most important contributions to the allied war effort, the British Commonwealth Air Training Plan.

The idea of training Commonwealth pilots in Canada had come up before the war, but the plan as implemented began with an initiative by Massey and his Australian colleague, Stanley Bruce, after the outbreak of hostilities. Massey assisted in drafting the telegram in which the British prime minister, Neville Chamberlain, made the proposal to King, thereby ensuring that it was couched so as to elicit a favourable reception. Massey knew that he was taking a chance in so acting and wondered what King would say "if he knew I helped to write what he receives!"[12] Fortunately for the plan, the prime minister did not find out until after the war.

At the time, King responded positively, although prolonged negotiations were required before agreement on all points was reached, at the end of the year. These proceeded under King's close control and with his active participation. Skelton was closely involved from the first, the prime minister having instructed him and Heeney to draft the reply to Chamberlain. The under-secretary was the point of contact in Ottawa for the British high commissioner and attended most of the cabinet committee meetings concerned with the implementation of the plan. He also was a member of the Canadian group dealing with the British and Commonwealth negotiating team that began work in Ottawa on October 14. Skelton was not the only go-between, however, for Heeney also served as a conduit between Canadian ministers and the negotiators from overseas.

Talks about the air training plan were closely bound up with the arrangement of other aspects of the wartime economic relationship with the United Kingdom. These were the subject of discussions that the British proposed to hold in London in the autumn of 1939 with ministerial representatives of the dominions. King agreed to send the minister of mines and resources, T. A. Crerar, "solely for the purpose of consultation, coordination and cooperation."[13] The British accepted this position, and both governments issued carefully worded press releases setting out the basis of the consultations in the terms desired by Canada.

In explaining to Chamberlain his position concerning the Crerar mission, King made it clear that he regarded the emerging network of high commissioners' offices as the preferred means of consultation among members of the Commonwealth. Thus Canada House rather than ministerial visits came to be looked upon as the ongoing medium for dealing with the subjects in Crerar's brief, that is "questions of supply and economic defence generally." "We consider it desirable, in order to ensure effective coordination of effort," Chamberlain was told, "that officers assigned to such work should act under the general supervision of the High Commissioner."[14]

Insistence on the use of Canada House did not imply that all the officers working under Massey's jurisdiction must be from External Affairs. From the first, it was recognized that wartime needs demanded participation of specialists from other departments. For the subjects covered by Crerar's mission, for example, the Canadian government had in mind using representatives of the departments of Trade and Commerce and of Agriculture stationed in Britain. This possibility does not seem to have been troubling to Massey, who had never lacked confidence in his ability to co-ordinate the work of the various departments represented in London. Indeed, he well knew the need for expertise in wartime dealings with the British and recommended that it be enhanced.

"Crerar and I," Massey informed Ottawa on November 1, "both feel that as problems of finance bulk very large in all the questions under consideration it would have been of great value if our special problems under the head of finance could have been expressed by a member privately representing the Department of Finance at Ottawa or the Bank of Canada. The United Kingdom Treasury will certainly be represented in all such committees here."[15] Soon afterward, Crerar's team was strengthened by the addition of the director of commercial intelligence at Trade and Commerce, Dana Wilgress, and the governor of the Bank of Canada, Graham Towers. Massey and others from the high commissioner's office continued to attend Crerar's meetings with the British but could rely on these experts to take the lead on technical matters.

New wartime responsibilities

In Ottawa, meanwhile, growth in the workload came not so much from the demands of policy making as from the practical aspects of belligerency. There were many legal problems, related to the movement and treatment of aliens in Canada, the interests of Canadians abroad, and recruitment by allied governments, for service in their own armed forces, of their ex-nationals in this country. There were also various economic activities, involving export controls and procurement of supplies. The result was substantial expansion of hitherto modest responsibilities or the addition of new ones. As in the past, some of these fell outside the mandate of a foreign office. In taking them on, the department was helping to fill a gap in the structure of the Canadian government: no single department handled many of the domestic responsibilities performed by Britain's Home Office.[16]

The department's new duties were not entirely divorced from its conventional functions. Out of its responsibility for relations with foreign states came involvement in regulations affecting enemy or neutral aliens. Under the defence-of-Canada regulations, the minister of justice had practically unlimited power to intern. Just days before the war began, the Royal Canadian Mounted Police indicated its intention to seize consular archives, with a view to outlawing and suppressing not only those identified with the declared enemy but members of eastern European ethnic groups and communists as well. Norman Robertson, who handled liaison between the department and the RCMP, was "appalled" by this prospect and warned Skelton that it

> involved a great deal of bitter inter-racial resentment and the prospect of endless labour troubles throughout industrial and mining areas, as well as the alienation of the sympathy and support of great blocs of opinion which, if properly handled, could be led to support any efforts the Government was making rather than to oppose them. I thought the Police should concentrate on their plans for the immediate arrest of persons suspected of treasonable activity, and that they would be ill-advised to destroy organizations about which they now know a good deal and with whose personnel they are familiar. It would drive them underground.[17]

The department could act on these precepts, since it became involved in dealing with complaints from wartime internees. In the view of Skelton and Robertson, evidence of subversive ideology or activity, not merely previous nationality, should be the justification for internment. Criticism of the government, they contended, was not necessarily seditious just because it came from radical sources.[18]

The RCMP's investigations reached into the department itself when, in August 1940, the commissioner of the force raised questions about an officer, Escott Reid, who had received from Moscow a bulletin describing publications on Communist propaganda. "Receipt of a book publisher's circulars," Skelton told the commissioner, "could hardly be considered to indicate an intention to buy, much less an indication of sympathy with the doctrines, though as a matter of fact several of the books listed in this case are well-known writings with which any one desiring a thorough knowledge of European forces and trends would have to be familiar." Skelton rightly pointed out that "Mr. Reid is one of the most valuable members of our Service and a man in whom we have complete confidence."[19]

The department's work with suspected subversives and enemy aliens went beyond questions of interpretation. Robertson took an interest in enemy aliens unable to find employment and in modifying the terms in which the status was defined. One result of his efforts was the eventual revocation of the regulation under which British subjects of former German and Italian nationality were automatically treated as enemy aliens even though their actions showed that they were fully behind the Canadian war effort.[20]

The department's involvement in questions of economic warfare, such as contraband, blacklisting, and the handling of enemy ships in Canadian ports, was also related to its function as the channel of communication with other governments. On September 14, 1939, the Advisory Committee on Economic Policy, composed of senior officials, was established to assist the cabinet in directing the government's wartime economic activities. Robertson, one of the acknowledged public-service experts on its subject-matter, was departmental representative.

While the department's wartime responsibilities were thus accumulating, at home and abroad, it was still possible to accommodate some time-consuming distractions from urgent business. One such occurred in London as an unpleasant offshoot of Alice Massey's interest in providing rest and recreation facilities for Canadian troops being sent overseas. Almost immediately tension developed between a women's committee headed by Alice Massey and a London advisory committee of the Canadian Red Cross, operating under the aegis of R. B. Bennett, now residing in Britain, where he was elevated to the peerage in June 1941. The resultant feud, embittered by the Masseys' resentment of Bennett's withdrawal of their original assignment to London in 1930, ended in dispersal of the women's committee and bad relations between Canada House and resident Canadians.

"Most diplomats," Massey observed sourly, "regard their local colony as a perennial problem, and I wonder if any of them have difficulties comparable to those created by the Canadian community here." He and his wife, however, soon recovered their equilibrium, and Alice Massey went on to establish three highly successful institutions for use by the Canadian forces in Britain during the war: the Beaver Club, in London, for non-commissioned members of the services (and men from other Commonwealth countries as well); an officers' club, also in London; and a convalescent hospital for officers, in the countryside.[21]

THE BLITZKRIEG

The phony war ended in the spring of 1940. In April and May, the Germans occupied Denmark, Norway, the Netherlands, Belgium, and Luxemburg. By June they controlled part of France and the remainder of that country was in the hands of a pro-German government under Marshal Henri Philippe Pétain, with its capital at Vichy. While the German armies stopped at the English Channel the air force did not. Britain itself was in peril and subject to savage bombing in the autumn of 1940. In the mean time, Chamberlain, his policies discredited by the collapse of allied fortunes on the continent, resigned as prime minister on May 10, to be succeeded by Winston Churchill, the foremost critic of Britain's lack of preparedness in the years before the war.

The closing of posts in Europe

German successes in western Europe required the closing of diplomatic and other offices maintained by the Canadian government in the countries affected. Although Switzerland remained neutral, the mission in Geneva was also closed down because of fears of German occupation.

The evacuation of personnel from enemy territory was not a task for which External Affairs was well prepared. Officials in Ottawa, like many of their counterparts in the defeated governments, had anticipated that the Maginot line along the Franco-German frontier would withstand the onslaught if Germany should turn toward the west. Warnings to the contrary had not produced contingency plans for Canadian posts. Even when the enemy was on the march, the department was reluctant to order withdrawal, for fear of harming morale in the host countries. "Safety of personnel is undoubtedly first consideration," Skelton acknowledged in a cable to The Hague in April 1940, "but it is also necessary to take into account possible repercussions on local and foreign opinion of any sudden departure of Canadian officials unless urgency is established."[22]

At the last minute, all was confusion. The minister in Brussels, Jean Désy, for example, followed the Belgian government to France, finding accommodation in farms and abandoned houses along the escape route. Then, having been warned to avoid entanglement in Poitiers, where the Belgian government was briefly located, he left for Portugal. Others took refuge in France, making their way to the coast and thence to the comparative safety of Britain. Some Canadian government employees were not so fortunate. Rumours abounded of their entrapment in the German advance, and hopes for rescue with the British troops evacuated from Dunkirk were disappointed. Fifty-eight employees of the government, including some trade commissioners, remained in enemy or enemy-occupied countries at the end of 1940.[23]

While all Canadian diplomatic staff members escaped from the continent, their journeys were arduous. Their experience was described by Pearson, who met the chargé d'affaires in The Hague, Kenneth Kirkwood, and other diplomatic evacuees after their voyage across the channel to Britain:

They looked tired, unkempt and unshaven and were pretty nearly all in. They had been bombed and machine-gunned on the way over, both on land and while they were on the destroyer. Scenes in The Hague around Kenneth's home were fantastic in the extreme. Parachutists landed close by and Fifth Column Nazis suddenly appeared out of buildings and adjoining Dutch Government Offices. Kenneth said that he was not able to leave the house at all because firing was going on all over the city. When they did get away they were only given half an hour's notice, when it seemed clear that The Hague would soon be cut off. As a result they got nothing away except the clothes they were wearing.[24]

The response of headquarters did not make these tribulations easier to bear. Because the chief clerk, Agnes McCloskey, continued to enforce rigorously the frugal regime she had introduced many years earlier, Kirkwood did not expect compensation for replacement of essential clothing. Nor, by contrast with the Department of Trade and Commerce, did External Affairs offer a formal expression of relief about the successful escape of staff from the continent.[25]

The speed of the German advance and the department's lack of preparation, meanwhile, immediately increased the workload, for the abrupt departure of Canadian staff had left behind myriad administrative and jurisdictional problems. Missing personal effects had to be found and keys located for the safes in the immigration office in Antwerp; there were arrangements to be made with the US authorities to move the contents of property rented by the Public Archives of Canada in Paris to the former British embassy; the dismissed locally engaged staff of the Commercial Intelligence Service had to be paid; and so on. All these questions required extensive correspondence before they were resolved or an impasse was reached.

Canada House during the blitz

At Canada House, there had to be adjustments to the austerity of war and the perils of the blitz. The Masseys made theirs with panache, giving up their house and moving into the Dorchester Hotel, a favourite of important residents of wartime London, which had its own air-raid shelter. At the office the changes, as described by Pearson, were more mundane, but none the less essential for work to be carried on with at least rudimentary precaution:

> So far, Canada House has been fortunate. We have had two high-explosive bombs—both at night—so near that it is surprising they did not shatter parts of the building. But they have only smashed some of our windows and thrown parts of the road on the roof! . . .
>
> Of course our work is interrupted during the day by alarms—in fact this letter has already been the victim of such an interruption and I have just returned to continue it from our shelter. In the early days of bombing, we issued orders that when the sirens were sounded all employees on the top and most vulnerable floor were to go to the shelter and a proportion of those on the lower floors. This, however, caused altogether too much interruption in our work, and in co-operation with Canadian Military Headquarters we have now a new system in effect. When the sirens sound, roofspotters, one of them from Canada House—we all take this duty in turn—go on duty at once and all other employees remain working. If the roof spotters see enemy planes approaching, or hear gunfire or bombs in the neighbourhood, they press a button which sounds an alarm throughout the building. On the second alarm all employees go to the shelter. This means that now we spend about four-fifths of the time during a raid at work. However, this system is not altogether satisfactory, since the Germans have started sending over single aeroplanes in daylight who take advantage of cloud and mist, glide down from a great height and drop bombs without any warning of any kind. Two or three times in the last week—and in fact only half an hour ago—our first warning that the second alarm was necessary took the form of a bomb whistling down from the air. I am afraid there is no completely satisfactory solution for this problem, but we do our

best to reconcile the necessity for carrying on our work with a reasonable regard for the safety of personnel.

Some of our personnel have already suffered from bombs, though fortunately we have had no casualties. Two or three of the members of our staff have lost their homes and others have had property damage of one kind or another. Some of our staff who have been living in particularly vulnerable areas have been sleeping in the shelters, which helps them and also helps us as we have thereby persons on duty night and day.

A good many of our girls are having extremely difficult times under present conditions. One can never be sure of having gas, water or heat these days. In fact, you are extremely lucky if you have. Life under such circumstances, especially when one is living alone, can be a pretty grim and depressing affair, and it speaks a great deal for the pluck and character of our girls who are working here that they keep so cheerful, in spite of everything. You would be proud of them.[26]

As with the response to the evacuation from Europe, Ottawa did little to maintain the spirits described by Pearson. A collection made in the East Block for Canada House at Christmas in 1940 was an undoubtedly welcome expression of warmth. At the same time, however, it was announced that, as a result of the war, the Civil Service Commission had frozen all but the most urgent promotions and that, since there was likely to be less entertaining, allowances would be reduced.

Relations with allied governments and with France

London became the home also of the missions accredited to Belgium, France, and the Netherlands. For the Canadian government, representation in unoccupied France was a complex political problem: Pétain's regime was unpopular in English Canada, because of its relationship with Germany, but gained credibility in Quebec from its claim to embody enduring French values. The example of the United States, which maintained an embassy at Vichy, was a further argument for continuing diplomatic relations.

Canada did not establish a resident office at Vichy, but neither did it break formally with the French government. The minister, Georges Vanier, returned to Canada but did not give up his title. The first secretary of the legation, Pierre Dupuy, became chargé d'affaires but performed the function from an office in London. He acted similarly for Belgium and the Netherlands, which had established governments in exile in the British capital. As a corollary, the offices in Canada representing Belgium, France, and the Netherlands remained open. In the autumn of 1940, the Canadian government agreed to recognize a provisional government of Czechoslovakia, also based in London, and to accept the consul general in Montreal as its representative in Canada.

As chargé d'affaires, Dupuy had legitimate reasons to travel to Vichy France to see to Canadian interests. This he did, at the request of the British (who had no accredited representative), on three occasions between November 1940 and August 1941, the real reason being to report on conditions and to assess the possibility of support for the allied side.[27]

New posts

Also affecting Canadian representation abroad was the status of overseas possessions, not under enemy control, of the defeated states in western Europe. Of particular importance to Canada was the future of Greenland, a dependency of Denmark. The island was a near neighbour and the source of cryolite, an esssential ingredient in the manufacture of aluminum.

Under pressure from the Aluminum Co. of Canada, the Canadian government seriously considered sending "a small defence force" to Greenland to protect the cryolite mines, guard against establishment of a German submarine base, and help maintain supply lines for the inhabitants. This project was supported by Skelton, Keenleyside, and the Department of National Defence. Although King had some doubts about it, it was discussed with the US and British governments. The latter gave enthusiastic support, but there were strong objections in Washington, where it was argued that the proposed Canadian action might provide a pretext for Japanese occupation of the Netherlands East Indies. While the US position was persuasive with Ottawa, there was need to monitor the situation in Greenland, and it was felt that, for reasons of "national prestige," the task could not be left entirely to the United States. The solution was similar to that adopted by the United States: dispatch of a coastal vessel carrying supplies (and a few weapons) to Greenland and establishment of a consulate, the first such office to be opened by Canada. Kenneth Kirkwood, former chargé d'affaires in The Hague, was appointed consul, with A. V. Porsild, a Danish-speaking officer of Mines and Resources, who had visited Greenland before, as vice-consul. They took up residence at Ivigtut, near the cryolite mines, and later moved to Godthaab, seat of the governor of the Southern District and the island's wartime administrative centre.[28]

German successes in western Europe also renewed the opportunity to achieve Skelton's ambition for representation in Latin America. The justification was the need to penetrate new markets to make up for the loss of those in Europe and to gain sure access to supplies necessary for the war effort. King still required persuasion. In August 1940, he suggested deferring any diplomatic appointments in "a trouble zone" until after the war: the Canadian interest in trade and war supplies could be met by augmenting the six trade commissioners already in the area with consular appointments. Skelton countered that "quasi-diplomatic standing" would be anomalous for Canadian consuls once the countries where they resided had opened legations in Ottawa; only diplomatic representatives could make formal representations to foreign governments, and, with the complex trade controls prevailing in Latin America at the time, British representatives should not be asked to act on Canada's behalf. To Skelton's advantage was the wartime situation and a surplus in the department's estimates, which made it unnecessary to ask Parliament for additional funds to open the new missions. In October 1940, King agreed to establishment of legations in Rio de Janeiro and Buenos Aires.[29]

While Désy was happy to go to Brazil, it was more difficult to find someone for Argentina. Because of the high cost of living in Buenos Aires, career diplomats found existing allowances inadequate, and some departmental candidates were unwilling to serve in a small, new post in a part of the world hitherto of little interest to the department.[30] In September 1941 King finally found a suitable appointee in W. F. A. Turgeon, chief justice of Saskatchewan. In May and June of that year, Brazil and Argentina respectively had opened legations in Ottawa.

The League of Nations and the ILO

While these changes were taking place, one former representational requirement, that arising from membership of the League of Nations, could be allowed to lapse altogether. After the German invasion of western Europe, the League's headquarters in Geneva became virtually inactive, and much of the remaining staff of the secretariat was transferred to temporary quarters in the Institute of Advanced Study in Princeton, New Jersey.

In the summer of 1940, arrangements were made for the International Labour Organisation to move to Montreal, where accommodation was provided at McGill University. The director, John Winant, an American, would have preferred to go to the United States, but, when this proved impossible to accomplish, he settled on Canada. Hume Wrong, still the official Canadian representative on the ILO's Governing Body after his transfer to London and on good terms with Winant, assisted with the arrangements. Montreal apparently was chosen in preference to other Canadian cities because of Winant's friendship with Dr Wilder Penfield, head of the Montreal Neurological Institute, who secured the co-operation of Cyril James, principal of McGill. Satisfactory terms for the organization's relocation, however, depended on the co-operation of the interested departments in Ottawa, External Affairs and Labour, which received warm tribute from the deputy director, Edward Phelan, in 1941.[31]

Wartime recruitment

The decisions taken in 1939 and 1940 to open and close posts produced a net increase of four. This in turn created a demand for more junior staff, which was met by a substantial recruitment of new officers in 1940 and 1941. Fifteen entered the foreign service by competitive examination in those years: P. A. Beaulieu, A. B. M. Bell, Marcel Cadieux, R. E. Collins, C. C. Eberts, R. A. D. Ford, G. W. Hilborn, George Ignatieff, Jules Léger, A. R. Menzies, A. J. Pick, S. F. Rae, R. G. Robertson, Gilles Sicotte, and Paul Tremblay. One-third of the number was francophone, a marked increase over the position in the late pre-war years. Two, Collins and Menzies, had been born in China. One, Ignatieff, was from outside the Anglo-Saxon and francophone mainstreams of the Canadian population. Not all at first enjoyed the rank of third secretary. Because nothing had been done to increase the officer establishment of External Affairs before a ban on new positions was imposed, some had to begin as principal clerks.[32]

The Passport Office

An unexpected demand for new officers arose as a result of problems in the Passport Office. With the outbreak of war in 1939, it had been assumed that fewer Canadians would be travelling and the staff of the Passport Office therefore had been reduced from fourteen to six through transfers and layoffs. Then, on June 6, 1940, the US government, concerned, as a result of recent events in Europe, about fifth columnists gaining easy access, suddenly announced that, as of July 1, Canadians crossing the border would require passports and visas. Since an estimated 500,000 Canadians entered the United States each year, the problem created was immense. Barriers were suddenly erected at ports of entry and tens of thousands of impatient travellers, including, on one occasion, the driver of a hearse, created chaos at the turnstiles. In Ottawa, a special eight-page passport, for travel to the United States only, was hastily prepared. A temporary staff numbering 113 was recruited from the civil service lists and quickly put to work in the premises occupied by the Passport Office at 38 Bank Street, a dismal place at the best of times and now crowded with the new arrivals.[33] Recently recruited foreign service officers were hastily dispatched to open regional passport offices in St Stephen, Montreal, Toronto, Sault Ste Marie, and Vancouver. There they remained until the following year, when the demand for passports began to decline as a result of foreign-exchange controls, and newly trained passport officers became available to take charge of operations outside Ottawa.[34]

The department in 1940

Because of recent recruitment, there were in the summer of 1940 13 officers at headquarters (including Skelton but not those on the prime minister's staff) and 220 clerical staff members, an increase of 182 in one year. In spite of the influx, the department continued to operate as it had before the war, without any change in organizational structure. When an officer joined the department or returned from a posting, he might be left for a couple of weeks to find his way around before Skelton gave him a mixture of assignments, in all likelihood consisting of tasks hitherto unassigned or matters that for one reason or another had not received the attention they required. Thus the workload remained disproportionately heavy at the higher levels while some on the junior staff were underemployed.

In an effort to deal with this problem, Keenleyside started on a scheme for organizing the department's work along lines of operational responsibility. In doing so, he encountered the problem of overlapping activities that had always bedevilled attempts to formalize departmental structure. Thus Keeleyside had difficulty deciding which division should handle air force files involving acquisition of US material and personnel for transfer to the United Kingdom. His solution was to treat the subject as a functional rather than a geographical responsibility, thereby making it possible to assign it to a single officer.

Keenleyside's achievement was limited to reorganization of his own "General Division" of three officers handling North American and Far Eastern affairs and publicity. In defining the duties of the officers, he made it clear who had to be consulted, and on what subjects.[35] Skelton, in contrast, never undertook a wholesale restructuring of the department along these lines. Instead, he added new activities to the established responsibilities of senior officers, who were given some help from newcomers. With the addition of new third secretaries, Skelton observed, "we have been able to organize the work to better advantage by assigning one or two secretaries to each senior officer. Even with the additions, they are all extremely busy, but the work is done more quickly and more effectively."[36]

With Skelton maintaining his close scrutiny of policy recommendations going forward to ministers, there was no marked change in established departmental positions. Thus the wariness toward closer association with the British continued, resulting, in Pearson's view, in the exclusion of Canada from allied policy-making generally. "So far as policy and planning in this war are concerned," he wrote to the minister of national defence, "our status is little better than that of a colony. We have practically no influence on decisions and little prior information concerning them. . . . A very important meeting of the [Supreme War] Council took place last Saturday but we have not yet received information as to what took place at that meeting; neither has North Borneo." Pearson had a number of suggestions for improvement, including insistence on the right to attend meetings of the British War Cabinet when matters of Canadian participation were being discussed,[37] but these were out of step with opinion in Ottawa.

The Canadian government was also unenthusiastic about consultation through a meeting of Commonwealth prime ministers. The British suggested such a gathering late in 1940, but King thought it unnecessary. In the war of 1914–18, he argued, lack of alternative means of consultation might have necessitated the premiers of the self-governing colonies gathering in London. Now, however, each dominion had its own department of external affairs, high commissioners, cable, cypher, and overseas telephones. Communications could thus be directed between prime ministers or through the network provided by the high commissioners' offices, their home departments, and the Dominions Office. To Massey, King observed that "the visit from time to time of ministers dealing with especially important aspects of coordination of effort [such as the Crerar mission had done], supplementing the regular system of information and consultation would appear to be fully adequate."[38] To a later suggestion for a Commonwealth meeting, he responded: "What I am more doubtful about is whether, in terms of hard fact, there is anything that we could accomplish in conference together in London that we cannot do more effectively and much more expeditiously by continuous exchange of views between our several posts of duty."[39]

There was greater interest, again in conformity with Skelton's established priorities, in discussions with the United States, made the more urgent by the increased danger to North America resulting from the German position in western Europe. Representation of the Canadian interest in Washington was complicated by the illness of Christie in 1940. A substitute was provided by Keenleyside, who made four visits to Washington between May 19 and June 7 as the prime minister's personal emissary for discussions with Roosevelt and senior members of his administration. After Christie's recovery, the legation became the usual vehicle for dealing with US authorities and the British embassy.

The most important development in Canadian-US relations arose from discussions between Roosevelt and King at Ogdensburg, New York, in August 1940. They agreed on a new body, the Permanent Joint Board on Defence (PJBD), to deal with the shared interest in North American defence. The achievement at Ogdensburg owed a good deal to the personal relationship between Roosevelt and King: the latter took no advisers with him, and his briefing seems to have been limited to a list of required military equipment provided by J. L. Ralston, who had become minister of national defence in June.

The PJBD was established at the operational level, with each country eventually naming six members. Most were from the services, but there was also civilian representation. For the United States, this was provided from the outset by Fiorello LaGuardia, mayor of New York and president of the US Council of Mayors, who, Roosevelt believed, "was well liked in Canada, and had had large experience in matters of the kind to be considered."[40] J. D. Hickerson of the US State Department (consul in Ottawa 1925-27 and assistant chief 1930-44 of the Division of European Affairs, which dealt with Canada) was secretary of the US section. External Affairs provided the civilian member on the Canadian side, Keenleyside. Since he was also the Canadian secretary, the department could anticipate heavy involvement in the board's work.

THE LEGACY OF SKELTON

Although required by the exigencies of war to compromise some of his principles, Skelton could take considerable satisfaction from the course of policy followed by the government, after as well as before the reverses suffered by the allies in Europe in the spring of 1940. Although he and King had not been entirely in accord over Greenland, their relationship was not upset by the type of open disagreement that had sometimes characterized it in the late 1930s. King indeed called on Skelton more and more for advice and was well aware of both the burden imposed and the willingness with which it was borne. "I have known no man with a sense of duty greater than Skelton," the prime minister wrote on February 1, 1940, "or who took on tasks more willingly and with less complaint. I am afraid that he will not be able to stand very long further indefinite strain."[41] Thereafter, notwithstanding King's concern about the possible consequences for the under-secretary, the workload continued to grow. Skelton was required, for example, to give attention to the dominion-provincial conference on the financial relationship between the two levels of government, which assembled in Ottawa on January 14, 1941, as well as to be available whenever King required him to discuss a speech or a telegram.

At this time, Skelton may well have been at the height of his influence, for the policies he supported had contributed to one of King's greatest successes, the election victory of 1940. He had a special relationship with the prime minister not only as deputy minister of the department that was King's direct responsibility but also as a trusted confidant. He was someone on whom King could test ideas, secure in the knowledge that, while Skelton would speak his mind, he had a keen sense of political reality and therefore would offer sound guidance.[42] As well, King could be certain of confidentiality and of loyal execution of policy decisions, even if they went against Skelton's recommendations.

Placing the trust he did in Skelton, King was disinclined to turn elsewhere for advice and support. The under-secretary never resisted any assignment, and, since he remained unwilling to delegate ultimate responsibility for much of his dossier, there was unrelieved pressure on a constitution already weakened by heart trouble. The strain was evident to others, but Skelton ignored medical advice to slow down. Suddenly the burden became too much. On January 28, 1941, at the age of sixty-two, Skelton suffered a heart attack while returning to his office after a quick lunch and died at the wheel of his car.

The death of Skelton was a grievous blow for the prime minister. "There is no question, " he wrote in his diary on the day it happened, "that so far as I am personally concerned, it is the most serious loss thus far sustained in my public life and work." There was now a vacuum at the centre of King's life as prime minister and secretary of state for external affairs. "I shall miss him particularly," he reflected later, "in not having one, outside the Cabinet, with whom I can talk over matters generally." Yet it had not taken King long to recall his wariness about becoming overly dependent on any counsellor, even one as close as Skelton. Searching for a lesson from the event, he observed on January 28 that the under-secretary's passing might "be meant to cause me to rely more completely on my own judgment in making decisions and to acquaint myself more meticulously with all that is happening so as to be able to meet each demand as it is occasioned." Three days later, as he was inclined to do, he reprimanded himself for "not concentrating more on work and perhaps mastering more myself, not trusting too greatly to the outside aides."[43]

The loss of Skelton was felt not just by the prime minister but by the public service and the government as a whole. Other ministers besides himself, King was aware, "not infrequently sought and received the invaluable assistance of his thoughtful intelligence. He was, as it were, the elder statesman in the Civil Service of Canada, trusted and honoured by all who knew him."[44] Thus he occupied, in the words of Wrong, "a permanent place in the Government which no one can fill."[45] His advice was sought on most major advances in government policy and also on the shaping and direction of many departments in addition to his own. As a result, according to the deputy minister of finance, Clifford Clark, he was responsible for "the enhancement of the power and prestige of the Canadian Civil Service of which he was so universally recognized as the leader, without peer."[46] In the judgment of the influential journalist Grant Dexter, in fact, Skelton was "actually . . . the deputy prime minister of Canada. . . . Down the years it became the custom of ministers, members of parliament and civil servants to turn to him for advice. When problems seemed completely unmanageable—no matter what kind of problems they happened to be—someone would hit on the happy idea of deferring the decision until Dr. Skelton had been consulted.''[47]

Skelton's activity outside his own mandate was part of his legacy to his department, which for many years continued to be a source of advice to the government and of personnel for special tasks, domestic as well as international, not normally within the purview of a foreign office. But his contribution was much greater, for the department as it existed in 1941 was his creation. So closely identified was he with the character of the department that the *New York Times* on January 29 described him as the first under-secretary, completely overlooking Sir Joseph Pope's sixteen years in the post.

Prominent among the achievements mentioned in comment on Skelton's death was the creation of a first-class foreign service.[48] Including Christie and the early wartime recruits of 1940 and 1941 (but not politically appointed heads of post), forty-three officers entered the department, mostly by competitive examination, after Skelton became under-secretary. Remarkable stability had been maintained: only one of his recruits had left permanently at the time of his death. In terms of education and previous experience abroad, the officer corps was highly qualified. Twenty-six had studied in the United Kingdom, nineteen of them at Oxford or Cambridge and nine on Rhodes scholarlships. Twelve had attended universities in the United States and ten in France. With twelve francophone officers, there was an approximate reflection of the balance between the two largest elements in the Canadian population, though in some respects the service was not at all characteristic of the country it represented. The language of work had become even more exclusively English than formerly, as a result of the closing of the legations in Paris and Brussels. Other ethnic groups were underrepresented: only two officers were from neither the anglophone nor the francophone community, and the service was entirely male.

Skelton did not leave the department with a sophisticated organizational structure, and so the training of junior officers was left to chance and they were often underemployed. Yet he did encourage them to make use of their intelligence and education: the approach he favoured to the work was thoughtful, thorough, and scholarly. These qualities were to be applied within a well-understood attitudinal framework. Part of that was Skelton's concept of the public servant, as source of frank advice, keeper of confidences, and loyal executor of policy, whether or not one's recommendations were accepted.

The other part of the framework was Skelton's view of Canada's position as an autonomous nation with interests unique to itself. During Skelton's lifetime, the imperial relationship had provided the context within which those interests were identified and advanced. By the time of his death, the context was changing, but the commitment to a foreign policy based on indigenous concerns remained. The department would have to develop new mechanisms and policies to meet changing requirements, but in doing so it would have the benefit of the human resources and the fundamental principles bequeathed to it by Skelton.

Chapter Nine
Adjusting to New Demands: 1941–1943

A NEW UNDER-SECRETARY

The appointment of Norman Robertson

NOT LEAST OF SKELTON'S BEQUESTS to the department was the strength of the senior ranks, which contained several suitable candidates (although no obvious successor) for the post of under-secretary. Thus there was no need, as there had been when Pope retired, to go outside the service for a new permanent head. The prime minister's first inclination was to appoint Loring Christie. He, however, had been hospitalized for two months, and medical reports revealed a rapidly deteriorating heart condition from which he was not expected to recover. The alternative was to choose from among Skelton's recruits of the late 1920s.

On paper, the most obvious candidate was the assistant under-secretary, Laurent Beaudry, who had assumed control during Skelton's recent absences. Beaudry, however, did not want the job, nor was he judged to have strong qualifications for the type of leadership the department required. His specialty was in matters of protocol and procedures rather than policy. The legal adviser, John Read, was also excluded. The quality of his legal mind had earned him great respect in both External Affairs and Justice, but he lacked experience in the economic and political fields that had been so important to Skelton's work.

Ranking behind these senior candidates were Keenleyside, Pearson, Robertson, and Wrong. The last, though abundantly endowed with the technical and intellectual qualifications for the post, suffered from a reputation for abrasiveness, a major negative consideration in the mind of the prime minister. Keenleyside had demonstrated his managerial skills in Tokyo and in the organization of the royal tour of 1939 but had fallen out of favour by persistently defending the interests of Japanese Canadians in British Columbia at a time when the political situation there made his position unpopular. Pearson, although likely to work well with ministers and other politicians, was an ocean away in London.

Robertson, in contrast, was present in Ottawa. His work as a trade negotiator had impressed the prime minister, he had avoided controversies that might put him at odds with politicians, and his manner was conciliatory. Thus, although at thirty-seven he was the youngest and most junior of the candidates and had neither pressed for nor expected the appointment, Robertson was chosen by King to take charge of the department immediately as acting under-secretary. His permanent tenure of the position was confirmed on June 24, 1941, with a salary increase of $4,000 per year (nearly doubling his previous rate of $6,000), retroactive to Skelton's death.

An idealist with leftward inclinations at the time he entered the department, Robertson had developed over his years of service a shrewd appreciation of political realities. This quality, combined with a self-effacing temperament, counted for much in getting along with King and adapting to his unpredictable work habits. Robertson, in other words, brought to the job many of the qualities that King had valued in Skelton. There was one important difference, however: Robertson had not been part of the pre-war group reluctant to make commitments overseas. The prospect, therefore, was for departmental leadership more directed to seeking opportunities for taking initiatives in international affairs.

As the youngest and the most junior of the candidates, Robertson was in a rather delicate position arising from the disappointment of the others. Perhaps because he at first had the office only in an acting capacity, however, this did not in fact cause problems. Robertson, acknowledged Wrong, "has in his hands more of the many threads which passed through Skelton's office than anyone else and his choice is intelligent as a temporary measure."[1]

Robertson himself was taken by surprise by the promotion and concerned about the managerial responsibilities involved. "The job," he wrote to his parents,

is a big one and calls for a number of qualities I simply have not got. . . . My senior colleagues without exception will be helpful—the P.M. is encouraging—but I dislike very much assuming so much responsibility in unfamiliar fields—and my inability to organize my own work is an ominous note for a department desperately in need of organization. Policy is not such a worry as personnel and the two questions are unfortunately not separable as matters stand. . . . Technically I suppose I have made a good promotion but feel pretty bleak and miserable about it.[2]

His introduction to his new responsibilities revealed that Skelton's burdens had become heavier than even those close to him in the department had realized. "It's only when you start taking an inventory," Robertson told Pearson, "that you realize what a range of responsiblities he took—and how we all lived and worked secure in the shadow of a great rock—. . . we unloaded—ultimately—almost every worry on him."[3]

Reorganization

At the time Robertson became under-secretary, the senior ranks in the department had been reinforced by Wrong's return to Ottawa, in early 1941. Wrong was soon posted again to Washington, his place at head-quarters being taken by Pearson. Along with Keenleyside, Pearson was to have the title (without any increase in pay) of assistant under-secretary. The responsibilities assigned to these positions were still undefined, and Pearson regarded the prospect with limited enthusiasm. "Of course," he confided to his diary, "I don't like the idea really of going back to the Department, except as Under-Secretary, and I am not quite sure what this post of Joint Assistant Under-Secretary means. My own view is that it means that Mr. King wants Norman Robertson as a sort of super personal assistant and is going to give him the rank of Under-Secretary for that reason, while I am to be brought back to do the work that the Under-Secretary would normally be doing, without being given the rank."[4]

Pearson's comment pointed to a need for reconsideration of the department's structure. Specific encouragement was provided by the lesson of Skelton's sudden death from overwork. Thus Wrong and Keenleyside, quite independent of each other, began preparing schemes for relieving "the intolerable heavy pressure" on the under-secretary.[5]

Wrong, like Keenleyside, had an appreciation of administrative efficiency, acquired while administering army camps after injuries had removed him from active service in the First World War and expressed over the years in various proposals for improvements in departmental operations. Now he turned his attention to the long-standing problem of dealing with both geographical and functional responsibilities. He suggested a mixture of geographical and functional divisions, the chiefs of which would sign routine correspondence and would provide a flow of information to the posts engaged in activities of interest to them. To maintain clear lines of demarcation, each division would retain its own registry of files, and office space would be assigned according to the divisional responsibility rather than the rank of the occupant. He also recommended a division that would prepare summaries and reviews of broad issues, such as war aims and peace terms, for the Cabinet War Committee.

Keenleyside's plan, like Wrong's, was based on "the rational principles . . . that subjects of like quality or inherent relationship should be grouped together, and . . . that there should be as clear a distinction as possible between the different units of the organization."[6] The proposed new structure involved only one assistant under-secretary, a legal adviser, four geographical divisions (American, Far Eastern, Europe, and Commonwealth and Empire), and six functional divisions (Administration, Consular, Legal, Commercial, Economic, and Information and Research). A personnel board would write and administer a "Service Code" of regulations governing work abroad, supervise admission examinations, and advise the under-secretary on personnel issues. Additional suggestions dealt with expediting the flow of paper and relieving the under-secretary of the requirement to sign routine correspondence.

Keenleyside's recommendations resulted in creation of a personnel board, to advise on all matters relating to personnel administration, but it became bogged down in minor matters. Otherwise, nothing was done about reorganization so long as Robertson remained only acting head. When Pearson arrived from London, therefore, he found the department still "a hive of unorganized activity."[7] Robertson was running the department much as Skelton had done, and decentralization continued to be impeded by two obstacles: "First the Prime Minister's insistence on dealing with one person and one person only, the Under-Secretary, on every matter, great and small. Secondly, the necessity under the present system of getting the Prime Minister's approval on practically every step—diplomatic, administrative or political—which the Department desires to take."[8]

The first problem, being a result of deeply entrenched prime ministerial habit, was not subject to alteration. The second arose from Treasury Board regulations, which required ministerial signatures to authorize even small expenditures, such as for flowers sent to members of the diplomatic corps and for the installation of new telephones. This was a responsibility that King took seriously. There was therefore little hope of escape from the requirements of Treasury Board regarding signing authority. Although the department persuaded the minister of finance that routine submissions to Treasury Board not exceeding $200 might go forward without the ministerial signature, King refused to sign the document authorizing the change. The only relaxation of the rules that Robertson was able to achieve was waiver of a stipulation that King sign applications, required in triplicate by the comptroller of the treasury, for the installation of new telephones.[9]

Operations overseas added to the burden. Posts had always come under the direct scrutiny of the under-secretary, and now, with the opening of new offices, there was an endless flow of issues for Robertson to deal with, covering support staff, finances, and administration. In a memorandum to Robertson, Pearson drew attention to the harmful consequences:

> I think the fundamental weakness of our departmental organization is shown by the fact that I have to write to you about matters like this. There should be some one to relieve you of this side of the work, so that you will only be approached on administrative matters when a final decision on some important matter is to be made. Personally, I don't see how you are going to show the Prime Minister how to win the war and make the peace if you have to spend two hours each day talking about the cost of Mr. Désy's table linen or the salary of the newest stenographer.[10]

Once he was confirmed as under-secretary, Robertson persuaded King to accept a scaled-down version of Keenleyside's proposals. Instead of ten divisions there were to be four, representing the interests of the senior officers under Robertson. Three were to be headed by assistant under-secretaries: Beaudry (Diplomatic and Economic Division, with five officers), Pearson (Commonwealth and European Division, five officers), and Keenleyside (American and Far Eastern Division, four officers). The legal adviser, Read, considered equal in rank to the assistant under-secretaries, was to be in charge of the Legal Division, with four officers. The divisions themselves were subdivided into ten sections, each with specialized responsibilities. Functional and geographical activities were kept separate, except in the Commonwealth and Europe Division, where two sections had special responsibilities related to the war. Now for the first time the department was organized according to levels of descending responsibility, with well-defined demarcation between its various activities.[11]

Not only the department as a whole but also the under-secretary's office was ripe for adjustment after Skelton's death. Marjorie McKenzie had long since given up secretarial duties in order to concentrate on other tasks: keeping up a set of working files,[12] preparing correspondence, writing periodic résumés of current events, summarizing British documents, and copying King's marginal notes onto the departmental copies of papers before the originals were returned to Laurier House. She also continued in her role as commentator, via marginalia of her own, on drafts coming up from the department for the under-secretary. Someone was needed to help, through organization of the paper flow, to establish and maintain priorities. For this purpose, one of the newly recruited officers, Saul Rae, was assigned to the under-secretary's office as special assistant.

Among the activities attracting Rae's attention were the newspaper clipping service, reception of visitors, distribution of documents, and methods of filing. Lack of space and shortage of manpower were also eventually identified as problems. Resistance from Marjorie McKenzie prevented major organizational changes, but, by the time he was posted abroad in November 1943, Rae had contributed to the more orderly preparation of the under-secretary's work.[13] On the basis that he laid, his successors helped ensure that the under-secretary's office functioned reasonably well, despite Robertson's unwillingness to turn visitors away or to terminate discussion. His personal secretary, Sybil Rump, who had been working with him before he became under-secretary, also did her best to ensure that urgent matters received his attention.

The Special Section

The organization of the department was also modified to provide for activities arising directly from the war. Thus the Special Section, under Alfred Rive, was created within the Commonwealth and European Division, to deal with matters related to interned civilians and prisoners of war.[14]

During the First World War, matters pertaining to Canadians interned abroad had been handled by the British. As a result of the constitutional changes during the intervening years, responsibility now was assumed by the Canadian government. The agency with nominal authority was the Immigration Branch of the Department of Mines and Resources, but it was unable to act, since it had no agents abroad during the war. Instead, External Affairs became the channel for liaison with the protecting power and the International Red Cross on such matters as arranging and verifying delivery of relief to Canadian internees, guaranteeing legal counsel, and securing cash allowances. There was also communication with the same authorities regarding the interests of enemy aliens in Canada.

Before long these activities grew to include more complex tasks, beginning with repatriation of 500 Canadian civilians from Europe in the summer of 1940. At about the same time, Canada began to receive civilian internees transferred from the United Kingdom.[15] These were later joined by prisoners of war. Particularly after the fall of Hong Kong in December 1941 and the failure of the Dieppe raid in August 1942, the fate of Canadian fighting men in enemy hands also became a major concern. Eventually, as a result of protracted negotiations through the Swiss, there were several exchanges of persons with the enemy.

The pressure on the Special Section was such by the summer of 1942 that voluntary help was sought from the wives of public servants. Among those working in the section on this basis were Lyla Rasminsky, Alexandra Stone, and Joyce Wrong. Knowledge of French, typing ability, and a minimum commitment of four hours a day were required. The volunteers collated reports on camp conditions into a weekly document for circulation to concerned government officials. They also kept complete and current records on each camp that held at least two Canadians.[16]

At its peak, the work of the Special Section consumed the time of eight officers and a large clerical staff plus the volunteers, making it, in terms of personnel, the largest single wartime activity of the department. The volume was so great that all had to work a substantial amount of overtime. Abroad, one officer at Canada House and another in Washington were engaged full-time on Special Section activities for most of the war. Among the responsibilities in London was service on Commonwealth committees, established in 1940 and 1944 respectively, to deal with the interests of interned civilians and prisoners of war. (A prisoners-of-war committee was also established in Washington, but it was not very active.)

In Ottawa, the growing complexity of the work demanded liaison with other departments and with several non-governmental agencies, such as the Red Cross and the YMCA. Unfortunately, a workable method of co-operation never developed. Although several interdepartmental committees were set up, they had no final authority to take decisions but could only make recommendations back to the departments. Lack of a single authority to hand down a final ruling, combined with reluctance to go to cabinet except on crucial issues, left a rather confused situation. Disputes with other agencies caused frustration in the Special Section and added to the workload.[17] In one such disagreement, the department, concerned about the effect on Canadian participation in exchanges of persons with the enemy, had to overcome the objections of the intelligence authorities to repatriation of uninterned German civilians. Heavy personal sacrifice of time was required of Rive and his staff in order to make sure that the interests of internees and prisoners of war were served, despite the problems caused by overlapping jurisdictions in Ottawa.

Conditions of work

As Rive's experience of overwork indicated, the structural changes initiated under Robertson did not shift responsibility, which remained firmly in the hands of those at the top. Even so, the situation became more satisfying for junior officers. There was still no training program, but newcomers now had more coherent assignments and a better sense of their responsibilities, and the organizational structure made more readily available consistent guidance and training from experienced staff. There was also a greater oppportunity to have at least a modest influence on policy, as a result of representation at a junior level on many more interdepartmental committees.

The authority vested in senior career officers was not fully reflected in conditions of service. The salary scale for assistant under-secretaries ($6,240 to $7,200 per year) in Ottawa was well below that for ministers and high commissioners abroad (up to $12,000, plus allowances), though duties at home were much the heavier. Wage and price controls, however, froze salaries of existing ranks. External Affairs did not make promotions to acting ranks in order to provide for advancement and for greater distinctions in pay among senior officers with varying levels of responsibility.

Another problem resulted from a ruling by the Department of Justice that a public servant, upon appointment as a head of post, could no longer contribute to the superannuation fund or receive the benefits of superannuation upon retirement. Both Jean Désy and Loring Christie were affected by this decision. In July 1942, an amendment to the External Affairs Act extended superannuation benefits to career officials who assumed charge of diplomatic or consular missions, with retroactive effect to January 1, 1938.[18] As a result, the income of Christie's widow was restored to the level it would have been had her husband remained in Ottawa.

Changes in representation

The most urgent problem at the posts arose from the need to replace Christie in Washington. In February 1941, King selected a wealthy Toronto lawyer, Leighton McCarthy. A trustee of the US National Foundation for Infantile Paralysis and of the Georgia Warm Springs Foundation, McCarthy had a long personal friendship with President Franklin Roosevelt. As a condition of accepting the appointment, McCarthy asked that Wrong come to Washington as his deputy. King agreed in February 1941, thus creating the requirement for Pearson's return to Ottawa from London. In Washington, the need for a seasoned deputy soon became apparent, for the new minister, seventy-one at the time of his appointment, kept short hours and, in Wrong's judgment, was starting a new career too late in life to make up for his inexperience. In the circumstances, Wrong became in all but name head of the mission.[19]

The legation in Japan meanwhile remained without a minister. Keenleyside and the chargé d'affaires in Tokyo, E. D. McGreer, both thought that appointment of a Canadian minister would improve Japan's relations with the democratic powers. In July 1941 the government acted as they recommended, choosing Brig. W. W. Foster, "a leading citizen of British Columbia'' with ''a sympathetic and friendly interest in the problems of Japanese Canadians,'' who was district officer commanding the Canadian Army in Saskatchewan. The United Kingdom and the United States, concerned about the conduct of the Japanese government, advised against going ahead. In the interest of maintaining solidarity, the Canadian government complied, and circumstances thereafter never favoured filling the vacancy.[20]

Solidarity with defeated allies that maintained governments in exile in London required reconsideration of the policy that Canada would not expand its diplomatic relations with European nations until after the war. By November 1941, Canada was prepared to accept legations from Czechoslovakia, Greece, Norway, Poland, and Yugoslavia, on condition that reciprocity was not required and that arrangements would be reviewed after the war. Poland elevated its consular representation in Ottawa; the other four countries, which maintained consulates general in Montreal, opened new offices in Ottawa.

Also requiring some flexibility on Canada's part was policy on relations with countries in Latin America, from which there was pressure to expand beyond Brazil and Argentina. Most effective, because the country was considered by the United States to be important to ''hemispheric defence,'' were representations from Chile. On September 28, 1941, W. F. A. Turgeon was accredited to Chile as well as to Argentina.

This was the first time that Canada had accredited a mission to a country in which it had no resident diplomatic representation. The attempt did not work well. The distance between Buenos Aires and Santiago was too great for easy commuting, and, with the transportation available, Turgeon found the journey too strenuous. In the next year, therefore, Canada established a separate legation in Santiago, with Warwick Chipman, a lawyer and professor of law at McGill with an interest in international affairs, as minister. Chile opened a counterpart in Ottawa in 1942.[21]

Of much more interest to Canada were neighbouring territories off the east coast of North America. Foremost among these was Newfoundland, which had had dominion status but reverted, as a result of financial difficulties, to a semi-colonial position in 1934, with a six-man commission to advise the governor. As a near neighbour with many overlapping interests, Canada was much concerned about the security of the island, the intentions of its government, and the activities of possible rivals there, especially the United States.

Newfoundland had been hurriedly garrisoned by Canadian troops and brought under an Atlantic command established in July 1940. Unease about US intentions none the less prevailed in Ottawa, as a result of Newfoundland's inclusion in the destroyers-for-bases arrangement with the United Kingdom in September 1940, arrival of American troops in the island in January 1941, and the leased-bases agreement of March 27, 1941. Despite Canadian objections, the United States thereby received long-term leases on three naval and air facilities and priority rights over the entire island during an emergency. Canada had had observers at the negotiations but had to be content with a protocol acknowledging its "special concern" for the defence of Newfoundland.[22] Then, confirming its interest in Newfoundland and further enhancing its position there, the United States followed up with appointment of a senior consul general at St John's.

Skelton had raised the idea of an exchange of representatives between Canada and Newfoundland earlier in the war, but it had been rejected by Newfoundland's Commission of Government as too expensive. Now there was an urgent need for someone in St John's with a rank at least equal to that of the US consul general. Bilateral issues—arising from Newfoundland's customs and fishing regulations and from competition in US markets for newsprint—could be handled more expeditiously between the two governments directly rather than through the Dominions Office. "Canada has more varied, more important and more urgent business with Newfoundland," Robertson told King, "than with all the self-governing Dominions in which we maintain High Commissioners put together."[23]

On July 31, 1941, the Canadian government chose as its representative in St John's the recently appointed high commissioner to Australia, Charles Burchell, an authority on admiralty and shipping law. Burchell was to be designated high commissioner in Newfoundland, a title that would give him precedence over the US consul general. The British, however, took the view that Newfoundland, as a territory lacking full self-government, could not use the same term if it established a presence in Ottawa. An acceptable form of representation was never worked out for the Canadian capital, and so all wartime matters involving Canada and Newfoundland were dealt with through the high commissioner's office in St John's.[24]

Like Newfoundland, St Pierre and Miquelon acquired heightened importance during the war. After the fall of France, the islands were considered a possible source of danger to shipping in the North Atlantic, especially once it became known that a high-powered radio transmitter had been built there, which might become a source of intelligence in support of submarine operations by the enemy. As well, Canada had longstanding bilateral concerns in the islands, the most persistent of which arose from illicit liquor traffic and other forms of smuggling.

For a number of reasons, it was concluded that Canada required a consular office in the islands. A British vice-consul who had represented Canadian interests had retired and not been replaced. If there were to be only one Commonwealth consulate, it was suggested in Ottawa, it would be more appropriate for the office to be maintained by the country with the most direct interests, Canada. Nor was it considered prudent to rely on the United States. "The public," it was observed in July 1941, "could not be told that Canada was receiving reports from the United States Consul in the Islands and in any event the public might not be sufficiently reassured by this." Independent Canadian representation, moreover, would assist in any effort to work out a policy of "equal responsibility" with the United States in the event that Vichy France became "actively hostile." With these considerations in mind, the Canadian government decided, on August 19, 1941, to open a consulate in St Pierre and Miquelon. Named to the post, as vice-consul with the local rank of acting consul, was one of the new officers, Christopher Eberts.[25]

Policy-making

As a result of the administrative changes introduced after Robertson became under-secretary, External Affairs became better equipped to contribute to the Canadian war effort. These resources could be put to good use, because of the rapport that developed between Robertson and King. Inevitably there was a period of settling in, but, as Robertson's confirmation in June 1941 indicates, he soon won the prime minister's confidence.

One reason for Robertson's success was his availability whenever he was called on. This filled an unquestioning expectation on King's part. On one occasion when he had returned unexpectedly to his office late in the evening, the under-secretary received a telephone call from King, who had an idea he wanted to discuss. "The old so-and-so took it for granted that I would be there," Robertson observed to a friend, J. D. Hickerson of the US State Department, on recalling the incident.[26] Robertson succeeded to Skelton's position as a regular participant in meetings of the Cabinet War Committee and, along with Heeney, drafted and redrafted many statements of government policy. With the broad knowledge thus gained, Robertson was well placed to assume another of Skelton's roles— confidant of the prime minister.

Not all policy decisions were ones about which the government had much choice. This was so with the growing list of countries with which Canada was at war, since there was little alternative once they had taken up arms on the side of Germany. On June 10, 1940, the Canadian government had decided on a declaration of war against Italy. In the autumn of 1941, the German attack on the Soviet Union, supported by Finland, Hungary, and Romania, added further to the roster of enemies. King, however, did not accept Robertson's recommendation that, without publicity, Canada follow the lead of the United Kingdom and declare war on Bulgaria. Britain had not requested such action, and King did not think that Canadian interests alone made it necessary. "Declaring war is a large order, or ought to be," he wrote, "and grounds sufficient to satisfy Parliament must exist."[27] No action, therefore, was taken.

Preparation of documents for declarations of war was squarely within the department's mandate, but some important aspects of international relations that developed after Robertson's appointment were not. An acute foreign exchange crisis occurred with the United States early in 1941. Robertson, Keenleyside, and Wrong all helped prepare for the meeting between King and Roosevelt that settled the problem in the Hyde Park agreement of April 20, 1941, but the lead was taken by Finance and by Munitions and Supply (created in 1940 to deal with war production). Those departments dominated the Canadian side of the joint economic committees created subsequently to study the economic relationship between the two countries. External Affairs was not a full participant in the committees, although liaison was maintained through Keenleyside.[28]

External Affairs, however, could co-ordinate interdepartmental projects. For a working group on export control, the department provided the chairman.[29] As the focal point of communications with Tokyo, London, and Washington, External Affairs also was central in preparation of the Canadian policy on trade with Japan. On this subject the department under Robertson was becoming more up-to-date in its communications, for the telephone was used on occasion to reach both Washington and Tokyo. Headquarters failed, unfortunately, to overcome another inefficient habit developed under Skelton. Those in Ottawa with access to information from all the sources available to the department were still careless about keeping the posts abreast of developments. "I am disappointed," Wrong wrote to Robertson from Washington on December 6, 1941, "that you have not sent me immediately on their arrival copies of the telegrams which you are receiving from London on the Far Eastern situation. I do not know how much to cover in the reports that I am making to you. Any light which you can throw on the views of the Canadian Government towards the Far Eastern crisis would also be valuable."[30]

There was no time to act on this request, for the next day the Japanese attacked Pearl Harbor. Canada had a new enemy across the Pacific but, more important, a new ally next door. Canada's comparative importance as a combatant was instantly diminished, and it had to develop means of working with the complex network of new organizations whereby the United States and Britain directed the allied war effort. Now much more than immediately after Skelton's death the department needed fresh approaches to policy, and the pressure on its resources was to become heavier than ever.

CANADA AND THE GRAND ALLIANCE

At war with Japan

Much more thorough arrangements had been made for the closing of the legation in Tokyo than had been done in Europe in 1939. Also well prepared was the procedure for going to war—indeed, Canada was the first Western country formally to enter the conflict against Japan, having taken all the necessary action even before the United States. Even so, there was no quick escape from Tokyo for the staff of the Canadian legation. Unlike their colleagues in Europe in 1940, they had to remain under house arrest in the Japanese capital until mid-1942, when an exchange of persons enabled them to return home.

House arrest in Tokyo was no prison camp, but conditions were very confined. On December 8 the chargé d'affaires, McGreer, was informed that the Canadian legation was no longer considered a diplomatic mission. All staff members were required to move immediately into the compound, the gates were closed, no one was permitted to leave without authorization, and all short-wave radios were seized. With McGreer's permission, the premises were searched. Police were posted not only outside but also, for a couple of weeks, inside the compound as well.

The Japanese foreign office arranged for adequate supplies of food, but fuel oil was provided only in very limited quantity. Since the staff preferred to use it to heat water for bathing, the building itself was unheated throughout the winter, except on Christmas day. Diversions were few: during the period of house arrest, four motion pictures were shown, occasional walks were allowed as well as visits to the doctor and the dentist, and one game of golf was permitted. Relief from boredom, therefore, depended much on conversation. In this regard, it has been observed, Herbert Norman was "an ideal fellow prisoner."[31]

The worst hardship was probably the sense of isolation, since contact with the diplomatic community was not permitted (even to say good-bye prior to departure) and there was little access to news, Japanese or foreign. Thus, when arrangements were being made for repatriation, McGreer asked the department through the protecting power for a "liberal supply of reading material covering world events particularly Canadian since December 1st."[32] On the whole, however, he found no cause for complaint in the treatment:

Once we had accepted the fact that we were to be isolated and that we were no longer considered by the Japanese to be a diplomatic mission, it can be honestly said that our treatment was most considerate and that

251

apart from the usual delays in getting things done in Japan, there was no real complaint to register against the Japanese authorities. We were shown every consideration and in this connection it may be of interest to note that on Christmas eve, a large turkey, amply sufficient for seven people, was sent to Mrs. McGreer by the wife of the Vice Minister for Foreign Affairs.[33]

For Canada, as for the United Kingdom, Argentina at first acted as the protecting power in Japan and Manchuria, and Switzerland performed the function in other parts of Asia under enemy control. In the spring of 1942, Switzerland was asked to take over responsibility for British and Canadian interests in Japan as well. The reason was pressure from the United States, which considered relations with the enemy of the former protecting power, Argentina, to have been too warm. In Canada, Spain was the protecting power for Japan, and Argentina assumed a similar role for Italy, taking over from Japan. With the United States now in the war, Switzerland became the protector of Canadian interests in Europe.

The treatment of Japanese in Canada

The outbreak of war in the Pacific added heavily to the department's workload. Even new subjects handled elsewhere often required substantial attention from External Affairs. The most immediate cause of concern to the government was the activity of people of Japanese origin in Canada, almost all of whom lived on the Pacific coast. Feeling against this community had been strong in British Columbia before Pearl Harbor, and in October 1940 the federal government had appointed the Special Committee on Orientals in British Columbia, under Keenleyside, to consider the security question. Among its recommendations were an end to Japanese propaganda, voluntary repatriation, and the exemption of Japanese from military call-up.[34]

Once the two countries were at war, anti-Japanese sentiment intensified and was brought forcefully to the federal government's attention by members of Parliament from British Columbia, including their spokesman in the cabinet, Ian Mackenzie. Their demands were controversial in at least two respects: they proposed harsher treatment than for other enemy aliens, and they wanted British subjects of Japanese origin, whether naturalized or native-born, treated the same way as citizens of Japan. The price for belonging to this visible minority was to be high: confiscation of property and forced relocation away from the coast.

These pressures were of concern to External Affairs for a number of reasons. Harsh measures were likely to have repercussions on Canadian and British internees and prisoners of war in Japanese hands. Unequal treatment, by comparison with other enemy aliens, could produce complaints from the protecting power, which would be difficult for the Special Section to answer. In the Permanent Joint Board on Defence, Canada had undertaken in November 1941 to co-ordinate its policies with those of the United States, but some of the actions being proposed were more draconian than those taken south of the border. To these were added civil libertarian and humanitarian considerations embraced by the External Affairs officers involved in the subject, including Robertson, Keenleyside, John Read, and Escott Reid. "We are ostensibly fighting in the cause of British liberty, British justice and Christian ethics," Robertson wrote in a memorandum to the prime minister at the end of January 1942. "We become exposed to the charge of hypocrisy if we derogate from these principles. Our own morale would be impaired if our government were believed to be departing from them."[35]

The department's concerns were expressed in a meeting in Ottawa, on January 8 and 9, 1942, of representatives from British Columbia, External Affairs, the police, and the military and subsequently in recommendations to King and Mackenzie from Robertson and Keenleyside. The political pressure behind a policy involving evacuation and confiscation of property, however, overwhelmed their arguments. Once the decisions had been taken, in February and March 1942, the department no longer had direct involvement, for it was not represented on the British Columbia Security Commission established to carry them out. Thereafter, its role was limited to dealing, in the Special Section, with representations from the protecting power about the interests of Japanese nationals, as it did for enemy aliens from other countries.[36]

Defence co-operation with the United States

The department also had an interest in the second major consequence of Pearl Harbor, closer defence co-operation with the United States. Arrangements for such projects as construction of the Alaska highway, made in the Permanent Joint Board on Defence, could profoundly affect relations between the two countries. Attention had to be given to Canadian control of the north, in view of the large number of Americans working there. The department was alerted to the situation in March 1943 by the British high commissioner, Malcolm MacDonald, on his return from a visit to the region. Robertson acknowledged the need for assertion of Canadian interests and, in association with Heeney, prepared for the appointment of Brig. W. W. Foster as special commissioner for defence projects in northwest Canada, with headquarters in Edmonton. Thereafter the department's direct role receded, for Foster reported to the War Committee, through Heeney.[37]

St Pierre and Miquelon

At the same time as it was dealing with new issues arising from the Pacific war, the department had to attend to an increasingly complicated European situation. Coinciding with Pearl Harbor, concern was mounting about the situation in St Pierre and Miquelon. Because the territory was one that King considered to be very sensitive politically, Robertson's handling of the matter was a severe test of his progress in gaining the prime minister's confidence, just as his first year as under-secretary was coming to a close.

On December 1, 1941, without apprising King of what he had in mind, Robertson placed before the Cabinet War Committee a proposal that Canada, without telling London or Washington, send a departmental officer (T. A. Stone) and military censors to the islands in a corvette. King was opposed and, although the idea was dropped, found the episode unsettling. Robertson's judgment, he decided, was "not anything comparable to what S[kelton]'s was in matters of the kind."[38] His dissatisfaction, some of which he communicated to Robertson by telephone, was recorded at length in his diary:

> I much resented having these matters brought before the War Committee without any discussion with myself in advance; . . . as P.M. and Secretary of State for E.A., I had responsibility to Parliament for what was done, and I thought I was entitled to the full confidence of my staffs in all matters pertaining to my two offices. I resented very much matters being settled behind my back with other Departments. No consultation with myself in advance. I tried to restrain myself in the way I spoke but I could not help showing a very strong feeling of indignation at the persistent way in which in matters affecting peace and war, others were trying to settle policies for which I would have to take the responsibility. The trouble is there is a little quota of men who are off by themselves, Robertson, Stone, and Keenleyside, Pearson, etc., a bureaucracy who are good enough men themselves but left to themselves without wide experience or political knowledge are liable to make many grave mistakes. It is very trying to have these contending forces about one from every side.[39]

Once asserted, the prime minister's authority prevailed without challenge by Robertson. When Vice-Adm. E. H. Muselier, commander in chief of the Free French naval forces, seized the islands on December 24, the response was non-committal. "In view of circumstances of Free French occupation of St. Pierre today," Massey was instructed, "do not send Christmas greetings to General de Gaulle."[40] When the US secretary of state, Cordell Hull, suggested in a press release on December 26 that

Canada (suspected in Washington of being in collusion with Muselier or at least aware of his intentions) should restore the status quo in the islands, King avoided being pressured into doing anything. By the time it had become apparent that public reaction in Canada, including Quebec, favoured the Gaullist takeover, no action was necessary. "The only possible policy," Robertson concluded in April, "seems to be to leave the situation as it is."[41]

Notwithstanding the satisfactory outcome, the turmoil over St Pierre and Miquelon left King with a lingering unease about advice from External Affairs, which lasted at least until April 1942. While his sensitivity was particularly acute regarding relations with France, it operated more generally as well. Thus he complained that Robertson was too assertive during a visit to Washington, in the wake of the crisis, for meetings with Roosevelt and Churchill. "It annoys me a little," King wrote, "that the members of my staff try to settle the Prime Minister's course of action. . . . Suggestions are all right, but I think I see many of these things much more clearly than either Robertson or Wrong. I do not intend to yield my judgement over to theirs in anything, unless convinced."[42]

Fortunately, Robertson soon became more attuned to what the prime minister would accept, and so the latter's confidence in him, and also in the department, was restored. That was a noteworthy achievement, since, as a result of US entry into the war, the department had some important new things to say. The prime minister did not always accept its recommendations, but the department regained the credibility needed to receive serious consideration.

The functional principle

During their meetings in Washington, Churchill and Roosevelt decided on the creation of an Anglo-American body, the Combined Chiefs of Staff, to direct the allied war effort. There were to be as well in Washington and London a number of subsidiary boards, concerned with such matters as shipping and supplies, also restricted to British and American membership. Like the other allies, Canada was excluded from these bodies, and it learned of the plans for them only informally, through information coming to the legation in Washington.

Canada did not aspire to membership in the Combined Chiefs of Staff, but, as a major producer, it wanted representation on some of the combined boards dealing with war production—on the basis of "functionalism." In brief, the argument was that, to be effective, international co-operation must reflect the comparative strengths of all the nations involved. Thus it was not realistic either for the largest powers to claim unquestioned dominance or for all participants to insist on an equal voice irrespective of strength. Rather, the level of involvement should vary from one activity to another, depending on the contributions of the countries concerned.[43]

The application of the principle to Canada's wartime position was first suggested (without using the term) by Wrong on January 20, 1942, in a report from Washington on plans for the combined war organizations. After his return to Ottawa, Wrong, according to J. L. Granatstein, "directed the battle" to promote the functional principle, working closely with Robertson at home and with Pearson at the legation in Washington.[44] Although Canada's claim was regarded with limited enthusiasm by the major allies, the effort eventually achieved modest success: membership of the Combined Production and Resources Board and the Combined Food Board, and limited association with the work of the Munitions Assignment Board.[45]

It was becoming apparent, meanwhile, that there were similar problems of recognition in many other aspects of the war effort, in planning for a post-war settlement, and in relations with other large states besides the United States and Britain. Initiatives, based on the functional principle, were required on a broad range of fronts. Thus pressure on the department's resources, already heavy, was further increased by the change in the alliance structure produced by US entry into the war.

Mutual aid

Other relationships as well increased the work of the department, as Canada's war effort moved from the Commonwealth context into one embracing a multiplicity of allies. Typical was the expansion in 1942 of financial arrangements, developed earlier to assist the United Kingdom and the Commonwealth, into a broader program of mutual aid, whereby other allies, including the Soviet Union, China, and the Free French, obtained war supplies from Canada.

Many aspects of the mutual aid program were of primary interest to departments other than External Affairs. The monetary arrangements were the concern of Finance, and the chief agent in implementation was Munitions and Supply. External Affairs handled much of the correspondence with representatives of the recipient countries. Often it was a go-between, but John Read and the staff of the Legal Division helped to draft mutual aid agreements between Canada and the other countries concerned. External Affairs was a member of the interdepartmental agency responsible for the program, the Mutual Aid Board (chaired by the minister of munitions and supply, C. D. Howe), usually being represented by Robertson or Wrong.

Canadian posts in the recipient countries all had work arising from mutual aid, and those in London and Washington had special functions. The initial arrangements governing supplies for the Soviet Union were set up by Canada House in the spring and summer of 1942, and the resulting agreement was signed by Massey in London on September 8, 1942. To co-ordinate the Canadian program with US lend-lease, a joint advisory committee of the Mutual Aid Board was established in Washington, with the industrialist E. P. Taylor of Munitions and Supply chairing the Canadian section. Pearson represented the legation.[46]

Alternatives to officer recruitment

Wartime limitations made finding officer staff for its new responsibilities the department's most difficult operational problem. "I am obsessed," Robertson complained about a year after his confirmation as undersecretary, "by the difficulties of staffing an expanding service, under wartime conditions."[47]

After long arguments with Treasury Board, the department had been exempted, because of new posts abroad, from the wartime freeze on hiring for permanent positions. After the recruitment of 1941, however, Robertson decided not to compete with the armed forces for officers. For the duration of the war, the department would take on no more men as third secretaries, unless there should be suitable candidates who were unfit for military service. Like other employers, the department looked to another pool of talent, university-educated women.

Because the position of third secretary was still open only to men, the women university graduates recruited during the war were hired as grade 4 clerks. The duties were advertised as administrative and secretarial, but a difficult entrance examination tested knowledge of Canadian and international affairs. Once in the department, these new clerks were given the same duties as male third secretaries, and some filled the positions of officers going abroad. The salary of $1,620, however, was only 60 per cent of that paid to probationary third secretaries. Despite representations from External Affairs, the Civil Service Commission refused an increase in salary by insisting on paying for the position advertised rather than the work performed. A few women clerks eventually received war-duty supplements, but no retroactive compensation was paid.

The salary scale was unfair in terms of work performed and qualifications. The latter were similar to those possessed by the men recruited over the years as third secretaries. One new clerk, Kathleen Bingay (later Dunton), was a lawyer, the only woman in her class at the University of Alberta and the graduate with the highest marks. Among her assignments in the department was assisting John Read in drafting the mutual aid agreements. Another, Dorothy Burwash, a graduate of Oxford and Mount

257

Holyoke, had a PHD from Bryn Mawr. Agnes Ireland had a master's degree from the same university; Mary Bridge, Elizabeth MacCallum, Margaret Meagher, and Hilda Reid all had master's degrees earned in Canada; and Mary Dench had graduated in both commerce and arts from Queen's. Hilda Reid was also a qualified librarian, but her work in the department was not confined to the library. Elizabeth MacCallum, born to missionary parents in Turkey, had studied at Columbia University after receiving her MA from Queen's and had been a researcher with the Foreign Policy Association in New York from 1925 until 1931. A recognized authority on the Middle East, she provided the department with expertise hitherto lacking. She had also worked as a school teacher, as had Mary Bridge, Agnes Ireland, and Margaret Meagher. Dorothy Burwash had been a university professor before entering the public service, and Mary Dench had had a career in business and with the Bank of Canada.

The unequal treatment accorded such well-qualified personnel caused discomfort in senior ranks. John Read told Kathleen Bingay that he considered it important in principle for women to be eligible for officer positions, provided they were willing to make a permanent commitment to the career. Although doubting that she wanted to be an officer, Bingay was dissatisfied with a classification inferior to that of male wartime assistants doing the same work. She also believed that exclusion from some departmental activities, such as an evening at Norman Robertson's house to hear Owen Lattimore, political adviser to Generalissimo Chiang Kai-shek, was the result of being female.[48]

Twelve women, all anglophones, entered the department in 1942 and 1943. Before long, however, it was concluded that the required skills were in limited supply. "We are scraping bottom," Robertson was told in October 1943, "in our search for Grade 4's."[49] No further competitions were held, therefore, after 1943.

Meanwhile, Robertson had to deal with the competing attractions of the armed services for the younger male officers. Some he was able to give a greater sense of involvement in the war by sending them to posts near the conflict. Even so, he was often called on to persuade an officer that his work in External Affairs was as important to winning the war as if he were in uniform. A threat to this argument was a proposal by National Selective Service in 1944 to enlist eligible officers in the armed forces and second them back to the department. If the plan had been successful, it would have destroyed Robertson's contention about equivalent service.[50] He therefore resisted the scheme, which never came into effect.

Also of concern was retention of francophone officers who had joined after the outbreak of the war. Not only did they give the department better linguistic balance, but also they were exceptionally useful at a time when relations with France required careful attention, for domestic as well as external reasons. They were familiar with the public mood in French Canada and could assess possible responses to Canadian policies. Thus, for example, Marcel Cadieux and Paul Tremblay co-operated with Saul Rae, who had been an associate of George Gallup at the American Institute of Public Opinion, in sampling opinion in Quebec on issues related to the war.[51]

Wartime Ottawa did not provide the ideal environment for holding the interest of young, professional francophones. War brought a large influx of workers, mostly English-speaking, from all over Canada. Accommodation was hard to find, restaurants were overcrowded, and diversions were limited. All newcomers of course were affected by these problems, but francophones also had to adjust to an essentially English-speaking workplace. As well there seemed to be a requirement to adapt to English-Canadian expectations: it was Cadieux's feeling that the acceptable French Canadian was one who had been to Oxford, spoke English with an accent, and watched baseball games on Saturday afternoon. Certainly it helped in the department to play baseball, for the occasional game against members of the US legation (and between the Canadian legation in Washington and the US State Department) was a favourite diversion, arranged by means of an elaborate burlesque of formal diplomatic notes.[52]

Despite the frustrations, French-speaking officers recruited at the beginning of the war all remained in the service. Compensating for a sense of isolation was the hospitality of the senior francophone, Beaudry, and his family.[53] As they settled in, these new officers developed some ideas about bringing more French Canadians into the public service. "The government," it was suggested to Robertson, "should announce a policy designed at putting an end to the French-Canadian grievances that they do not have their share in the federal administration."[54] A further recommendation was that the Civil Service Commission seek a working relationship with educational authorities in Quebec in order to improve recruitment from the province. "There has never so far been such an imperative need," the submission concluded, "of having in Ottawa persons who earned the respect and the confidence of the Quebec upper classes."

The department, unfortunately, had little time for long-range planning. It needed staff of officer quality to perform the ever-increasing array of tasks generated by the war. Temporary wartime appointments between 1941 and 1944 added twenty-six men, all but two of whom were anglophones. Some were taken on for special tasks lasting only a brief period, but others remained for the duration of the war and then moved into permanent positions.

Temporary appointments strengthened middle management at headquarters, through secondments from outside the public service, the usual title being special wartime assistant to the under-secretary. Most, including H. F. Angus, G. P. de T. Glazebrook, R. A. Mackay, S. M. Scott, Goldwin Smith, and F. H. Soward, were university professors. Some, however, came from other walks of life. Of the two recruited in 1944, T. W. L. MacDermot had been principal of Upper Canada College, and S. D. Pierce was a former journalist and businessman who had been in Washington as a representative of the Department of Munitions and Supply.

A number of other temporary assistants performed work comparable to that of departmental officers recruited in the conventional manner. The two francophones, J. R. B. Chaput and J.-L. Delisle, were in this group. Others included J. M. S. Careless, J. J. Deutsch, H. S. Ferns, J. W. Holmes, and R. G. Riddell. When recruitment was for service outside Canada, a diplomatic designation normally was used. Thus A. E. Ritchie was named a temporary third secretary when he joined the staff of the legation in Washington in 1944. The practice, however, was not entirely consistent. G. L. Magann, a former businessman, had been designated special assistant to the minister to the United States when appointed to the same legation in 1941.

Apart from Delisle, who was assigned to the prime minister's staff from 1942 to 1946, the temporary appointees represented a net gain in the department's resources. On the whole, the expedient worked well, if not entirely without friction.[55] It was, moreover, part of an impressive increase in the bank of talent available to the government as a result of the war, which changed forever the character of Ottawa. Now for the first time, it has been observed, it was possible "to talk in terms of a 'brains trust' in the sense that the term was used during the American New Deal—to describe a group of intellectuals with direct access to the levers of power." No longer was the capital the domain of a small coterie of influential public servants of whom the foremost were "the relatively isolated figures of Skelton at External and Clark at Finance."[56]

Temporary assistants, however, were too few to meet the demands of war. The only means that Robertson could see of acquiring more professional staff, he told King in March 1942, was a merger of External Affairs and the trade commissioner service, since the latter possessed officers experienced in representational and quasi-consular work.[57] The project was also of interest to Keenleyside, who saw trade commissioners as potential manpower for a consular service he wanted to establish in the United States. Diplomats, he argued, might at one time have disdained commercial work, but they had recently come to recognize that "trade and other economic factors are fundamental to ninety percent of all international relations and are thus worthy of, and in fact demand, consideration by the most competent and responsible officials available." What was required, in Keenleyside's view, was a selective rather than a wholesale approach to Trade and Commerce, because of what he considered to be "the inadequacy of some of the members of the Trade Commissioner Service for senior posts in External Affairs."[58]

King gave no encouragement to these initiatives, but amalgamation of the British services in May 1943 allowed Robertson to propose to Trade and Commerce a committee to consider a closer relationship. Although Trade and Commerce agreed to take part, both the minister, J. A. MacKinnon, and his acting deputy, Oliver Master, were opposed to amalgamation. As well, before the committee met, the trade commissioners on duty in Ottawa warned Master in a collective submission that "it would be very desirable that some definite understanding be arrived at which will prevent Trade and Commerce personnel, the only Government Department personnel at present trained in foreign trade, being relegated to a status in foreign posts inferior to that of junior officials appointed abroad for the first time by External Affairs."[59] Their position had support from the prime minister, expressed, also before the committee met, in an interchange in the House of Commons with Gordon Graydon of the Conservatives. In his view, stated King, the two services were quite distinct in training and purpose, and External Affairs did not have time to look after commercial interests abroad.[60]

When the committee met, Keenleyside was able to present his plan, but amalgamation was not treated as an immediate or early concern.[61] Instead, the committee concentrated on the need—identified by Trade and Commerce—for closer co-ordination at posts, always a lively subject in view of the recurrent friction between members of the two services. In its recommendations late in 1943, the committee rejected amalgamation but made various proposals for co-ordination, including creation of a personnel and administration committee, representing the two departments, to ensure common practice abroad. Fusion of the two services remained a distant prospect, which continued to receive attention but was not fully achieved until 1982.

Without access to manpower from the trade commissioner service, External Affairs remained shorthanded. In 1944, Robertson made one last effort to relieve the pressure, trying informally to get some help from the prime minister's staff, but King warned that External Affairs' work must be done in the department.[62] Thus throughout the war Robertson and his senior colleagues had to meet the demand the same way Skelton had done, by putting in long hours, six and often seven days a week. As in Skelton's time, too, the burden was not evenly distributed. The longest hours were worked by those on war-related subjects. Units that were not so affected, George Glazebrook has recalled, were "sedate and peaceful," and those in charge were able to keep normal working hours.[63]

Overcrowding at headquarters

Inadequate though it might be, recruitment of wartime staff put severe pressure on the space available to the department in the East Block. The search for relief was complicated by the government's decision in 1940 to make a distinction between war and non-war departments. Classified as one of the latter, External Affairs did not qualify for the benefits conferred on "a unit engaged exclusively in war work" and so had low priority in allocation of supplies and accommodation. Overcrowding therefore was relieved only slowly and marginally. In 1941 the governor general made available three additional offices by giving up his space in the East Block. In November 1942 the Legal Division and the Special Section were installed in the New Post Office Building at the corner of Sparks and Elgin streets, the first in a series of moves that over the next twenty years dispersed the department's offices among a number of buildings around Confederation Square.

Shortage of support staff

Also as a result of being a non-war department, External Affairs could not exempt its employees from the Treasury Board's freeze on promotions, reclassifications, and statutory increases, which made it difficult to hold on to support staff. The attraction of enlistment in the armed forces was not the main problem. Prior to July 1942, only seven employees of External Affairs left for military service. Intensified recruiting campaigns in late 1942 and the summer of 1944 drew twenty-four more into uniform. Throughout the war, however, External Affairs lost only thirty-nine from headquarters and five from Canada House to the armed services. The main reason for going elsewhere was better pay and working conditions offered by competing employers.

Despite the benefits deriving from Stone's reorganization early in the war, the code room suffered from the turnover of staff. Conditions were also difficult in the file room. Files were being created at the rate of approximately 12,000 per year, without a systematic method of retiring old ones. There was no space for orderly storage and retrieval in the main file room, since cabinets were stored on top of one another, making the whole area a depressing and dangerous place in which to work. The practice of creating new files each year was abandoned after 1940. New files were opened with the suffix "40," regardless of the year, and some of those created earlier remained in use as well.[64] There were long delays in retrieving documents. The once-orderly system having outgrown itself, much now depended on the memory of individual staff members, but rapid turnover often removed this resource. Because officers took to keeping their own records in order to have ready access to frequently required documents, there were many gaps in the registry files.

The department was also short of messengers. In order to free men for active service, the department at first tried to make do with boys too young to enlist, but they very soon proved to be unreliable and unimpressed by threats of dismissal. Later girls were hired, but they were not allowed to carry classified documents outside the East Block, even across the street to the New Post Office Building. There were also discipline problems, similar to those experienced earlier with the unruly boys. External Affairs then asked National Defence for some discharged soldiers, but the candidates were not suitable.[65] Much of the urgent messenger work therefore had to be done by officers or their secretaries.

Wartime problems in administration were alleviated by the skill and commitment of the senior secretaries. While there were complaints that letters had to be "done over and over again," most correspondence and memoranda leaving the department went through senior officers who had retained a group of experienced, competent, and dedicated secretaries who willingly shouldered the extra burden.[66] On them devolved many of the tasks that in better conditions would have been assumed by other staff.

Increased work at the posts

The broadening of the war increased pressures not only on headquarters but also on posts abroad. One result was the augmentation of staffs by specialists, most notably service attachés, who were appointed to several missions besides Washington. There was also a financial attaché in Washington, and an administrative secretary was added to the staff in London.

In addition to personnel accorded places in the diplomatic list, and thus at least nominally under the jurisdiction of the head of post, there were other Canadian officials active abroad whose relationship was less clear. This was particularly true of Washington, because of the vast amount of trans-border business created by Canada's need to obtain war supplies even before Pearl Harbor. Prominent examples were the office of the Department of Munitions and Supply and the Canadian Joint Staff Mission, established under Maj.-Gen. Maurice Pope (Sir Joseph's son) in 1942 to maintain liaison with the Anglo-American Combined Chiefs of Staff. As well, there was a good deal of business transacted between officials of various departments in Ottawa and their counterparts in Washington.

After Washington, the capital most affected by the extension of the war to the Pacific was Canberra. Managing the Canadian response fell to an inexperienced high commissioner, because of Burchell's transfer to

Newfoundland. King's choice as successor was Maj.-Gen. Victor W. Odlum, a prominent British Columbian who was commander of the Second Canadian Division in England. King was under pressure from the British to ease Odlum out of his command, and the posting to Canberra offered a means of doing so. Odlum was not keen on the transfer but reluctantly agreed to go.

Australian anxiety about security after Pearl Harbor was something Odlum was prepared to address from his military background: on his own initiative, he raised the possibility in Canberra of the dispatch of a Canadian force to help out. This idea was not well received in Ottawa, but Odlum did not take readily to guidance. "You'll never make a real diplomat out of me while the war is on," he told Robertson, "so don't try too seriously." He was not the best spokesman, therefore, for a country disinclined to commit forces to the war in the Pacific. The resultant confusion, which was resented particularly by Australia's forceful external affairs minister, Herbert Evatt, made for some awkward moments in relations between the two countries after Pearl Harbor.[67] Much smoother was the relationship with New Zealand, which named a cabinet minister, Frank Langstone, high commissioner to Canada in April 1942, thereby completing the network of communications with the other dominions envisaged by Skelton.

Given much more serious attention than the Pacific situation was France, because of the domestic political ramifications. Although the Canadian government indicated disapproval of the Pétain regime by ordering the French consulates to close in May 1942, the legation in Ottawa was allowed to remain open until relations were broken with Vichy at the time of the allied landings in North Africa in November of that year. In addition to the political considerations for leaving the legation in operation as long as possible, there was a practical advantage to the allies, since Canada was able to monitor communications with Vichy.[68] Georges Vanier's position, meanwhile, remained ambiguous, for his resignation as minister to France in May 1941 had never been formally acknowledged by the Canadian government. The same was true of the Free French presence in Canada. In 1941, Canada had agreed to receive a permanent representative of de Gaulle, to the opening of an information office, and to the appointment of a naval liaison officer in Halifax but was careful to avoid the semblance of official recognition.

After the break with Vichy, Vanier, recently named minister to the allied governments in exile in London, was also authorized to deal with de Gaulle's organization, although not on the basis of formal diplomatic relations. The ambiguity continued after Vanier was transferred to Algiers, which had become de Gaulle's headquarters, at the end of 1943. (Vanier remained minister to the allied governments in exile, but Pierre Dupuy, as chargé d'affaires in London, was responsible for dealing with all except those of Greece and Yugoslavia, which had relocated to Cairo.) Not until de Gaulle had established a provisional government in Paris in October 1944 did Canada, along with the United Kingdom, the United States, and the Soviet Union, grant formal recognition and resume full diplomatic relations.[69]

The situation was more straightforward regarding two new allies, the Soviet Union and China. With both countries, the main problem was not the decision to establish diplomatic relations but implementing it effectively at a time when normal travel routes were cut off and the host governments were directly engaged in combat.

Hitler's invasion made the Soviet Union an ally in June 1941. In October of that year, the ambassador in London approached Commonwealth representatives with a proposal to appoint consular officers in their countries. It was thought that in Canada such officials could usefully handle problems arising from shipments of war supplies. King considered acceptance advisable, and an agreement for an exchange of consular officers was ready for signature in February 1942, although it seemed unlikely that Canada would reciprocate very soon.

Robertson wanted the exchange upgraded to the level of minister. "The general public," he pointed out, "would find it extremely difficult to understand why our representation in Russia should take the same form as our representation in Greenland and St. Pierre."[70] This recommendation was accepted. The Soviet Union's legation in Ottawa opened in October 1942, and the following month Dana Wilgress (deputy minister of trade and commerce) was appointed the first Canadian minister to that country. Having been a trade commissioner in Omsk and Vladivostok between 1916 and 1919, he was one of the few Canadians who had served in the Soviet Union.

Establishing the mission in Kuibyshev, the temporary wartime location of some government departments, including the foreign ministry, was difficult. Because of the extensive territory covered by Axis operations, the eight-week air journey, early in 1943, had to be made via Brazil, the Gold Coast, Cairo, and Tehran. As anticipated, there were limitations on information gathering in Kuibyshev, and Moscow, where many senior officials of the foreign ministry remained, was out of bounds to all but a few diplomats. Even so, the new legation embarked on an energetic program of reporting while awaiting the move to Moscow in 1944.[71]

A diplomatic exchange with China was first mentioned in a memorandum of June 1941 and approved by King a month later. The Chinese minister, who was a senior member of the Foreign Office, arrived in Ottawa in February 1942. After considering several candidates, King decided that the Canadian minister should be Edgar J. Tarr, a prominent member of the Canadian Institute of International Affairs with an interest in Asia and president of the Monarch Life Insurance Co. Tarr, however, was a critic of the government's foreign policy, which he considered to have lacked sufficient assertiveness, and therefore did not accept the post.[72] The appointment went instead to Odlum, who had been frustrated in Australia and who wanted to be nearer to a theatre of war. His place in Canberra was taken by T. C. Davis, deputy minister of the new Department of National War Services. Well aware of the Canadian government's priorities, Davis could be relied on to avoid misunderstandings of the sort that had arisen after Odlum's arrival in Canberra.[73]

Chungking, temporary wartime capital of China, was, like Kuibyshev, difficult to reach. The Canadian party travelled there via India, flying (without supplementary oxygen) "over the hump" of the Himalayas from Calcutta. Since Chungking was in the war zone, supplies had to be brought in by the same route, and the damage inflicted by the Japanese made working and living conditions difficult. Odlum's headstrong qualities also continued to be a problem. His staff consisted of a counsellor, G. S. Patterson, who had been with the YMCA in Japan; a third secretary, Ralph Collins, who had been born in China; a military attaché, Brig. O. M. Kay; and an assistant military attaché, Maj. (later Lt.-Col.) H. F. Wooster. Odlum was at odds with the attachés, especially the senior, and, though lacking background knowledge of China, did not (contrary to Robertson's hope) seek guidance from Patterson. The result was a certain amount of tension, combined with a desire for escape from the constraints imposed by Odlum. Before the war was over, Patterson was asking Robertson for a posting that offered "a chance to do some worthwhile work."[74]

The war also brought extension of Canadian representation in the United States, provoked by concern about misconceptions there of Canada's international position and its role in the conflict. The government therefore decided to open an information office in New York. Such an operation, it was believed, would be more effective if it had consular status. Early in 1943 a consulate general was opened in New York. It incorporated the existing trade commissioner's office and was to carry out information work and to perform the consular services for Canadians hitherto available from the British.

Hugh D. Scully, commissioner of customs, was named consul general, and the first appointees as consul and vice-consul were trade commissioners. External Affairs was represented in the person of Agnes McCloskey. As vice-consul with the personal rank of first secretary, she was the department's first woman employee given representational duties abroad. The question of the consul general's authority over the trade commissioners was referred to the co-ordinating committee formed with Trade and Commerce, which ruled that the senior member of any joint office (in this instance, Scully) "should be responsible for the general administrative activities of all personnel."[75]

Overhauling headquarters administration

Agnes McCloskey's posting to New York resolved a difficult administrative problem at headquarters. The practices she had devised, which had worked well so long as the department's operations were simple, were inadequate to the volume and complexity of work arising from the war. Her unmodified practices became, in the view of senior officers, an obstacle to departmental efficiency, the more so because she insisted on consulting the under-secretary frequently on minor matters. Robertson avoided a confrontation, even after receiving strong representations in November 1942 from Angus, Glazebrook, Keenleyside, Stone, and Wrong,[76] but he seems for a time to have despaired of solving the department's administrative problems.

On December 13 Robertson drafted a letter to the prime minister in which he said: "I have come to the conclusion that the [under-secretary's] job is not one which I am cut out to do satisfactorily. It is in large and growing measure, an administrative post, requiring qualities of temperament and character which I, unfortunately, lack. . . . I believe I can be a more useful member of the public service in an advisory than in an executive capacity."[77] The letter was not sent, but a solution did not come to hand until Keenleyside conceived the idea of posting Agnes McCloskey to New York. On hearing the announcement in Washington, in April 1943, Pearson noted in his diary: "For anyone who has had to pry expense accounts out of her, the significance of this move will be obvious. In the legation, it overshadowed all the war news; even the advance of the 8th Army had to take second place."[78]

McCloskey was replaced by a special assistant to the under-secretary, Donald Matthews, a lawyer who had been with the Foreign Exchange Control Board. Matthews had served as an unpaid attaché at the legation in Washington in 1929 and 1930, earning a favourable report from Massey, and he was well regarded by Henry Borden of Munitions and Supply. He was soon handling an enormous number of administrative and personnel issues without unduly troubling Robertson. Regulations for post operations were drafted by the staff in Washington. With Wrong's help, bottlenecks were gradually removed and departmental committees established to coordinate and make written recommendations for administrative policy.[79] Keenleyside made his division—American and Far Eastern—a model of administrative efficiency, with job descriptions and procedures for meeting deadlines. He also set out to chart and define the complex interaction of wartime agencies in Canada, the United States, and the United Kingdom.

Censorship and intelligence

The administrative improvements introduced by Matthews, combined with the other organizational changes, supported both the expansion of the traditional work and movement into new areas. Important among the latter were the interrelated subjects of censorship and intelligence. These, closely linked with communications, attracted Stone once he had reorganized the code room early in the war.

External Affairs had been involved in censorship since the beginning of the war. The British had complained about the publication in Canadian newspapers of information that might be useful to the enemy. The Canadian reply should have come from an interdepartmental committee set up to direct and harmonize censorship activities, but it seldom met. Stone therefore began to call ad hoc meetings to resolve problems of co-ordination with the British.[80]

These efforts not only restored confidence in Canada's ability to protect sensitive information, but they also revealed the utility of intercepted messages, if properly organized and analysed, as a source of intelligence. Stone therefore instituted a system whereby censorship workers sorted out the intercepts as they came in and put them in appropriate files.[81] By the end of 1941 the current material was available for analysis. Since Stone was too busy, the task was passed to Glazebrook.

Glazebrook soon saw that, with so many jurisdictions, effective exploitation of the information available through censorship was impossible.[82] He therefore recommended a central supervision mechanism. The Cabinet War Committee agreed, and in May 1942 Col. O. M. Biggar was appointed director of censorship, responsible to National War Services for all branches of the activity. His office produced broad reports of use to several departments, on such subjects as German morale and the impartiality of neutral countries. External Affairs relied considerably on these digests and received intercepted texts only on matters of particular concern, such as St Pierre.

For its own purposes, the department also analysed the mail of enemy prisoners of war and internees in Canada, which was intercepted notwithstanding an international protocol to the contrary. Despite the sensitivity of this operation, arrangements for destroying the evidence were not very sophisticated. On one occasion junior officers had to be deployed on Parliament Hill to rescue intercepts blown about when an unexpected updraft in an East Block fireplace sent them swirling up the chimney before they could be burned.[83]

External Affairs was not merely a passive recipient of information coming in via censorship; it also gathered intelligence. It helped to set up a cryptographic unit and to oversee its operations and was a prime consumer of the information produced by the unit.

The chiefs of staff had been presented by the Signals Corps with a proposal to create a cryptographic bureau late in 1940 but had turned it down. They believed that such an establishment would be too expensive and that Canada could rely on British facilities and, once the United States entered the war, American as well. External Affairs was informed of this view in January 1941, when National Defence discovered that Keenleyside and Dr. C. J. Mackenzie, acting president of the National Research Council (NRC), were discussing the same idea. They none the less persisted with their project, with the support of Robertson and Stone, and a small unit was established under an American cryptographic expert, Herbert Osborn Yardley (who, for purposes of secrecy, used the name Herbert Osborn). The NRC provided the administrative support. The name "Examination Unit" was chosen as being sufficiently ambiguous to mask the true purpose yet not irrelevant to the NRC's work.

The Examination Unit soon ran into difficulties, since Britain and the United States did not co-operate. Yardley was persona non grata with both because his book, *The American Black Chamber*, published in 1931, had compromised British and American cryptography. Yardley therefore was replaced when his contract expired in December 1941 by a British expert, Oliver Strachey.

The unit could now play a more useful role in allied intelligence activities. A committee to oversee its operations was established under Pearson, with representatives from the services and the Royal Canadian Mounted Police. Another body, the "Y" Committee, prevented duplication of effort between the unit and the service intelligence operations. External Affairs also chaired that committee. More technical subjects were handled by a subcommittee.

At first, the Examination Unit monitored communications between the French legation in Ottawa and Vichy. Following Pearl Harbor it also intercepted Japanese traffic. Apparently at the urging of William Stephenson, a Canadian by origin who had established British Security Coordination (to represent the major British security and intelligence agencies and maintain liaison with their US counterparts) in New York after the fall of France, the department decided to form the Special Intelligence Section to analyse the product. It came into being in September 1942, and, though housed with the Examination Unit next door to King's residence, Laurier House, its members remained officers of External Affairs.

Chosen to head the section, because of his academic background and Japanese expertise, was Herbert Norman. The reports prepared by the Special Intelligence Section were sent to the under-secretary, the service directors of intelligence, and British Security Coordination in New York. As well, it was arranged for Norman to hold discussions in New York and Washington shortly after his appointment. "I feel," Stone wrote to Stephenson, "that the establishment of these close connections will be of much benefit to everyone. We clearly appreciate that in the field particularly, a constant interchange of information and ideas is highly desirable. From our end we will do everything we can to facilitate this."[84]

This co-operation, according to an unpublished history of the Examination Unit, contributed to the common cause: "From practically nothing in 1941, Ottawa grew in three years to the stature of London and Washington in those two fields (French and Japanese) on which we have worked. We have pulled our own weight in these fields and made many worthwhile contributions to the common pool of knowledge, while at the same time feeding a continuous stream of intelligence to the Department of External Affairs and to the Directors of Intelligence."[85]

More modest was the department's role in the best-known allied intelligence operation in Canada during the war: the training of agents at the so-called Camp X (nicknamed the "country house" by Robertson), located on the shore of Lake Ontario near Oshawa. Camp X (Special Training School 103) was a British project under the direction of the Special Operations Executive (SOE), established in Canada because, at the time the idea was conceived, the United States had not entered the war. External Affairs functioned as the principal channel for liaison with British Security Coordination and Stephenson in New York. Most of the routine liaison was handled in turn by Stone and Glazebrook.

Camp X opened its doors two days after Pearl Harbor and closed in April 1944. It fostered co-operation between SOE and its US counterpart, the Office of Strategic Services (forerunner of the Central Intelligence Agency). "For Canadians," David Stafford observes in his study of the subject, "Camp X provided an opportunity to demonstrate their commitment to the British war effort, their friendship for the United States, and their competence and independence in the face of both."[86]

Stafford's generalizations about Camp X are applicable to Canadian objectives generally at the midpoint of the war. Fully committed to the war effort, the government wanted a voice in allied councils commensurate with its contribution. After Pearl Harbor, the department developed the rationale on which Canadian arguments for recognition were based. Better organization, greater resources, and expanded representation abroad enabled the department to make the case for Canada and contributed to credibility as an ally. The pressure on the department, meanwhile, was continually increasing, as the fortunes of war turned in favour of the allies and planning began for the peacetime reconstruction of the international system. Thus the country needed vigorous promotion of its interests abroad, and the department had to grow and adapt in order to make its contribution effectively.

Chapter Ten
Preparing for Victory: 1943–1945

REORGANIZATION AND EXPANSION

The challenge

GENERATIONAL CHANGE AFFECTED DEPARTMENTAL LEADERSHIP striking-ly from 1943 onward. The under-secretary, Norman Robertson, had been too young to fight in the First World War, but a number of his senior colleagues had experienced that conflict, and he shared their determination that this time a basis should be found for a lasting peace. The department's new leaders, in the words of John Holmes, "sought for things Canada might do rather than things Canada might avoid doing."[1] They worked in particular to secure a voice for Canada in post-war international relations appropriate to its strength and its contribution to the defeat of the enemy.

Conditions in Canada early in 1943 were more favourable than formerly to governmental endorsement of the department's objectives. With the plebiscite of 1942 behind him, King for a time was less preoccupied by the divisive issue of conscription; he, like everyone, was reassured by improved allied fortunes overseas; and he did not consider the recently renamed Progressive Conservative party under John Bracken a serious threat. "There was no period in the war," J. W. Pickersgill has observed in *The Mackenzie King Record*, "when the war itself seemed so remote from Canada as the first six months of 1943: the fear of defeat had passed and the Canadian Army was not yet engaged in actual hostilities."[2]

At the same time, King doubtless knew that domestic stability was subject to disruption, as happened after Canadian troops became actively engaged on the European continent and concerns about a manpower shortage produced a new conscription crisis in 1944. He therefore was still no enthusiast for parliamentary discussion of foreign policy. The subject received attention there mainly when departmental estimates were presented, and until October 1945 the prime minister resisted attempts to create a House of Commons standing committee on external affairs to supersede the moribund Committee on Industrial and International Relations.[3]

Lack of parliamentary debate disappointed those who wanted to encourage public awareness of Canada's external interests, but the department saw advantages in low exposure. Robertson by nature preferred to avoid the limelight,[4] and senior officers saved the time that frequent responses to debate would have consumed. King, meanwhile, could deal with the changing international situation without as many second thoughts as vigorous and contradictory public discussion might have produced. In the circumstances, the department was able to concentrate on the evolving agenda of international issues and on organizational and other requirements for dealing with it effectively.

Economic Division

The area of departmental activity perhaps most in need of better organization in 1943 was the economic. Ottawa had a growing community of decision-makers in this field, which included some of the most powerful public servants of the day. Among them were Clifford Clark, deputy minister of finance; Graham Towers, governor of the Bank of Canada; Louis Rasminsky, alternate chairman of the Foreign Exchange Control Board and later executive assistant to Towers; W. A. Mackintosh, special assistant to the deputy minister of finance; R. B. Bryce of the same department; and Donald Gordon, chairman of the Wartime Prices and Trade Board. Robertson, a veteran of the trade negotiations in the 1930s, was part of this group. A member of the Advisory Committee on Economic Policy (commonly known as the Economic Advisory Committee) and the Foreign Exchange Control Board, he had helped to formulate wartime commercial policy, even before becoming under-secretary.

Robertson's advice was valued by his peers in the economic community, and his closeness to King made him an effective channel to convey their views to the prime minister.[5] The department's resources for dealing with these subjects, however, were thin: at the time Robertson became under-secretary, commercial policy and agreements were assigned to T. A. Stone, part-time. In the US State Department, by contrast, the work was divided among six divisions. At Hume Wrong's urging, Robertson used the US example in an effort to secure King's approval for substantial expansion in Ottawa. "We are trying to cover the same ground in the Department here," the under-secretary reported. "Stone, single-handed, except for such assistance as I can give him, performs in the Department the functions of five of the six divisions under the Board of Economic Operations in the Department of State, and looks after questions of censorship as well. He, among others, is slipping behind in his work which is steadily increasing beyond the capacity of our establishment."[6]

King did not authorize enhancement of the department's resources for economic work, nor did the reorganization of 1941 bring coherence to the activity. Despite creation of the Diplomatic and Economic Division, responsibility was fragmented. Shipping questions were separated from export controls and economic warfare from war production, and a number of other tasks were distributed haphazardly. By April 1942, as a result, Stone was complaining to the under-secretary about disorganization both at home and in Washington, where much of the activity took place. "I believe," Stone wrote,

> that unless the Department can organize itself efficiently to work more expeditiously, to take more effective decisions based on considerations of the whole field, to co-ordinate its relations with other departments and agencies in one division, we should resign ourselves to playing a secondary role in a good many matters where it should be considered essential for us to take the lead. It is not only impossible, under present circumstances, for us to make the running but also not right for us to try. It is essential to face the fact that as a result of our lack of staff, lack of organization and resulting lack of efficiency in the economic fields External Affairs is being most severely criticized by other departments of the government and that whenever these other departments can short-circuit us they do so. Officers of the department have been told this in so many words . . . when in point of fact our real role—we are the only department that can play this part—is to bring some kind of order into chaotic crises which arise from time to time.[7]

In February 1943 an economic division was created to handle a broad range of subjects, such as commercial relations, foreign exchange control, merchant shipping, compensation for war damage, economic warfare, liaison with other departments, the economic side of war supplies and relief, and the international economic aspects of post-war planning.[8] The leadership (first Scott Macdonald and then Henry Angus), however, did not become part of the team of key economic decision-makers in Ottawa.

Economic work in External Affairs was now better organized, but the department's influence continued to depend on Robertson's expertise and his closeness to the prime minister.

Information work

The departmental organization expanded to accommodate also public relations, which, before the war, had been left to the initiative of heads of post. Departmental headquarters had no resources to support their efforts, nor any considered policy on the subject. War, however, created a requirement to mobilize public opinion in support of the government's policies at home and in allied countries. The resultant publicity campaigns dealt with aspects of external relations and formed part of the government's operations abroad.

The department became involved only gradually, for it had little to do with the establishment of the agencies responsible for the federal government's programs. The first of these, the Directorate of Public Information, was created in December 1939, to operate only within Canada.[9] As the war effort increased, a more structured and wider-ranging operation was sought, to make Canada's contributions to the allied cause better known not only at home but also abroad, especially in the United States.

In September 1942 the Directorate of Public Information was replaced by the Wartime Information Board (WIB), intended to facilitate distribution of Canadian war news and information in Canada and elsewhere, particularly in the United States, and "to establish offices within and without Canada, as it may deem appropriate."[10] In due course, such offices were opened in New York, Washington, London, Canberra, and Paris. Although under the jurisdiction of the heads of post, these offices on occasion acted quite independently, thereby causing friction between the department and the board. When their work was co-ordinated with other activities, however, they could assist Canadian missions. In Canberra, the board's representative worked with the high commissioner to ease strains developed earlier in the war. There was also a good relationship between the posts in Latin America and a special section of the board created in 1943 to deal with the region.

The board's external activities gave the department a substantial interest in the operations of its governing body, which met regularly to determine priorities at home and abroad. Robertson sometimes attended, depending on the agenda, although the department was usually represented by Pearson and, after his posting to Washington, by Wrong.[11]

Also of interest to the department was the International Service of the Canadian Broadcasting Corporation (CBC-IS), which began operation early in 1945. The order-in-council creating the service recognized that international broadcasting would be closely related to Canada's external relations and that the department therefore would play an important role, particularly in policy. The department was a very active member of the Short Wave Advisory Committee and laid claim to something more than the consultative role envisaged by the order-in-council. In one early meeting of the committee, on June 23, 1944, the general manager of the CBC, Augustin Frigon, acknowledged that "External Affairs was the final authority on all policy decisions."[12]

As Frigon's statement indicated, information work was gaining recognition as part of the department's mandate and necessitated organizational change. The department's interests were identified in a memorandum of May 26, 1944, by Gordon Robertson, who was serving in the under-secretary's office. His proposals arose from two main considerations: that the Wartime Information Board was not designed to meet the posts' information and cultural needs and that this resource, though inadequate, would presumably disappear once peace returned. He therefore suggested that the department develop its own mechanism to meet these requirements during the post-war period. Among the activities he envisaged were press relations at home and abroad, as well as information work generally, all to be carried out independently, without the problems of policy co-ordination that had occurred with the WIB. He also put forward a strong case for a program of cultural relations, including distribution of books, films, radio programs, and music, exchanges with other countries of works in those media and of scholars and lecturers, visits abroad by Canadian cultural leaders, and provision of scholarships and fellowships.

Wide circulation of the memorandum in the department produced a generally favourable response. Even Hume Wrong, who was not enthusiastic, acknowledged that some action should be taken. "I am myself allergic to proposals for expanding our activities in this field at the present time," he wrote, "because I think that they do not rank high enough in our priorities to warrant the expenditure of time, personnel, and money involved. I feel sure, however, that we shall have to undertake greater activities in this field and it might clear the path somewhat if we were to make progress towards settling policy and defining responsibility."[13]

The Information Division came into being in September 1944 under the direction of one of the special wartime assistants, T. W. L. MacDermot, but with fewer duties than Robertson had envisaged. It was to answer inquiries from the public, the press, and the posts; prepare a monthly news bulletin, primarily for the offices abroad; circulate reports and memoranda of interest to them; and arrange press conferences. A good deal of time was spent on liaison work with the National Film Board, the WIB (on which MacDermot became departmental representative), and CBC-IS. There was no mandate for the promotion of cultural relations.

The Information Division did virtually no writing of its own but distributed material obtained from other sources. It therefore was not equipped to replace the WIB, which in September 1945 was succeeded instead by the Canadian Information Service (CIS). This service was exclusively to provide information and news outside Canada, which it did partly through the offices established abroad by the WIB. Because of its international mandate, External Affairs was represented on the supervisory committee of the CIS. The under-secretary occasionally attended meetings, but the usual departmental participant was MacDermot.[14]

Reorganization

Creation of two new divisions, together with changing wartime demands, required some alterations to the organizational structure devised in 1941. These came about in two stages. The first, approved in December 1944 with retroactive effect to July 1 of that year, gave the title deputy under-secretary to Wrong and Read, who had assumed part of Robertson's responsibility for overseeing the various divisions.[15] The second, the work of Wrong, was a reorganization of the divisional structure, which came into operation in January 1945.

Reflecting the expansion in the department's activities, the reorganization of 1945[16] increased the number of divisions. People in charge of most units were now known as chiefs or heads of division, with four senior officers ranged above them. One of these four was the under-secretary, to whom the Economic and Information divisions and the Administrative Branch reported. Wrong, given the personal rank of associate under-secretary in recognition of his close relationship to Robertson,[17] oversaw the political divisions. Known as First, Second, and Third Political, these dealt respectively with international organizations; with the Commonwealth, Europe, the Middle East, and Africa; and with the United States, Latin America, and Asia. Laurent Beaudry, as assistant under-secretary, was in charge of the Diplomatic Division (dealing with protocol, questions pertaining to the diplomatic corps in Ottawa, immigration, and consular matters) and supervised the work of the Passport Office.

John Read remained legal adviser, in charge of the Legal Division. Beginning about April 1946, a treaty division, reporting to Read, registered and published international agreements of interest to Canada; this was incorporated into the Legal Division in the spring of 1947. In recognition of the growing volume of work it handled as the war ended, the Special Section was raised to divisional status in the reorganization of 1945, also under Read. Once the war was over, however, the workload began to decrease, and in the autumn of 1945 the division again became a section, within the Legal Division, where it remained until, its tasks having been completed, it was closed at the end of 1946.[18]

Wrong's reorganization confirmed that the division would be the key operational unit. The problem remained of co-ordinating activities that involved both area and functional divisions. Weekly meetings of heads of division were for exchange of information on work in progress rather than for collegial decision-making. Co-ordination depended on the under-secretary and his associate, who reviewed all proposals going forward to ministers from the department. The workload, therefore, continued to be unevenly distributed, and success in an activity depended on the attention it received at the top.

The latter consequence was reinforced by another feature of Wrong's changes, which would characterize the department for some years to come. As indicated by the vague names he gave to the political divisions, Wrong wanted to allow flexibility so that the organization could be altered according to the availability and interests of personnel. At least at the top, jobs were to be made for men rather than men for jobs.[19] Thus the department's strength in its various branches would depend not so much on its organizational structure as on the interests, abilities, and reputations of those in charge.

The under-secretary

In the new framework as in the old, the under-secretary was the principal source of foreign policy advice for the prime minister. By 1943, Robertson's relationship with King had long since recovered from the momentary disruption over St Pierre and Miquelon, and Robertson was firmly established as the prime minister's most trusted confidant. "No one ever completely took Skelton's place," J. W. Pickersgill observed later, "although Norman Robertson . . . quickly gained and retained a greater measure of Mackenzie King's confidence than any other adviser of the closing years of his life."[20]

There was a heavy price to be paid for such closeness, as King himself was aware. There was, he acknowledged in November 1942, "a much too great pressure upon Robertson himself, inadequate staff in his office as well as in mine. Gave him authority to use some of the money provided by Parliament for entertaining guests, when persons here on diplomatic missions, whom it is necessary for him to see. Told him I would initial the outlays up to a thousand dollars. It is really shameful the burdens we have been throwing on our staffs, financial as well as official; far beyond their capacity to bear."[21] Such concern was no more lasting for Robertson than it had been for Skelton. Busier than ever as a result of the war, the prime minister remained a demanding and unpredictable employer. To serve him effectively, therefore, Robertson had to commit all his time to public service. His hobby, observed an officer of the British high commissioner's office in 1944, was "work, more work."[22]

Arnold Heeney's appointment in 1940 as secretary to the cabinet and clerk of the privy council had lessened the department's responsibility for the prime minister's requirements while introducing a new participant in policy-making. Robertson and Heeney had a close working relationship, reinforced by the latter's inevitable involvement in the international aspects of the prime minister's work. Also helpful was the presence of departmental officers on the prime minister's staff. James Gibson, for example, handled much of the paper work dealing with external affairs, and the department was a beneficiary of his growing sensitivity to the importance of timing in getting prompt decisions from the prime minister. As well, Gibson was normally in the party when King travelled abroad on official business, looking after many of the prime minister's practical requirements, participating in drafting and briefing, and taking notes in meetings with other international figures.[23]

Increasing the officer staff

Valuable though such outside help might be, more officers were needed if the department's objectives were to be prosecuted effectively. Already stretched to the limit by wartime assignments, the permanent staff in this category could expect no relief with the return of peace. In a survey of future requirements in 1943, Wrong estimated that within five years there would be work for approximately seventy-five officers abroad and between forty and fifty in Ottawa.[24] In other words, the officer strength would have to be doubled by 1948.

To meet anticipated demand, the department had to reverse its earlier decision to forgo making appointments to career positions until after the war. It was still policy that such positions should be filled exclusively by men: recruits therefore would be found primarily within the armed forces, since the majority of able-bodied university graduates were in uniform. In accordance with the requirements of the Civil Service Commission, preference would be given to veterans who had served overseas.

A committee of senior departmental officers was established in October 1943 to study recruiting.[25] Because the war was assumed to have interrupted the education of many potential candidates, it was decided that a special category of "learner" should be created to accommodate those who did not possess the academic qualifications normally demanded of third secretaries. Entrants with this designation would be expected to complete their degrees and at some future date would be given educational leave to do so. Graduates would be unlikely to have attained the educational level common in pre-war candidates, and so less emphasis than formerly was to be placed on the written part of the examination.

In January 1944, the department decided to embark on a three-year program of recruitment. The positions were to be advertised to all ranks on active service overseas, to discharged members of the forces who had served overseas, and to prisoners of war who had been Canadian residents at the time of their enlistment. Beginning in August 1944, examining boards conducted interviews at Canada House in London and on the continent of Europe. Writing skills and knowledge were also tested by the requirement to compose an essay. This procedure was followed until the end of 1945. By then, as a result of repatriation, there were many eligible candidates in Canada, and the last set of interviews in London had suggested, according to one examiner, that the department was reaching "the bottom of the barrel" there.[26] In 1946, therefore, the selection process was carried out in Canada.

The recruiting drive brought sixty-four officers to the department between 1944 and 1946. Most entered as third secretary or equivalent, but a few were learners, and some, because of their rank in the armed services or other special qualifications, were given higher standing. Starting in September 1944, the old designations, based on diplomatic rank, were replaced by a new one, foreign service officer (FSO), divided into six numerical grades, with level 1 being that at which most recruits entered.

Of the sixty-four new officers, twelve were francophones, a somewhat smaller proportion than in the competitions held at the beginning of the war. Thus the department acquired a more heavily anglophone character, although four were from outside the Anglo-French mainstream.

As anticipated, the educational level was somewhat lower than before the war. Most new officers were university graduates, but only thirty-three are shown as having any post-graduate education. Four were Rhodes scholars, but two did not attend Oxford and one did so, on educational leave, only after joining the department. All but eight are listed as veterans of the armed forces. Although the educational standard established when Skelton was under-secretary may have been somewhat relaxed, the criterion of maturity, which he had also emphasized, was observed to the full. As a result, the department was well supplied with new officers able to move quickly into positions of responsibility.

The ability of the new officers to handle their duties was enhanced by the development, for the first time, of a training program, which eventually became known as "the university of the East Block." At the request of the under-secretary, the plans were laid by John Holmes and Gordon Robertson, and the course was in place when the first group of probationary officers arrived in the autumn of 1944. It took the form of a combination of seminars, intended to introduce the newcomers to the practical side of their work, and discussion groups, in which senior officers spoke about various aspects of Canadian policy.[27] The training provided had to be a crash course. "Pressure on staff," Robertson noted, "has been such that we will probably find ourselves compelled to send them abroad sooner than would have been desirable."[28]

The recruitment of servicemen did not supply needed additional strength in the higher grades. One possible solution was to retain the services of the temporary wartime assistants. The department did not consider all such officers suitable for a diplomatic career,[29] but it did encourage likely candidates to stay on. A number returned to teaching positions in the universities: student enrolments swelled with returning veterans, and the attraction was strong.

A letter from F. H. Soward to an academic colleague is perhaps typical of those who regarded work in the department as an interruption, for a national emergency, in a scholarly career:

> From the standpoint of seeing from the inside the operations of diplomacy and having access to material which otherwise would not be available, the experience is invaluable. There is also a real stimulus being in Ottawa at a time when it has considerable claim at being a world capital. On the other hand, I find the hours rather trying (in contrast to university hours) and the regular routine at a desk 50 weeks in the year is quite a sharp change from our way of living. I look on it essentially as a war job and will gladly return to the academic hall when the need for assistance is less great in the department. There is also the sense of feeling that perhaps I am making some contribution to the war effort in a more direct way than I could in university life.[30]

Some, however, were attracted by the possibilities of the public service. In 1946, a special competition was held whereby they could qualify for permanent senior positions.

Working conditions

The influx of new officers was not accompanied by a corresponding change in conditions of service: the only innovation of note was the consolidation into a single list of the permanent establishments for headquarters and offices abroad, to give the department greater flexibility in moving staff from one location to another.[31] New officers, therefore, were required to adapt to a regime designed by and reflecting the interests of their seniors, and not all of what they found was to their liking. One cause of dissatisfaction was the salary level, which was particularly hard on junior staff members in Ottawa.[32] They might fare better on posting, since there was still no income tax on the salaries of those outside the country. Some new recruits, however, were attracted by better pay elsewhere and left after a brief period in the service.

Also a problem was uneven distribution of work. One new recruit might be plunged directly into important activities, but another might find himself less than fully taxed. John Starnes, posted to the legation to the allied governments in London as third secretary in 1944, considered the mission overstaffed, a situation he found disquieting with the war still going on. "There is only one good reason," he wrote, "why people such as . . . myself have not been fighting—and that being that there was work to be done which required whatever skill and talents we could muster—and if one doesn't do that job then what bloody right have we to be sitting by while others are really doing something worthwhile?"[33]

Back in Ottawa in the autumn of 1945, Starnes found the same problem. Senior officers remained under intense pressure, eased somewhat by a carefully cultivated nonchalance that played down the urgency and importance of matters at hand. Some enjoyed the detached, university-like atmosphere that resulted,[34] but Starnes would have liked more vigorous activity. Some of the work seemed boring: the Diplomatic division was "but one step removed from the grave," and an officer being posted to Washington from there was badly in need of a "chance to exercise his brain." When Starnes was doing assignments for the First and Second Political divisions, he had insufficient work and "considered that most of it could be done by a good, intelligent policeman!"

Also underused, in Starnes's view, were the women employees, with results harmful to the department: "They make the requirements for a stenographer something comparable to post-graduate work and then having obtained the services of such girls they put them on the difficult task of typing or filing—the results: the girls, or the better ones at least, simply leave for better jobs. . . . Seems to me that there *must* be something for such girls to do other than filing or typing? Prejudices, coupled with the argument that these girls are apt to marry after being carefully trained, seem to be the greatest stumbling blocks."[35] Clearly, staffing arrangements did not meet the challenges of the post-war world. Just as clearly, recruitment of veterans brought in officers who recognized the problems, who had ideas about how to solve them, and who had the experience, self-confidence, and drive to become a force for change.

Diplomatic and consular representation

Meanwhile, new pressures affected representation abroad. A discussion between Roosevelt and King in the spring of 1943 led to the decision to establish embassies rather than legations. Most countries had come to designate their offices abroad embassies. Doubt could arise about Canada's independence, since British embassies maintained officers (six in Washington) enjoying the title of minister, the same as that held by the heads of Commonwealth missions. As well, the prime minister was advised, constitutional considerations need no longer be an inhibition. "I think," the under-secretary told him, "that events have destroyed any validity that there may have been in the argument that the King could only be represented by one Ambassador in any country. This argument rests on the ancient doctrine that an Ambassador represented the person of the Sovereign in a way which gave him readier access to the Head of the foreign state."[36]

The first to be raised to embassy level was the legation in Washington, at the end of 1943. There was also a change within the Commonwealth, for South Africa was persuaded to follow the custom of the other members by designating its head of post in Ottawa high commissioner rather than accredited representative.[37]

Liberation in Europe made it possible to resume Canada's pre-war representation there and to reciprocate for some of the missions opened in Ottawa. Canadian diplomats returned not only to Paris but also to Brussels and The Hague. The ambassador to Belgium was now accredited also as minister to Luxemburg, and a resident minister was appointed to the Netherlands.[38] The new missions were an embassy in Greece, a legation in Norway, accredited also to Denmark, and a consulate general in Portugal. The prospect of peace also made possible the return of provincial representatives to London (where the only remaining such office, that of British Columbia, had been "used largely as a soldier's club during the war"[39]), beginning with an agent general of Ontario in 1944.

Despite the successes of the Allies, the conduct of diplomacy in Europe was not without its hazards. Marcel Cadieux, posted to London as third secretary in January 1944, vividly recalled the attacks on that city by incendiary bombs and the unmanned German V-1 aircraft late in the war:

> Une nuit je m'éveille. Il est deux heures du matin. L'alerte a été donnée. Les canons des environs font rage. La maison, à chaque salve, vibre. Quand les détonations s'apaisent, j'entends le grondement plein, précipité, terrible des engins ennemis.
>
> Des boules de feu s'avancent au-dessus de la ville. Elles disparaissent dans une grande lueur suivie d'une explosion sourde.
>
> J'ai peur. . . .
>
> Il n'y a rien à faire pour vous protéger. Les métros sont fermés. Et il est bien inutile de descendre dans la cave. Contre les bombes incendiaires, un abri improvisé sous un escalier de béton peut suffire. Mais

contre les bombes d'une tonne . . . vous êtes autant en sûreté dans votre chambre. . . .

Un matin, je mettais la dernière main à une dépêche sur les allocations familiales: je relisais mes notes et j'allais rédiger la conclusion quant la cloche m'obligeait à quitter mon bureau pour l'abri. Je n'étais pas aussitôt revenu et remis des émotions de la dernière alerte—parfois, les bombes passaient si bas que toutes les fenêtres de Canada House en tremblaient—qu'une nouvelle sonnerie me ramenait à l'abri. Il m'a fallu presque toute la matinée pour arriver à terminer mon dernier paragraphe.[40]

Diplomatic response to the advance of the allied forces was also difficult to arrange. "The good news of the liberation," the chargé d'affaires to the allied governments in London was told in September 1944, "is coming in faster than our preparations for it." There would, it was expected, have to be "a good deal of improvisation and, often entirely temporary assignments." The posting of female clerks to the continent "in the first instance" was discouraged; their functions should be performed temporarily instead by men on secondment from the armed forces.

Despite the problems, the government urgently wanted a presence in the newly liberated allied countries.[41] As a result, resources had to be husbanded carefully, and not all exchanges were reciprocal. Not only was dual accreditation from Oslo the response to the appointment of a Danish minister in Ottawa, there was for the time being no Canadian counterpart to representatives received from Sweden, Switzerland, and Turkey. As in the past, there was a shortage both of potential heads of post and of experienced staff. Certainly the prospect of peace did not give much opportunity to redeploy personnel through the closing of war-related missions. Only three such posts, all of them small, suffered that fate: the legation to the allied governments and the consulates in St Pierre and Miquelon and in Greenland.

There were decisions to be made about representatives of countries regarded as unfriendly or worse during the war. Easiest to agree to was the reopening of the former French consulates, no longer a problem when not controlled by Vichy, although Canada wanted the informal designation "consular office" to be used until a provisional government in Paris was recognized.[42] A representative was also accepted from Italy, to be located, at the suggestion of the Canadian government, in Ottawa rather than in Montreal as the Italians proposed and to have the status of "agent with the personal rank of Consul General."[43] Much cooler was the attitude toward Spain, neutral throughout the war. In 1943, the government had received evidence indicating that a Spanish consular officer in Vancouver was acting as an enemy agent, and it was dissatisfied with the way the matter had been handled in Madrid. Partly for that reason, Canada rejected an overture from Spain to exchange diplomatic missions. The new consulate general in Lisbon was given responsibility for commercial but not other relations with Spain.[44] As well, Spain continued to maintain a consulate general in Montreal.

The department had also to attend to other parts of the world in which there were growing Canadian interests. One such was Latin America. Because of the manpower problem, no early action could be taken to extend Canadian representation there beyond the posts opened in Argentina, Brazil, and Chile. Other countries in the region, however, sought similar exchanges, and Ottawa knew the usefulness to the allied war effort of a positive response. As an interim gesture, the government encouraged countries wishing to open diplomatic missions to establish consular offices instead.

When, by 1944, it became possible to consider expansion in Latin America, the preference was for the larger states and those in which there was a substantial Canadian business interest. Thus embassies were opened in Mexico and Peru in 1944, a legation was established in Cuba in 1945, and a consulate general in Venezuela in 1946. There was not much interest in the smaller countries with little economic potential. In this context, Haiti, the only other francophone nation in the Americas, posed a rather awkward problem. "The acceptance of a minister from the Dominican Republic," Robertson wrote privately to Pearson, "would immediately involve a parallel request on the part of Haiti. . . . In view of the special cultural ties shared by Haiti and the Province of Quebec, it would be inadvisable to extend to the Dominican Republic a concession that was not granted to Haiti." It would be better, therefore, not to exchange diplomatic representatives with either.[45] The possibility that the government of Adélard Godbout in Quebec might open offices of its own in Haiti or elsewhere in the region was not regarded with enthusiasm, but discreet pressure from the department was sufficient to keep such plans from coming to fruition.

Initially, none of the new missions in Latin America was headed by a career officer from External Affairs. The situation soon changed in Mexico, however, for in November 1944 Keenleyside was posted there as ambassador. Appointed acting consul general in Venezuela was C. S. Bissett, a trade commissioner with considerable experience in Latin America.

Also of much interest to the department was the Canadian presence in the United States, where Pearson succeeded Leighton McCarthy as ambassador in 1945. The focus of attention was consular representation. One reason was the appearance in 1943 of an office to represent the interests of Quebec in New York. This was considered "normal," so long as it only promoted trade, tourism, and social contacts. At the same time, the possibility that such agencies established abroad by Quebec might some day be given rather grander assignments produced "a certain impression" in the department. Apparently in response, the consulate general in New York was made more representative of the Canadian population by the posting there of a francophone officer as vice consul.[46] Since the government of Quebec seemed unlikely to go beyond the "normal" in its activities abroad in the foreseeable future, action of this kind could be assumed to be a sufficient departmental response.

Taken more seriously was the desirability of assuming the consular functions still performed on behalf of Canadians by British representatives in the United States. The prospect of expanding Canadian representation across the country was of much interest to Pearson, and the subject was thoroughly studied both at the embassy and in Ottawa. The immediate result was modest in the extreme—a temporary vice consulate in Portland, Maine. Portland was a rail and oil-pipeline terminal important to Canada, and the British office that had handled Canadian interests was being closed.

The new post, which became an honorary vice consulate in April 1946, meant almost nothing in terms of a distinctive Canadian presence in the United States, and Pearson was exasperated that so little had resulted from the plans that had been made. "I can't refrain from registering my disappointment," he told Robertson,

> that our consular service in the United States is being extended in this way and for the reason that a British Vice Consulate is being closed. Solvitur ambulando has its merits, but surely should not be the basis for the development of a Canadian Consular Service. Isn't there something absurd about Canadian consular representation in Portland, and no such representation in places like Detroit, Buffalo, Chicago, or Los Angeles. I feel very strongly that our consular service in this country must be set up according to a carefully worked out plan and that we are only on the road to trouble and confusion if we try to do it in any other way.[47]

This temporary expedient, however, was not intended to be a substitute for the larger plans already formulated. They would continue to receive attention and to produce a network of consulates in the United States that would develop as resources became available.

Property abroad

Even though all the department's plans were not immediately carried out, expansion during and immediately after the war raised numerous questions about acquisition of property for chanceries and official residences and furnishing of new premises. Early in 1944 an advisory committee was formed, consisting of three officers' wives—Katherine Keenleyside, Alexandra Stone, and Joyce Wrong—to look into acquiring characteristically Canadian furnishings for the posts. In April, it submitted a report listing Canadian sources for various household requirements such as silverware, china, linen, and furniture. The department was also pressured by an interdepartmental committee on Canadian hand arts and crafts, chaired by the director of the National Gallery.[48]

It was clear that more professional expertise would also be required. Robertson had his eye out for a suitable candidate and by the fall of 1945 had settled on Antoine Monette, a Montreal architect trained in France. During the war he had served in the armed forces and had been Canadian representative on a mission headed by Sir Leonard Woolley, a distinguished archaeologist, advising the allied authorities on the preservation of works of art and architecture in liberated areas. In recommending to the prime minister Monette's appointment, Robertson noted that under wartime conditions the department had had to rent premises abroad, an expensive and hence unsatisfactory procedure. Now it would be appropriate to buy, but he was

> reluctant to recommend purchasing for permanent occupation on the sole advice of the Ambassador or High Commissioner who happens to be on the spot. This is a responsibility which can only be adequately handled by a really experienced man who can look over alternative properties, relate standards of accommodation in one post to what we may be able to provide in another, and generally take a more informed view of what the long-run interests of the Canadian diplomatic service will require. In addition to the question of from time to time purchasing or building quarters for our permanent representation abroad, there is the related question of furnishing them appropriately. This too is becoming a sizeable commitment and one that Matthews cannot continue to handle with his present staff.

Robertson's memorandum was "read with pleasure" by the prime minister, but, when the approval of Treasury Board was sought, the suggestion was made that the required services be obtained from the Architectural Branch of the Department of Public Works.[49] Robertson countered that, because of the overseas operations of External Affairs, it would be false economy to rely on architects who had only domestic experience, particularly in view of the size of the investment involved: "This Department anticipates the need of spending from $6,000,000 to $7,000,000 in the next few years in acquiring and furnishing offices and residences for its over-

seas missions. It is, in my opinion, essential that the man selected to supervise and in some measure to standardize these purchases should come under
the immediate control of this Department. Only then, could he give the
necessary full-time study to our needs and be sent without any delay to
posts requiring urgent attention in the matter of accommodation and
furnishings."[50]

The board relented, and Monette was hired as special adviser to the
under-secretary on property and furnishings. His appointment, however,
did not produce immediately the round of purchases contemplated by
Robertson, for the prime minister was reluctant to authorize the expenditures involved. His feelings were brought to a head in August 1946, when,
on a visit to Paris, he was informed of plans to buy a new residence for
the ambassador. "I felt the time had come," he told his diary

> when I should speak out plainly as to where we were getting and said
> to R[obertson] I had become very deeply concerned about expenditures
> in connection with E.A. . . . Also that I felt we had to consider together
> various suggestions that had been made. . . . I did not think our people
> would understand. . . . I did not want the last of my associations with
> E.A. to be one concerning which there might be great public discussion
> in Canada as to questionable expenditures, etc. . . . At any rate, I was
> not prepared to take them on myself without going over the whole situa-
> tion with the Cabinet and having them share responsibility. I added that
> I might leave all that business to whoever I shall appoint as a successor.
> Let him take responsibility as he would be the one who would have to
> continue to face it in Parlt. I then said that I thought what would be
> the best plan, was to have the committee on E.A. go into the whole
> question of outlays for conferences, buildings, etc. Robertson saw pretty
> quickly that I thought things were going too far. Did not press very
> much. I told him I would do nothing while on this side at all until I
> had a chance for a conference with colleagues.[51]

At a cabinet meeting in October, King raised the matter of referring
property acquisition to the House of Commons Standing Committee on
External Affairs; the recommendation was approved at a further meeting
in December.[52] There was little acquisition of property, but at least the
means of bringing it about were now in place.

ENDING THE WAR

Clearly the government was not ready to confront all the administrative
implications of a more assertive position in international affairs. The
department therefore had to interpret its mandate carefully so as to apply

its resources effectively toward its most important objectives. Activities related only to the conduct of the war could be wound up quickly as the fighting came to an end. Others, for example, involving resettlement of persons displaced by the war, remained active well after the cessation of hostilities. A number of temporary wartime activities consequently had to be continued even as the department planned for peacetime.

The Quebec conferences

The war-related events that attracted the most attention in Canada were not necessarily those that imposed the heaviest burden on the department. This was true of the Quebec conferences of 1943 and 1944, in which the active participants were Roosevelt and Churchill, with King serving as host and engaging in private discussions with the other leaders. Both conferences also provided an opportunity for Churchill and others from the United Kingdom to meet with the Cabinet War Committee and therefore required substantial Canadian ministerial presence.

Organization was co-ordinated not by External Affairs but by the under-secretary of state, E. H. Coleman, with support from a number of sources. Press relations were handled by the Wartime Information Board, and the armed forces assisted—most notably, the army communications service looked after such facilities as telephones. External Affairs set up a cypher unit for Canadian use on both occasions. Robertson attended both conferences. In 1943 he was supported by three members of his office: Marjorie McKenzie, Saul Rae, and Sybil Rump. The following year, he was accompanied by Sybil Rump and Joe Boyce, who was also in the under-secretary's office at the time.[53]

Conduct of the war

The conduct of the war itself continued to be outside the purview of the department, although certain negotiations with the allies involved Canadian representatives abroad, especially Massey in London. Among the subjects engaging Massey's attention were the government's concern to secure suitable public recognition of Canadian participation in the allied landings in Sicily in 1943 and Normandy in 1944 and allocation of transport for repatriation of Canadian troops after the end of the war in Europe. There was also communication between the prime ministers (especially on Sicily) and between the department and the Dominions Office. Normally, the simultaneous operation of several centres did not cause confusion, but on one occasion Massey was embarrassed, when a press release by National Defence suggested that Canada would settle for a slower pace for repatriation of troops than the high commissioner had been arguing for in London.[54]

With the approach of peace in Europe, the department had to look at plans for the use of Canadian forces against Japan. Strict limitations on the possibilities were set by the prime minister. "The Canadian people excepting the province of B.C.," he observed in his diary on January 5, 1944, "are not going to be enthusiastic about going on with the war against Japan."[55] Canada in his view should show solidarity with the United States, the United Kingdom, and Australia, but only by making a modest commitment to the Pacific theatre.

Development of means to fulfil this objective was chiefly the work of National Defence, but public servants from other branches of government were involved as well, notably Heeney, Robertson, and Pope, the last after his appointment as military secretary to the Cabinet War Committee on September 5, 1944. In June of that year, Heeney and Robertson, at the request of the War Committee, collaborated with the chiefs of staff on a memorandum considering action Canada might take, "in relation to probable Allied strategy at the close of the European war and the particular interests of Canada as a member of the Commonwealth and as an American nation."[56] In due course, the government agreed to make available ships carrying approximately 15,000 naval personnel, an army division, and five RCAF squadrons, all volunteers, for service in the Pacific. Before they could become engaged, however, the war against Japan came to an end, on August 14, 1945.

Psychological warfare

The department continued also to have direct responsibility for certain aspects of the Canadian war effort. An activity attracting mixed response was psychological (or political) warfare, that is, propaganda directed against the enemy. The department's engagement had begun in 1942 in response to a request from the Political Warfare Executive in London, which operated under the Foreign Office, for recorded messages from interned German merchant seamen and prisoners of war for use in British propaganda broadcasts. Senior officers, notably Robertson and Wrong, were sceptical, considering personnel resources already overstretched. There was an enthusiastic response, however, from George Glazebrook, after he joined the department as a special wartime assistant in 1943, and Stone. As a result, the department agreed to go ahead,[57] with Stone becoming the main protagonist when Glazebrook moved into intelligence work.

Lack of suitable Canadian radio transmitters made it necessary to co-operate with the British Broadcasting Corporation and the US Office of Wartime Information in order to make use of material produced in this country. To ensure that the Canadian contribution be readily identifiable, Stone was determined that the product have a distinctive national character, particularly through broadcasts in French. Since German propaganda directed to France was intended to demonstrate that French Canadians did not want to fight, Stone was convinced that his country had a special role to play in the counter-offensive, as well as helping to bridge "the English-French gap" in Europe.[58] There was as well concern to establish a Canadian presence in this as in other fields of international endeavour, with a view to achieving greater influence after the war. "Only by participating in Allied political warfare directed towards Europe and the Far East," a memorandum to the Cabinet War Committee maintained, "can the Canadian authorities have a voice in the policies followed, control and direct the distribution of information related to Canada and strengthen our position in an important section of world information, not only in wartime but also with a view to Canada's place in the post-war world."[59]

In 1944, Stone was posted to London for work on psychological warfare. There he was close to the BBC, considered to be more effective than the Office of Wartime Information in reaching listeners behind enemy lines. Robertson supported the move, but made it clear that he still wanted the department's commitment to psychological warfare to be limited: "I have stipulated that activities of the psychological warfare committee involving External Affairs personnel should be cut to the bone, and that supplementary sideshows, however intriguing, should be eschewed. I feel our participation in Canada in psychological warfare should be limited to questions: (1) arising out of the presence of German prisoners of war in Canada; (2) directly concerning the liberation of France. Applications for our assistance in psychological warfare activites directed toward other targets should be discouraged."[60]

Stone was not deterred. From London, he began to deluge Ottawa with requests for scripts, leading Wrong to complain that, as he had feared, the transfer had "not in fact really reduced our responsibility in psychological warfare."[61] Rather, the prospect was for an increase in demand, for Stone decided to move his headquarters from Canada House to the centre of the BBC's operations in Bush House. Soon after he learned of this, Robertson removed Stone from psychological warfare activities by having him appointed chargé d'affaires to the allied governments. At the same time, his assistant was posted back to Ottawa, leaving no provision for full-time liaison with the BBC in London. Clearly international recognition in psychological warfare had little appeal to Ottawa; other priorities called for resources as wartime requirements began to scale down.

Intelligence work

The intelligence function, closely related as it was to the needs of war, also received reconsideration as peace approached. By January 1945 the department concluded that it could dispense with the Special Intelligence Section. The staff was badly needed elsewhere, and there was some doubt about the continuing value of the work being done on Japanese traffic. The section therefore was closed, although Herbert Norman continued to read and summarize Japanese intercepts. Now only brief summaries of the most important messages were made for senior officers, along with the occasional memorandum based on Japanese intelligence.[62]

The future of the Examination Unit meanwhile remained to be settled. This had been under discussion for some time, with Stone in particular favouring a unified cryptography facility that would serve as the Canadian counterpart to Britain's Bletchley Park and lay the foundation for a permanent international presence in the field. Stone's posting to London in June 1944 deprived the scheme of its chief exponent, and it never got off the ground.[63] By October 1944 the interdepartmental committee supervising the Examination Unit had decided that its future should depend on the attitude of External Affairs, which was having second thoughts about permanent commitment of the resources required. A draft letter to the chief of the general staff, prepared by Glazebrook in April 1945, explained the department's position: "The cost of the machinery alone would be prohibitive and it is generally recognized that only with modern machinery and a large staff can such a unit fill a useful role. The present Unit, set up for particular purposes under unusual conditions has been valuable. We are still receiving most useful intelligence from it, but the reasons for its establishment have, in part, disappeared." Accordingly, it was decided to close the Examination Unit at the end of July, transferring the Japanese section, which would continue to function, to army intelligence.[64]

Refugees

Persons displaced early in the war still needed resettlement. As before the war, the most urgent cases involved Jewish refugees in Europe. The Canadian government, based on its perception of the national mood, continued to be restrictive. Until his retirement in 1943, the director of immigration, F. C. Blair, remained as committed as ever to a strict interpretation of the government's intentions. Robertson and Wrong locked horns with Blair over treatment of refugee children, and disharmony between the two departments contributed to a negative response when US authorities (without consulting the Canadian government) suggested a conference on refugees in Ottawa in 1943. There had been "a regular guerrilla warfare" between External Affairs and the Immigration Branch, Robertson told Malcolm MacDonald, and a meeting in Canada would only "add to the embarrassment."[65] In due course, the conference took place in Bermuda, but, largely owing to the government's unwillingness to assume a high profile in refugee matters, Canada did not attend.

Although Blair's successor, A. L. Jolliffe, was somewhat more flexible, obstacles at home and abroad inhibited help to Jewish refugees while the war was on. In 1942, despite objections from the Immigration Branch, the cabinet agreed to a proposal, supported by External Affairs, for admission to Canada of 1,000 Jewish children in southern France, but the project fell through. Before the details of transfer via Switzerland could be worked out, the allies invaded North Africa, Germany moved into unoccupied France, and most of the children eventually fell into the hands of the Nazis.

In 1943, the cabinet, over the objections of the Immigration Branch, accepted another External Affairs recommendation, that Canada give haven to 200 Jewish refugee families who had managed to reach Spain and Portugal. This time the result was more successful. The Immigration Branch sent an officer to Lisbon to screen the candidates, and by 1944 a total of 114 families had been accepted.

Repatriation and resettlement

Other questions required new arrangements as need arose. These included repatriation of prisoners of war and interned civilians and resettlement of displaced persons. External Affairs was only one of the government departments involved. National Defence and the Immigration Branch were the most heavily engaged, but National Health and Welfare (Pensions and National Health until October 1944), Labour, and Reconstruction (created in 1944) were also active.

In External Affairs, repatriation and resettlement were dealt with primarily by the Special Division, with assistance from the Legal and the political divisions when necessary. Robertson and Wrong kept the whole subject under close scrutiny, partly because of its international implications but also because of its domestic political importance, since various ethnic groups were pressing members of Parliament and the government for favourable treatment of their communities in Europe.[66]

Meetings with the British and the Americans, both at home and abroad, were frequent, and correspondence with them was heavy, for Canada often depended on their facilities, especially in Asia, for repatriating civilians and servicemen. Dealings with the Soviet Union, in contrast, were fairly infrequent, since few questions of repatriation arose with that country.

There were, for instance, only five soldiers of Soviet origin among the thousands of German prisoners of war in Canada.[67] Abroad, posts in Europe and the embassy in China were in the front line. At times, special missions were sent overseas to deal with particular problems. External Affairs officers were invariably included in such missions and on occasion headed them. Herbert Norman, for example, was in charge of a team sent to Manila during the late summer of 1945 to assist in evacuation of Canadians in the area.

The return of Canadian and German prisoners of war was carried out expeditiously in 1945 and 1946. Repatriation and resettlement of civilians took longer, because shipping was in short supply. As well, decisions regarding displaced persons seeking to come to Canada had to await determination of the government's general policy on immigration after the war.

The future of the Japanese-Canadian community

Also demanding attention as the war drew to a close was a domestic problem with international implications, the future of the Japanese-Canadian community. On this issue the department took a cautious approach, notwithstanding public opinion surveys indicating a softening of attitudes.[68] There was still hostility to Japanese Canadians in Parliament and the cabinet, and the prime minister wished to avoid controversy on the subject. Policy recommendations were formulated with these considerations in mind, but, because of the efforts of advocates of a more generous regime, public discussion produced further liberalization.

The prime minister's caution worked against change in the government's policy until the late winter of 1944. At that time, Gordon Robertson, in a long memorandum on the subject, recommended segregating disloyal from loyal Japanese in order to advance the interests of the latter. His suggestions gained the approval of other departmental officers, including Henry Angus, one of the strongest defenders of the Japanese Canadians.[69]

Robertson's approach thus became the basis of the departmental position. A memorandum to the prime minister which he drafted for the undersecretary's signature recommended the segregation of disloyal Japanese, with those considered loyal being allowed to buy land outside British Columbia in order to encourage them to establish roots in other provinces. The prime minister, still more cautious than the department, "generally approved but not re buying land," which he considered "questionable so long as the war lasts."[70] On this basis, the matter went to the Cabinet War Committee, which on April 19 agreed on appointment of a special commissioner to determine which Japanese should be segregated and hence become liable to deportation. The subject then returned to the public-service level, for interdepartmental consultation on details of implementation and drafting and redrafting of the requisite orders-in-council.

In the mean time, a statement of policy in Parliament from the prime minister was necessary. This was prepared by Norman Robertson to take account of the continued activity by anti-Japanese groups and a statement by Ian Mackenzie (until October 17, 1944 minister of pensions and national health and the most influential BC member of the cabinet) that he would resign from any government that authorized the return of Japanese to the province. These circumstances, the under-secretary believed, made it "almost impossible for the Government to lay down a liberal and realistic policy on this question." He hoped, however, that the prime minister, while announcing the policy of segregation and deportation, coupled with an end to permanent immigration, would also stress that "the Government is convinced that the principles involved in the stand we are taking in the present war against persecution and intolerance and in the British traditions of justice and fair play, require that unjust persecution should not be visited on innocent individuals who have lived in peace in Canada and most of whom are citizens of Canada merely because they are of a particular race."[71] The statement King made in the House on August 4 generally followed the lines recommended, although he did not accept another suggestion, that Japanese Canadians be allowed to volunteer for active service overseas as a way of proving their loyalty to Canada and lessening the feeling against them.[72]

At the end of 1944, action was taken to set in motion the government's announced policy. Details of implementation had required much consultation between External Affairs and the Immigration Branch, the Royal Canadian Mounted Police, and the departments of Labour, Justice, and the Secretary of State. In February 1945, the cabinet decided to proceed with the segregation of Japanese who agreed to voluntary repatriation and to encourage Japanese to relocate outside British Columbia but to defer establishment of the proposed loyalty commission.[73]

By the end of the war with Japan, some 10,000 had agreed to repatriation from Canada, although some had requested revocation of their signatures. On September 5, 1945, the cabinet established a special committee, consisting of the ministers of labour (chairman), of national defence, and of veterans' affairs, the solicitor general, and the under-secretary of state for external affairs, to make recommendations on the process.[74] In its report, laid before the cabinet on September 19, the committee recommended negotiations with the allied commander in Japan, Gen. Douglas MacArthur, for repatriation of all those who had been interned and had requested repatriation, except for Canadian citizens who had revoked their request before September 1. Establishment of a loyalty commission was once again deferred.

Although the cabinet approved the committee's suggestions,[75] it soon became apparent from protests by religious and other organizations that the government's plans were not going to be accepted quietly. Gordon Robertson concluded that the government would find itself embarrassed unless the policy were moderated, particularly with regard to the desire of British subjects to revoke agreements to be repatriated. Hume Wrong, to whom this report was addressed, agreed, as did John Read, the External Affairs representative on an interdepartmental committee preparing the orders-in-council.[76]

Norman Robertson, however, remained convinced that only limited modification of the announced policy was feasible. As he explained to the prime minister in December, he could see "no possibility of taking a completely consistent, reasonable and humane line on these matters. We should, however, avoid purely racial discrimination as much as we can." Within those constraints, he suggested ways of responding to the critics. He pointed out that the aspect of the policy that was drawing the most criticism involved the denationalizing and deportation of native-born Japanese Canadians; the cabinet itself indeed was divided. Thought therefore should be given to modifying this policy. He also recommended that the orders be phrased in general terms that would be applicable to other enemy nationalities and not to Japanese alone.[77]

The effect of Robertson's recommendations can be seen in the orders-in-council approved by the cabinet on December 15: only Canadian-born Japanese who requested repatriation would be sent to Japan, and the Loyalty Commission, for the present, would concern itself only with Japanese nationals and naturalized Canadians. Canadian-born Japanese could withdraw their request for repatriation up to the actual issuance of a deportation order. As well, the order concerning revocation of status was couched in general terms applicable to any enemy national.[78]

Notwithstanding these modifications, the government's policy still aroused much criticism from religious groups and civil libertarians. Norman Robertson despaired of further concessions "until my native province of British Columbia achieves some change of heart,"[79] but in fact public outcry and the passage of time brought amelioration. Pending a decision of the Privy Council in London, which the government asked to rule on the validity of the orders-in-council, the deportation policy was suspended. By the time the Privy Council made its decision, upholding the orders, in December 1946, the situation had drastically altered. Resettlement of Japanese across Canada had decreased the proportion of the community residing in British Columbia from over 95 per cent to 33 per cent, while a total of 3,671 had been voluntarily repatriated. In the circumstances, and in light of public opinion, the government saw no point in proceeding. The orders-in-council were repealed in January 1947.[80]

Chapter Eleven
Planning a New International Order: 1943–1946

PREPARING FOR THE FUTURE

THE PROLONGED ACTIVITY ARISING FROM such war-related problems as those involving Japanese Canadians had to be accommodated while the department was considering the new international order which began to take shape through consultations among the major allies as the prospects for victory brightened in 1943. All the plans that emerged were of interest to the department, but some consumed more of its time than others. Some initiatives from outside Canada came not from foreign offices but from domestic departments, which dealt with their counterparts in Ottawa; also, with its senior personnel heavily overextended, External Affairs could not take the lead on all fronts. Both these circumstances affected the handling of international economic relations during the latter part of the war.

International trade and finance

Post-war commercial policy began to require attention as early as 1941, as a result of Anglo-American discussions, arising fron the lend-lease agreement, about liberalization of international trade. Robertson followed these closely, but policy-making in Canada was no longer dominated by the pre-war triumvirate of trade negotiators: himself, Dana Wilgress, and Hector McKinnon, chairman of the Tariff Board. Of the three, only the last was able to continue his role. As under-secretary, Robertson no longer had the time for prolonged direct involvement in negotiations, and Wilgress was not available after his posting to the Soviet Union. The discussion of international trade, moreover, was often bound up with that of post-war monetary organization, a subject in which External Affairs personnel were not the acknowledged experts. Thus the team that formulated and gave effect to commercial policy became more diverse, and External Affairs, although still influential, had a more modest place vis-à-vis new participants, most notably the Department of Finance.[1]

That department was even more prominent in dealing with the related subject of post-war monetary relationships. In the United States and the United Kingdom, the leading exponents of planning in this field were the treasury departments, which communicated with their counterpart in Ottawa. Robertson, who briefed the prime minister from time to time on developments and who participated or was represented in interdepartmental discussions in Ottawa, did not question this relationship. Rather, he recognized the expertise of Finance and the Bank of Canada and commended the results to King. Thus the lead remained with the economic branches of government, Canada's chief exponent being Louis Rasminsky. The minister of finance, J. L. Ilsley, headed the Canadian delegation at the conference at Bretton Woods, New Hampshire, in the summer of 1944, which established the International Monetary Fund and the International Bank for Reconstruction and Development. Of the seven Canadian officials present, only two, John Deutsch and Paul Tremblay, were from External Affairs. The most prominent were W. A. Mackintosh, acting head of the delegation when Ilsley was absent, and Rasminsky.[2]

Also primarily for discussion between treasury departments was Canada's balance of payments with the United States and the United Kingdom. Concerning financial relations with the United States, the presence of a Canadian financial attaché in Washington, A. F. W. Plumptre, made it easy for Finance to carry out unmediated cross-border dealings. Lack of consultation caused concern in External Affairs and could leave the ambassador in Washington insufficiently informed. The under-secretary, however, seems to have been kept in the picture and did not object to Finance's practice.[3]

External Affairs assigned the subject to two officers, A. E. Ritchie and Douglas LePan, recently recruited in Washington and London, respectively. Although Ritchie came to the department from the British Ministry of Economic Warfare mission in Washington, LePan was not an economist, a circumstance that puzzled Whitehall when he set out to inform himself by means of interviews with British experts:

> Most of those I interviewed were polite and friendly and tolerably forth-coming, even though I could often detect some bewilderment at a caller

of seeming intelligence who nevertheless came equipped with questions that were either simple-minded or ill-based or unwittingly embarrassing. Their cordiality was almost invariably proof against such provocations, which, God knows, I didn't intend. The one exception was Lionel Robbins, now Lord Robbins. He was at that time the head of the Economic Section of the Cabinet Office and was the most senior of all those I interviewed on my earliest rounds. For all his courtly manner, his reception was distinctly frosty. I was unnerved by the chill, so unnerved that I could hardly go on, until I realized that he simply couldn't believe that the Canadian Government would send as one of its representatives into the fastnesses of Whitehall a neophyte with such innocent questions. He thawed only gradually as he came to accept me at face value for the innocent I was, an innocent abroad in the highly subtle and cameralist world of international finance.[4]

Economic expertise was scarce in the junior ranks of the department, but LePan mastered the subject quickly and in May joined Mackintosh and Graham Towers in a memorable meeting at Cambridge to discuss sterling balances with a British delegation headed by Lord Keynes. Despite its relatively low profile on some international economic issues at the end of the war, the department had by no means lost interest in the activity and, through the involvement of recruits such as LePan and Ritchie, was preparing a new generation of experts.

UNRRA

The department was interested above all in the creation of a new order for the maintenance of international peace and security. The likely shape of that order was suggested by the plans of the great powers for the United Nations Relief and Rehabilitation Administration (UNRRA). While the activities of UNRRA—provision of economic assistance to areas devastated by the war—were not within the conventional mandate of the department, the implications for Canada's future place in the world made it a subject of major interest. As a result, the Canadian response to plans for and requirements of the organization became a preoccupation of External Affairs.

The first organization to encompass all the United Nations, as the allies collectively had been known since the beginning of 1942, UNRRA was constituted differently from the combined war organizations, dominated as they were by the United States and the United Kingdom. The executive (ultimately named the Central Committee) of the new agency was to have four members, the United Kingdom, the United States, the Soviet Union, and China. As a country expected to be a major contributor of relief supplies, Canada had an interest, justified by the functional principle,[5] in being represented on the Central Committee. UNRRA would establish the model for post-war international organization, and restoration of the pre-war concept of great-power dominance would leave little room for influence by smaller states such as Canada, however important their contribution to international life.

As had happened regarding the combined war organizations, proposals for the Canadian response to the plans for UNRRA were formulated in External Affairs, with decisions being reached, because of the importance of the subject, in the Cabinet War Committee. The negotiations took place mostly in Washington, where Pearson was the Canadian spokesman in dealing with the State Department and the British embassy.

Initially, the department favoured pressing the case for full representation on the Central Committee, but eventually it was persuaded that the opposition of the Soviet Union to expanding that body made compromise necessary. The proposed solution, advanced by the British via Pearson, was that Canada provide the chair of the Committee of Suppliers, who could take part in meetings of the Central Committee when supplies were under discussion. In a memorandum heavily influenced by Pearson, the department provided the War Committee with the options for and against this proposal. As in the days of Skelton, the argument was subtly slanted in the direction favoured by the department, that is, acceptance.

The War Committee, when it considered the memorandum on April 7, 1943, did not accept the department's reasoning without question. The deputy minister of finance, Clark, wanted to hold out for full membership of the Central Committee, and his arguments were given voice by his minister, Ilsley, with support from the minister of national defence for air, Charles Power. The prime minister, in contrast, was sensitive to the possibility that "the Canadian government would be subject to severe criticism both inside and outside Canada if it could be alleged that we were responsible for the failure of the whole United Nations relief plan."[6] Accordingly, the War Committee, "in the circumstances," agreed to the compromise, with the proviso that it was not to be a precedent for other United Nations organizations and did not imply Canadian acceptance of the principle of four-power control.

Pearson continued as the Canadian negotiator while the details of the UNRRA agreement were worked out and by September was able to report that the decision to compromise (still regretted by Clark, and also by Massey in London) had been vindicated by the acceptance of Canadian proposals to improve the position of smaller states by strengthening the council (in which all members were represented) at the expense of the Central Committee. In due course, Pearson was named the Canadian member of the council and in that capacity headed the delegation to its first meeting, which took place in Atlantic City, New Jersey, immediately after the signature of the agreement at the White House on November 9, 1943. Pearson's alternate on the council was Brooke Claxton, who had been appointed parliamentary assistant to the president of the privy council in May and who in that capacity assisted King in dealing with external affairs. In December, accompanied by Claxton, Pearson reported on the meeting to the War Committee. Among the achievements of the Canadian delegation had been the right, as anticipated, to provide the chairman of the Supplies Committee. The office was to be occupied by Pearson, and the other Canadian member, John Deutsch, also came from External Affairs.[7]

An event of signal importance for Canada in the history of UNRRA was the decision to hold the second meeting of the council in Montreal, in September 1944. Not only would the conference draw attention to Canada's importance as a supplier, but, as administrative arrangements were left to the UNRRA secretariat, the burden on the government would probably be light. "All that would be required," the department was told, "would be the goodwill of the Canadian Government, their good offices in securing a suitable hotel, and the appointment of a few persons who might act in a liaison capacity to ensure that there were adequate facilities available, telegraph, press, etc."[8] The conference undoubtedly helped to consolidate Canada's position in the organization and was a personal success for Pearson, who served as chair.[9] He led the delegation to the third session of the council in London in the spring of 1945, at which Canada was at last asked to join the Central Committee.

Post-hostilities planning machinery

The long struggle to obtain a seat on the Central Committee of UNRRA was part of a larger process of adjustment by the department to a new international structure and to an equally rapid evolution of domestic expectations of Canada's place in it. In these circumstances special arrangements were made, for the first time in the department's history, to plan for the future.

Some officers, notably Wrong and Reid, had as early as 1942 suggested long-term thinking about the problems it faced. The stimulus to action, however, came from the British. Early in the summer of 1943, the Dominions Secretary asked whether Canada would wish to participate in a proposed United Nations Commission for Europe and in a European policing system. At the same time he sought Canada's opinions on the principles for the ending of hostilities and the maintenance of law and order in occupied countries. The department's reaction was expressed in a memorandum by Wrong. "The question of Canadian participation," he pointed out, "may well involve a preliminary decision on our part to play an active role in a new world security system," a commitment that would require close co-operation and policy co-ordination between External Affairs and the armed forces.[10] This memorandum was placed before the War Committee, which instructed Robertson to convene a meeting to study the question and to come up with agreed recommendations. The clerk of the privy council, the chiefs of staff and their planning specialists, and appropriate officials from External Affairs were to attend. This ad hoc group unanimously recommended, and the War Committee accepted, the principle of Canada's involvement in post-war Europe.

Owing to the number and complexity of the issues involved, the War Committee decided on a more formal planning body. A small working committee was set up under Wrong, with representatives from the Privy Council Office, the armed forces, and External Affairs, to recommend more permanent arrangements. The resulting proposals, primarily the work of Wrong, received the War Committee's approval in December 1943. Two committees were created. The senior group—the Post-Hostilities Advisory Committee, under Robertson—was responsible for policy, and a working committee, directed by Wrong, would produce detailed studies. In addition to Robertson, the advisory committee consisted of the secretary to the cabinet, the chiefs of staff, the deputy minister of finance, and the vice-chairman of the National Harbours Board, J. E. St Laurent. The working committee reflected the membership of the senior body, but with more junior officers. John Holmes was appointed secretary, being replaced, when posted to London in January 1945, by George Ignatieff.[11]

Initially, much of the work consisted of commentaries on British papers, but the approach of a Commonwealth prime ministers' conference, scheduled for May 1944, prompted Wrong to propose that the working committee deal with broad political and economic questions of particular concern to Canada. On March 28, 1944, this approach was accepted by the advisory committee, which also approved for study Canadian post-war defence arrangements with the United States, Canada's military interests in Greenland, Canada's position in the event of strained relations between the Soviet Union and the United States, Canada's role in the defence of the North Pacific and the defence of Newfoundland, and the advantages and disadvantages for Canada of a regional security organization. Owing to time constraints, Wrong suggested a planning staff to work on studies and prepare reports between meetings. Known as the Junior Drafting Group, it worked under Ignatieff's direction, with representatives from the department and the three services.[12]

By the spring of 1945, the main studies had been completed and operations began to wind down. Attempts to keep some planning machinery in place in the department met with little success, in part because those who had been involved were posted abroad. There were, however, more fundamental limitations. Since the international agenda was unpredictable, especially for a small state, the departmental routine was always subject to disruption: the urgent frequently had to be given priority over the desirable. Continued limitations of staff further eroded the resources for planning.

Thus the department, as it appeared to the head of the First Political Division, Charles Ritchie, just after the war, continued to handle its business by making do:

> All morning a stream of interesting and informative telegrams and despatches from missions abroad comes pouring across my desk. I am tempted to read them all and try to understand what is really happening, but if I do that I have not time to draft answers to the most immediate telegrams and despatches crying out for instructions. I must skim through everything with my mind concentrated on immediate practical implications. If I try to be objective and to comprehend all the issues I am lost. I draft telegrams and speeches under pressure, short-term considerations uppermost.[13]

The approach of peace had made orderly planning both possible and necessary. Even then, however, it was but one component in policy-making, and the process did not become well enough established to be preserved, against competing calls on the department's resources, once the large questions of the day had been addressed.

The Commonwealth

Still an important starting-point in dealing with those questions was Canada's relationship with the United Kingdom and the Commonwealth. This received concentrated attention in Ottawa early in 1944 as a result of a celebrated speech in Toronto by the British ambassador in Washington, Lord Halifax, expressing a degree of enthusiasm for Commonwealth solidarity that King found alarming. One lesson to be learned from the furore caused by the speech, Pearson pointed out, was that the department would have to give some attention to Canada's position in the Commonwealth and its implications for other post-war activities, especially in whatever world organization might replace the League of Nations.[14]

Despite the creation of planning machinery, Canadian preparations were informal for the meeting of Commonwealth prime ministers in London in May 1944. As usual, this gathering was very much in the domain of the prime minister. After long experience, he was an adept participant. As well, he had advisers who could anticipate his requirements on the basis of long acquaintance and meet them with a minimum of paper work. Preparations for the conference, therefore, were carried out by a combination of old and new methods.

In a memorandum to the prime minister in March 1944, the under-secretary informed him that "some consideration" had been given to the draft agenda by himself, Heeney, and Wrong, who provided comments. In due course, briefing papers were prepared by various officials, including Heeney, Pickersgill, and Robertson. As well, the planning process was to be used for two topics, possible Canadian involvement in post-war policing of Europe and plans for post-war international security and defence.[15] In London, King was assisted by Robertson and Massey; by Lt.-Gen. Kenneth Stuart and Air Marshal L. S. Breadner of Canadian forces headquarters in London; and by one of the planners, Holmes. The planning process continued to have its attractions afterward, to help respond to British proposals for Commonwealth defence co-operation, a sensitive subject in Canada because of the implications for centralization. Owing to continuing uncertainty about the responsibilities that an international security organization might assume, however, the planners were unable to reach agreed conclusions. Informal consultation at the senior level, therefore, remained important, the participants being Robertson, Wrong, Heeney, and the military secretary to the Cabinet War Committee, Pope.[16]

This combination of formal and informal planning defined Canada's attitudes, as Pearson had recommended after Halifax's speech. In brief, this stance represented the evolution of the position long associated with King: that members of the Commonwealth were first and foremost independent nations, which should not be expected to form a bloc in the pursuit of international objectives. Opportunities arose outside the immediate Commonwealth context for Canada to act on this premise. One such involved the international regulation of civil aviation. Canadian policy on this matter was formed in a similar way to that on the Commonwealth: formal planning and informal consultation. As a prototype for other forms of co-operation among states, the negotiations on the subject were of considerable interest to External Affairs. They also had a high technical component, however, and therefore required heavy involvement by other branches of government.

Civil aviation

In planning for the post-war regime governing civil aviation Canada found it much easier to secure a satisfactory role than it did, for example, in UNRRA. Having become a major air power and lying astride important routes linking the Americas, Europe, and Asia, Canada was able, on the basis of the functional principle, to claim a leading and independent role in new regulatory arrangements. The department took advantage of the opportunity thus offered, assigning the subject for study to the post-hostilities planners working under Wrong's direction.[17] They rejected a strictly Commonwealth civil aviation system, initially preferred by the British, in favour of broad international arrangements in which Canada would have greater scope and influence.

In the cabinet the leading voice on civil aviation was C. D. Howe's, but support for his activity came not so much from his department, Munitions and Supply, as from Transport, the Air Transport Board, Trans-Canada Airlines, the Privy Council Office, and External Affairs. The departmental officers dealing most closely with the subject were Escott Reid, then first secretary in Washington, and R. M. Macdonnell, in the Third Political Division, which was responsible for US affairs. Reid took part in tripartite negotiations in Washington, and he and Macdonell both attended the international conference on civil aviation held in Chicago in the autumn of 1944, at which the Canadian delegation was headed by Howe. The convention discussed and approved at Chicago was based on a Canadian draft, largely the work of John Baldwin of the Privy Council Office, Macdonnell, and Reid. In addition, Canada was proposed by the United States as the future site of the headquarters of the proposed regulatory organization. In 1946, during the first meeting of the interim assembly of the Provisional International Civil Aviation Organization, Montreal was selected for the purpose.[18]

The United Nations

Not being technical in nature, the prospective United Nations organization required less formal co-operation between External Affairs and other departments. For External Affairs, the United Nations was a central concern, both because it was seen as a means of promoting collective security and because of a desire that, unlike wartime allied organizations, it be established so as to give an effective voice to smaller but influential states such as Canada. Thus the department from the first was the motive force behind Canadian planning for the organization, although other senior public servants, including Heeney, Mackintosh, Pope, Rasminsky, and Towers, also made contributions, often through casual discussions outside the normal working environment.[19]

The idea of a United Nations organization received careful consideration and an enthusiastic response in the department from the time it was first broached by the major allies in 1943. Most prominent in formulating the department's position were Pearson in Washington and Wrong

in Ottawa, the latter in particular being quick to see functional representation as a means of advancing Canada's interests. When aspects of the
subject came under study by the post-hostilities planners in London, they
received attention from their counterparts in Ottawa,[20] but the conventional departmental policy-making process, with approval when required
from the prime minister and his cabinet colleagues, remained dominant.

The association between Wrong and Pearson was especially important
during the drafting of the proposed United Nations charter by the four
great powers (the United States, the United Kingdom, the Soviet Union,
and China) at the Dumbarton Oaks estate in Washington in the summer
of 1944. Although not a participant, Canada was able to make its views
known, chiefly via the British. As worked out by Wrong and Pearson,
these were transmitted in two ways, from Ottawa to the Dominions Office
and in meetings of Commonwealth representatives in Washington, chaired
by Sir Alexander Cadogan, the permanent under-secretary of state for
foreign affairs, and attended by Pearson on behalf of Canada. In Ottawa,
Wrong took the lead, often communicating with King and other ministers.
Wrong, along with Massey, also represented Canada at a Commonwealth
meeting held in London early in 1945 to discuss the Dumbarton Oaks
proposals. This assignment was a considerable tribute to Wrong's standing
with his government as an authority on the subject, for most representatives
were ministers.[21]

The drafting powers revealed little flexibility with regard to modifications that might be of benefit to smaller countries. Since the involvement
of major states was considered essential to effective operation of the organization, the Canadian delegation to the founding conference of the United
Nations in San Francisco in the spring of 1945 had to accept constraints
on action to pursue such objectives as limitations on the veto power of
permanent members of the Security Council. The primary goal, rather,
was to be establishment of an organization as well equipped as possible
to preserve international security. The press, the party learned as it
commenced its work, was to be told that "the Canadian delegation was
of one mind in its desire to do everything possible to assist the work of the
conference and to ensure its success. . . . The primary aim . . . was to
ensure that the world organization would be brought into being in as large
a way as might be possible."[22]

That this commitment was taken seriously by the government was
evident from the composition of the Canadian party. King led the delegation with Louis St Laurent as his deputy, and all the other accredited representatives were parliamentarians: two senators (J. H. King, the government leader, and Lucien Moraud, a Conservative), Gordon Graydon, who
acted for John Bracken as leader of the opposition in the House of
Commons because the latter had not yet been elected to Parliament, the

leader of the CCF, M. J. Coldwell, and Cora Casselman, Liberal member of Parliament for Edmonton East. A future Conservative prime minister, John Diefenbaker, member of Parliament for Lake Centre, Saskatchewan, was also present, as an adviser to Graydon.[23] Of the thirteen public-service advisers to the delegation, all but two (Maurice Pope and Louis Rasminsky) were from External Affairs, including Robertson, Wrong, and Pearson. The three-man secretariat of the delegation was also drawn from the department,with Gordon Robertson in charge. Press relations were handled by the Wartime Information Board.

With the prime minister and so many senior officials present in San Francisco for the opening of the conference, most early decisions could be taken in delegation meetings, with Ottawa consulted primarily for technical guidance. To some extent, in fact, decision making on foreign policy in general was transferred to San Francisco, with Ottawa finding it necessary to consult King or senior officials there when action had to be taken on major issues. After May 14, however, the delegation in San Francisco had to consult King by telegram, since he had returned to Canada, where a general election had been called for June 11. After the election, the prime minister went back to San Francisco (arriving on June 23) for the closing sessions of the conference, which came to an end on June 26.

In Wrong's judgment, the Canadian party "shaped up very well," with "no serious rifts among the delegates and the group of advisers . . . working together harmoniously." Such a smooth operation was of vital importance, for the demands of the conference were intense, leaving little time for reporting to Ottawa:

> It has not been physically possible to keep the Department properly informed of developments here. Usually about ten of the twelve Technical Committees of the Conference meet each day with the final batch of three sitting, as someone put it, from 8:30 p.m. until unconditional surrender. In addition, there are a good many sub-committees and meetings of the various controlling committees. We are represented on all three of these latter, the Steering Committee, the Executive Committee and the Coordination Committee. What time one has between attending meetings and preparing for them is given up to ensuring reasonable liaison inside the delegation and a good deal of inter-delegation contact.

The burden on officials, moreover, was about to increase, as the parliamentarians followed the prime minister's example and began returning to Canada.[24]

In conformity with guidance received from the prime minister at their first meeting, the Canadians at San Francisco kept a low profile and did much of their work behind the scenes. Some improvements of importance to Canada were secured in the charter, including two affecting the position of smaller states vis-à-vis the permanent members of the Security Council. One of these changes ensured that non-members of the council could participate in the relevant decisions of that body if called upon by it to contribute to a United Nations force. The other acknowledged the functional principle by establishing that the primary criterion for election to the Security Council should be a member's contribution to the preservation of peace and security and to the other activities of the organization.[25]

The work at San Francisco was regarded by the government as a valuable asset in the election campaign, offsetting the damage done by the conscription issue and enabling King and his colleagues to stand forth as men who would move easily among the leaders of the post-war world.[26] Thus the result of the election, which sustained the Liberals in power, though with a reduced majority, could be interpreted as endorsement of the more active foreign policy recently being conducted on the advice of the department. With the war in Europe having ended on May 8 and that against Japan drawing to a close, the department could anticipate the continuation, probably at an accelerated pace, of the role it had assumed during the latter part of the conflict.

ADJUSTING TO PEACE

Atomic energy

Even before the surrender of Japan on August 14, it was apparent, as a result of the use by the United States of atomic weapons in the closing days of the conflict, that hopes for a stable international regime might well be jeopardized by the advance of technology. The application of atomic energy was of major interest to Canada, a source of uranium and one of the contributors, along with the United States and the United Kingdom, to wartime research on the subject. Only a very small number of people in Canada had been involved, however, and the issue had not hitherto been a concern of the department. Those in the Canadian government most closely engaged were the minister of munitions and supply, Howe, and C. J. Mackenzie, of the National Research Council. They were in direct communication with the British high commissioner and the British and US authorities concerned with the subject. Robertson and to some extent Wrong were au courant, but others in the department were not.

As soon as the new weapon had been used, the subject received the attention of others as well, as the department started to assess the consequences for the international order. With the end of the war in the Pacific and the beginnings of United Nations work in the atomic field, responsibility was assigned to the First Political Division under Charles Ritchie. As ambassador, Pearson was a participant when King met in Washington with US President Harry Truman and British Prime Minister Clement Attlee to produce the Potomac agreement of November 15, 1945, recommending creation of the United Nations Atomic Energy Commission. An advocate of international control, Pearson wrote the document on which the Canadian position was based and was a member (with US and British representatives) of the three-man team that drafted the agreement.

In April 1946, Gen. A. G. L. McNaughton became Canada's first representative on the Atomic Energy Commission. Instructions were necessary for the numerous meetings of this body (commencing in June 1946), especially when the chairmanship, which rotated, passed to McNaughton. Agreed interdepartmental positions were reached in the Advisory Panel on Atomic Energy, created on March 27, 1946, under the chairmanship of Wrong. The National Research Council, the Department of Reconstruction and Supply (created by the merger of Howe's portfolios in December 1945), and the Defence Research Board were members, in addition to External Affairs. Wrong was assisted by Ignatieff, and the department also supplied the secretary.[27]

The occupation of Germany and Japan

Another post-war subject of concern to the department was the occupation of former enemy territory, which affected Canada's position vis-à-vis the other allies and future interests in the countries concerned. As a result of dissatisfaction with arrangements for involving smaller states, Canada declined to make a commitment to the occupation of Germany. It was considered necessary, however, to have a representative there, because of Canadian civilian and military interests. In the autumn of 1945, therefore, the government decided on establishment of a military mission in Berlin, accredited to the Allied Control Council (on which the United States, the United Kingdom, the Soviet Union, and France were represented).

Placed in charge of the office in Berlin, responsible jointly to the departments of External Affairs and National Defence, was Lt.-Gen. Maurice Pope. In addition to a staff officer, he was supported by Morley Scott of External Affairs as head of a consular section, an economic adviser, and a representative of the custodian of enemy property. Although the civilians on the staff were given honorary military rank, Robertson told Pope that in practice he would represent the government in the same way as any ambassador. The establishment of the military mission, therefore, marked the effective beginning of diplomatic relations between Canada and Germany.[28]

The opportunity to influence events was somewhat greater in the Pacific than in Europe. The Far Eastern Commission in Washington, created to deal with "political matters connected with fulfilment by Japan of its obligations under the terms of surrender,"[29] was not confined to the great powers but admitted as well representatives of smaller states with an interest in the area, including Canada. Pearson was named representative, and Canada was in a position to make a modest contribution through chairing the constitutional committee. The commission, which met in the premises of the Japanese embassy, remained in operation until made obsolete by the Japanese peace treaty of 1951.

Also important was the activity of the department's expert on Japan, Herbert Norman, who was seconded, at their request, to the occupation authorities in Japan for counter-intelligence work. Early in 1946, he was transferred to Washington as Pearson's alternate on the Far Eastern Commission, and in the summer of that year he was posted back to Japan as head of a Canadian liaison mission accredited to the Supreme Commander Allied Powers, Gen. Douglas MacArthur. Norman himself had prepared the recommendation for establishing this mission, making it clear that, as in Germany, the functions would include those performed by Canadian diplomats elsewhere. Among his duties would be dealing with problems of relief for Canadian nationals in Japan, doing general consular work, assisting American authorities in dealing with Japanese deportees from Canada, looking after Canadian commercial interests, and providing political reports.

In effect, creation of the liaison mission restored diplomatic relations with Japan, although Norman was the only officer from External Affairs on the staff. It also resulted in the reoccupation of the fine legation built by Sir Herbert Marler, after Norman, making use of contacts established with MacArthur's staff during his secondment, secured the removal from the building of the Commonwealth members of the international prosecution section of the war crimes trials and the Commonwealth member of the Allied Council.[30]

Beginning the work of the UN

These arrangements for representation were overshadowed by creation of the new international organization, the United Nations. An indication of the high level of interest in Canada was the government's decision to make parliamentary approval of the charter (October 19, 1945) the occasion for one of the few House of Commons debates on external policy not related to the department's estimates. Acceptance of the charter had an important and immediate effect on the department. Since the San Francisco conference, said the annual report for 1945, "the work of the Department, in both the political and the economic field, [had] been more and more largely concerned with the United Nations Organization and its auxiliaries."[31]

Initially, much of the new UN work arose from practical arrangements to launch the organization. To this end, a preparatory commission was created at San Francisco, with members from all the countries attending the conference. The commission as a whole did not go to work immediately, the way being prepared by its Executive Committee, representing fourteen states, of which Canada was one. The committee, followed by the commission, met in London in the summer and autumn of 1945. Their work involved the "nuts and bolts" of the new organization but was none the less important for that. "UN politics," John Holmes has observed, "would have been far worse if there had not been this notable effort to devise procedures in the reasonably calm atmosphere of Westminster during the summer of victory."[32] Canada therefore needed effective representation, although other demands on manpower made it impossible to field large delegations.

When the Executive Committee began its meetings, Pearson, who was in London for the UNRRA Council, was named Canadian representative but was expected to attend only the opening meetings. His alternate, assigned for as long as necessary, was Escott Reid, who had attended the San Francisco conference as an adviser to the Canadian delegation. "We are not at present," the dominions secretary was told, "able to attach further staff to the Canadian representative."[33]

The Executive Committee proved to be a forum more favourable to Canadian operations than the San Francisco conference had been, because it was less dominated by the great powers. "The most significant development," Ottawa was informed, was "that there are no penthouse meetings taking place as at San Francisco."[34] Reid kept in close touch with the department throughout, but, being alone most of the time, had to work enormously hard to take advantage of this situation. "We are concerned in the Department," Wrong told him, "at not being able to supplement your efforts by providing further help for the Executive Committee. . . . The trouble is the old familiar one—in the first place we are desperately short of people and, secondly, we are not in a position to try to give you very much guidance on the issues that will arise because of the pressure of work and the large number of urgent and important matters coming up for decision."[35]

Eventually, Pearson was replaced by the ambassador to Belgium, W. F. A. Turgeon, but even so, as Reid reported to Ottawa, it was impossible to cover all the meetings:

Turgeon is attending Committees 5, 9, 10 on the [International] Court [of Justice], League and General respectively. I am attending Committees 1, 2, 6 on the Assembly, Security Council and Secretariat respectively. The number of Committee meetings per week is being increased and Sub-Committees are also being formed. We regret, therefore, that we have no time to attend any of the meetings of the four other Committees, or even to read their documents. Consequently, if any contribution is to be made by Canada to the work of these four Committees, it will be necessary for you to send us memoranda in a form suitable for transmission, without change, to the Secretary of the Committee concerned.[36]

To help, Canada House was asked to make staff available, enabling the delegation to take part in more, but not all, of the meetings. The result, Reid concluded in his report, was an effective contribution to an international exercise in institution building, in an atmosphere conducive to co-operation. With such slender resources, the Canadian effort had depended above all on Reid's skill and tenacity as a draughtsman. He was, Holmes has said, "a major and dynamic force during this period. Reid was a superb and a compulsive draftsman, with a zealous sense of mission about international organization. Lester Pearson once said, 'Escott would bring the Archangel Gabriel to the mat for a comma'."[37]

In accordance with the plans made at San Francisco, the report of the Executive Committee was reviewed by the full Preparatory Commission, which met, also in London, in November and December 1945. This meeting was no rubber stamp; like that of the Executive Committee, it was "a hard working conference which . . . split up into committees."[38] Once again the department was concerned about putting together an effective delegation. "Our difficulties," Wrong told Reid in September, "arise in part from the extraordinarily congested programme of international meetings, combined with the additional volume of work which has fallen on the Department with the end of hostilities. I think there will be between 7 and 10 international conferences or meetings of one sort or another between now and the end of the year at which Canada will have to be represented, and in many of the cases this Department will have the main responsibility."[39] The leader was the ambassador to the Soviet Union, Dana Wilgress, and the delegates were four members of Parliament, including Gordon Graydon who had been at San Francisco, and one senator. There were four advisers, including Reid, from External Affairs, and one with economic expertise from outside, A. F. W. Plumptre of Finance.

Although Wilgress was given guidance on "certain particular points of importance" and was encouraged to consult Ottawa as the need arose, he was to a considerable degree left on his own. Awareness of what had transpired at San Francisco and in the Executive Committee was expected to make the delegation familiar with the Canadian position on the most important issues. It was considered that the delegation should formulate its own response to unexpected developments. In keeping with successful practice at San Francisco, Wilgress was advised to hold daily delegation meetings "to discuss the lines to be followed at the meetings of the Committees."[40]

As indicated by Reid's schedule for November 29, the workload was extremely heavy, keeping members occupied until after midnight:

9:00–10:00 a.m.	Delegation meeting
10:30–1:00	Committee meeting
1:00–3:00	Lunch with US adviser
3:00–4:45	Office drafting telegrams to Ottawa
5:00–7:15	Committee
7:30–8:00	Massey cocktail party
8:00–9:15	Dinner with delegation
9:30–12:15	Delegation meeting

'This life," he told his wife a few days later, "is madness."[41]

The effort, according to the delegation, was worthwhile, enabling Canada to be the fifth most important participant in the conference, after the United Kingdom, the Soviet Union, the United States, and China. An important vehicle for achieving influence was the network of subcommittees. "In order to get on as many . . . as possible," said the report, "the delegation submitted proposals or amendments as early in the conference as it could." The result was an active delegation that played a distinctive role, appropriate to Canada's position in international affairs. "So far in the Executive Committee and the Preparatory Commission," the report concluded, "Canada has steered a middle course, and has been able, on the merits of the questions which have come up, to vote against the Great Powers about as frequently as it has voted with them. It is to be hoped that this happy situation will continue."[42]

There was an immediate opportunity to test the situation, in the first part of the first General Assembly, held in London at the beginning of 1946. Anticipating an important session, Robertson recommended a high-level delegation, formulated on lines similar to those followed at San Francisco. He wanted two or three members of the government as delegates, with representatives of opposition parties and possibly of the Senate as alternates and senior officials as delegates or alternates. Most 'of the officials he suggested were from External Affairs, but Rasminsky, "who . . . made a fine name for himself at San Francisco,"[43] was included for economic and social questions and Mackenzie for atomic energy. In accordance with these suggestions, the delegation was led by the minister of justice, Louis St Laurent, and included the minister of agriculture, J. G. Gardiner, and the secretary of state, Paul Martin. The other delegates were Massey and Wrong. Two members of the opposition were among the alternates, Graydon of the Conservatives and Stanley Knowles of the CCF, as were three officers from External Affairs: Read, Wilgress, and Pierre Dupuy, minister to the Netherlands. Of the ten advisers, all were from External Affairs but two, Rasminsky and G. C. Andrew, of the Canadian Information Service, the latter being also one of the press officers. Mackenzie did not take part. As with earlier UN meetings, it was impossible to give detailed instructions in advance on all issues, partly because the guidelines had to be prepared before the complete report of the Preparatory Commission was available and partly because "the attitude to be adopted on a number of contentious questions must depend on the situation which develops in the Assembly itself and in its committees."[44]

Canada's standing was recognized during the session in a number of ways, including election to the Economic and Social Council and the successful candidacy of John Read for the International Court of Justice. A major disappointment was failure to secure one of the non-permanent seats on the Security Council. This was a defeat of considerable importance, for it revealed that, notwithstanding the charter, regional considerations would outweigh the functional principle in determining membership.

The utility of the functional principle was being eroded by another and more sobering circumstance evident during the General Assembly: the rapidly deepening tension between the Soviet Union and the Western powers. "What took place in London," Wrong reported,

> has shown that the General Assembly and in particular the Security Council can be and are being used as instruments in the war of nerves, especially by the Soviet Government. . . . Without a great alteration . . . in the attitude towards each other of the great powers—and it should be emphasized that this alteration is required not only on the part of the Soviet Government—the first meetings of the Security Council and the Assembly leave open the question whether the establishment of the United Nations has in fact furthered its primary purpose—the maintenance of international peace and security.[45]

Clearly, the opportunity for Canada to enjoy the "happy situation" noted by Wilgress at the Preparatory Commission had been fleeting. Instead, the preoccupation of Canadian diplomacy late in the war—the country's position among the victors against the Axis powers—would be overshadowed by the need to work in common cause in an alliance led by a single superpower, the United States.

The Gouzenko affair

By the time of the first meeting of the UN General Assembly, the department was already well aware of prospective post-war tension, as a result of the defection, on September 6, 1945, of a cypher clerk in the Soviet Union's embassy in Ottawa, Igor Gouzenko. With him Gouzenko brought documents revealing that his government was carrying out espionage.

Gouzenko's story and the documents revealed that there were spies in the State Department in Washington, in the atomic research laboratories in Montreal, and in the Cypher Division of External Affairs. A registry clerk in the office of the British high commissioner was also passing on information. Were there other informers active in Canada? Gouzenko did not know. Time was needed to work out the full story, to locate all the contacts, and to ensure concerted action with the British and the Americans. Fortunately, there was one secure means of communication with London, the British Security Coordination link. Thus the Soviet authorities were prevented from discovering what was being said, and time was provided for identification of other suspected collaborators, not only in Canada but elsewhere. Since the Royal Canadian Mounted Police had little experience in counter-espionage, two British intelligence experts were sent to assist in the investigation.

Robertson and Wrong now had to spend long hours, day and night, meeting with the men from British Security Coordination, the British high commissioner and his deputy, and Supt. C. E. Rivett-Carnac of the RCMP. Each night the documents were stored in a Corby's whisky box in Robertson's office. Hence the matter became known as the "Corby" case. Access to information on the subject was on a strict need-to-know basis. Pearson in Washington was informed early on because King wanted him to break the news to the US secretary of state, James Byrnes. Wilgress, however, was not informed until December, when he was in London for the United Nations Preparatory Commission, and Massey remained completely unaware until February 1946, just before the story became public.[46]

Once the news was out, a royal commission was quickly appointed in Canada, under two justices of the Supreme Court, R. L. Kellock and Robert Taschereau. Arnold Smith of External Affairs, recently returned from three years' service in Moscow, acted as secretary. A worrisome aspect of the royal commission's proceedings for External Affairs was the possible impact on the relationship with the Soviet Union. While wanting to send a strong message to Moscow, the department hoped to avoid lasting damage. Wrong, after testifying before the commissioners, offered them some guidance on how to shape their report:

I felt that the investigation and the consequent trials should be regarded as a surgical operation and that we must make an effort to reestablish working relations with the Soviet Government. I indicated that the report ought not to draw general conclusions about Soviet activities in foreign countries but should confine itself to describing the detailed sample of the way they carried on in Canada and the way in which these activities were directed by Soviet agencies in Moscow. They appeared to be in general agreement with this line. I have asked Arnold Smith to watch the drafting closely as we do not want the report to contain vague generalizations or loose ends which might be exploited in rebuttal.[47]

The royal commission's report was released on July 15, 1946. The department did not figure prominently except in two respects: the activities of a cypher clerk, Emma Woikin, and the use of a false Canadian passport by a Soviet agent. Emma Woikin was a Russian-speaking Canadian who had joined the Passport Office in 1943 and was transferred to the Cypher Division in March 1944. After recruitment by the Soviet embassy, she would memorize the contents of Dominions Office telegrams, write out the texts at home, and pass them to her contact. One of her colleagues later noted that "she did not have any particularly close friends in the Cypher Division and seemed to me to be an average Canadian girl. She did not at any time arouse any suspicions in our minds of the interest in anything but the work in hand."[48]

The material Woikin handed over consisted of political assessments of eastern Europe. Although the information was not highly sensitive, the commissioners were perturbed because it had been received from another government and its betrayal might have resulted in an embargo on the future provision of such data to Canada. The report recommended that each department or agency that had been breached take steps "to prevent further unauthorized transmission of information and to set up further safeguards." It also recommended, with reference to the misuse of a Canadian passport, that "the practice and procedure in connection with the issue of Canadian passports be revised."[49]

Despite the department's efforts, relations with the Soviet Union deteriorated dramatically as a result of the Gouzenko affair. The ambassador in Moscow, Wilgress, was forced to conclude that Canada's position had reached a nadir. Particularly stung by "their ferocious attack against Mr. King," he counselled Ottawa in April 1946 against a visit being contemplated by the prime minister.[50] Wilgress himself found a distinct cooling off in the attitude of the host government. "During the war," he noted in his memoirs, "I had felt myself at the very top in Soviet esteem, ranking just after the British and American ambassadors. Now, I had fallen to the very bottom. . . . I could feel that my days of usefulness as Ambassador to the Soviet Union were over.''[51]

Meanwhile, the recommendations of the royal commission had further ramifications at home, resulting in the establishment of a system of internal security within the government. Norman Robertson, who played the key role in determining the nature of that system, recommended following British practice. The result was formation of an interdepartmental body, the Security Panel, chaired by the clerk of the privy council, with permanent representation from External Affairs, National Defence, and the RCMP. Individual departmental security officers were to be appointed to maintain liaison with the panel. Security checks on government employees were to be carried out by the RCMP, with the departments, not the Security Panel, retaining the right to decide on employability.[52] Once the system began to function at the end of 1946, the immediate domestic adjustment to the Gouzenko affair could be regarded as complete. The international consequences, of course, were part of something much larger and would be a central preoccupation of the department in the years to come.

The war and the department

The department that would confront post-war dangers and opportunities had changed much since 1939, but many of the characteristics, including some of the weaknesses, remained from its earlier years. In the judgment of Edgar Tarr, expressed at the time he was considered for appointment as minister to China in 1942, the cautious approach of King's government to foreign policy had hurt the department at home and abroad. Canada, Tarr told King, counted for little because it had "not given the impression that it is interested in counting." The principal reason for "this failure on Canada's part to serve itself and at the same time contribute to the general welfare," he went on, was

> the functioning, or rather the lack of functioning, of the External Affairs Department.
> . . . There has to all appearance been nothing like the same interest in having Canada function effectively as a nation, as there was in the mere establishment of the right to act as such. The absence of this interest has had ill effects both at home and abroad, not the least of which is to lessen the possibilities of really useful service by members of our Diplomatic Service. At home the Service does not rank high in our thinking, and abroad Canada's apparent indifference naturally means that other countries don't assess our diplomats more seriously than we do ourselves.
> Consider our record of delays in making diplomatic appointments.

It is difficult to over-estimate the effect of this in lessening in the Canadian mind the importance of these diplomatic posts. Too many people have come to think of them as jobs being hawked around without any takers.[53]

While the government's approach to foreign policy became more vigorous after Tarr's words were written, some earlier inadequacies remained. One was the slowness in making diplomatic appointments. In response to questioning in the House of Commons, King might announce exchanges long before he could follow through with nominations. In the case of Cuba the wait stretched to eighteen months; for China it was twenty-one. Thus tardy reciprocation by Canada came to characterize the exchanges agreed to during the war, unless, as happened with Cuba and Mexico, the other government deliberately delayed making its appointment to Ottawa.[54]

The department was still too small to fill all the positions available. As well, most allowances continued to be so low that few public servants could afford the representational costs borne by heads of post. Pearson, for example, could accept appointment as ambassador in Washington in 1944 only after the allowances had been raised, since he lacked the private means available to his predecessor.[55] As a result of these factors, only nine of the eighteen high commissioners, ambassadors, and ministers in office at the end of the war were from External Affairs. There were a few heads of post from other departments, such as Wilgress in Moscow and Hugh Scully, the consul general in New York, but a number still had to be recruited from outside the public service.

Whether from the public service or the private sector, heads of newly created posts were on their own in preparing for their assignments. Apart from letters of instruction, which the department began to issue in 1943, there was no organized system of briefing.[56] There were many competing pressures on the attention of senior officers at headquarters during the war. As well, Robertson, like Skelton and Pope before him, had never (apart from a brief period in Washington just after he joined the department) been posted abroad. All had been on missions outside Canada, but always on assignment from headquarters. The perspective of the under-secretary's office, therefore, was very much oriented from Ottawa and may have reinforced a tendency created by war-related preoccupations to give only occasional attention to the posts, especially the smaller ones.

The need for better communications with the posts was recognized in Ottawa, for example, by Wrong, but improvement was dependent both on a more pervasively outward-looking attitude at headquarters and on enhanced resources. In the mean time, despite improvements, there was continuing complaint from the posts about being out of touch.[57] In such circumstances, the department's missions could be underused.

Without frequent acknowledgment, instruction, or admonition for inadequacies, reporting might become haphazard. Nor was frequent use made of posts other than London and Washington to exert pressure in foreign capitals in favour of positions being advanced by Canada in international forums. Rather, Robertson, like Skelton, tended to rely more on contacts with the missions of other countries in Ottawa, and, since most of the exchanges were oral, Canadian representatives overseas might have to learn of them, if at all, from the governments to which they were accredited. The consequence could be felt not only in the bilateral but also in the multilateral context. Escott Reid, for example, considered that the task of the delegation to the civil aviation conference in Chicago in 1944 would have been eased by effective lobbying in the capitals where Canada was represented.[58]

Another result of loose surveillance by Ottawa was that the department could find itself, in response to the initiative of a head of post, endorsing action that did not accord with its priorities. Thus, on May 24, 1944, Canada exchanged notes with Brazil on the promotion of cultural relations. The project had originated with the ambassador to that country, Jean Désy. The department, which gave a much higher priority to war-related activities and was not keen to become heavily involved in cultural promotion, was not enthusiastic, but by the time it became aware of Désy's activities the negotiations had proceeded too far to be turned back.[59]

The department's response to Désy's initiative was consistent with the desire during the latter stages of the war to bring responsibilities more into line with resources. Although numerous new tasks related to the war had been undertaken as need arose, these had not been regarded as permanent and were phased out as circumstances permitted. Hitherto unexplored branches of diplomacy, such as information and cultural work, meanwhile, were regarded with a wary eye, and less attention was given even to some of the responsibilities that the department had assumed without question prior to 1939. The growing complexity of international relations, staffing constraints, especially in the senior ranks, and increasing demands of conference diplomacy were causing the department to concentrate more and more on its traditional mandate.

A consequence was that the making of external policy in Ottawa became a more diffuse process during the war. There was a similar tendency abroad, as various departments and agencies sent representatives of their own to important capitals, especially London and Washington. As indicated by the difficulties with the Wartime Information Board and those experienced earlier with Trade and Commerce and other departments, such a variety of offices could cause problems of focus for the Canadian presence. A further complication was the frequency of travel outside Canada by officials of various agencies, over whom the local representatives of

External Affairs had no control. In London, where Massey had never been troubled by the multiplicity of Canadian offices, there continued to be quite good co-ordination during the war, but the effort was less successful in Washington, because of the ease of cross-border communication.

The war therefore brought not only a heavy if unevenly distributed workload but also a measure of frustration. This was not confined to the business of the office, for wartime restrictions prevented promotions and improvements in salaries and allowances to compensate for increased responsibility. There was not even the prospect of recognition through the award of honours. Canada had no orders of its own, and at the end of 1943 the prime minister announced that the king's forthcoming new year's honours list would be the last to include Canadian civilians until after the war. When a post-war list was prepared in July 1946, it was decided not to recommend departmental officers for inclusion, a position that was considered to preclude them from accepting awards from other governments as well. "In principle," Robertson observed, "the task of selection is an invidious and ungrateful one, and in the present case the awards available, viz., the junior grades in the established United Kingdom Orders, are not suitable for the recognition of senior Canadian diplomatic officers."[60]

The decision attracted a wry comment in verse from Alfred Rive, who succeeded Walter Riddell as high commissioner to New Zealand in 1946:

When first I was an F.S.O.,
"third Sec." was the designation,
I thought, "Some day my chest will show
Some simple decorations."
And so, as slow I struggled through
External's permutations,
I saw myself in distant view
Bedecked with decorations.
Through thick and thin, as near or far
Were my perambulations,
I hitched my wagon to a star
And other decorations.
But as I neared the goal apace
And told all my relations,
External sent a blunt ukase
"You'll get no decorations."
"We'll put you in no Honours List
With flattering citations.
We think your name will not be missed
No stars—no decorations![61]

The following was composed in reply:

> Abandoning the ancient style
> Of formal salutations
> Herewith I venture to reply
> To yours on decorations.
> We've known you now for many years
> Enjoyed your aberrations
> But never did we realize
> You yearned for decorations.
> We thought the Special Section toil
> With all its tribulations
> Would be for you an ample prize
> Transcending decorations.
> Or junkets to the ILO
> And intervening stations
> Would compensate your noble soul
> For bauble decorations.
> But ah! tis clear no man escapes
> These tinsel aspirations
> Even New Zealand cannot slake
> The greed for decorations.
> And so I have the honour, Sir
> To send congratulations
> Because you've reached your lofty post
> Not needing decorations.[62]

The last two lines contained an important message about the effect of the war. The events of the period, by increasing the importance of the department's work to an extent never before experienced, had created an unprecedented opportunity for middle- and senior-ranking officers to demonstrate their abilities and to establish the basis for advancement after the war. This process was of benefit not only to the people concerned but also to the department and indeed to the country as a whole. Having earned a high reputation in government circles at home before the war, the department by 1945 was gaining similar standing abroad as a result of the activities of its personnel. "It came to be known," wrote I. Norman Smith in the Ottawa *Journal* on June 28, 1945, "that when Mr. Robertson or Mr. Wrong or Mr. Pearson put forth a suggestion [at the San Francisco conference] it was likely to be a good one, was certainly not to be an old one and was unlikely to be a selfish one."

Thus, as it was becoming more specialized, the department was also building a reputation for handling its particular functions well. This reputation undoubtedly enabled the department to make good use of its limited resources and to take advantage of the fact that they were growing, although not as rapidly as those in charge might have desired. In 1946 the department had twenty-six posts abroad (including the consular offices in New York, Portland, Maine, Caracas, and Lisbon), two of which had dual accreditation, and there were twenty-nine representatives (including the agent of Italy and two consuls general) of other countries in Ottawa. The appropriation for the fiscal year 1946–47, including grants to the United Nations and its specialized agencies, was nearly $7 million. The staff at the beginning of that fiscal year numbered 151 (65 at home and 86 abroad), of whom 67 were officers.

Those who served in the department during the war, John Holmes has observed, had a comparatively safe time of it, even in London: "Dodging v-bombs and eating bread sausages were very minor discomforts" by contrast with those of the battlefield. The work was none the less vital to the winning of the war, and the prospects were exciting, despite the horrors of the recent past and the uncertainties of 1945. "There was another side of 1945," Holmes has recalled of the atmosphere in Britain, where he was stationed at the end of the war, "and that always leads me to Wordsworth: 'Bliss was it in that dawn to be alive, [but] to be young was very heaven.' If you had survived, that is. . . . Now peace was upon us. It was daunting but exhilarating."

Some of the exhilaration came from the mood Holmes observed in Trafalgar Square on VE day. Despite the damage done in the blitz and afterward and recent revelations about German concentration camps, there were "no effigies being burned," and he did not hear Hitler's name mentioned. "They seem to want to express their pride and confidence in what they have done," he concluded at the time, "rather than to enjoy a good hate." The same spirit was observable in the election campaign that returned a Labour government to power. "The sense that a new and more blissful dawn was round the corner in Britain as well as the world at large," Holmes reflected later, "explains something about 1945—some of the ingenuousness perhaps, more hope than optimism."[63] The department, this recollection suggests, emerged from the war not only strengthened in resources and reputation but also with confidence that it would be possible to prevent a recurrence of world crisis on the scale just experienced. All these assets would be deployed to the full in dealing with the tensions, still only dimly appreciated, yet to come.

Note on Sources

The principal source for this history is the archival record of the Department of External Affairs (DEA). Central registry files created before 1940 and those of the office of the under-secretary down to 1946 were consulted at the National Archives of Canada and are cited, with the abbreviation RDEA, according to their location there. Central registry files originating in 1940 and later were in the process of transfer to the archives while work was in progress. Since permanent volume numbers have not yet been assigned by the archives, these records have been cited using the abbreviation DEA and the file number only, whether they were located at the archives or were still held in the department.

The records of other governments, of other branches of the Canadian government, and of individual persons have been consulted when necessary to supplement the story contained in the files of the department. In addition, interviews have been conducted with some of the participants in the events described. Except where indicated, the record of these interviews is held by the Historical Section, Academic Relations Division, Department of External Affairs.

Notes

ABBREVIATIONS

AI   Access to Information
DCER   Department of External Affairs, *Documents on Canadian External Relations*
DEA   Department of External Affairs
DND   Department of National Defence
HC   Canada, House of Commons
NA   National Archives of Canada, Ottawa
PCR   Privy Council Records, National Archives
PRO   Public Record Office, London, England
RDEA   Records of the Department of External Affairs, National Archives
RGG   Records of the Governor General, National Archives
SSEA   Secretary of State for External Affairs
TBR   Treasury Board Records, National Archives

CHAPTER ONE

1 *Report of the Commissioners from British North America Appointed to Inquire into the Trade of the West Indies, Mexico and Brazil* (Ottawa: G. E. Desbarats, 1866), p. v, also pp. 2n, 4-5. The commissioners did not visit Mexico, where conditions were unsettled. See also David M. L. Farr, *The Colonial Office and Canada, 1867-1887* (Toronto: University of Toronto Press, 1955), pp. 216-18, 220-21, and, on Hincks's role in the negotiations of 1854, D. C. Masters, *The Reciprocity Treaty of 1854* (London: Longmans Green, 1937; Carleton Library edn., Toronto: McClelland and Stewart, 1963), p. 6, and Ronald Stewart Longley, *Sir Francis Hincks* (Toronto: University of Toronto Press, 1943), pp. 249-50, 271-74.

2 G. V. LaForest, *Extradition to and from Canada*, 2nd edn. (Toronto: Canadian Law Book Ltd., 1977), pp. 1-5; M. Hancock in "The Status of Aliens in Canada," Canadian Political Science Association, *Proceedings* 6 (1934): 79-80; Department of External Affairs, "Historical Sketch of Canadian Passports" (1949), in K. P. Kirkwood, "The Department of External Affairs: A History" (unpublished MS, mimeo.: 1958), Department of External Affairs Library, vol. II, part 1, pp. 478 ff.

3 J. E. Hodgetts, *Pioneer Public Service: An Administrative History of the United Canadas, 1841-1867* (Toronto: University of Toronto Press, 1955), pp. 30-31, 35-37, 77-80, 87, 270-84.

4 G. P. de T. Glazebrook, *A History of Canadian External Relations*, rev. (Carleton Library) edn., vol. I: *The Formative Years to 1914* (Toronto: McClelland and Stewart, 1966), p. 19. The first version of this work, covering the years until 1939, was published in Toronto by Oxford University Press in two parts, 1942 and 1950.

5 H. Gordon Skilling, *Canadian Representation Abroad: From Agency to Embassy* (Toronto: Ryerson, 1945), p. 107; Wesley Barry Turner, "Colonial Self-Government and the Colonial Agency: Changing Concepts of Permanent Canadian Representation in London, 1848 to 1880," PHD thesis, Duke University, 1971, pp. 2-14, 44-49; Shirley B. Elliott, *Nova Scotia in London: A History of Its Agents General 1762-1988* (London: Office of the Agent General of Nova Scotia, 1988), pp. 2-24.

6 Paul W. Gates, "Official Encouragement to Immigration by the Province of Canada," *Canadian Historical Review* 15, no. 1 (March 1934): 24-38; Hodgetts, *Pioneer Civil Service*, pp. 240-55; Skilling, *Canadian Representation*, p. 2; Farr, *Colonial Office*, pp. 254-5. At this time, the activity was commonly designated "emigration," reflecting the perspective of the country of origin, rather than "immigration."

7 On these developments, see Roger F. Swanson, *Intergovernmental Perspectives on the Canada-U.S. Relationship* (New York: New York University Press, 1978), pp. 54-60; and Pierre Savard, *Le consulat général de France à Québec et à Montréal de 1859 à 1914* (Quebec: Laval, 1970), pp. 28-29, 57-58, 77-80.

8 G. Neuendorff, *Studies in the Evolution of Dominion Status: The Governor-General of Canada and the Development of Canadian Nationalism* (London: George Allen and Unwin, 1942), p. 126.

9 P. Stevens and J. T. Saywell, eds., *Lord Minto's Canadian Papers*, vol. I (Toronto: Champlain Society, 1981), p. xxiv. On the practices described here, see Farr, *Colonial Office*, p. vii; Glazebrook, *History*, vol. I, pp. 201-2; and, for the conduct of relations with the United States, RGG, vol. 1, file 4, vol. 7, file 1221, vol. 9, file 33, and vol. 81, file 173-1c.

10 See, for example, Secretary of State Records, NA, vol. 107, files 2528 and 2790.

11 LaForest, *Extradition*, pp. 5-7.

12 The Canadian government could after March 1872 recognize the permanent appointments of vice-consuls or consular agents made by resident consuls general or consuls. Lord Granville (foreign secretary) to Count von Bernsdorff (German ambassador), March 23, 1872, Secretary of State Records, NA, vol. 11, file 693.

13 Governor general to colonial secretary, no. 98, June 2, 1868, enclosure, report of Council, June 2, 1868, Colonial Office Records, CO 42/669/6344, NA, microfilm reel B-486. Order-in-council PC 749D, October 8, 1877, RGG, series G21, vol. 382, file 3625, microfilm reel T-1484.

14 Governor general to colonial secretary, no. 29, February 5, 1891, enclosure, minute of Council, February 2, 1891, and Colonial Office minute, Colonial Office Records, CO 42/806/4094, NA, microfilm reel B-639.

15 D. Owen Carrigan, comp., *Canadian Party Platforms 1867–1968* (Toronto: Copp Clark, 1968), pp. 2–7. On the early public service, see Hodgetts, *Pioneer Public Service*, pp. 36, 279–80; cf. Sandra Gwyn, *The Private Capital: Ambition and Love in the Age of Macdonald and Laurier* (Toronto: McClelland and Stewart, 1984), pp. 83, 90–91.

16 Farr, *Colonial Office*, p. 17.

17 On emigration agents, see *Canada in London: An Unofficial Glimpse of Canada's Sixteen High Commissioners 1880–1980*, comp. Nancy Gelber (London: Canada House, n.d. [1980]), p. 9; Skilling, *Canadian Representation*, pp. 2–3, 6–9; also Gates, "Official Encouragement," pp. 25–35.

18 Order-in-council PC 716, October 2, 1869, PCR, series 1, vol. 17.

19 On Rose in London, see *Canada in London*, pp. 9–10; Skilling, *Canadian Representation*, pp. 86–87; Morden H. Long, "Sir John Rose and the Informal Beginnings of the Canadian High Commissionership," *Canadian Historical Review* 12, no. 1 (March 1931): 23–43; and David M. L. Farr, "Sir John Rose and Imperial Relations: An Episode in Gladstone's First Administration," *Canadian Historical Review* 33, no. 1 (March 1952): 19–38.

20 Quoted in Donald Creighton, *John A. Macdonald: The Old Chieftain* (Toronto: Macmillan, 1955), p. 77. See also Ronald D. Tallman, "Warships and Mackerel: The North Atlantic Fisheries in Canada-American Relations, 1867–1877," PHD thesis, University of Maine, Orono, 1971, pp. 82, 275–84.

21 C. P. Stacey, *Canada and the Age of Conflict: A History of Canadian External Relations*, vol. I: *1867–1911* (Toronto: Macmillan, 1977), p. 19; also Farr, *Colonial Office*, p. 223.

22 On the Washington conference, see Goldwin Smith, *The Treaty of Washington* (Ithaca: Cornell University Press, 1941; New York: Russell and Russell, 1971); also Creighton, *Macdonald: The Old Chieftain*, pp. 82–105; Lester Burrell Shippee, *Canadian-American Relations, 1849–1874* (New Haven: Yale; Toronto: Ryerson, 1939), pp. 348–73, 388–401, 415–16; Tallman, "Warships and Mackerel", pp. 294, 327–29.

23 Farr, *Colonial Office*, pp. 21–22; Sir Richard Cartwright, *Reminiscences* (Toronto: William Briggs, 1912), p. 173; Dale C. Thomson, *Alexander Mackenzie: Clear Grit* (Toronto: Macmillan, 1960), pp. 311–12; R. A. Shields, "Imperial Policy and the Role of Foreign Consuls in Canada 1870–1911," *Dalhousie Review* 59, no. 4 (Winter 1979–80): 717–47.

24 Skilling, *Canadian Representation*, pp. 85–88; *Canada in London*, p. 9; Farr, *Colonial Office*, pp. 255–56; Thomson, *Alexander Mackenzie*, p. 269.

25 Thomson, *Alexander Mackenzie*, pp. 188–89, 203–7; J. M. S. Careless, *Brown of the Globe*, vol. II: *Statesman of Confederation, 1860–1880* (Toronto: Macmillan, 1963), pp. 312–24; Farr, *Colonial Office*, p. 230. See also Cartwright, *Reminiscences*, pp. 173–76.

26 The negotiations with France and Spain are dealt with in P. B. Waite, *Canada 1874–1896: Arduous Destiny* (Toronto: McClelland and Stewart, 1971), pp. 74–77; Creighton, *Macdonald: The Old Chieftain*, pp. 247, 256; Oscar Douglas Skelton, *The Life and Times of Sir Alexander Tilloch Galt* (Toronto: Oxford University Press, 1920), pp. 516–17, 521–22, and 534–35; Farr, *Colonial Office*, pp. 225–26. On the exemption from British treaties, see Farr, *Colonial Office*, pp. 232–40.

Older British treaties were more difficult to deal with, since the United Kingdom's trading partners were naturally reluctant to give up privileges in colonial markets they had enjoyed for years. Two of these treaties, with Belgium (1862) and with the German Zollverein (1865), were objectionable to Canada because they gave these countries any preference that Canada might offer Britain. The self-governing colonies, led by Canada, collaborated in a campaign to force the United Kingdom to alter the treaties. In the end Britain agreed to denounce them, a step that was taken a year after Canada granted the United Kingdom a preference in its tariff.

27 Creighton, *Macdonald: The Old Chieftain*, p. 271; also Farr, *Colonial Office*, p. 227.

28 HC *Debates*, April 29, 1880, p. 1859.

29 HC *Debates*, April 21, 1882, p. 1078.

30 Skelton, *Galt*, pp. 529–31; Farr, *Colonial Office*, pp. 264–68; Glazebrook, *History*, vol. I, pp. 132–34; Stacey, *Canada and the Age of Conflict*, vol. I, p. 34; Wilfrid I. Smith, "The Origins and Early Development of the Office of the High Commissioner," PHD thesis, University of Minnesota, n.d. [1969], p. 396.

31 Galt to Macdonald, March 13, 1881, cited in Skilling, *Canadian Representation*, p. 96.

32 Cited in ibid., p. 99.

33 Farr, *Colonial Office*, p. 253. Tupper's leadership of the colonial representatives is described in Tupper to Sir Robert Borden, December 5, 1913, Borden Papers, NA, vol. 183.

34 Under-secretary of state for external affairs to prime minister, October 27, 1911, in *DCER*, vol. I: *1909–1918* (Ottawa: Queen's Printer, 1967), p. 9.

35 HC *Debates*, April 21, 1882, p. 1078.

36 Quoted in Creighton, *Macdonald: The Old Chieftain*, p. 525.

37 Farr, *Colonial Office*, pp. 191, 214–15, 228–30.

38 Quoted in Farr, *Colonial Office*, p. 231. See also Skilling, *Canadian Representation*, p. 137. A Canadian representative first enjoyed full plenipotentiary powers at a postal union conference in 1906.

39 Robert Craig Brown, *Canada's National Policy, 1883–1900: A Study in Canadian-American Relations* (Princeton: Princeton University Press, 1964), p. 218.

40 On the early development of the Department of Trade and Commerce, see ibid., p. 227, and O. Mary Hill, *Canada's Salesman to the World: The Department of Trade and Commerce, 1892–1939* (Montreal: McGill-Queen's, 1977), pp. 1, 7–8, 11–14, 21, 25–29, 44–46, 71–72, 79–81.

41 The Ripon circular is quoted in Stacey, *Canada and the Age of Conflict*, vol. I, p. 47. On the conference and the circular, see also Brown, *National Policy*, p. 228; Hill, *Canada's Salesman*, pp. 72–74; R. A. Shields, "Imperial Policy and the Ripon Circular of 1895," *Canadian Historical Review* 47, no. 2 (June 1966): 119–35; Glazebrook, *History*, vol. I, p. 144.

42 Maurice Pope, ed., *Public Servant: The Memoirs of Sir Joseph Pope* (Toronto: Oxford University Press, 1960), p. 41. On the public service at the time Laurier came to office, see Doug Owram, *The Government Generation: Canadian Intellectuals and the State, 1900–1945* (Toronto: University of Toronto Press, 1986) pp. 45–46.

43 Russell to Pope, October 4, 1893, Sir Joseph Pope Papers, NA, vol. 1.

44 See D. J. Hall, *Clifford Sifton*, vol. I: *The Young Napoleon, 1861–1900* (Vancouver: University of British Columbia Press, 1981), p. 126, and Pope, ed., *Public Servant*, p. 129. Pope was not the first deputy minister to abstain from voting.

45 Pope, ed., *Public Servant*, p. 115.

46 On the development of the trade commissioner service during this period, see Hill, *Canada's Salesman*, pp. 52–68. Hill does not include the representative in London in her list of trade commissioners abroad in 1911.

47 The promotion of immigration under Sifton is dealt with in Hall, *Sifton*, vol. I, pp. 132–33, 257–63. See also Skilling, *Canadian Representation*, pp. 9–10.

48 Skilling, *Canadian Representation*, pp. 107–10; David E. Smith, "Provincial Representation Abroad: The Office of Agent General in London," *Dalhousie Review* 55, no. 2 (Summer 1975): 315–20.

49 Cited in Brown, *National Policy*, p. 379.

50 Laurier to Davies, August 1, 1898, Laurier Papers, NA, vol. 791D.

51 Norman Penlington, *The Alaska Boundary Dispute: A Critical Reappraisal* (Toronto: McGraw-Hill Ryerson, 1972), p. 86. Pope's activities are described in Pope, ed., *Public Servant*, pp. 144–47.

52 HC *Debates*, October 23, 1903, p. 14817.

53 Minto to Alfred Lyttleton (colonial secretary), October 25, 1903, Minto Papers, NA, letter book 4, microfilm reel A132.

54 John G. Foster (consul general) to Francis B. Loomis (assistant secretary of state), des. 40, October 23, 1903, Records of Foreign Governments–USA, Department of State: Consular Records, NA, microfilm reel M-4440.

55 Oscar Douglas Skelton, *Life and Letters of Sir Wilfrid Laurier* (Toronto: Oxford University Press, 1921), vol. II, p. 160. See also Glazebrook, *History*, vol I, p. 220.

56 Cited in Shields, "Imperial Policy," p. 731.

57 For a detailed discussion of the Lemieux mission, see R. J. Gowen, "Canada's Relations with Japan, 1895–1922: Problems of Immigration and Trade," PHD thesis, University of Chicago, 1966, pp. 142–91.

58 Minute, January 1, 1908, Colonial Office Records, CO 42/922/78, NA, microfilm reel B-2243.

59 Pope to Laurier, December 9, 1907, Pope Papers, NA, vol. 134.

60 Grey to Lord Elgin (colonial secretary), March 1, 1906, Grey of Howick Papers, NA, vol. 13, no. 83.
61 Elgin to Grey, March 22, 1906, ibid., vol. 13, no. 87.
62 On the International Joint Commission, see N. F. Dreisziger, "Dreams and Disappointments," in Robert Spencer, John Kirton, and Kim Richard Nossal, eds., *The International Joint Commission Seventy Years On* (Toronto: Centre for International Studies, University of Toronto, 1981), pp. 8–21; Alan O. Gibbons, "Sir George Gibbons and the Boundary Waters Treaty of 1909," *Canadian Historical Review* 34, no. 2 (June 1953): 124–38; and, for an American perspective, James Morton Callahan, *American Foreign Policy in Canadian Relations* (New York: Macmillan, 1937), pp. 499–510.
63 John B. Stewart, *The Canadian House of Commons: Procedure and Reform* (Montreal: McGill-Queen's, 1977), p. 45.
64 Grey to Bryce, November 28, 1907, Grey of Howick Papers, vol. 7. no. 98.
65 Pope to Anderson, July 10, 1899, Pope Papers, vol. 49.

CHAPTER TWO

1 Pope to Laurier, December 27, 1904, Laurier Papers, NA, vol. 348. Evans's proposal for a ministry of imperial and foreign affairs is in his book on Canada's participation in the South African war, *The Canadian Contingents and Canadian Imperialism* (Toronto: Publishers' Syndicate, 1901).
2 Robert MacGregor Dawson, *The Civil Service of Canada* (London: Oxford University Press, 1929), p. 74.
3 The complete text of Pope's memorandum is printed in James Eayrs, "The Origins of Canada's Department of External Affairs," *Canadian Journal of Economics and Political Science* 25, no. 2 (May 1959): 111–13. A revised version of the article, with a partial text of the memorandum, is in Hugh L. Keenleyside et al., *The Growth of Canadian Policies in External Affairs* (Durham, NC: Duke University Press, 1960), pp. 14–32. The existing procedure is dealt with in chapter 1 above.
4 Pope to Lemieux, February 24, 1908, Pope Papers, NA, vol. 20, file 228.
5 Peter Neary, "Grey, Bryce, and the Settlement of Canadian-American Differences, 1905–1911," *Canadian Historical Review* 49, no. 4 (December 1968): 358. See also Alvin C. Gluek, Jr, "Pilgrimages to Ottawa: Canadian-American Diplomacy, 1903–13," Canadian Historical Association, *Historical Papers* (1968): 75.
6 Bryce to Sir Edward Grey, February 11, 1908, Foreign Office Records, PRO, FO 115/1476, pp. 153–54. For Bryce's claim about the embassy's workload (made in 1912), see Robert Bothwell, "Canadian Representation at Washington: A Study in Colonial Responsibility," *Canadian Historical Review* 53, no. 2 (June 1972): 126.
7 Bryce to Sir Edward Grey, des. 84, March 6, 1908, Foreign Office Records, PRO, FO 115/1476, pp. 204–7.
8 Grey to Lord Elgin, March 23, 1908, Grey of Howick Papers, NA, vol. 14, no. 181.

9 Sir Francis Hopwood (permanent under-secretary of state for the colonies) to under-secretary of state in the Foreign Office, April 3, 1908, ibid., vol. 14, No. 214.

10 Diary, April 22, 1908, Pope Papers, vol. 45. On Mackenzie's problems with Pope, see Arthur R. Ford, *As the World Wags On* (Toronto: Ryerson, 1950), p. 45.

11 Bryce to Grey, August 22, 1908, Grey of Howick Papers, vol. 8, no. 187.

12 Crewe to Grey, July 4, 1908, ibid., vol. 15, no. 29.

13 Grey to Bryce, August 22, 1908, ibid., vol. 8, no. 187.

14 Diary, September 9, 1908, Pope Papers, vol. 45.

15 Confidential memorandum for the prime minister, March 11, 1912, ibid., vol. 115, no. 8.

16 Grey to colonial secretary, May 3, 1909, Grey of Howick Papers, vol. 15, no. 241. See also Paul Stevens, "Laurier, Aylesworth and the Decline of the Liberal Party in Ontario," Canadian Historical Association, *Historical Papers* (1968): 96-97.

17 Diary, February 11, 1909, and March 4, 1909, Pope Papers, vol. 45. For a clause-by-clause comparison of Pope's draft with the bill as passed, see Eayrs, "Origins," pp. 119-21.

18 Grey to colonial secretary, May 3, 1909, Grey of Howick Papers, vol. 15, no. 241.

19 HC *Debates*, March 4, 1909, pp. 1978-2008, presents the complete debate.

20 Pope to Walker, March 10, 1909; Walker to Pope, March 12, 1909, Pope Papers, vol. 22, file 375.

21 Quoted in B. Pénisson, "Le Commissariat canadien à Paris (1882-1928)," *Revue d'histoire de l'Amérique française* 34, no. 3 (December 1980): 362-63.

22 Memorandum from the second assistant secretary to the secretary of state, March 13, 1909, State Department Records, National Archives, Washington, file 4863/10.

23 Laurier to Grey, May 6 and 7, 1909, and Grey to Laurier, May 7, 1909, Grey of Howick Papers, vol. 4, nos. 418 and 419.

24 Ronald Hyam, *Britain's Imperial Century 1815-1914: A Study of Empire and Expansion* (London: B. T. Batsford, 1976), pp. 126-29. On the Dominions Department, see J. A. Cross, "The Colonial Office and the Dominions before 1914," *Journal of Commonwealth Political Studies* 4, no. 2 (July 1966): 138-48. The importance of the change seems to have been largely symbolic, although the department can be regarded as the forerunner of the Dominions and Commonwealth Relations Offices.

25 Minute by A. B. Keith on Grey to Crewe, May 8, 1909, Colonial Office Records, NA, CO 42/930/18380, reel B-2249.

26 Great Britain, House of Commons, *Debates*, March 3, 1909, cols. 1421-22. Provision for a department of external affairs had been made in the constitution of the Commonwealth of Australia in 1901.

27 Murphy to Pope, November 29, 1909, RDEA, vol. 1093, file 48-09. For the text of the act, see *DCER*, vol. I: *1909-1919* (Ottawa: Queen's Printer, 1967), pp. 3-4. The proclamation officially launching the department was dated

June 1, 1909, but Grey was not in the country to sign it. While Pope acted as if it had been signed, it did not in fact bear Grey's signature until June 21, 1909. Order-in-council PC 1391, PCR, series 1, vol. 725.

28 Murphy to Laurier, April 22, 1910, Laurier Papers, vol. 627.

29 Grey to Bryce, June 2, 1909, Grey of Howick Papers, vol. 9, no. 283.

30 Eayrs, "Origins," p. 123.

31 Grey to Bryce, June 2, 1909, Grey of Howick Papers, vol. 9, no. 283.

32 Pope to Murphy, June 30, 1909, RDEA, vol. 1093, file 48-09.

33 Diary, March 12, 1910, Pope Papers, vol. 45. The emphasis on "him" is in the original. On Murphy, see Ford, *As the World Wags On*, p. 71.

34 Memorandum, January 10, 1912, RDEA, vol. 1125, file 666-12.

35 Pope to Mulvey, June 13, 1912, ibid.

36 On departmental structure, see J. E. Hodgetts, William McCloskey, Reginald Whitaker, and V. Seymour Wilson, *The Biography of an Institution: The Civil Service Commission of Canada 1908–1967* (Montreal: McGill-Queen's, 1972), p. 27. Figures on the size of the departments are from *The Civil Service List of Canada, 1909*, Sessional Papers, 1910, no. 30 (Ottawa: King's Printer, 1910).

37 The term was also current in the United Kingdom. See J. E. Hodgetts, *The Canadian Public Service: A Physiology of Government 1867–1970* (Toronto: University of Toronto Press, 1973), p. 29.

38 On the reforms, see Hodgetts et al., *Biography*, pp. 25–28, and Dawson, *Civil Service*, pp. 74–80.

39 Hodgetts, *Canadian Public Service*, p. 35.

40 Canada, *Civil Service Commission, 1908: The Report of the Commissioners*, Sessional Papers, 1907–08, no. 29a, "Minutes of Evidence," vol. I (Ottawa: King's Printer, 1908), p. 42. The testimony of senior civil servants before this royal commission is a rich source of material on the position of women in 1909. Sir George Murray's *Report on the Organization of the Public Service of Canada*, Sessional Papers, 1912, no. 57a (Ottawa: King's Printer, 1913), pp. 12–23, provides valuable information on the immediate effects of the reforms of 1908. An analysis of the role of women in the federal government can be found in Dawson, *Civil Service*, pp. 190–95. *The Report of the Royal Commission on the Status of Women in Canada* (Ottawa, 1970; reprinted Ottawa: Department of Supply and Services, 1977) is also useful.

41 McCloskey, Miss Kathryn Agnes, notes prepared for insertion in Mr. [P.] Renaud's compilation "Canadian Diplomatic History: Biographical Notices," n.d., Records of the Public Service Commission, NA, vol. 335. On McCloskey, see also Madge Macbeth, "Efficiency Does It," *Mayfair* (June 1943): 19, 37.

42 The scale at the University of Toronto was somewhat higher. See Hilda Neatby, *Queen's University*, vol. I: *1841–1917* (Montreal and Kingston: McGill-Queen's, 1978), pp. 258, 442, 466. Choice steaks could be had in Ottawa for roughly fifteen cents per pound; the finest orange pekoe tea for forty-nine cents per pound; a dozen bottles of beer (large) for two dollars; shirts for less than a dollar. There were no provincial sales taxes. A large house could be acquired for less than $1,500 (three bedrooms, living and dining

rooms, kitchen, usually only one bath). Accommodation rentals varied between eighteen and thirty dollars per month. See *Canada Year Books*, the Special Report on Wholesale Prices in Canada (1890–1909), issued by the Department of Labour, and also the *Labour Gazette* for the period.

43 Grey to Laurier, November 3, 1909, Grey of Howick Papers, vol. 4, no. 438.

44 Grey to Laurier, November 5, 1909, ibid., no. 439, and Grey to Pope, November 5, 1909, ibid., no. 439a.

45 Grey to Laurier, December 22, 1909, ibid., no. 450; see also Laurier to Grey, November 3, 1909, ibid., no. 437.

46 Grey to Pope, December 11, 1911, in Maurice Pope, ed., *Public Servant: The Memoirs of Sir Joseph Pope* (Toronto: Oxford University Press, 1960), p. 239.

47 Pope to H.P. Biggar (chief archivist for Canada in Europe), October 25, 1910, quoted in Eayrs, "Origins," p. 128.

48 Pope to Murphy, May 2, 1910, RDEA, vol. 1093, file 48-09.

49 Pope to president of privy council, May 10, 1920, Borden Papers, NA, vol. 11, file OC552.

50 Bryce to Grey, July 1, 1911, Grey of Howick Papers, vol. 10, no. 453.

51 HC *Debates*, December 15, 1909, p. 1584. See also Bryce to Grey, December 13, 1909, Grey of Howick Papers, vol. 9, no. 311.

52 On this achievement, see Gluek, "Pilgrimages to Ottawa," p. 82, and Pope, ed., *Public Servant*, p. 234.

53 Ernest J. Chambers, ed., *The Canadian Parliamentary Guide* (Ottawa: Mortimer Co., 1909), pp. 498–500.

54 HC *Debates*, December 7, 1910, p. 953. An earlier statement is in ibid., December 2, 1909, pp. 854–55. See also Grey to Lord Elgin, March 26, 1906, Grey of Howick Papers, vol. 13, no. 89; Crewe to Grey, March 30, 1910, ibid., vol. 16, no. 268a; and general correspondence in ibid., vol. 26.

55 J. G. Foster to Rep. D. J. Foster, March 15, 1910, D. J. Foster to J. G. Foster, March 26, 1910, and J. G. Foster to Sen. W. P. Dillingham, May 13, 1911, J. G. Foster Papers, Queen's University Archives.

56 H. J. Morgan, *The Canadian Men and Women of the Time* (Toronto: W. Briggs, 1912), p. 910.

57 Bryce to Grey, July 4, 1910, Grey of Howick Papers, vol. 10, no. 387.

58 Alvin C. Gluek, Jr, "Programmed Diplomacy: The Settlement of the North Atlantic Fisheries Question, 1907–12," *Acadiensis* 6, no. 1 (Autumn 1976): 59–60.

59 On the last point, see Pope to G. J. Desbarats (deputy minister of naval service), January 14, 1911, Desbarats to Pope, January 19, 1911, RDEA, vol. 1107, file 18-11.

60 Pope to Griffith, July 9, 1909, ibid., vol. 1092, file 1-09; Griffith to Pope, March 1, 1911, ibid., vol. 1112, file 304-11.

61 Pope to Griffith, January 27, 1911, ibid., vol. 1110, file 101-11.

CHAPTER THREE

1 Quoted in C. P. Stacey, *Canada and the Age of Conflict: A History of Canadian External Policies*, Vol. I (Toronto: Macmillan, 1977), p. 159.

2 Grey to Bryce, September 26, 1911, Grey of Howick Papers, NA, vol. 11, no. 476.

3 For the text of the act see *DCER*, vol. I: *1909-1918* (Ottawa: Queen's Printer, 1967), p. 12.

4 Comment on "Effect of Canada's Position in the Empire on Her Own Political Life," in *Round Table Studies* (London: R. Clay, n.d. [1911?]), p. 133.

5 "Small Display but Big Import to Borden's Job," Edmonton *Journal*, December 18, 1912.

6 Pope to Borden, January 10, 1912, RDEA, vol. 1125, file 666-12.

7 W. Griffith to Borden, October 3, 1911; G. Perley to Borden, February 7, 1912, Borden Papers, NA, vol. 173, file 198.

8 *DCER*, vol. I, pp. 8-10; Roy to George Foster (minister of trade and commerce), May 28, 1912, order-in-council PC 3278, December 20, 1912, Pope to Borden, January 4, 1913, and Roy to W. S. Roche (minister of the interior), November 21, 1913, RDEA, vol. 1129, file 29-13.

9 Canada, Senate, *Debates*, 1911-12, p. 118.

10 *Report on the Organization of the Public Service of Canada*, Sessional Papers, 1912, no. 57a (Ottawa: King's Printer, 1913).

11 Pope to Borden, February 26, 1912, Pope Papers, NA, vol. 115, file 8. On the red ensign see Pope to G. B. van Blaricon (editor, *The Busy Man's Magazine*), May 15, 1909, ibid., vol. 22, file 388.

12 Robert Bothwell, *Loring Christie: The Failure of Bureaucratic Imperialism* (New York: Garland Publishing, 1988), pp. 7-20. On Christie's early life and career in the department, see also Michael F. Scheuer, "L. C. Christie and the North Atlantic World, 1913-1941," PHD thesis, University of Manitoba, 1986, pp. 1-132.

13 Walker to A. E. Blount (private secretary to Borden), February 20, 1913, Borden Papers, vol. 255, file 2997.

14 Bothwell, *Loring Christie*, p. 52.

15 See Pope to Borden, June 23, 1914, Pope Papers, vol. 116, file 9.

16 Memorandum, n.d., Loring Christie Papers, NA, vol. 2, file 3. The term *commonwealth* was gaining currency at this time among persons concerned with the future of the empire, including members of the Fabian Society and of the Round Table movement.

17 J. Castell Hopkins, ed., *The Canadian Annual Review of Public Affairs* (Toronto: Canadian Review Co., 1914), p. 161-62.

18 Diary, August 4, 1914, Pope Papers, vol. 46.

19 E.g. J. Pope, "Confidential Memorandum upon the Subject of the Annexation of the West India Islands to the Dominion of Canada," January 31, 1917, ibid., vol. 127, file 71.

20 Borden to Christie, August 6, 1914, Christie Papers, vol. 3, file 9.

21 For the contrasting attitudes of Asquith and Lloyd George, see Borden to Perley, January 4, 1916, *DCER*, vol. I, p. 104, and Lloyd George to colonial secretary, December 12, 1916, in David Lloyd George, *War Memoirs*, vol. IV (Boston: Little, Brown, 1933), p. 1733.

22 Quoted in Robert Craig Brown, *Robert Laird Borden: A Biography*, vol. II: *1914-1937* (Toronto: Macmillan, 1980), p. 81. See also "Extracts from Minutes

of Proceedings of the Imperial War Conference," April 16, 1917, in *DCER*, vol. I, pp. 308-12. The effect of the war on the imperial relationship is examined in detail in Philip G. Wigley, *Canada and the Transition to Commonwealth: British-Canadian Relations 1917-1926* (Cambridge: Cambridge University Press, 1977), p. 19-66.

23 Perley to Borden, August 15, 1914, ibid., pp. 18-22.

24 Comments on CO 42/989/42072, Colonial Office Records, NA, microfilm reel B-3244.

25 Perley to colonial secretary, August 30, 1915, and comments thereon, ibid.

26 Andrew Bonar Law (colonial secretary) to governor general, des. 820, August 26, 1915, enc., Perley to Kitchener, August 4, 1915, RDEA, vol. 1154, file 5-15.

27 On the Overseas Ministry see Desmond Morton, *A Peculiar Kind of Politics* (Toronto: University of Toronto Press, 1982).

28 Griffith to Perley, February 1919, Borden Papers, vol. 45, file 205.

29 R. Reid to Borden, February 3, 1914, L. Gouin to Borden, August 26, 1914, and Borden to Gouin, May 6, 1914, together with Pope's "Notes on a Memorandum by Dr. Pelletier on the subject of the status of the representatives of Canadian Provinces in London," April 30, 1914, Borden Papers, vol. 48, file 217; J. Reid to A. L. Sifton, July 7, 1916, and Borden to A. L. Sifton (Premier of Alberta), September 8, 1916, Pope Papers, vol. 116, file 11; Pope to Borden, September 20, 1920, Pope to governor general's secretary, October 5, 1920, and Viscount Milner (secretary of state for the colonies) to Duke of Devonshire (governor general), November 10, 1920, RDEA, vol. 1274, file 964-20.

30 Sen. C. P. Beaubien to Borden, April 20, 1918, ibid., vol. 281, file P8/92. Unfortunately, not much is known of Roy's wartime work in Paris because his office records were subsequently destroyed and he still was not submitting an annual report to Ottawa.

31 Pope to C. Spring Rice, June 4, 1917, Pope Papers, vol. 115, file 7.

32 Spring Rice to Pope, January 31, 1918, ibid., vol. 115, file 7; Spring Rice to Borden, February 2, 1915, ibid.

33 Spring Rice, "Notes on the Manner in which Canadian Business is Transacted in Washington," January 29, 1918, ibid., file 6. On Christie, see Bothwell, *Loring Christie*, p. 91.

34 A. J. Johnston (deputy minister of marine and fisheries) to Pope, June 15, 1916, RDEA, vol. 1189, file 4445-16.

35 Robert Bothwell, "Canadian Representation at Washington: A Study in Colonial Responsibility," *Canadian Historical Review* 53, no. 2 (June 1972): 133-36.

36 R. D. Cuff and J. L. Granatstein, *Canadian-American Relations in Wartime: From the Great War to the Cold War* (Toronto: A. M. Hakkert, 1975), pp. 45-50. On Flavelle see also Michael Bliss, *A Canadian Millionaire* (Toronto: Macmillan, 1978), pp. 366-67.

37 Maurice Pope, ed., *Public Servant: The Memoirs of Sir Joseph Pope* (Toronto: Oxford University Press, 1960), p. 276.

38 PC 272, February 2, 1918, *DCER*, vol. I, pp. 32-34.

39 W.A.. Matheson, *The Prime Minister and the Cabinet* (Toronto: Methuen, 1976), pp. 68–69.

40 Diary, July 9, 1920, Pope Papers, vol. 47. See also Margaret Prang, "N. W. Rowell and Canada's External Policy, 1917–1921," Canadian Historical Association, *Annual Report* (1960): 86, and, on the war committee (intended to co-ordinate the work of several departments), Brown, *Borden*, vol. II, p. 131.

41 Christie to Rowell, January 22, 1926, together with Christie, "Notes on the Organization of the Foreign Office," May 25, 1920, RDEA, vol. 1281, file 1576-20.

42 *Reports of the Secretary of State for External Affairs . . . 1915– . . . 1920* (Ottawa: King's Printer, 1916–21).

43 Pope to Borden, October 16, 1917, RDEA, vol. 1223, file 330-18.

44 Pope to J. Hunter, October 17, 1917, ibid.

45 Pope to Rowell, December 24, 1918, ibid.

46 D. M. Page, "Canadians and the League of Nations before the Manchurian Crisis," PHD thesis, University of Toronto, 1972, pp. 81–88.

47 R. Borden to L. Borden, January 18, 1919, as quoted in Brown, *Borden*, vol. II, p. 152. On Canadian objectives in the negotiations, see Wigley, *Canada and the Transition to Commonwealth*, pp. 67–95.

48 Pope to Foster, January 20, 1923, Pope Papers, vol. 31, file 966.

49 Diary, December 11, 1920, Pope Papers, vol. 47, and Maurice Pope, ed., *Public Servant*, p. 287.

50 "The League of Nations and its consequences in National Policy," n.d., Christie Papers, vol. 2, file 1.

51 For Christie's several reports see RDEA, vol. 1281, file 1576-20.

52 Sir Robert Laird Borden, *Canadian Constitutional Studies* (Toronto: University of Toronto Press, 1922), p. 124.

53 Minute of June 29, 1919, Foreign Office Records, PRO, FO 371/4249.

54 HC *Debates*, May 17, 1920, pp. 2457–58.

55 Diary, January 29, 1919, Pope Papers, vol. 46.

56 Keefer to Pope, April 10, 1919, RDEA, vol. 1242, file 460-19.

57 Diary, August 23, 25, and 29, 1919, Pope Papers, vol. 46.

58 J. E. Hodgetts, *The Canadian Public Service: A Physiology of Government, 1867–1970* (Toronto: University of Toronto Press, 1973), pp. 266–69; Pope to W. Foran (secretary, Civil Service Commission), July 26, 1919, RDEA, vol. 1256, file 66-A-20; and J. E. Hodgetts et al., *The Biography of an Institution: The Civil Service Commission of Canada, 1908–1967* (Montreal: McGill-Queen's, 1972), pp. 66–75.

59 Pope to W. W. Cory (deputy minister of the interior), July 7, 1922, in Maurice Pope, ed., *Public Servant*, p. 288.

60 J. Pope, memorandum to the Civil Service Commission, February 1, 1920, W. Foran to Pope, July 8, 1920, and Roche to Pope, June 27, 1922, RDEA, vol. 1256, file 66-A-20. The study by Arthur Young and Co. is dealt with in Robert MacGregor Dawson, *The Civil Service of Canada* (London: Oxford University Press, 1929), pp. 95–96.

61 Rowell to King, November 30, 1925, King Papers, NA, series J1, vol. 123.

62 Meighen to Graham, February 16, 1953, Meighen Papers, NA, vol. 226, file 55. See Bothwell, *Loring Christie*, p. 312, and Roger Graham, *Arthur Meighen*, vol. II: *And Fortune Fled* (Toronto: Clark, Irwin and Co., 1963), p. 55.

63 See also Bothwell, *Loring Christie*, p. 319.

64 Extract, "Annual Report for United States, 1920," Colonial Office Records, NA, CO 42/1038/55887, microfilm reel B-3364.

65 As a result of a decision taken at the Imperial Conference in 1917, Canada had begun receiving a weekly "British Empire and Africa Report." In 1919, this became the "British Empire Report," and a "Western and General Report" and an "Eastern Report" were added. Besides these weekly reports, in 1920 the department received 195 cabinet papers, 25 war cabinet papers, 3 British Empire delegation papers, and 9 others of various classes.

CHAPTER FOUR

1 Diary, July 10, 1922, Pope Papers, NA, vol. 47, and, on the imperial conferences, May 14 and September 20, 1923.

2 Christie to Sir Robert Borden, March 15, 1926, Borden Papers, NA, vol. 264, file 59; diary, April 1 and November 9, 1922, William Lyon Mackenzie King Papers, NA; Michael F. Scheuer, "L. C. Christie and the North Atlantic World 1913-1941," PHD thesis, University of Manitoba, 1986, pp. 171-218.

3 Diary, February 26 and April 25, 1924, Pope Papers; HC *Debates*, June 15, 1923, p. 3988.

4 Diary, January 28 and February 1, 1922, King Papers.

5 Ibid., September 26, 1922. See also ibid., September 18, 19, and 20, 1922. A discussion of the Chanak crisis in the imperial context is in Philip G. Wigley, *Canada and the Transition to Commonwealth: British-Canadian Relations 1917-1926* (Cambridge: Cambridge University Press, 1977), pp. 160-66.

6 On Canada and the treaty, see C. P. Stacey, *Canada and the Age of Conflict*, vol. II: *1921-1948* (Toronto: University of Toronto Press, 1981), pp. 35-42, and Wigley, *Canada and the Transition to Commonwealth*, pp. 167-72, 209-16; also diary, December 30, 1922, and January 1, 1923, King Papers, and governor general to colonial secretary, October 31, 1922, in *DCER*, vol. III: *1919-1925*, ed. Lovell C. Clark (Ottawa: Information Canada, 1970), pp. 85-86.

7 The halibut treaty is dealt with in R. MacGregor Dawson, *William Lyon Mackenzie King: A Political Biography 1874-1923* (Toronto: University of Toronto Press, 1958), pp. 431-39, Stacey, *Canada and the Age of Conflict*, vol. II, pp. 48-56, and Wigley, *Canada and the Transition to Commonwealth*, pp. 175-85.

8 Skelton to King, June 27 and September 24, 1911, King Papers, series J1, vol. 19; Skelton to King, August 8, 1919, and King to Skelton, August 22, 1919, ibid., vol. 51.

9 Diary, January 21, 1922, King Papers. For the speech referred to see O. D. Skelton, "Canada and Foreign Policy," in Arthur S. Bourinot, ed., *The Canadian Club Year Book, 1921-1922* (Ottawa: Dadson-Merrill Press,

1922), pp. 58–69. King was already aware of Skelton's view on these matters, for the latter had sent him his article "Canada, the Empire, the League," *The Grain Growers' Guide* (February 25, 1920): 7, 71–73; (March 3, 1920): 7, 12–16.

10 Diary, January 21, 1922, King Papers. For an examination of Skelton's views, see Norman Hillmer, "The Anglo-Canadian Neurosis: The Case of O. D. Skelton," in Peter Lyon, ed., *Britain and Canada: Survey of a Changing Relationship* (London: Frank Cass, 1976), pp. 61–84.

11 King to Skelton, October 16, 1922, King Papers, series J1, vol. 82.

12 Diary, March 17, 1923, King Papers.

13 Ibid., September 11, 1923. On Skelton's meeting with Pope, see diary, July 20 and September 20, 1923, Pope Papers, vol. 47. On the Canadian role in the imperial conferences of 1923, see Wigley, *Canada and the Transition to Commonwealth*, pp. 185–205, and John M. Carland, "Shadow and Substance: Mackenzie King's Perceptions of British Intentions at the 1923 Imperial Conference," in Gordon Martel, ed., *Studies in Imperial History: Essays in Honour of A. P. Thornton* (London: Macmillan, 1986), pp. 178–200.

14 Diary, January 18, 1924, King Papers. On the work of the Canadian delegation in London, see Dafoe's report in Ramsay Cook, "J. W. Dafoe at the Imperial Conference, 1923," *Canadian Historical Review* 41, no. 1 (March 1960): 19–40.

15 Diary, March 24, 1924, King Papers. Ewart's contribution is also referred to in ibid., March 23 and April 22, 1924.

16 King to Sir Lomer Gouin (minister of justice and attorney general), September 6, 1923, ibid., series J1, vol. 86; D. M. Page "Canadians and the League of Nations before the Manchurian Crisis," PHD thesis, University of Toronto, 1972, p. 224.

17 Order-in-council PC 105, January 19, 1924, RDEA, vol. 1371, file 190-24.

18 King to Peter Larkin, April 23, 1924, King Papers, series J1, vol. 102. Christie's comment is in Christie to Biggar, February 29, 1924, Christie Papers, NA, vol. 9, file 30.

19 E. M. Macdonald, *Recollections, Political and Personal* (Toronto: Ryerson, 1938), pp. 433–38. For Skelton's views, see "A Summary of the Meetings of the British Empire Delegation, August 31–September 30, 1924," RDEA, vol. 1386, file 1424-24.

20 The text of Dandurand's speech is in W. A. Riddell, ed., *Documents on Canadian Foreign Policy—1917–1939* (Toronto: Oxford University Press, 1962), pp. 462–65. See also Page, "Canadians and the League of Nations," pp. 235–38.

21 Baldwin to King, February 5, 1925, RDEA, vol. 814, file 629. In due course, the protocol was killed as a result of rejection by Britain.

22 Rowell to G. D. Robertson, May 13, 1920, Records of the Department of Labour, NA, vol. 3173, file 628A-2-2.

23 A complete list of delegates to the ILO is in ibid., vol. 3245, file 8-2-2-8. On External Affairs' responsibility for submissions to cabinet, see G. Brown (assistant deputy minister of labour) to Pope, April 5, 1921, and minister of

labour to Skelton, December 29, 1930, ibid., vol. 3173, file 628A-2-2.

24 W. A. Riddell, *World Security by Conference* (Toronto: Ryerson, 1947), p. 28. The arrangements for Riddell's appointment are discussed in Riddell to Skelton, March 2, 1925, Skelton to King, January 16, 1925, Skelton to Riddell, November 17, 1924, and February 12, 1925, and order-in-council PC 2174, December 17, 1924, RDEA, vol. 1400, file 74-A-25. See also John Mainwaring, *The International Labour Organization: A Canadian View* (Ottawa: Minister of Supply and Services, 1986), pp. 37–81.

25 On Pope's retirement and on Walker, see diary, July 10, 1924, and January 26, January 27, March 16, and March 30, 1925, Pope Papers, vol. 47. Skelton was still expressing doubts about taking the job of under-secretary in February 1925, but by that time Pope was confident he would agree to do so. Ibid., February 7, 1925.

26 Diary, April 1, 1925, King Papers.

27 King to Rowell, December 7, 1925, ibid., series J1, vol. 123.

28 Because King was unable to convince the cabinet of the wisdom of appointing parliamentary under-secretaries, Pacaud's position was informal, and he received no extra remuneration. W. A. Matheson, *The Prime Minister and the Cabinet* (Toronto: Methuen, 1976), p. 69.

29 King to Rowell, December 7, 1925, King Papers, series J1, vol. 123.

30 F. W. Gibson, *Queen's University*, vol. II: *1917–1961: To Serve and Yet Be Free* (Montreal and Kingston: McGill-Queen's, 1983), p. 23.

31 "Marjorie McKenzie," *External Affairs* 10, no. 1 (January 1958): 32; Corolyn Cox, "Safekeeper of the Secrets and Conscience of External Affairs," *Saturday Night* (March 17, 1945): 2.

32 Quoted in Alison Taylor Hardy, "Women: Always Diplomatic and More Recently Diplomats," *Liaison* 1, no. 6 (February 1985): 3.

33 "Competition for a Counsellor," RDEA, vol. 787, file 408.

34 Skelton to King, December 9, 1925, King Papers, series J1, vol. 125.

35 T. W. King to W. L. M. King, October 24, 1922, King Papers, series J1, vol. 75. See also diary, October 20, 1922, King Papers, and Skelton to T. W. King, April 17, 1925, RDEA, vol. 1855, file 64-38. Tom King was still reporting to the prime minister and being paid $100 per month by the department in 1939 "as resident correspondent connected with the press at Washington." Agnes McCloskey to King, December 17, 1939, ibid.

36 A. Geddes (British ambassador, Washington) to Lord Curzon (foreign secretary), November 3, 1922, Colonial Office Records, NA, CO 42/1043/55643; Byng to Duke of Devonshire (colonial secretary), January 19, 1923, CO 42/1043/63214. Devonshire agreed with King's position "that if Canada is to be represented at Washington it should be only for questions of trade and tariff etc., and not for diplomatic purposes." Devonshire to Byng, February 7, 1923, ibid.

37 HC *Debates*, June 2, 1925, p. 3839. See also H. B. Neatby, *William Lyon Mackenzie King 1924–1932: The Lonely Heights* (Toronto: University of Toronto Press, 1963), p. 69.

CHAPTER FIVE

1 *DCER*, vol. IV: *1926–1930*, ed. Alex I. Inglis (Ottawa: Information Canada, 1971), p. 15. The precedent established by Ireland is dealt with in chapter 4 above.

2 While Massey claimed that he, along with King, requested the presence of the British ambassador, the foreign secretary appears to have engineered the operation. See Vincent Massey, *What's Past Is Prologue: The Memoirs of the Right Honourable Vincent Massey, C. H.* (Toronto: Macmillan, 1963), p. 123, and Norman Hillmer, "Anglo-Canadian Relations 1926–1937: A Study of Canada's Role in the Shaping of Commonwealth Policies," PHD thesis, Cambridge University, 1974, p. 103.

3 Diary, October 18, 1927, King Papers, NA.

4 Diary, September 29, 1928, King Papers. See also ibid., August 26, 1928, and Norman Hillmer, "The Foreign Office, the Dominions and the Diplomatic Unity of the Empire 1925–29," in David Dilks, ed., *Retreat from Power: Studies in Britain's Foreign Policy of the Twentieth Century*, vol. I: *1906–1939* (London: Macmillan, 1981), pp. 68–72.

5 Diary, October 18, 1927, King Papers. The immigration question is dealt with in W. P. Ward, *White Canada Forever: Popular Attitudes and Public Policy towards Orientals in British Columbia* (Montreal: McGill-Queen's, 1978), pp. 128–39.

6 HC *Debates*, January 30, 1928, p. 29.

7 William Lyon Mackenzie King, "The Canadian Legations Abroad," *Canadian Nation* 2, no. 1 (March–April 1929): 5–7, 24–26.

8 Hillmer, "The Foreign Office, the Dominions, and the Diplomatic Unity," pp. 72–76. See also Hillmer, "Anglo-Canadian Relations," pp. 109–32.

9 Willingdon to L. S. Amery (dominions secretary), December 29, 1926, Dominions Office Records, DO 35/24/259, NA, reel B-4719. The establishment of the Dominions Office is dealt with in Joe Garner, *The Commonwealth Office 1925–68* (London: Heinemann, 1978), pp. 6–14. On the Imperial Conference of 1926, see James G. Wigley, *Canada and the Transition to Commonwealth: British-Canadian Relations 1917–1926* (Cambridge: Cambridge University Press, 1977), pp. 248–77.

10 Diary, October 25–27, 1926, King Papers.

11 Norman Hillmer, "A British High Commissioner for Canada, 1927–28," *Journal of Imperial and Commonwealth History* 1, no. 3 (May 1979): 340–41.

12 Precedence and uniforms are dealt with in *Canada in London: An Unofficial Glimpse of Canada's Sixteen High Commissioners, 1880–1980*, comp. Nancy Gelber (London: Canada House, n.d. [1980]), p. 38. Diplomatic status was conferred in 1952 by 15 and 16 Geo. 6 and 1 Eliz. 2, cap. 18, Diplomatic Immunities (Commonwealth Countries and Republic of Ireland) Act, 1952.

13 Claude Bissell, *The Young Vincent Massey* (Toronto: University of Toronto Press, 1981), p. 143.

14 Vincent Massey, *What's Past Is Prologue*, p. 123.

15 On Massey's career in Washington, see Bissell, *Young Vincent Massey*, pp. 112–45.

16 Hugh L. Keenleyside, *Memoirs*, vol. I: *Hammer the Golden Day* (Toronto: McClelland and Stewart, 1981), p. 247.

17 Diary, January 5, 1929, King Papers.

18 Skelton to Civil Service Commission, August 15, 1928, RDEA, vol. 787, file 408.

19 J. E. Hodgetts et al., *The Biography of an Institution: The Civil Service Commission of Canada—1908-1967* (Montreal: McGill-Queen's, 1972), p. 98. See also Doug Owram, *The Government Generation: Canadian Intellectuals and the State 1900-45* (Toronto: University of Toronto Press, 1986), pp. 77, 129-30.

20 Hickerson to Biggar, July 18, 1941, United States National Archives and Record Service, State Department, Records of European Affairs, Box 4. See also Hickerson interview, Washington, September 1979.

21 Willingdon to King, July 26, 1928, RDEA, vol. 787, file 408.

22 Skelton to W. Henderson (director, Australian Department of External Affairs), September 27, 1930, RDEA, vol. 787, file 408.

23 Skelton to Australian external affairs minister, October 27, 1940, ibid.

24 Skelton to Keith Crowther, July 27, 1928, ibid., file 409.

25 For related correspondence, see ibid., vol. 786, file 407. The subject is also dealt with in NA interview with John E. Read, Read Papers, NA, vol. 10.

26 R. H. Hadow (first secretary, United Kingdom high commissioner's office) to G. G. Whiskard (assistant secretary, Dominions Office), April 4, 1929, Dominions Office Records, DO 35/68/6765, NA, reel B-4764.

27 The information on Skelton and King was supplied by Sheila Menzies and Blair Neatby, respectively.

28 Hadow to P. A. Koppel (counsellor, Foreign Office), April 24, 1929, Foreign Office Records, PRO, FO 627-12, file U 310/315/750.

29 On Keenleyside's early activities in Japan, see Keenleyside, *Memoirs*, vol. I, pp. 246-85.

30 Ibid., pp. 287-90; Bissell, *Young Vincent Massey*, pp. 125-26.

31 Diary, August 7, 1929, King Papers. The description of the working environment is based on interviews with three early recruits: J. Scott Macdonald, Napanee, February 11, 1980; H. F. Feaver, Ottawa, September 14, 1979; and Hugh L. Keenleyside, Victoria, October 23, 1978. On Skelton's objectives in recruitment, see Keenleyside, *Memoirs*, vol. I, p. 232.

32 HC *Debates*, May 20, 1929, p. 2666.

33 Keenleyside, *Memoirs*, vol. I, p. 231; also interviews with G. Hilborn, Ottawa, August 1, 1985, and H. F. Feaver, Ottawa, July 7, 1985. Grace Hart described her work in "The Library of the Department of External Affairs: An Historical Outline," May 15, 1951, DEA file 1066-D-40. The early development of the library is also dealt with in K. P. Kirkwood, "The Department of External Affairs: A History," unpublished MS (mimeo: 1958), pp. 1152, 1155-56, DEA Library.

34 Skelton to Roy, October 7, 1929, RDEA, vol. 794, file 162; Skelton to Wrong, November 12, 1930, ibid., vol. 851, file S-12-D.

35 HC *Debates*, April 13, 1927, pp. 2457-61.

36 Pearson, "Memorandum on the Work of the Department of External

Affairs,'' November 17, 1930, RDEA, vol. 787, file 408.

37 Skelton to King, July 5, 1929, King Papers, series J4, vol. 66, file 451.

38 Sir Harry Batterbee (assistant secretary, Dominions Office, in 1926) inter-view, Washington, December 1970. On the reports from the high commis-sioner's office, see Hillmer, ''Anglo-Canadian Neurosis,'' pp. 75–76.

39 Diary, September 10, 1929, King Papers. For Skelton's adaptation to the prime minister's position, see Skelton to Dandurand, December 30, 1924, in M. Hamelin, ''L'honorable Raoul Dandurand et la participation du Canada à la Société des Nations dans les années 1920s,'' diplôme d'études supérieures en histoire, Université Laval, 1964, p. 62, and Skelton to King, February 16, 1925, King Papers, series J4, vol. 112, file 801.

40 Papers of the Imperial Conference of 1926, RDEA, Briefing Book 1-1926/9; Hillmer, ''Anglo-Canadian Relations,'' pp. 49–50. MacRae's comments were in letters to Dafoe. See Ramsay Cook, ''A Canadian Account of the 1926 Imperial Conference,'' *Journal of Commonwealth Political Studies*, 3, no. 1 (March 1965): 54, 58, 61.

41 Memorandum, January 5, 1929, King Papers, series J4, vol. 58, file 379. Burchell's assessment is in C. J. Burchell, *The Statute of Westminster and Its Effect on Canada* (Johannesburg: South African Institute of International Affairs, 1945), p. 9.

42 Diary, September 4, 1927, King Papers. See also ibid., June 8, 1927, and Lapointe to King, August 12, 1927, quoted in M. Hamelin, ed., *Les Mémoires du Sénateur Raoul Dandurand (1861–1942)* (Quebec: Les Presses de l'Université Laval, 1967), p. 298.

43 Skelton to King, September 19, 1927, King Papers, series J1, vol. 149.

44 For an evaluation of the Canadian delegations between 1920 and 1939, see Richard Veatch, *Canada and the League of Nations* (Toronto: University of Toronto Press, 1975), pp. 24–26.

45 Dandurand to King, July 8, 1928, King Papers, series J1, vol. 151.

46 Skelton, ''Pending Arbitration and Conciliation Questions,'' December 12, 1928, King Papers, series J4, vol. 127, file 965.

47 HC *Debates*, June 21, 1926, p. 4759; James Eayrs, *The Art of the Possible: Government and Foreign Policy in Canada* (Toronto: University of Toronto Press, 1961), p. 106. For expressions of the view that division on foreign policy should be avoided, see HC *Debates*, June 22, 1920, p. 3962; April 27, 1921, pp. 2631–32, 2642, and 2658; and June 21, 1926, p. 4770.

48 HC *Debates*, June 15, 1923, p. 4001; April 8, 1924, pp. 1125–26; April 24, 1924, p. 1440; May 19, 1924, p. 2266; February 25, 1926, p. 1335; March 15, 1926, p. 1561; June 21, 1926, p. 4771; May 28, 1928, pp. 3489 and 3597; February 19, 1929, pp. 257 and 269; April 8, 1930, pp. 1387–90.

49 Ibid., April 8, 1930, p. 1391; Kirkwood, ''History,'' pp. 1153–54; Eayrs, *Art of the Possible*, p. 118.

50 HC, *Report, Proceedings and Evidence of the Select Standing Committee on Industrial and International Relations . . .* (Ottawa: King's Printer, 1930), p. 12.

51 ''Notes on the function, organization, practices and personnel of the Depart-ment of External Affairs,'' June 28, 1927, RDEA, vol. 787, file 408.

52 King to Rowell, December 7, 1925, King Papers, series J1, vol. 123.

53 Note by Skelton, January 17, 1928, RDEA, vol. 1489, file 242-27.

54 Walker to Wrong, August 18, 1927, ibid., vol. 1498, file 686-27.

CHAPTER SIX

1 HC *Debates*, April 13, 1927, p. 2472, January 30, 1928, p. 29, and June 11, 1928, p. 4164.

2 J. M. Beck, *Pendulum of Power: Canada's Federal Elections* (Scarborough: Prentice-Hall, 1968), pp. 194, 197; HC *Debates*, July 30, 1931, pp. 4341, 4345. The text of Bennett's claim is in John Robert Colombo, ed., *Colombo's Canadian Quotations* (Edmonton: Hurtig, 1974), p. 48.

3 Exports fell from $1.368 billion in 1929 to $528 million in 1933, while imports went from $1.265 billion to $406 million during the same period. The price of wheat plummeted from $1.69 to 38 cents per bushel between 1929 and 1932. Statistics Canada, *Historical Statistics of Canada*, 2nd edn., ed F. H. Leacy (Ottawa: Minister of Supply and Services, 1983). On the Depression and its effects on Canada, see John Herd Thompson and Allen Seager, *Canada 1922–1939: Decades of Discord* (Toronto: McClelland and Stewart, 1985), pp. 193–221, and Robert B. Bryce, *Maturing in Hard Times: Canada's Department of Finance through the Great Depression* (Kingston and Montreal: McGill-Queen's, 1986), pp. 39–59.

4 Bennett's work habits are described, in the context of various policy issues, in Thompson and Seager, *Canada 1922–1939*, pp. 193–276. For the assessment of a severe critic, see Norman Ward, ed., *A Party Politician: The Memoirs of Chubby Power* (Toronto: Macmillan, 1966), pp. 288–93. A more favourable view is in Donald C. Story, "Canada's Covenant: The Bennett Government, the League of Nations and Collective Security, 1930–1935," PHD thesis, University of Toronto, 1976, pp. 34–36.

5 On the Department of Finance at this time, see Bryce, *Maturing in Hard Times*, pp. 67–76.

6 On Bennett's early relations with the department, see NA interview with John E. Read, Read Papers, NA, vol. 10, and Hugh L. Keenleyside, *Memoirs*, vol. I: *Hammer the Golden Day* (Toronto: McClelland and Stewart, 1981), p. 459.

7 Pearson interview, Ottawa, September 23, 1970.

8 NA interview with John E. Read, Read Papers, vol. 10.

9 Ibid.

10 Corolyn Cox, "Safekeeper of the Secrets and Conscience of External Affairs," *Saturday Night* (March 17, 1945): 2; "Canadian External Affairs: Pending Questions," n.d. (1930), RDEA, vol. 796, file 488.

11 Lawrence Martin, *The Presidents and the Prime Ministers: Washington and Ottawa Face to Face: The Myth of Bilateral Bliss, 1867–1982* (Toronto: Doubleday, 1982), pp. 105–106.

12 Rowell to Bennett, August 8, 1930, Bennett Papers, NA, microfilm reel M1213, pp. 136,147–50.

13 Ibid.

14 Diary, August 13 and 14, 1930, King Papers, NA.

15 Marler to Skelton, August 7, 1930, RDEA, vol. 792, file 433.

16 HC *Debates*, September 20, 1930, p. 491; May 15, 1931, p. 1660.

17 Ibid., May 15, 1931, p. 1658. See also ibid., pp. 1665-69 and 1674, RDEA, vol. 842, file S-2-E, and Peter Oliver, *G. Howard Ferguson: Ontario Tory* (Toronto: University of Toronto Press, 1977), pp. 378-80 and 382.

18 HC *Debates*, May 15, 1931, p. 1651, also ibid., p. 1674.

19 Grant Dexter, "Young Canada Goes to Washington," *Canadian Magazine* 75, no. 4 (April 1931): 3, 45. See also *New York Times*, March 4, 1931, and Toronto *Mail and Empire* and Montreal *Gazette*, March 9, 1931.

20 Hume Wrong to Skelton, "The Representation of the United States in Foreign Countries," December 13, 1930, Wrong Papers, NA, vol. 1, file 6. On US practice, see also W. F. Ilchman, *Professional Diplomacy in the United States 1779-1939: A Study in Administrative History* (Chicago: University of Chicago Press, 1961), pp. 213-14.

21 For the results of the examination, see RDEA, vol. 788, file 412. Marjorie McKenzie wrote the best paper on international affairs. She did not take the oral examination. Bennett's defence of recruitment is discussed in NA interview with John E. Read, Read Papers, vol. 10.

22 RDEA, vol. 1566, file 318, vol. 1573, file 704, and vol. 1561, file 80G. On the shortage of economists in the public service, see Bryce, *Maturing in Hard Times*, p. 27.

23 Skelton to Herridge, February 2, 1934, RDEA, vol. 793, file 454. See also Ian M. Drummond, *Imperial Economic Policy 1917-1939: Studies in Expansion and Protection* (Toronto: University of Toronto Press, 1974), pp. 219-99; O. Mary Hill, *Canada's Salesman to the World: The Department of Trade and Commerce, 1892-1939* (Montreal: McGill-Queen's, 1977), pp. 522-23; and Bryce, *Maturing in Hard Times*, pp. 79-81, 90-94.

24 Watson Sellar (comptroller general) to secretary of the Treasury Board, September 6, 1933, RDEA, vol. 831, file 2.

25 N. Allen (Office of the Comptroller General) to Skelton, February 18, 1932, ibid., file 1. See also HC *Debates*, April 3, 1941, p. 2142, Roy to Skelton, November 26, 1935, RDEA, vol. 849, file 194; Roderick Duncan MacLean, "An Examination of the Role of the Comptroller of the Treasury," *Canadian Public Administration* 7, no. 1 (March 1964): 1-133; and Bryce, *Maturing in Hard Times*, pp. 73-76.

26 Skelton to R. K. Finlayson (prime minister's secretary), February 28, 1934, RDEA, vol. 831, file 2.

27 Agnes McCloskey to Skelton, November 22, 1935, ibid., vol. 786, file 406.

28 Agnes McCloskey to Pierre Dupuy (second secretary), July 13, 1937, and Dupuy to Agnes McCloskey, July 15, 1937, ibid., vol. 849, file 196.

29 Canada, *Report of the Auditor General for the Year Ended March 31, 1938* (Ottawa: King's Printer, 1938), vol. I, p. 302.

30 Ferguson to Bennett, October 27, 1933, RDEA, vol. 853, file 221.

31 Skelton to Sellar, December 30, 1935, ibid., vol. 854, file 234. For the comptroller's suggestion, see Sellar to Skelton, November 20, 1935, ibid., vol. 853, file 221.

32 Agnes McCloskey to Skelton, October 9, 1936, ibid., vol. 842, file 1-1-3; HC *Debates*, March 24, 1937, pp. 2173–74. On financial administration, see also RDEA, vols. 786, 787, and 831–57.

33 Canada, *Reports of the Auditor General for the Years Ended March 31, 1932, 1933, 1936* (Ottawa: King's Printer, 1932, 1933, 1936), vol. 11, p. E-2. See also HC *Debates*, February 8, 1932, p. 59.

34 Lester B. Pearson, *Mike: The Memoirs of the Right Honourable Lester B. Pearson*, vol. I: *1897-1948* (Toronto: University of Toronto Press, 1972), p. 78. On Robertson, see J. L. Granatstein, *A Man of Influence: Norman A. Robertson and Canadian Statecraft 1929-1968* (Ottawa: Deneau, 1981), pp. 47–48.

35 Skelton to Marler, January 24, 1933, RDEA, vol. 792, file 435.

36 Skelton to Sellar, June 15, 1933, ibid., vol. 791, file 421; Treasury Board minute TB 148837B, March 31, 1933, and order-in-council PC 8/608, March 24, 1938, ibid., vol. 833, file E-4/26-28. Employees in the United States were not affected by these arrangements, because salaries and allowances there were set in local currency.

37 Marler to Bennett, April 12, 1933, Bennett papers, microfilm reel M891, p. 165641.

38 Skelton to Herridge, February 2, 1934, RDEA, vol. 793, file 454.

39 On Christie's return to the department, see Michael F. Scheuer, "L. C. Christie and the North Atlantic World, 1913-1941," PHD thesis, University of Manitoba, 1986, pp. 386–89.

40 Roy to Skelton, January 8, 1935, RDEA, vol. 794, file 462. Crowther's resignation is dealt with in Wrong to Skelton, January 9, February 10, and September 23, 1931, ibid., vol. 793, file 454. On Pacaud, see Robert Speaight, *Vanier: Soldier, Diplomat and Governor General* (Toronto: Collins, 1970), pp. 170–71.

41 Duplessis to Bennett, May 8, 1933, and January 5, 1934, Dupré to Bennett, May 2, 1933, C. Bourgeois to Bennett, May 5 and December 22, 1933, Bennett Papers, microfilm reel M1215, pp. 136303, 136307, 136322–30.

42 Beaudry, "Canadian Representation Abroad," December 27, 1930, RDEA, vol. 791, file 428. At this time Canadian trade commissioners served in more than twenty countries in Europe, South America, and the Pacific. The handicaps they faced are described in Hill, *Canada's Salesman*, pp. 421–29. Pearson's defence of the department is in "Memorandum on the Work of the Department of External Affairs," November 17, 1930, RDEA, vol. 787, file 408.

43 SSEA to secretary of state for dominion affairs, July 6, 1931, RDEA, vol. 1585, file 142; Skelton, "Canadian Representation in the East," July 8, 1931, ibid., vol. 796, file 480; British high commissioner, Ottawa, to secretary of state for dominion affairs, July 7, 1931, and British consul general, Shanghai, to British minister, Peking, March 22, 1930, Dominions Office Records DO 35/165/6210/3, reel B-4816, NA; high commissioner to Dominions Office, July 9, 1931, DO 35/165/6210/21, ibid.; Sir Miles Lampson (British minister in China) to Marquis of Reading (foreign secretary), September 14, 1931, DO 35/6210/23, ibid. The episode was the occasion for one of the comments

on policy, for which she was well known in the department, by Marjorie McKenzie, who suspected that the motives of the British were economic. McKenzie's undated minute is on Skelton, "Canadian Representation in the East."

44 HC *Debates*, July 30, 1931, p. 4336.

45 Ibid., February 3, 1933, p. 1786. Marler's proposals and the response are in "Report of His Majesty's Minister for Canada in Japan on Conditions in China—March 1930 to the Right Hon. The Secretary of State for External Affairs, Canada," p. 64, RDEA, vol. 1561, file 80G-30; Stevens to Bennett, June 5, 1931, and Marler to Stevens, June 9, 1931, Stevens Papers, NA, vol. 12, file 3; J. P. Manion, *A Canadian Errant: Twenty-Five Years in the Canadian Foreign Service* (Toronto: Ryerson, 1960), p. 41. For other proposals to integrate the two services, see Vincent Massey, "The British Commonwealth Relations Conference," in *Proceedings of the Canadian Club of Toronto 1933-34* (Toronto: Warwick Brothers and Rutter, 1934), pp. 134-36, and Montreal *Standard*, May 5, 1934.

46 HC *Debates*, February 23, 1934, pp. 925-26.

47 Oliver, *Ferguson*, p. 385; Skelton to Herridge, February 2, 1934, RDEA, vol. 793, file 454. The staff of the high commissioner's office is listed in Canada, *Report of the Auditor General for the Year Ended March 31, 1934* (Ottawa: King's Printer, 1934), vol. I, pp. E3-4. On the cost of operating the high commissioner's office and of other departmental activities, see ibid., vol. I, pp. E-1-11, ZZ27.

48 Skelton to Herridge, February 2, 1934, RDEA, vol. 793, file 454. On Ferguson and reporting, see Oliver, *Ferguson*, p. 386.

49 Quoted in Oliver, *Ferguson*, p. 414. The suggestion of the Foreign Office was that the Canadian government should rely on reports from Canada House (in this instance dealing with the Geneva disarmament conference) rather than the press.

50 Similar direct channels were used between Canada and the other dominions.

51 Joe Garner, *The Commonwealth Office, 1925-68* (London: Heinemann, 1978), pp. 73-79, also p. 28.

52 Skelton to Bennett, February 21, 1933, Bennett Papers, microfilm reel M1229, p. 160192.

53 "Possible changes in staff of offices abroad," n.d. (probably 1934), RDEA, vol. 788, file 408. On the activities of the high commissioner's office, see report for the year ended December 31, 1933, ibid., vol. 1644, file 40E.

54 Bennett to Stevens, October 7, 1931, ibid., vol. 1580, file 39A-31. See also Vanier to Skelton, August 21, 1931, ibid.

55 Wrong to Skelton, September 25, 1930, and Wrong to Bennett, February 4, 1931, ibid., vol. 793, file 450.

56 Wrong, "The Canadian Legation at Washington," May 29, 1931, ibid., file 454.

57 Story, "Canada's Covenant," pp. 67-70.

58 Herridge to Bennett, March 22, 1933, Bennett Papers, microfilm reel M1025, p. 184854. See also Story, "Canada's Covenant," pp. 69-70, and Toronto *Telegram*, June 1, 1933.

59 Herridge to Skelton, June 23, 1931, Bennett Papers, reel M1025, pp. 184400-2.
60 Dean Acheson, *Morning and Noon* (Boston: Houghton Mifflin, 1965), pp. 178–80. See also diary, October 25, 1935, King Papers; Charlottetown *Guardian*, August 11, 1932; Regina *Leader-Post*, May 15, 1933; Winnipeg *Free Press*, October 11, 1935. Skelton, according to King, also thought Herridge had some weaknesses: "He was nothing of a speaker, and did not show well in public; also, he never quite succeeded in getting things across."
61 Montreal *Star*, November 25, 1931; *New York Times*, April 8 and 18, 1932, and April 26, 1933; Martin, *Presidents and Prime Ministers*, p. 108.
62 Herridge to Skelton, December 19, 1933, RDEA, vol. 793, file 454.
63 Skelton to Herridge, February 2, 1934, ibid.
64 "Possible changes in staff."
65 Roy to Skelton, December 14, 1934, RDEA, vol. 794, file 462. See also Roy to Bennett, December 16 and 23, 1930, and Roy to Skelton, January 12, 1931, ibid.
66 Skelton to Herridge, February 2, 1934, ibid., vol. 793, file 454; "Possible changes in staff."
67 For this story, see RDEA, vol. 1562, file 80L-30.
68 Marler to Bennett, April 19, 1933, Bennett Papers, microfilm reel M891, p. 165644.
69 "Possible changes in staff."
70 Skelton to Riddell, April 13, 1934, RDEA, vol. 848, file 183.
71 "Explanatory Notes Concerning Estimates for Representation at Geneva, 1930–31," ibid., vol. 847, file 179.
72 "Duties," n.d. (probably 1933), ibid., vol. 831, file D-1.
73 "Possible changes in staff."
74 Skelton to Riddell, February 16, 1935, RDEA, vol. 847, file 181.
75 This account of family life is based on Gordon Riddell interview, Ottawa, October 10, 1985.
76 Pearson, *Mike*, vol. I, p. 85. See also Keenleyside, *Memoirs*, vol. I, pp. 283–341, and, for an account of life at a Canadian mission abroad in a later period (1957–59), P. K. Page, *Brazilian Journal* (Toronto: Lester & Orpen Dennys, 1987).
77 Garner, *Commonwealth Office*, p. 75.
78 Cf. chapter 5. Short-staffing in Ottawa is dealt with in Skelton to Riddell, February 16, 1935, RDEA, vol. 847, file 181.
79 F. C. T. O'Hara (deputy minister of trade and commerce) to Skelton, February 21, 1931, Department of Trade and Commerce Records, NA, vol. 152, file 2G491.
80 "Draft Points for Consideration," London Wheat Conference, May 18, 1931, Bennett Papers, microfilm reel M1066, p. 224403; Oliver, *Ferguson*, p. 384.
81 Granatstein, *Man of Influence*, p. 67.
82 Riddell to Skelton, March 5, 1935, RDEA, vol. 847, file S-1(181).
83 Treasury Board minute T159147B, August 20, 1935, ibid., vol. 839, file 88.
84 W. A. Found to Skelton, July 20, 1931, ibid., vol. 1585, file 135-31. There is no indication on the file that the conference was held.

85 Skelton to prime minister, n.d. (September 1931), ibid., vol. 1575, file 864-30. On the Department of Trade and Commerce during this period, see Hill, *Canada's Salesman*, pp. 435-538.

86 Norman Hillmer, "Anglo-Canadian Relations 1926-1937: A Study of Canada's Role in the Shaping of Commonwealth Policies," PHD thesis, Cambridge University, 1974, pp. 220-22.

87 Perley and Winnifred Kydd left Geneva in May 1932. Dupré remained until the adjournment of the first phase of deliberations in July of that year. Ferguson and Skelton were the Canadian delegates when the conference reconvened in 1933. The arrangements are dealt with in Skelton to G. J. Desbarats (deputy minister of national defence), April 14, 1931, "Inter-departmental Committee on Disarmament," July 17, 1931, and "Report of the Inter-departmental Committee on Disarmament," n.d., RDEA, vol. 1567, file 377-30. See also Pearson, *Mike*, vol. I, p. 91; Walter A. Riddell, *World Security by Conference* (Toronto: Ryerson, 1947), pp. 46-48; Richard Veatch, *Canada and the League of Nations* (Toronto: University of Toronto Press, 1975), pp. 62, 117; Story, "Canada's Covenant," pp. 62, 83-180.

88 Donald C. Story, "Canada, the League of Nations and the Far East, 1931-3: The Cahan Incident," *International History Review* 3, no. 2 (April 1981): 244-45.

89 *DCER*, vol. V: *1931-1935*, ed. Alex I. Inglis (Ottawa: Information Canada, 1973), p. 322.

90 Ibid., pp. 324-27. The special session of the assembly, December 3-11, 1932, was summoned following the regular session to deal with the situation in Manchuria.

91 On this phase of the Ethiopian crisis, see Skelton, "Pros and Cons of Canadian Participation," c. August 1935, King Papers, series J4, vol. 165, file 1507; *DCER*, vol. V, pp. 390-91; R. K. Finlayson, "Life with R. B.: That Man Bennett," p. 305, Finlayson Papers, NA, vol. 1; and Oliver, *Ferguson*, pp. 416-26.

CHAPTER SEVEN

1 H. Blair Neatby, *William Lyon Mackenzie King*, vol. III: *1932-1939: The Prism of Unity* (Toronto: University of Toronto Press, 1976), p. 129.

2 Ibid., pp. 133, 262-64.

3 On the senior public service, see J. L. Granatstein, *The Ottawa Men: The Civil Service Mandarins 1935-1957* (Toronto: Oxford University Press, 1982), pp. xi-xii, 1-18.

4 Quoted in Neatby, *King*, vol. III, p. 136.

5 Diary, April 17, 1936, King Papers, NA.

6 Ibid., July 1, 1936, and Neatby, *King*, vol. III, pp. 134-35.

7 Ibid., p. 134.

8 SSEA to advisory officer, November 4, 1935, telegram 77, in *DCER*, vol. V: *1931-1935*, ed. Alex I. Inglis (Ottawa: Information Canada, 1973), pp. 405-6, 408.

9 Robert Bothwell and John English, "Dirty Work at the Cross-Roads:

New Perspectives on the Riddell Incident," Canadian Historical Association, *Historical Papers* (1972): 281.

10 Diary, February 11, 1936, King Papers, also King diary, August 3, 1936, and Riddell diary, January 30, 1936, Riddell Papers, York University.

11 On the conduct of the negotiations, see Neatby, *King*, vol. III, pp. 142-45.

12 J. L. Granatstein, *A Man of Influence: Norman A. Robertson and Canadian Statecraft 1929-68* (Ottawa: Deneau, 1981), p. 52.

13 Wrong to Finlayson, October 18, 1935, Bennett Papers, NA, microfilm reel M1025, pp. A18462-63.

14 Skelton, "Canadian External Affairs Service," January 16, 1936, King papers, series J4, vol. 154, file 1340.

15 Dafoe to J. M. Macdonnell, September 16, 1940, Dafoe Papers, NA, vol. 11. For Dafoe's views on the League of Nations, see Ramsay Cook, *The Politics of John W. Dafoe and the Free Press* (Toronto: University of Toronto Press, 1963), pp. 246-47.

16 Claude Bissell, *The Imperial Canadian: Vincent Massey in Office* (Toronto: University of Toronto Press, 1986), pp. 5-6, 35; diary, July 24, 1936, King Papers; HC *Debates*, February 9, 1937, p. 698, and January 31, 1938, pp. 37-38, 66.

17 Diary, July 24, 1936, King Papers, also Dafoe to Macdonnell, September 16, 1940, Dafoe Papers, vol. 11.

18 Charles Ritchie, *The Siren Years: A Canadian Diplomat Abroad, 1937-1945* (Toronto: Macmillan, 1974), pp. 15-16.

19 Bissell, *Imperial Canadian*, p. 75.

20 King to Massey, January 25, 1936, King Papers, series J1, vol. 223.

21 Quoted in Massey, *What's Past Is Prologue*, p. 231. See also Bissell, *Imperial Canadian*, p. 75. This message was in response to Massey's request for information to enable him to state the Canadian position on the German decision to enter the Rhineland.

22 Massey, *What's Past Is Prologue*, pp. 240-41, 258; Bissell, *Imperial Canadian*, pp. 76-78.

23 Lester B. Pearson, *Mike: The Memoirs of the Right Honourable Lester B. Pearson*, vol. I: *1897-1948* (Toronto: University of Toronto Press, 1972), p. 109.

24 Ritchie, *Siren Years*, pp. 11-12.

25 Bissell, *Imperial Canadian*, pp. 14-28, 55, 72-80; Pearson, *Mike*, vol. I, pp. 107-9; Massey to King, January 30, 1936, King Papers, series J1, vol. 223. Although not much consulted, Massey was asked for his assessment of the European situation shortly before the outbreak of war. King to Massey, August 15, 1939, ibid., vol. 274.

26 Massey, *What's Past Is Prologue*, pp. 225-26, 243-44; Bissell, *Imperial Canadian*, pp. 49-52, 59. On trade promotion from the point of view of the Department of Trade and Commerce, see O. Mary Hill, *Canada's Salesman to the World: The Department of Trade and Commerce 1892-1939* (Toronto: McGill-Queen's, 1977), pp. 337-43.

27 Bissell, *Imperial Canadian*, pp. 36-49; Massey, *What's Past Is Prologue*, pp. 254-57.

28 King to Massey, November 1, 1936, King Papers, series J1, vol. 224. See also Bissell, *Imperial Canadian*, pp. 29, 58–61. On differences that arose between King and Massey about the representational side of diplomacy, cf. Massey, *What's Past Is Prologue*, pp. 240–41.

29 Marler discussed his approach in Marler to King, December 30, 1936, King Papers, series J1, vol. 222. On King and Roosevelt, see Lawrence Martin, *The Presidents and the Prime Ministers: Washington and Ottawa Face to Face: The Myth of Bilateral Bliss* (Toronto: Doubleday, 1982), pp. 117–29.

30 Toronto *Star*, August 12, 1937; Ottawa *Citizen*, August 17, 1937; Canadian League against War and Fascism to King, August 13, 1937, League of Nations Society to King, August 14, 1937, Skelton to Bruce, August 16, 1937, E. D. McGreer to Skelton, September 24, 1937, H. L. Keenleyside, memorandum, November 20, 1937, RDEA, vol. 794, file 465. Bruce's views were also reported in the Ottawa *Journal*, August 12, 1937, but this item was not controversial.

31 Bruce to Skelton, August 20, 1937, Skelton to Bruce, August 25, 1937, Skelton to King, September 27, 1937, RDEA, vol. 794, file 465.

32 E. D. McGreer, extract from letter, n.d., ibid. See also Bruce to King, March 8, 1938, ibid.

33 Kenneth Kirkwood (?) to Keenleyside, extract from letter, n.d., RDEA, vol. 1769, file 80-F-36.

34 King to Bruce, October 14, 1938, King Papers, series J1, vol. 247.

35 Skelton, "Expansion of Canada's External Affairs Service," October 5, 1937, ibid., series J4, vol. 158, file 1415.

36 *DCER*, vol. VI: *1936–1939*, ed. John A. Munro (Ottawa: Information Canada, 1972), pp. 48–55. Of much help in preparing the account of representation abroad in this chapter has been E. A. Kelly, "Diffident Diplomacy: The Expansion of Canadian Diplomatic Representation Abroad 1930–1939," paper presented to Canadian Historical Association annual meeting, University of Manitoba, June 1986.

37 Skelton, "Extension of Canada's External Affairs Service," October 5, 1937, King Papers, series J4, vol. 158, file 1415.

38 Christie, "Notes on the Placing of New Legations," September 23, 1937, RDEA, vol. 791, file 428.

39 Diary, December 9, 1937, King Papers.

40 Skelton, "Resumption of Development of Canadian Representation Abroad. Summary of Memorandum," January 11, 1938, and "Memorandum re Establishment of New Offices, Finance and Personnel," January 17, 1938, RDEA, vol. 791, file 428.

41 Skelton, "Extension of the Canadian Service Abroad," January 21, 1938, ibid. South Africa wanted its representative to have full diplomatic status and therefore objected to the title "high commissioner." The Canadian government agreed to use the term *accredited representative* but granted only the status, privileges, and immunities of a high commissioner. See B. D. Tennyson, *Canadian Relations with South Africa: A Diplomatic History* (Washington: University Press of America, 1982), pp. 87–90.

42 Skelton to King, "Re: Canadian Service Abroad," December 23, 1938, RDEA, vol. 788, file 408.

43 Minister for external affairs of Ireland to SSEA, March 1, 1939, ibid., vol. 227; A. D. P. Heeney (principal secretary to the prime minister) to Skelton, March 7, 1939, ibid., vol. 788, file 408.

44 Skelton to Wrong, March 2, 1939, Wrong Papers, NA, vol. 3, file 17. The proposal is in Wrong to Skelton, February 24, 1939, RDEA, vol. 1894, file 125-39. See also Vanier to Skelton, February 28, 1939, ibid.

45 Skelton, "Ministerial Appointments to Legations," April 11, 1938, ibid., vol. 788, file 428.

46 HC *Debates*, May 26, 1938, p. 3260.

47 King to Bruce, October 14, 1938, King Papers, series J1, vol. 247. It seems improbable that Vanier's transfer to London from Geneva in 1931 was part of a long-range plan to make him minister in Paris. Although Skelton favoured him for that post, he was prepared to consider sending him elsewhere and proposed other candidates for the French capital. Cf. Bissell, *Imperial Canadian*, p. 53, and Robert Speaight, *Vanier: Soldier, Diplomat and Governor General: A Biography* (Toronto: Collins, 1970), p. 176.

48 King to Massey, December 20, 1938, King Papers, series J1, vol. 255, also King to Bruce, October 14, 1938, ibid., vol. 247.

49 Bissell, *Imperial Canadian*, p. 56; Massey to King, November 25, 1938, King to Massey, December 20, 1938, King Papers, series J1, vol. 255.

50 Information supplied by Escott Reid, November 27, 1986.

51 Max Wershof interview, Ottawa, February 1, 1980. The department was still far from representative of the ethnic balance of the population, which according to the 1941 census included approximately 2,300,000 persons of neither British nor French origin in a total of 11,506,655.

52 On Norman's entry into the department, cf. Roger Bowen, *Innocence Is Not Enough: The Life and Death of Herbert Norman* (Vancouver and Toronto: Douglas and McIntyre, 1986), pp. 65–71, and James Barros, *No Sense of Evil: Espionage, The Case of E. Herbert Norman* (Toronto: Deneau, 1986), published in rev. ed. as *The Espionage Case of Herbert Norman* (New York: Ivy Books, 1987), pp. 29–31. Contemporary practice in the US State Department is dealt with in Barry Rubin, *Secrets of State: The State Department and the Struggle over U.S. Foreign Policy* (New York: Oxford University Press, 1985), p. 34. On the language problems of the legation in Tokyo, see chapter 6 above.

53 Salary scales as of January 1, 1938, RDEA, vol. 788, file 408.

54 Cabinet ministers were paid $10,000 per year, the rate set in 1921. The cost of living was rising only slowly (9.4 points between 1935 and 1940).

55 Wrong to Skelton, March 16, 1939, RDEA, vol. 847, file 177.

56 Wrong to Skelton, February 20, March 16, and March 24, 1939, and Skelton to Wrong, June 20, 1939, ibid.

57 Quoted in Granatstein, *Man of Influence*, p. 53.

58 Bennett to Clark, n.d., Bennett Papers, microfilm reel M3169, p. A588938. Comment by Bennett on Clark's obituary of Skelton.

59 Robertson to Pearson, November 4, 1936, Pearson Papers, NA, series N1, vol. 13.

60 Diary, January 1, 1936, ibid.

61 J. W. Pickersgill interview, Ottawa, June 17, 1971; also information supplied by Pickersgill, October 16, 1986, and Benjamin Rogers, October 30, 1986, and Norman to Keenleyside, April 24, 1941, RDEA, vol. 1562, file 80-L-30. In Washington, Wrong was conscientious in guiding the work of junior officers. See Charles Ritchie, *Storm Signals: More Undiplomatic Diaries* (Toronto: Macmillan, 1983), pp. 66–67.

62 Diary, October 9, 1937, King Papers.

63 Ibid., October 28 and 29, 1937.

64 Ibid., December 9, 1937.

65 Neatby, *King*, vol. III, p. 264.

66 Massey to King, March 3, 1939, King Papers, series J1, vol. 274.

67 RDEA, vol. 787, file 408.

68 Diary, July 24, 1936, King Papers.

69 *DCER*, vol. VI, p. 24. The death of the king and related subjects are covered in ibid., pp. 1–25.

70 The abdication crisis is dealt with in Neatby, *King*, vol. III, pp. 178–79, 182–85; Bissell, *Imperial Canadian*, p. 8; and Gordon Beadle, "Canada and the Abdication of Edward VIII," *Journal of Canadian Studies* 4, no. 3 (August 1969): 33–46. On the reluctance of the department to use the telephone, see Massey, *What's Past Is Prologue*, p. 258. "Ottawa dislikes the telephone," he observed on September 16, 1938, after his first telephone consultation with Skelton since his arrival in London. The occasion was the Munich crisis.

71 Bissell, *Imperial Canadian*, pp. 58–60. On the coronation address, see *DCER*, vol. VI, pp. 25–30.

72 Massey, *What's Past Is Prologue*, pp. 251–52. See also RDEA, vol. 1773, file 129-A-36.

73 Pearson, *Mike*, vol. I, p. 116.

74 Imperial Conference Directory, May 28, 1937, RDEA, vol. 1787, file 318-36; Imperial Conference 1937, list of files brought back from conference prepared by Marjorie McKenzie on the basis of the conference's agenda, n.d., ibid. The importance of McKenzie's role is indicated by her description as "delegation secretary" in a later article on her career. Corolyn Cox, "Safekeeper of the Secrets and Conscience of External Affairs," *Saturday Night* (March 17, 1945): 2.

75 C. P. Stacey, *Arms, Men and Governments: The War Policies of Canada 1939–1945* (Ottawa: Information Canada, 1970), p. 89; *DCER*, vol. VI, pp. 169–70. See also Imperial Conference, *Summary of Proceedings* (Ottawa: Queen's Printer, 1937), pp. 13, 19, in RDEA, vol. 1787, file 318-36; Stacey, *Canada and the Age of Conflict*, vol. II, pp. 202–209; James Eayrs, *In Defence of Canada: Appeasement and Rearmament* (Toronto: University of Toronto Press, 1965), pp. 53–59, 85–91; Neatby, *King*, vol. III, pp. 212–19.

76 On the tour, see RDEA, vol. 1879, file 787-B-38. The work of the interdepartmental committee is outlined in its first interim report, n.d., ibid.

77 Quoted in Robert B. Bryce, *Maturing in Hard Times: Canada's Department of Finance through the Great Depression* (Kingston and Montreal: McGill-Queen's, 1986), p. 100.
78 HC *Debates*, February 14, 1939, p. 899. On the negotiations, see Granatstein, *Man of Influence*, pp. 58-79; Richard N. Kottman, *Reciprocity and the North Atlantic Triangle, 1932-1938* (Ithaca: Cornell University Press, 1968), pp. 149-271; Hill, *Canada's Salesman*, pp. 558-62; Neatby, *King*, vol. III, pp. 203-4, 217-18, 221, 273-74, 283-87; Bryce, *Maturing in Hard Times*, pp. 99-102; Dana Wilgress, *Memoirs* (Toronto: Ryerson, 1967), pp. 108-9.
79 Administrative Circular No. 2, January 14, 1939, RDEA, vol. 1894, file 125-39. For later problems, see Marjorie McKenzie to Skelton, July 28, 1939, and Skelton to Désy, July 28, 1939, ibid., vol. 1783, file 254-36.
80 Neatby, *King*, vol. III, pp. 279-83, 294-99; Stacey, *Arms, Men and Governments*, pp. 2, 7, 71; Eayrs, *In Defence of Canada: Appeasement and Rearmament*, pp. 53-54; Granatstein, *Man of Influence*, p. 80; Michael F. Scheuer, "L. C. Christie and the North Atlantic World, 1913-1941," PHD thesis, University of Manitoba, 1986, pp. 451-601; Keenleyside, *Memoirs*, vol. I, pp. 510-13; Bissell, *Imperial Canadian*, pp. 88-106; Speaight, *Vanier*, pp. 194-95; Stacey, *Canada and the Age of Conflict*, vol. II, pp. 264-65; Granatstein, *Ottawa Men*, pp. 62-91, 121-23; information supplied by Benjamin Rogers, October 30, 1986.
81 A brief account of the Canadian response to the Spanish Civil War is in Thompson and Seager, *Canada 1922-1939*, pp. 317-18. See also Victor Hoar, *The Mackenzie-Papineau Battalion* (Toronto: Copp Clark, 1969). The documentary record is in RDEA, vol. 1801, files 631-36, 631-A-36, 631-D-36.
82 On the visit, see diary, December 26, 1936, and June 28, 1937, King Papers; Neatby, *King*, vol. III, pp. 222-23; C. P. Stacey, "The Divine Mission: Mackenzie King and Hitler," *Canadian Historical Review* 61, no. 4 (December 1980): 502-12; Stacey, *Canada and the Age of Conflict*, vol. II, pp. 209-13; Eayrs, *In Defence of Canada: Appeasement and Rearmament*, pp. 44-70.
83 High commissioner in Great Britain to SSEA, February 12, 1936, dispatch 102, RDEA, vol. 1661, file 342-33.
84 High commissioner in Great Britain to SSEA, November 29, 1938, telegram 269, ibid., vol. 1871, file 327-38.
85 Memorandum, "Canada and the Refugee Problem," November 29, 1938, ibid.
86 Robertson to Skelton, July 3, 1939, ibid. See also Ritchie to Robertson, November 29, 1938, ibid.
87 High commissioner in Great Britain to SSEA, February 17, 1939, dispatch A37, ibid. Cf. Bissell, *Imperial Canadian*, pp. 100-106, and Irving Abella and Harold Troper, *None Is Too Many: Canada and the Jews of Europe, 1933-1948* (Toronto: Lester and Orpen Dennys, 1983), pp. 1-66.
88 Stacey, *Arms, Men and Governments*, pp. 9, 100; Eayrs, *In Defence of Canada: Appeasement and Rearmament*, pp. 82-83; information supplied by J. W. Pickersgill, October 15, 1986.
89 For examples of Christie's rather crisp approach to these questions, see Eayrs, *In Defence of Canada: Apeasement and Rearmament*, p. 83; Stacey, *Arms, Men and Governments*, p. 71.

90 On the committee, see Stacey, *Arms, Men and Governments*, p. 69. See also Eayrs, *In Defence of Canada: Appeasement and Rearmament*, pp. 137–38.

91 Quoted in Stacey, *Arms, Men and Governments*, p. 74.

92 British high commissioner to dominions secretary, March 24, 1938, and Hankey to Harding, May 9, 1938, Cabinet Records, PRO, CAB 21/670/4636. See also British high commissioner to under-secretary of state for dominion affairs, January 20, 1939, and letter to Maj.-Gen. H.L. Ismay, March 1939, ibid., CAB 21/671/4627.

93 Eayrs, *In Defence of Canada: Appeasement and Rearmament*, pp. 134–53. On the Imperial Conference, see ibid., pp. 84–85.

94 Diary, November 13, 1938, King Papers. See also ibid., August 31, October 8, and October 24, 1938, and Stacey, *Canada and the Age of Conflict*, vol. II, pp. 231–43.

95 Diary, April 28, 1939, King Papers. The occasion was Hitler's response to remarks critical of Britain by the prime minister of Ireland, Eamon de Valéra. A further British commitment, to Turkey, was announced on May 12.

96 Christie, "Alternative Canadian Procedures If Great Britain Becomes at War," August 24, 1939, RDEA, vol. 1946, file 769-39. For the text of Skelton's memorandum (abridged), see Stacey, *Arms, Men and Governments*, p. 9.

97 Skelton, "Canada and the Polish War. A Personal Note," August 25, 1939, RDEA, vol. 726, file 74. On Christie, see diary, September 13, 1939, L. B. Pearson Papers, NA.

98 King to governor general in council, August 30, 1939, RDEA, vol. 1946, file 769-39; Stacey, *Arms, Men and Governments*, p. 113. Departmental reports on preparations in Canada and elsewhere are in RDEA, vol. 1944, file 756-39.

99 See Stacey, *Arms, Men and Governments*, pp. 9, 71.

100 Wilfrid Eggleston, *While I Still Remember: A Personal Record* (Toronto: Ryerson, 1968), pp. 253–54. The relationship between King and Skelton as war approached receives attention in J. L. Granatstein and Robert Bothwell, "A Self-Evident National Duty: Canadian Foreign Policy, 1935–1939," *Journal of Imperial and Commonwealth History* 3, no. 2 (January 1975): 212–33. For a survey of defence policy during the same period, see Stephen J. Harris, *Canadian Brass: The Making of a Professional Army, 1860–1939* (Toronto: University of Toronto Press, 1988), pp. 160–66.

101 See *DCER*, vol. VI, pp. 1292–1320, and Skelton's memoranda in RDEA, vol. 726, file 74.

102 Pearson, *Mike*, vol. I, pp. 138–39.

103 Pearson to Massey, July 16, 1939, quoted in Massey, *What's Past Is Prologue*, p. 295.

CHAPTER EIGHT

1 J. L. Granatstein, *Canada's War: The Politics of the Mackenzie King Government, 1939–1945* (Toronto: Oxford University Press, 1975), pp. 19, 24–25.

2 C. P. Stacey, *Arms, Men and Governments: The War Policies of Canada 1939-1945* (Ottawa: Information Canada, 1970), p. 118.

3 Vanier to SSEA, September 12, 1939, King Papers, NA, series J1, vol. 281.

4 Montreal *Gazette*, February 8, 1941, quoted in Michael F. Scheuer, "L. C. Christie and the North Atlantic World, 1913-1941," PHD thesis, University of Manitoba, 1986, vol. 2, p. 669. Not all the comment was unfavourable. Christie was supported by the Montreal *Star*, the Ottawa *Journal*, and his friend J. W. Dafoe of the *Winnipeg Free Press*. There were also impressive tributes, in Canada and the United States, at the time of his death. Ibid., pp. 670-74.

5 On Christie's service in Washington, see ibid., pp. 601-725. A military attaché was also appointed to Paris early in 1940. The Royal Canadian Air Force and the army had had representatives in London for some time. See Stacey, *Arms, Men and Governments*, pp. 76-78.

6 Skelton's views on the appointment of heads of post are dealt with in chapter 7 above.

7 N. A. Robertson to King, September 28, 1943, and October 18, 1944, DEA file 93 (s).

8 On Riddell in Washington, see Scheuer, "Christie," pp. 604, 619-20.

9 Rogers to D. M. Page, May 31, 1985, DEA file 7-5-2-7.

10 *DCER*, vol. VII: *1939-1941, Part I*, ed. David R. Murray (Ottawa: Information Canada, 1974), p. 724.

11 On this point, cf. Vincent Massey, *What's Past Is Prologue: The Memoirs of the Right Honourable Vincent Massey* (Toronto: Macmillan, 1963), pp. 294-96; diary, October 17-20, 1939, Pearson Papers, NA, series N8, vol. I, file 3; Claude Bissell, *The Imperial Canadian: Vincent Massey in Office* (Toronto: University of Toronto Press, 1986), pp. 118-20, 124; and James Gibson, "Root and Branch in Canadian Foreign Policy, 1938-1947," *Bulletin of Canadian Studies* 5, no. 2 (October 1981): 50-51.

12 Quoted in Norman Hillmer, "Vincent Massey and the Origins of the British Commonwealth Air Training Plan," *Canadian Defence Quarterly* 16, no. 4 (Spring 1987): 53. Documents on the negotiations are in *DCER*, vol. VII, pp. 549-671. See also F. J. Hatch, *The Aerodrome of Democracy: Canada and the British Commonwealth Air Training Plan, 1939-1945* (Ottawa: Minister of Supply and Services, 1983), pp. 1-31, and W. A. B. Douglas, *The Creation of a National Air Force: The Official History of the Royal Canadian Air Force*, vol. II (Toronto: University of Toronto Press, 1986), pp. 193-219, and, on Massey, Bissell, *Imperial Canadian*, pp. 137-38, and Massey, *What's Past Is Prologue,* pp. 303-6.

13 *DCER*, vol. VII, p. 378.

14 Ibid., p. 377.

15 Ibid., p. 380. For documents on the Crerar mission, see ibid., pp. 375-408.

16 G. P. de T. Glazebrook to J. W. Holmes, February 4, 1987, Holmes Papers, Canadian Institute of International Affairs, Toronto.

17 Robertson, memorandum to Skelton, August 28, 1939, RDEA, vol. 1964, file 855-E-39.

18 Robertson to Supt. E. W. Bavin (Intelligence Section, RCMP), August 2, 1940, ibid. See also Skelton, "Subversive Activities," December 13, 1939, King Papers, series J4, vol. 230, file 2218, and J. L. Granatstein, *A Man of Influence: Norman A. Robertson and Canadian Statecraft 1929–68* (Ottawa: Deneau, 1981), pp. 81–91.

19 Skelton to Col. S. T. Wood (commissioner, RCMP), August 12, 1940, and Wood to Skelton, August 10, 1940, Escott Reid Papers, Ste Cecile de Masham, Quebec, private collection of Escott Reid.

20 Saul Rae (office of the under-secretary), memorandum for prime minister, November 17, 1942, RDEA, vol. 1964, file 855-E-39. As drafted by External Affairs and Justice, Cabinet War Committee document 341 of November 17, 1942, was approved on December 2, 1942.

21 On these activities, see Bissell, *Imperial Canadian*, pp. 149–60, and Massey, *What's Past Is Prologue*, pp. 282–88.

22 Skelton to Kirkwood, April 16, 1940, RDEA, vol. 1904, file 385-39.

23 "Memorandum Respecting Employees of Canadian Government Offices in Enemy and Enemy-Occupied Countries," c. December 1940, ibid., vol. 846, file W-10.

24 Diary, May 14, 1940, Pearson Papers, series N8, vol. 1, file 3.

25 Ibid., May 15, 1940. Kirkwood's request (May 14, 1940) is found in DEA file 555-E-40 (London to External, May 14, 1940).

26 Pearson to Skelton, October 29 and 30, 1940, RDEA, vol. 792, file 448. On the Masseys' experience of the attacks on London, see Bissell, *Imperial Canadian*, pp. 107–11, and Massey, *What's Past Is Prologue*, pp. 289–92.

27 On the Dupuy missions, see *DCER*, vol. VIII: *1939–1941 Part II*, ed. David R. Murray (Ottawa: Minister of Supply and Services, 1976), pp. 631–66, also Pierre Dupuy, "Mission à Vichy: novembre 1940," *International Journal* 22, no. 3 (Summer 1967): 395–401.

28 For the story of Canadian policy on the cryolite mines and the decision to open the consulate in Greenland, see *DCER*, vol. VII, pp. 105–14, 947–1039. The subject is also dealt with in Graeme S. Mount, "Canadian-American Relations and Greenland, 1940–1941," paper presented to Canadian Historical Association annual meeting, University of Montreal, 1985.

29 Prime minister to Skelton, August 13, 1940, DEA file 261-40; Skelton to King, September 12, 1940, *DCER*, vol. VII, pp. 51–52. See also HC *Debates*, November 14, 1940, pp. 90–91, and February 17, 1941, pp. 816–17.

30 L. B. Pearson, *Mike: The Memoirs of the Right Honourable Lester B. Pearson*, vol. I: *1897–1948* (Toronto: University of Toronto Press, 1972), p. 194.

31 John Mainwaring, *The International Labour Organization: A Canadian View* (Ottawa: Minister of Supply and Services, 1986), pp. 107–21.

32 Secretary, Treasury Board, to under-secretary, August 13, 1940, RDEA, vol. 835, file 0-1-B. Ignatieff describes his family and his early life, including his entry into the foreign service, in George Ignatieff, in association with Sonja Sinclair, *Memoirs: The Making of a Peacemonger* (Toronto: University of

Toronto Press, 1985), pp. 3-73.

33 Laurent Beaudry, "Memorandum for the Prime Minister re Passports," July 25, 1940, Beaudry Papers, NA, vol. 1, file 8. On conditions in the Passport Office, see HC *Debates*, March 29, 1946, pp. 393-94, and HC, Standing Committee on External Affairs, *Minutes of Proceedings and Evidence*, June 13, 1947, p. 300.

34 Because of the decline in applications, the branch offices in Winnipeg, Toronto, and Montreal were closed on March 15, 1941. A branch in Windsor was under the local collector of customs.

35 Keenleyside to Skelton, September 5, 1940, and "Department of External Affairs, General Division, Assignment of Duties," September 25, 1940, DEA file 1086-40.

36 Skelton to King, October 11, 1940, RDEA, vol. 788, file 408.

37 Pearson, "War-time Intergovernmental Consultation and Communication," May 1, 1940, quoted in Stacey, *Arms, Men and Governments*, pp. 141-42. See also Massey to Skelton, April 20, 1940, RDEA, vol. 1976, file 902-A-39. The Supreme War Council was established by France and Britain, who were represented by their prime ministers and one other minister. Other allies were to take part through their ambassadors or other diplomatic representatives. Canada did not seek membership.

38 King to Massey, December 6, 1940, DEA file 572-40; also King to Skelton, November 3, 1940, *DCER*, vol. VII, pp. 433-35.

39 King to Massey for Churchill, June 14, 1941, DEA file 65-AS.

40 *DCER*, vol. VIII, p. 140. On the negotiations leading up to the meeting at Ogdensburg and establishment of the PJBD, see ibid., pp. 65-152. The subject is also dealt with in J. W. Pickersgill, ed., *The Mackenzie King Record*, vol. I: *1939-1944* (Toronto: University of Toronto Press, 1960), pp. 130-36, Lawrence Martin, *The Presidents and The Prime Ministers: Washington and Ottawa Face to Face: The Myth of Bilateral Bliss, 1867-1982* (Toronto: Doubleday, 1982), pp. 133-34, and Stacey, *Arms, Men and Governments*, pp. 336-43.

41 Diary, February 1, 1940, King Papers.

42 James A. Gibson interview, St Catharines, February 17, 1987.

43 Diary, January 28 and 31, 1941, King Papers, and J. W. Pickersgill, ed., *Mackenzie King Record*, vol. I, pp. 166-67.

44 Ottawa *Journal*, January 29, 1941.

45 Hume Wrong to Marga (Margaret) Wrong (his sister), February 2, 1941, Wrong Family Papers, Toronto, private collection of Mrs. C. H. A. Armstrong.

46 W. C. Clark, "Oscar Douglas Skelton," *Minutes of Proceedings of the Royal Society of Canada* (May 1941): 146.

47 Grant Dexter, "Oscar Douglas Skelton," *Queen's Quarterly* 48, no. 1 (Spring 1941): 1.

48 Toronto *Globe and Mail*, January 29, 1941; Montreal *Star*, January 29, 1941; *The Times*, London, January 30, 1941.

CHAPTER NINE

1 Hume Wrong to Marga (Margaret) Wrong (sister), February 2, 1941, Wrong Family Papers, Toronto, private collection of Mrs. C. H. A. Armstrong.

2 Robertson to parents, January 30, 1941, Robertson Papers, NA, vol. 2, Personal and Family file. See also J. L. Granatstein, *A Man of Influence: Norman A. Robertson and Canadian Statecraft 1929–68* (Ottawa: Deneau, 1981), pp. 102–5.

3 Robertson to Pearson, January 30, 1941, Pearson Papers, NA, series N1, vol. 13.

4 Diary, March 29, 1941, ibid., series N8, vol. 1, file 3.

5 Wrong, "Notes on Departmental Organization," February 26, 1941, DEA file 1086-40.

6 Keenleyside, "Scheme of Organization for the Department of External Affairs," March 1941, ibid.

7 L. B. Pearson, *Mike: The Memoirs of the Right Honourable Lester B. Pearson*, vol. I: *1897–1948* (Toronto: University of Toronto Press, 1972), p. 188.

8 Pearson to Massey, May 27, 1941, Pearson Papers, series N1, vol. 10.

9 See TBR, vol. 555, file 2-7, RDEA, vol. 846, file T-6.

10 Pearson to under-secretary, October 6, 1941, ibid., vol. 799, file 524.

11 Keenleyside, memorandum for members of the staff: departmental organization, August 2, 1941, DEA file 1086-40.

12 Known as the "Skelton-Robertson Papers," these files are in RDEA, vols. 714–829.

13 "Clipping Service for the Department of External Affairs," August 12, 1941, and "Suggestions in Connection with Proposed Departmental Reorganization," August 1941, DEA file 1086-40. See also Saul Rae, "Organization Suggestions," April 14, 1942, Marjorie McKenzie's comments on his suggestions, and Marjorie McKenzie to Robertson, September 18, 1942, RDEA, vol. 799, file 524.

14 Unless otherwise indicated, this survey is based on B. M. Meagher, "Draft History of the Special Division, Department of External Affairs," n.d. [October 1948], DEA file 7202-40.

15 On the inclusion of anti-Nazis among the civilian internees sent to Canada, see E. Koch, *Deemed Suspect: A Wartime Blunder* (Toronto: Methuen, 1980), pp. 26–35.

16 "Work of the Volunteers in the Special Section," n.d., DEA file 7202-40.

17 S. M. Scott to Margaret Meagher, September 29, 1948, ibid.

18 6 Geo. 6, cap. 24, pp. 79–80. On the problem, see E. P. Laberge (Civil Service Commission), "Memorandum to the Civil Service Commission," September 20, 1941, DEA file 1086-40; John E. Read, "Note—An Act to Amend the Department of External Affairs Act," May 26, 1942, RDEA, vol. 835, file O-1; and Robertson to W. C. Ronson (assistant deputy minister of finance), November 5, 1941, TBR, vol. 555, file 2-7.

19 J. L. Granatstein, *The Ottawa Men: The Civil Service Mandarins, 1935–1957*

(Toronto: Oxford University Press, 1982), pp. 123–24; Wrong to Marga, July 10, 1941, Wrong Family Papers. McCarthy was aware of his limitations and recognized that Wrong was the "sheet-anchor" of the legation. In 1942, he expressed the hope for early release from the position. McCarthy to King, March 18, 1942, King Papers, NA, series J1, vol. 327. On McCarthy's friendship with Roosevelt, see Pearson, *Mike*, vol. I, p. 201.

20 *DCER*, vol. VII: *1939–1941, Part I*, ed. David R. Murray (Ottawa: Information Canada, 1974), pp. 97–104.

21 On the exchange of missions with Chile, see Skelton to prime minister, November 28, 1940, Robertson to prime minister, April 2, 1941, DEA file 1621-40; Roosevelt to King, June 7, 1941, quoted in D. R. Murray, "Canada's First Diplomatic Missions in Latin America," *Journal of Interamerican Studies and World Affairs* 16, no. 2 (May 1974): 167; and Robertson to prime minister, July 18, 1942, King Papers, series J1, vol. 323.

22 See C. P. Stacey, *Arms, Men and Governments: The War Policies of Canada 1938–1945* (Ottawa: Information Canada, 1970), pp. 357–60; *Documents on Relations between Canada and Newfoundland*, vol. I: *1935–1949, Defence, Civil Aviation and Economic Affairs*, ed. Paul Bridle (Ottawa: Information Canada, 1974), pp. 42–321; P. F. Neary, "Newfoundland and the Anglo-American Leased Bases Agreement of 27 March 1941," *Canadian Historical Review* 77, no. 4 (December 1986): 491–519; and Neary, *Newfoundland in the North Atlantic World, 1929–1949* (Montreal and Kingston: McGill-Queen's, 1988), pp. 146–62.

23 Robertson to prime minister, July 15, 1941, DEA file 1793-40.

24 These questions are dealt with in Robertson to prime minister, October 10, 1941, Burchell to King, January 5 and January 6, 1942, and Keenleyside to Robertson, "Canadian Representation in Newfoundland," March 27, 1941, ibid.; and Malcolm MacDonald (United Kingdom high commissioner) to Wrong, September 16, 1942, Robertson to MacDonald, December 1, 1942, R. A. MacKay (special wartime assistant to the under-secretary) to Robertson, "Newfoundland Representative in Canada," September 20, 1943, DEA file 3768-40. See also David MacKenzie, *Inside the North Atlantic Triangle: Canada and the Entrance of Newfoundland into Confederation, 1939–1949* (Toronto: University of Toronto Press, 1986), pp. 62–65.

25 On events related to the establishment of the consulate, see *DCER*, vol. VII, pp. 115–21, vol. VIII: *1939–1941, Part II*, ed. David R. Murray (Ottawa: Minister of Supply and Services, 1976), pp. 723–840.

26 J. D. Hickerson interview, Washington, September 27, 1979.

27 Robertson to prime minister, December 30, 1941, and minute by King, DEA file 2983-40. Cf. Pearson, *Mike*, vol. I, p. 199.

28 On Hyde Park, see *DCER*, vol. VIII, pp. 277–351; C. P. Stacey, *Canada and the Age of Conflict*, vol. II: *1921–1948: The Mackenzie King Era* (Toronto: University of Toronto Press, 1981), pp. 315–17; J. W. Pickersgill, ed., *The Mackenzie King Record*, vol. I: *1939–1944* (Toronto: University of Toronto Press, 1960), pp. 189–204; Lawrence Martin, *The Presidents and the Prime Ministers: Washington and Ottawa Face to Face: The Myth of Bilateral Bliss,*

1867–1982 (Toronto: Doubleday, 1982), pp. 135–36; and R. D. Cuff and J. L. Granatstein, *Canadian-American Relations in Wartime: From the Great War to the Cold War* (Toronto: Hakkert, 1975), pp. 69–92.

29 Documents on this subject are in RDEA, vol. 1952, file 836-U-39.

30 *DCER*, vol. VIII, p. 1544. Canada's relations with Japan in 1941 are covered in ibid., pp. 1355–1561.

31 Charles Taylor, *Six Journeys: A Canadian Pattern* (Toronto: Anansi, 1977), p. 124.

32 British minister, Berne, to External Affairs, Ottawa, telegram 43, June 4, 1942, DEA file 2864-40.

33 McGreer, "Report on Treatment of Legation Staff in Tokyo and Allied matters Covering the period December 8, 1942—June 17th, 1942," August 20, 1942, ibid. Except where indicated, the foregoing description is based on this report. The treatment of Japanese diplomatic and consular officials in Canada was similar but less restrictive. The record is in DEA file 2863-40. On the declaration of war, see Stacey, *Canada and the Age of Conflict*, vol. II, p. 322. Canada did not declare war on Thailand.

34 On the recommendations of the special committee, see Granatstein, *Man of Influence*, p. 158.

35 Robertson to King, January 27, 1942, King Papers, series J4, vol. 361, file 3849. For a particularly vigorous statement of revulsion, see Escott Reid, "The Conscience of a Diplomat: A Personal Testament," *Queen's Quarterly* 74, no. 4 (Winter 1967): 587–88. Robertson's position is discussed in Granatstein, *Man of Influence*, pp. 157–67, and Keenleyside's in his *Memoirs*, vol. II: *On the Bridge of Time* (Toronto: McClelland and Stewart, 1982), pp. 168–79.

36 There is an extensive literature on this subject. See especially W. Peter Ward, *White Canada Forever: Popular Attitudes and Public Policy toward Orientals in British Columbia* (Montreal: McGill-Queen's, 1978); Ken Adachi, *The Enemy That Never Was: A History of the Japanese Canadians* (Toronto: McClelland and Stewart, 1976); Ann Gomer Sunahara, *The Politics of Racism: The Uprooting of Japanese Canadians during the Second World War* (Toronto: Lorimer, 1981); and F. E. LaViolette, *The Canadian Japanese and World War II: A Sociological and Psychological Account* (Toronto: University of Toronto Press, 1948). Cf. J. L. Granatstein and Gregory A. Johnson, "The Evacuation of the Japanese-Canadians, 1942: A Realist Critique," in Norman Hillmer, Bohdan Kordan, and Lubomyr Luciuk, eds., *On Guard for Thee: War, Ethnicity, and the Canadian State, 1939–1945* (Ottawa: Minister of Supply and Services, 1988), pp. 101–29; Howard Palmer, "Commentary," ibid., pp. 233–40; Granatstein, "The Enemy Within?" *Saturday Night* (November 1986): 32–34, 39–42; and "Letters," ibid. (February 1987): 5–6. The main DEA files are 3464-B-40 and 3464-J-40.

37 Documents on the situation in the north and Foster's appointment are in *DCER*, vol. IX: *1942–1943*, ed. John F. Hilliker (Ottawa: Minister of Supply and Services, 1980), pp. 1565–94. The subject is dealt with in Shelagh D. Grant, *Sovereignty or Security? Government Policy in the Canadian North, 1936–1950* (Vancouver: University of British Columbia Press, 1988), pp. 103–28.

See also Curtis R. Nordman, "The Army of Occupation: Malcom MacDonald and U.S. Military Involvement in the Canadian Northwest," and Richard J. Diubaldo, "The Alaska Highway in Canada–United States Relations," in Kenneth Coates, ed., *The Alaska Highway: Papers of the 40th Anniversary Symposium* (Vancouver: University of British Columbia Press, 1985), pp. 83–115.

38 King diary, December 1, 1941, quoted in Granatstein, *Ottawa Men*, p. 100.

39 Diary, December 2, 1941, King Papers. See also ibid., May 21, 1941.

40 *DCER*, vol. IX, p. 1649. Christopher Eberts, acting Canadian consul, described the takeover in dispatch No. 4 to SSEA, January 4, 1942, file 2984-40. See also Elisabeth de Miribel, *La liberté souffre violence* (Paris: Plon, 1981), pp. 81, 86–94.

41 *DCER*, vol. IX, p. 1701. Documents relevant to the episode are in ibid., vol. VIII, pp. 830–62, and vol. IX, pp. 1629–1701. There is an excellent description, including an analysis of Robertson's behaviour, in Granatstein, *Ottawa Men*, pp. 97–106. For an extended treatment of the crisis, see Douglas G. Anglin, *The St. Pierre and Miquelon "Affaire" of 1941: A Study in Diplomacy in the North Atlantic Triangle* (Toronto: University of Toronto Press, 1966).

42 Diary, December 28, 1941, King Papers. See also J. F. Hilliker, "The Canadian Government and the Free French: Perceptions and Constraints 1940–44," *International History Review* 2, no. 1 (January 1980): 97.

43 For a contemporary expression of these ideas, see Lionel Gelber, *Peace by Power* (Toronto: Oxford University Press, 1942). Cf. A. J. Miller, "The Functional Principle in Canada's External Relations," *International Journal* 35, no. 2 (Spring 1980): 309–28.

44 Granatstein, *Ottawa Men*, p. 129.

45 On this campaign, see *DCER*, vol. IX, pp. 102–249.

46 Ibid., pp. 380–452.

47 Robertson to David Johnson (Department of Finance), May 2, 1943, Robertson Papers, NA, vol. 2, Personal Correspondence file, 1940–43.

48 Kathleen Bingay to parents, May 5, 1942, and to mother, October 1, 1943, Kathleen Dunton papers, Ottawa, Dunton family private collection. Biographical information is in Ottawa *Citizen*, March 10, 1987, "Kathleen Dunton Died Monday," and Ann Trowell Hillme[r], "A Remembrance: Elizabeth Pauline MacCallum," *Bout de Papier* 2, no. 3 (Summer 1985): 14–15.

49 W. D. Matthews (chief administrative officer) to Robertson, c. October 14, 1943, RDEA, vol. 677, file 111. See also Robertson to prime minister, April 26, 1943, and Read, "Wartime Assistants Grade IV," May 6, 1943, ibid.

50 Robertson to Massey, January 4, 1943, and Robertson to A. MacNamara (deputy minister of labour), February 2, 1945, King Papers, series J4, vol. 250, file 2585.

51 E.g., "Quebec and the Present War: A Study of Public Opinion," July 1942, DEA file 54-B (s).

52 Examples are in T. A. Stone Papers, Sorrento, Maine, private collection of Ellen Devine, and in DEA files 2519-40 and 5526-40. See also Pearson, *Mike*, vol. I, p. 206, and Sidney A. Freifeld, "Freifeld on the Sporting Life," *Bout*

de Papier 5, no. 3 (Fall 1987): 13-15. Cadieux's views are in Marcel Cadieux interview, Ottawa, June 27, 1979.

53 Cadieux interview, June 27, 1979; Paul Tremblay interview, Ottawa, October 25, 1979.

54 Memorandum from Cadieux and Tremblay, "Quebec and the Conscription Issue," May 6, 1942, King Papers, series J4, vol. 358, file 3831.

55 See Henry Ferns, *Reading from Left to Right: One Man's Political History* (Toronto: University of Toronto Press, 1983), pp. 167-73. Cf. John W. Holmes, "Frederic Herbert Soward 1899-1985," *International Journal* 40, no. 1 (Winter 1984-5): 203-6.

56 Doug Owram, *The Government Generation: Canadian Intellectuals and the State 1900-1945* (Toronto: University of Toronto Press, 1986), pp. 257, 260.

57 Robertson to King, March 25, 1942, RDEA, vol. 799, file 524. Since the beginning of the war, External Affairs had appointed officers to perform consular functions in Tokyo and Buenos Aires as well as in Greenland and St Pierre and Miquelon.

58 Keenleyside, "Considerations Relating to the Proposed Amalgamation of the External Affairs Service and the Commercial Intelligence Service and the Incorporation Therein of a Canadian Consular Service," October 9, 1942, DEA file 1446-A-40. For the further development of Keenleyside's ideas, see "Memorandum for Members of the External Affairs-Trade and Commerce Advisory Committee on Canadian Representation Abroad," July 29, 1943, ibid.

59 "Submission Concerning the Trade Commissioner Service by Trade Commissioners and Assistants Resident in Ottawa 1942-43," Department of Trade and Commerce Records, NA, vol. 1035, file 18251, p. 38.

60 HC *Debates*, July 12, 1943, pp. 4772-74.

61 *DCER*, vol. IX, pp. 89-91.

62 King to Robertson, February 19, 1944, King Papers, series J4, vol. 250, file 2585.

63 Glazebrook to Holmes, February 4, 1987, Holmes Papers, Canadian Institute of International Affairs, Toronto.

64 The main series of files, known as the "40 series," continued to expand until 1963 without any system of grouping by subject. There were two refinements based on security classifications. Files with secret material were given the suffix "s" rather than "40." Another series, numbered in the 50,000s and with the suffix "40," was classified top secret. Thus it might be necessary to consult more than one series of files if a subject were dealt with in documents of varying levels of sensitivity.

65 Letter to Maj.-Gen. H. F. G. Letson (adjutant general), drafted for Robertson's signature but never sent. It appears that Robertson relayed the message to him orally. RDEA, vol. 679, file 136-0-1.

66 Keenleyside to Agnes McCloskey, December 23, 1942, ibid., vol. 678, file 136.

67 J. F. Hilliker, "Distant Ally: Canadian Relations with Australia during the Second World War," *Journal of Imperial and Commonwealth History* 13, no. 1 (October 1984): 52-56.

68 Peter St. John, "Canada's Accession to the Allied Intelligence Community 1940–45," *Conflict Quarterly* 4, no. 2 (Fall 1984): 9–12.

69 Hilliker, "Canadian Government and the Free French," pp. 93–108.

70 Robertson to prime minister, "Canadian Representation in the U.S.S.R.," February 27, 1942, *DCER*, vol. IX, p. 445. The agreement on consular representation is in Canada, *Treaty Series*, 1942/9 (Ottawa: King's Printer, 1942). See also Massey to King, October 15, 1941, *DCER*, vol. VII, p. 95, and December 15, 1941, DEA file 2462-40; and King to Massey, October 31, 1941, *DCER*, vol. IX, pp. 42–3.

71 Wilgress's instructions are in SSEA to Wilgress, January 6, 1943, King Papers, series J1, vol. 336. See also R. M. Macdonnell, "The Mission to Kuibyshev," *International Perspectives* (July–August 1973): 54; Aloysius Balawyder, "Canada in the Uneasy War Alliance," and Donald M. Page, "Getting to Know the Russians, 1943-1948," in Balawyder, ed., *Canadian-Soviet Relations 1939–1980* (Toronto: Mosaic Press, 1982), pp. 1–40; Dana Wilgress, *Memoirs* (Toronto: Ryerson, 1967), pp. 124–37; and Denis Smith, *Diplomacy of Fear: Canada and the Cold War 1941-1948* (Toronto: University of Toronto Press, 1988), pp. 25–49.

72 Tarr to King, September 21, 1942, RDEA, vol. 799, file 524.

73 On Davis in Australia, see Hilliker, "Distant Ally," pp. 56–64.

74 Patterson to Robertson, June 28, 1945, RDEA, vol. 799, file 523. See also Robertson to King, January 18, 1943, King Papers, series J4, vol. 310, file 3291; Odlum to under-secretary, July 29, 1943, DEA file 4558-E-40; and Kim Richard Nossal, "Chungking Prism: Cognitive Process and Intelligence Failure," *International Journal* 32, no. 3 (Summer 1977): 559–76.

75 Under-secretary to Scully, April 3, 1944, DEA file 2446-40.

76 Memorandum for under-secretary on "Division of Office Accommodation," November 26, 1942, by Keenleyside, Stone, Glazebrook, and Angus, Stone to Robertson, November 26, 1942, and Wrong to Robertson, November 26, 1942, DEA file 30 (s). See also Pearson to Massey, April 1, 1942, quoted in Granatstein, *Man of Influence*, p. 189.

77 Robertson to King, December 13, 1942, quoted in Granatstein, *Man of Influence*, p. 191.

78 Diary, April 9, 1943, Pearson Papers, series N8, vol. 1.

79 Report to under-secretary by Wrong, October 16, 1943, DEA file 9240-40. Matthews is dealt with in Massey to Skelton, March 5, 1930, and Borden to Heeney, February 20, 1943, Civil Service Commission Records, NA, vol. 334, file 1247.

80 Stone, "Memorandum on the Activities of the ad hoc Censorship Committee which has been meeting in the Department of External Affairs," August 11, 1941, RDEA, vol. 199, file 724-AD-39.

81 Paul Tremblay, "Postal Censorship Reports and External Affairs," December 15, 1941, and Pearson to F. E. Jolliffe (chief postal censor), February 23, 1942, ibid., vol. 1934, file 724-BZ-39.

82 Glazebrook to Pearson, February 26, 1942, Annex I, "Censorship, Intelligence and Security," ibid., vol. 1915, file 724-A-39.

83 J. M. S. Careless interview, Toronto, September 18, 1979.

84 Stone to Stephenson, October 21, 1942, DND, AI request 1463-86/10047.

85 Gilbert de B. Robinson, ed., "A History of the Examination Unit, 1941–1945" (1945), p. ii, ibid. The foregoing account is based principally on this history and on other material released in response to the same access-to-information request. See also Wesley K. Wark, "Cryptographic Innocence: The Origins of Signals Intelligence in Canada in the Second World War," *Journal of Contemporary History* 22, no. 4 (October 1987): 639–65, and St. John, "Canada's Accession to the Allied Intelligence Community," pp. 5–21.

86 David Stafford, *Camp X: Canada's School for Secret Agents 1941–45* (Toronto: Lester and Orpen Dennys, 1986), p. 286.

CHAPTER TEN

1 John W. Holmes, *The Shaping of Peace: Canada and the Search for World Order 1943–1957*, vol. I (Toronto: University of Toronto Press, 1979), p. 25. The impact of generational change on the department has also been dealt with in Mary Halloran, "Canada and the Origins of the Post-War Commitment," paper presented to a conference on Canada, the United States, and the Atlantic Alliance, Toronto, May 21, 1987, pp. 4–6, and in addresses to the conference by Robert Bothwell, May 21, 1987, and Charles Ritchie, May 22, 1987.

2 J. W. Pickersgill, ed., *The Mackenzie King Record*, vol. I: *1939–1944* (Toronto: University of Toronto Press, 1960), p. 466.

3 James Eayrs, *The Art of the Possible: Government and Foreign Policy in Canada* (Toronto: University of Toronto Press, 1961), pp. 118–19; Howard Green interview, Vancouver, March 2, 1980. Green, member of Parliament for Vancouver South from 1935, was one of the advocates of the standing committee and served as secretary of state for external affairs from 1959 to 1963.

4 J. L. Granatstein, *A Man of Influence: Norman A. Robertson and Canadian Statecraft 1929–68* (Ottawa: Deneau, 1981), p. 190. Cf. Green interview, March 2, 1980.

5 Robertson to prime minister, April 26, 1943, DEA file 6000-A-40; diary, February 13, 1943, King Papers, NA; and Granatstein, *Man of Influence*, p. 116.

6 Wrong to Robertson, October 16, 1941, and Robertson, memorandum to prime minister, October 25, 1941, DEA file 1086-40. On November 1, 1941, Wrong warned Robertson of a potential credibility problem, on matters of export control and blacklisting: "Unless we develop an adequate staff in Ottawa to handle these matters, I think that they may be compelled in Washington to pass over our position and interests because we have not proper machinery for co-operation." See Wrong to Robertson, November 1, 1941, RDEA, vol. 788, file 408.

7 Stone to Robertson, April 22, 1942, ibid.

8 "Establishment of an Economic Division," March 3, 1943, DEA file 1086-40.

9 Order-in-council PC 4073, December 8, 1939, DEA file 8100-G-40.

10 Order-in-council PC 8099, September 8, 1942, ibid.

11 The department's relations with the Wartime Information Board are dealt with in L. A. D. Stephens, "Study of Canadian Government Information Abroad," 1977, DEA, chapter 1, and William R. Young, "Making the Truth Graphic," PHD thesis, University of British Columbia, 1978, chapters 2 and 4. On activity in Australia, see J. F. Hilliker, "Distant Ally: Canadian Relations with Australia during the Second World War," *Journal of Imperial and Commonwealth History* 13, no. 1 (October 1984): 57, 64.

12 Minutes of Advisory Committee meeting, June 22, 1944, DEA file 8100-40. The CBC-IS was created by order-in-council PC 8168, September 18, 1942, DEA file 8100-G-40.

13 Wrong to under-secretary, July 26, 1944, DEA file 6633-40.

14 The creation of the Information Division is dealt with in Stephens, "Study," chapter 2, pp. 7–14. The CIS was created by order-in-council PC 6300, September 28, 1945, DEA file 8100-G-40.

15 King to G. H. Bland (chairman, Civil Service Commission), July 8, 1944, Civil Service Commission Records, NA, vol. 359, Hume Wrong personnel file.

16 "Organization of the Department of External Affairs," January 2, 1945, King Papers, series J4, vol. 242, file 2454.

17 Robertson to King, December 11, 1944, ibid., vol. 250, file 2580.

18 On the Special Section, see chapter 9. The closing of this unit is dealt with in M. H. Wershof to under-secretary, October 19, 1946, RDEA, vol. 678, file 136-D.

19 The reorganization was explained in "Note for the Information of Officers of the Department of External Affairs," January 23, 1945, DEA file 1086-40.

20 Pickersgill, ed., *Mackenzie King Record*, vol. I, p. 167. On the earlier relationship between Robertson and King, see chapter 9.

21 Diary, November 2, 1942, King Papers.

22 A. G. Maitland to J. D. Greenway, April 25, 1944, Foreign Office Records, PRO, FO 371/42682/w6731.

23 James Gibson interview, St Catharines, February 17, 1987; Gibson, "Travelling with the SSEA (1942–1946)," *Bout de Papier* 2, no. 4 (Spring/Summer 1986): 7–10; Gibson, "At First Hand: Recollections of a Prime Minister," *Queen's Quarterly* 61, no. 1 (Spring 1954): 16.

24 Wrong to Pearson, February 13, 1943, with enclosure, February 5, 1943, Pearson Papers, NA, series N1, vol. 31.

25 Robertson to Read, October 16, 1943, King Papers, series J4, vol. 240, file 2585.

26 Douglas LePan (second secretary, London) to Donald Matthews (chief administrative officer), December 13, 1945, RDEA, vol. 681, file 156.

27 Holmes to R. G. Robertson, November 30, 1944, DEA file 1086-40. See also R. G. Robertson to Holmes, January 15, 1945, and "Note for Officers of the Department," August 29, 1945, ibid.

28 Robertson to King, August 24, 1945, King Papers, series J4, vol. 242, file 2454.

29 On this point, see H. S. Ferns, *Reading from Left to Right: One Man's Political History* (Toronto: University of Toronto Press, 1983), pp. 169–72. Cf. J. M. S. Careless interview, Toronto, February 15, 1987.

30 Soward to Watson Kirkconnell (head, English Department, McMaster University, and chairman, Humanities Research Council of Canada), January 19, 1944, Kirkconnell Papers, Acadia University Archives, file 8/1972.

31 Robertson to prime minister, October 17, 1943, King Papers, series J4, vol. 242, file F2454.

32 John Starnes to Stone, March 30, 1946, Stone Papers, Sorrento, Maine, private collection of Ellen Devine. The salary range for third secretaries was $2,400 to $3,000. By comparison, university lecturers were paid $2,000 to $3,000 at Queen's and up to $3,500 at the University of Toronto. F. W. Gibson, *Queen's University*, vol. II: *1917–1961: To Serve and Yet Be Free* (Kingston and Montreal: McGill-Queen's, 1983), p. 466 n76. The average salary for a secondary-school principal in Ontario was $3,169 and for a male assistant $2,627. *Canada Year Book 1947* (Ottawa: King's Printer, 1947), pp. 279–80.

33 Starnes to Stone, April 20, 1945, Stone Papers.

34 G. P. de T. Glazebrook to J. W. Holmes, May 12, 1987, Holmes Papers, Canadian Institute of International Affairs, Toronto; Freeman Tovell interview, Victoria, March 4, 1980.

35 Starnes to Stone, October 23, 1945, Stone Papers.

36 *DCER*, vol. IX: *1942–1943*, ed. John F. Hilliker (Ottawa: Minister of Supply and Services, 1980), pp. 78–79.

37 SSEA to high commissioner in South Africa, February 3, 1944, dispatch 14, DEA file 3011-A-40, and acting accredited representative of South Africa to SSEA, May 21, 1945, note 9, King Papers, series J1, vol. 388.

38 Representation in Paris is dealt with in chapter 9. Canada did not agree to a request that Luxemburg's minister in Washington be accredited to Ottawa. Luxemburg's political interests in Canada were handled by the Netherlands and its commercial interests by Belgium.

39 Memorandum for prime minister, October 18, 1944, DEA file 7073-40.

40 Marcel Cadieux, *Premières armes* (Ottawa: Le cercle du livre de France, 1951), pp. 28–31.

41 SSEA to chargé d'affaires to allied governments, September 3, 1944, telegram 39, DEA file 4700-N-40.

42 Under-secretary to delegate of French Committee of National Liberation, February 14, 1944, DEA file 4761-40.

43 SSEA to high commissioner in Great Britain, April 8, 1945, telegram 824, DEA file 9676-40.

44 Acting high commissioner in Great Britain to SSEA, October 27, 1945, dispatch A521, DEA file 8150-40. See also *DCER*, vol. IX, pp. 1167–72.

45 Robertson to Pearson, February 24, 1945, DEA file 26-DY-40. See also Cadieux to Wrong, May 19, 1943, and John Deutsch, "Conversation with Prime Minister Godbout," November 22, 1943, DEA file 54-C(s), and, on the manpower problem affecting representation in Latin America generally, Keenleyside to Thomas M. Snow (British minister in Colombia), January 29, 1942, DEA file 3104-40.

46 Cadieux to Wrong, May 19, 1943, DEA file 54-C(s).

47 Pearson to Robertson, December 8, 1945, DEA file 8310-K-40.

48 Deane H. Russell (secretary, Committee on Canadian Hand Arts and Crafts) to Matthews, March 31, 1944, Katherine Keenleyside to Matthews, April 5, 1944, DEA file 6302-40.

49 Robertson to prime minister, September 3, 1945, minuted by King, September 5, Civil Service Commission Records, vol. 819; W. L. Ronson (assistant deputy minister of finance) to Wrong, November 14, 1945, King Papers, series J4, vol. 242.

50 Under-secretary to Ronson, November 19, 1945, ibid.

51 Diary, August 24, 1946, King Papers. See also J. W. Pickersgill and D. F. Forster, eds., *The Mackenzie King Record*, vol. III: *1945–1946* (Toronto: University of Toronto Press, 1970), pp. 324–25.

52 Cabinet Conclusions, October 16 and December 18, 1946, PCR, vol. 2365.

53 Documents on the Quebec conferences are in DEA files 3510-40 (1943) and 6960-40 (1944) and in King Papers, series J4, vol. 414, file 3992.

54 High commissioner in Great Britain to SSEA, July 4, 1945, telegram 1872, DEA file 22-U(s). Documents on Sicily are published in *DCER*, vol. IX, pp. 334–46. Those on Normandy are in DEA file 49(s) and on repatriation in file 22-U(s).

55 Quoted in Stacey, *Arms, Men and Governments*, p. 54.

56 Memorandum to Cabinet War Committee, June 14, 1944, PCR, vol. 5681. On Canada and the Pacific war, see Stacey, *Arms, Men and Governments*, pp. 54–62.

57 Stone, memorandum, "Psychological Warfare," February 10, 1944, DEA file 5335-P-40. See also D. M. Page, "Tommy Stone and Psychological Warfare in World War Two," *Journal of Canadian Studies* 16, nos. 3–4 (Fall–Winter 1981): 110–20.

58 Stone to Glazebrook, September 2, 1944, DEA file 5353-P-40. See also Stone to Pearson, May 22, 1942, ibid.

59 Memorandum to Cabinet War Committee, October 11, 1943, King Papers, series J4, vol. 426.

60 Robertson to Wrong, May 2, 1944, RDEA, vol. 2120, file 1046-2. The psychological warfare committee dealt with the use of prisoners of war in Canada for psychological warfare purposes.

61 Wrong to Robertson, June 16, 1944, ibid., vol. 676, file 136.

62 Gilbert de B. Robinson, ed., "A History of the Examination Unit, 1941–1945" (1945), pp. 58–59, DND, AI request 1463-86/10047; Peter St. John, "Canada's Accession to the Allied Intelligence Community 1940–45," *Conflict Quarterly* 4, no. 2 (Fall 1984): 16. On creation of the Special Intelligence Section and of the Examination Unit, see chapter 9 above.

63 St. John, "Canada's Accession," p. 16; Memorandum on Most Secret Intelligence, March 4, 1944, and Stone to William Stephenson (British Security Coordination), May 3, 1944, enclosure, DND, AI request 1463-86/10047.

64 Memorandum to Pope, April 7, 1945, enclosure, also Associate Committee minutes, October 4, 1944, ibid. The decision to close the Examination Unit was subsequently reversed. The subject will be dealt with in volume II.

65 MacDonald, quoted in Irving Abella and Harold Troper, *None Is Too Many: Canada and the Jews of Europe, 1933–1948* (Toronto: Lester and Orpen Dennys, 1982), p. 131. See also ibid., pp. 120, 122, and DEA file 4300-40. Also used for this account were RDEA, vol. 1839, file 583-37, and DEA file 4637-40.

66 See R. G. Riddell (Second Political Division) to Wrong, November 28, 1945, DEA file 8296-40, also DEA file 7648-40 for background information.

67 The five claimed to be not Russians but naturalized Germans. Two, however, decided to go to the Soviet Union without demur and two others eventually opted to return. The one remaining convinced the Soviet embassy that he was in fact a naturalized German, and it expressed no further interest in him. See Robertson to Read, December 11, 1944, DEA file 621-MA-40, and Rive to Robertson, February 2, 1945, DEA file 621-LY-40.

68 See Ann G. Sunahara, *The Politics of Racism: The Uprooting of Japanese Canadians during the Second World War* (Toronto: Lorimer, 1981), p. 116.

69 R. G. Robertson to N. A. Robertson, March 3, 1944, and H. F. Angus, "Memorandum on Mr. Robertson's Note on Policy With Regard to Japanese in Canada," March 22, 1944, DEA file 104(s). See also A. R. Menzies, "Policy With Regard to Japanese in Canada," March, 22, 1944, ibid. Earlier developments are dealt with in Granatstein, *Man of Influence*, p. 164, and *DCER*, vol. IX, pp. 552–53.

70 N. A. Robertson to prime minister, March 27, 1944, minuted by King, March 29, 1944, King Papers, series J4, vol. 361, file F3850, also Cabinet War Committee minutes, April 19, 1944, PCR, vol. 5681.

71 N. A. Robertson to prime minister, June 13, 1944, DEA file 104(s).

72 HC *Debates*, August 4, 1944, pp. 5915–17; N. A. Robertson to prime minister, June 22, 1944, King Papers, series J4, vol. 361, file F3850; Ken Adachi, *The Enemy That Never Was: A History of the Japanese Canadians* (Toronto: McClelland and Stewart, 1976), pp. 292–96.

73 Cabinet Conclusions, February 2, 1945, PCR, vol. 2636.

74 Cabinet Conclusions, September 15, 1945, ibid., vol. 2637.

75 On September 19, 1945, ibid.

76 R. G. Robertson to Wrong, October 24, 1945, Wrong to John Baldwin (Privy Council Office), October 30, 1945, and Read to under-secretary, December 6, 1945, and to acting under-secretary, November 1, 1945, DEA file 104(s).

77 N. A. Robertson to prime minister, December 14, 1945, ibid.

78 Cabinet Conclusions, December 15, 1945, PCR, vol. 2637; orders-in-council PC 7355-57, December 15, 1945, DEA file 104(s). The text of PC 7355 is printed in Adachi, *Enemy That Never Was*, pp. 429–30.

79 N. A. Robertson to prime minister, January 5, 1946, DEA file 50076-40.

80 *DCER*, vol. XII: *1946*, ed. Donald M. Page (Ottawa: Minister of Supply and Services, 1977), pp. 328–30; R. G. Robertson to prime minister, December 3, 1946, DEA file 50076-40; Adachi, *Enemy That Never Was*, p. 317.

CHAPTER ELEVEN

1 On the interrelationship of commercial and monetary policy, see *DCER*, vol. IX, pp. 604-96.

2 Robertson's comment on the expertise of Finance and the Bank of Canada is in ibid., p. 651. On the activity of Rasminsky and Mackintosh at Bretton Woods, see A. F. W. Plumptre, *Three Decades of Decision: Canada and the World Monetary System 1944-75* (Toronto: McClelland and Stewart, 1977), pp. 39-42, and Douglas H. Fullerton, *Graham Towers and His Times: A Biography* (Toronto: McClelland and Stewart, 1986), pp. 189-90. Towers and Plumptre were both at Bretton Woods. The recollections of several Canadian participants are in Louis Rasminsky, William A. Mackintosh, A. F. W. Plumptre, and John J. Deutsch, "Canadian Views," in A. L. K. Acheson, J. F. Chant, and M. F. J. Prachowny, eds., *Bretton Woods Revisited: Evolution of the International Monetary Fund and the International Bank for Reconstruction and Development* (Toronto: University of Toronto Press, 1970), pp. 34-47.

3 *DCER*, vol. IX, pp. 1403-22; SSEA to ambassador in United States, July 13, 1945, teletype EX-2583, DEA file 749-F-40.

4 Douglas LePan, *Bright Glass of Memory: A Set of Four Memoirs* (Toronto: McGraw-Hill Ryerson, 1979), p. 59.

5 See chapter 9.

6 *DCER*, vol. IX, p. 757.

7 On the establishment of UNRRA as it involved Canada, see ibid., pp. 768–839. Claxton's appointment as parliamentary assistant is discussed in James Eayrs, *In Defence of Canada: Peacemaking and Deterrence* (Toronto: University of Toronto Press, 1972), p. 20.

8 Ambassador in United States to SSEA, March 3, 1944, teletype WA-1321, DEA file 2295-Q-40.

9 Angus to under-secretary, September 27, 1944, ibid.

10 Dominions secretary to SSEA, June 19, 1943, telegrams D364-65, and Wrong to under-secretary, July 5, 1943, DEA file 7-AB(s). See also Reid, "The United States and Canada: Domination, Cooperation, Absorption," January 12, 1942, DEA file 1415-40. Reid subsequently had a "Report on Canadian Representation in and Relations with the United States of America" (March 31, 1942) prepared as a basis on which plans could be devised for achieving policy objectives.

11 Memorandum to Cabinet War Committee, "Post-Hostilities Problems," November 24, 1943, DEA file 7-AB(s); also DEA file 7-AD(s) for the War Committee's reaction.

12 Wrong, "Canadian Planning for the International Settlement," February 23, 1944, and minutes of the third meeting of the Advisory Committee on Post-Hostilities Problems, March 28, 1944, DEA file 7-AQ(s); working committee minutes, August 10, August 25, September 7, and September 21, 1944, DEA file 7-AB(s).

13 Charles Ritchie, *The Siren Years: A Canadian Diplomat Abroad 1937–1945* (Toronto: Macmillan, 1974), p. 208. See also Don Munton and Don Page, "Planning in the East Block: The Post-Hostilities Problems Committees in Canada," *International Journal* 32, no. 4 (Autumn 1977): 687–726.

14 Pearson to Robertson, February 1, 1944, DEA file 6133-40.

15 Under-secretary to prime minister, March 18, 1944, King Papers, NA, series J1, vol. 369.

16 Minutes of eighth meeting of Advisory Committee on Post-Hostilities Planning, March 15, 1945, DEA file 7-AQ(s); Pope, memorandum, August 2, 1945, DEA file 7-CM-1(s).

17 See DEA files 7-AD(s) and 7-AQ(s).

18 Documents on the work of the Canadian delegation at Chicago are in DEA files 72-MK-40 and 72-MK-1-40. Establishment of the organization's headquarters in Montreal is dealt with in *DCER*, vol. XII, pp. 520–24. See also Robert Bothwell and J. L. Granatstein, "Canada and the Wartime Negotiations over Civil Aviation: The Functional Principle in Operation," *International History Review* 2, no. 4 (October 1980): 585–601.

19 Holmes, *Shaping of Peace*, vol. I, pp. 230–31.

20 See note by the Canadian Working Committee on Post-Hostilities Problems, March 6, 1944, DEA file 7-CB(s). Early discussion of this subject is in *DCER*, vol. IX, pp. 865–82.

21 Documents on the Dumbarton Oaks proposals are in DEA file 7-V(s).

22 Minutes of meeting of Canadian delegates and advisers, San Francisco, April 24, 1945, ibid.

23 For Diefenbaker's recollection of the conference, see John G. Diefenbaker, *One Canada: The Memoirs of the Right Honourable John G. Diefenbaker*, vol. I: *The Crusading Years 1895–1956* (Toronto: Macmillan, 1975), pp. 233–35.

24 Wrong to Read (acting under-secretary), May 13, 1945, DEA file 7-V(s). Compromise was required to preserve the harmony described, for Wrong and at least one other adviser favoured a firmer line in dealing with the Soviet Union than the delegation adopted. See Denis Smith, *Diplomacy of Fear: Canada and the Cold War 1941–1948* (Toronto: University of Toronto Press, 1988), p. 85. The departmental officers at San Francisco received a warm tribute in I. Norman Smith, "Canada at San Francisco: That Competent Team from the East Block," Ottawa *Journal*, June 28, 1945. Similar sentiments were expressed by Graydon in HC *Debates*, October 16, 1945, pp. 1203–4.

25 The literature on Canadian involvement in organization of the United Nations is extensive. See Escott Reid, *On Duty: A Canadian at the Making of the United Nations 1945–1946* (Toronto: McClelland and Stewart, 1983), pp. 18–70; Holmes, *Shaping of Peace*, vol. I, pp. 229–68; Eayrs, *Peacemaking and Deterrence*, pp. 137–67; Granatstein, *Man of Influence*, pp. 145–56; C. P. Stacey, *Canada and the Age of Conflict: A History of Canadian External Policies*, vol. II: *1921–1948* (Toronto: University of Toronto Press, 1981), pp. 378–86; Ritchie, *Siren Years*, pp. 187–204; Pearson, *Mike*, vol. I, pp. 264–78; J. W. Pickersgill and D. F. Forster, eds., *The Mackenzie King Record*, vol. II: *1944–1945* (Toronto: University of Toronto Press, 1968),

pp. 375–90. The prime minister's guidance to the delegation is in minutes of a meeting of Canadian delegates and advisers, April 24, 1945, DEA file 7-V(s).

26 On the election of 1945, see J. Murray Beck, *Pendulum of Power: Canada's Federal Elections* (Scarborough: Prentice-Hall, 1968), pp. 241–58, especially p. 248; Pickersgill and Forster, eds., *King Record*, vol. II, pp. 314, 381; and J. L. Granatstein, *Canada's War: The Politics of the Mackenzie King Government, 1939–1945* (Toronto: Oxford University Press, 1975), p. 398. The foreign policy planks in the various party platforms are to be found in D. Owen Carrigan, comp., *Canadian Party Platforms 1867–1968* (Toronto: Copp Clark, 1968), pp. 149–50, 156–58, 160, 163, 165.

27 External Affairs documents on atomic energy are in files 201(s), 201-B(s), and 50219-W-40, also *DCER*, vol. XII, pp. 411–510. See also Brian L. Villa, "Alliance Politics and Atomic Collaboration, 1941–1943," in Sidney Aster, ed., *The Second World War as a National Experience* (Ottawa: Canadian Committee for the History of the Second World War, 1981), pp. 140–62; Wilfrid Eggleston, *Canada's Nuclear Story* (Toronto: Clarke, Irwin, 1965), pp. 29–206; and Smith, *Diplomacy of Fear*, pp. 92–94. Pearson's role is described in Pearson, *Mike*, vol. I, pp. 258–63.

28 Maurice Pope, *Soldiers and Politicians: The Memoirs of Lt. Gen. Maurice A. Pope* (Toronto: University of Toronto Press, 1962), p. 283. Documents on establishment of the military mission are in DEA file 7-CA-9(s). See also J. F. Hilliker, "No Bread at the Peace Table: Canada and the European Settlement, 1943–7," *Canadian Historical Review* 61, no. 1 (March 1980): 69–86.

29 Cabinet Conclusions, October 10, 1945, PCR, vol. 2637.

30 Memorandum for associate under-secretary, February 21, 1946, note for file, May 22, 1946, ambassador in United States to SSEA, May 24, 1946, teletype WA-2195, and June 18, 1946, teletype WA-2505, DEA file 4606-C-10-40. On Norman's work in Japan at this time, cf. Roger Bowen, *Innocence Is Not Enough: The Life and Death of E. Herbert Norman* (Vancouver and Toronto: Douglas and McIntyre, 1986), pp. 114–39, and James Barros, *No Sense of Evil: Espionage, The Case of E. Herbert Norman* (Toronto: Deneau, 1986), rev. edn., *The Espionage Case of E. Herbert Norman* (New York: Ivy Books, 1987), pp. 43–53. The Allied Council, with one member each from the United States, the Commonwealth, the Soviet Union, and China, was created to advise the supreme commander.

31 *Report of the Secretary of State for External Affairs for the Year Ended December 31, 1945* (Ottawa: King's Printer, 1946), p. 5. See also HC *Debates*, October 16, 1945, pp. 1185–87, 1195–1209, October 18, 1945, pp. 1249–90, October 19, 1945, pp. 1303–34.

32 Holmes, *Shaping of Peace*, vol. I, p. 263.

33 SSEA to dominions secretary, August 4, 1945, telegram 178, DEA file 5475-E-40.

34 Delegation to SSEA, September 1, 1945, dispatch 17, ibid.

35 Wrong to Reid, August 30, 1945, ibid.

36 High commissioner in Great Britain to SSEA, September 21, 1945, telegram 2734, ibid. The General Committee was responsible for maintaining continuity with the work of the San Francisco conference, for questions related to

the site of United Nations headquarters, and for all subjects not otherwise allocated.

37 Holmes, *Shaping of Peace*, Vol. I, p. 262. Also "Report by the Canadian Delegation on the Work of the Executive Committee of the Preparatory Commission of the United Nations held at London, 16 August–22 November, 1945," second draft, November 22, 1945, DEA file 5475-E-1-40, SSEA to acting high commissioner in Great Britain, September 23, 1945, telegram 2200, DEA file 5475-E-40, and Reid, *On Duty*, pp. 71–100.

38 "Report on the Work of the Preparatory Commission," January 4, 1946, DEA file 5475-J-40.

39 Wrong to Reid, September 29, 1945, ibid.

40 SSEA to high commissioner in Great Britain, November 27, 1945, telegram 2791, ibid. A subject about which Wilgress consulted Ottawa, by telephone, was the permanent headquarters of the organization.

41 Reid, *On Duty*, p. 109.

42 "Report," January 4, 1946, DEA file 5475-J-40. The work of the Preparatory Commission is dealt with in Reid, *On Duty*, pp. 101–32.

43 *DCER*, vol. XII, p. 657.

44 Ibid., pp. 660–61.

45 Ibid., p. 680. On the first session of the assembly, see ibid., pp. 656–81; also Reid, *On Duty*, pp. 133–41, and Paul Martin, *A Very Public Life*, vol. I: *Far from Home* (Ottawa: Deneau, 1983), pp. 399–416.

46 L. B. Pearson, *Mike: The Memoirs of the Right Honourable Lester B. Pearson*, vol. III: *1957–1968,* ed. John A. Munro and Alex I. Inglis (Toronto: University of Toronto Press, 1975), p. 165; Massey, *What's Past Is Prologue: The Memoirs of the Right Honourable Vincent Massey* (Toronto: Macmillan, 1963), p. 434; Dana Wilgress, *Memoirs* (Toronto: Ryerson, 1967), p. 145.

47 Wrong to Robertson, May 15, 1946, RDEA, vol. 2620, file N-1.

48 H. (A. L. Hall, Cypher Division?) to G. G. Crean (Second Political Division), April 3, 1946, ibid. On Emma Woikin, see June Callwood, *Emma* (Toronto: Stoddart Publishing, 1984). Emma Woikin had lived for several months in the home of Leo Malania, who had joined the department as a wartime assistant in 1943. Although there was no indication of Malania's involvement, his career, according to a recent study, was affected. Late in 1946, he acepted a position in the office of the UN secretary general, arranged with the assistance of Hume Wrong. Smith, *Diplomacy of Fear*, pp. 115–16.

49 *The Report of the Royal Commission Appointed under Order in Council P.C. 411 of February 5, 1946 to Investigate the Facts Relating to and the Circumstances Surrounding the Communication, by Public Officials and Other Persons in Positions of Trust of Secret and Confidential Information to Agents of a Foreign Power* (Ottawa: King's Printer, 1946), pp. 496, 689–90. For a selection of the evidence presented to the royal commission, see Robert Bothwell and J. L. Granatstein, eds., *The Gouzenko Transcripts* (Ottawa: Deneau, n.d.).

50 *DCER*, vol. XII, pp. 2053–55.

51 Wilgress, *Memoirs*, p. 147.

52 Granatstein, *Man of Influence*, p. 181; Reginald Whitaker, "Origins of the Canadian Government's Internal Security System, 1946–1952," *Canadian Historical Review* 65, no. 2 (June 1984): 156–88.

53 Tarr to King, September 21, 1942, RDEA, vol. 799, file 524.

54 The government was prepared to receive a Mexican minister before reciprocating, but Mexico declined. Robertson to King, December 6, 1942, King Papers, series J4, vol. 307, file 3218.

55 Pearson, *Mike*, vol. I, pp. 221–22.

56 On this problem as it affected John Hall Kelly before he went to Ireland in 1940, see diary, March 7, 1940, Pearson Papers, series N8, vol. 1, file 3.

57 In February 1943, Wrong wrote: "To use our Missions properly we shall require even after the Peace Settlement a stronger Department than that which we now have." Wrong to Pearson, February 13, 1943, enclosing Wrong, "Probable Expansion of Canadian Missions abroad and Department of External Affairs," February 5, 1943, Pearson Papers, series N1, vol. 31. On the problems of the posts, see Stone to ambassador, July 9, 1945, and Starnes to Stone, October 23, 1945, Stone Papers.

58 Reid, "International Conference on Civil Aviation, Chicago, 1944—Part III: The Reasons for the Partial Failure of the Conference," December 1944, Reid Papers, NA, vol. 5, file 6.

59 Désy to SSEA, December 17, 1942, Robertson to Désy, January 26, 1943, and August 18, 1943, DEA file 5836-40; Stone to Soward, March 18, 1944, DEA file 2727-C-40. See also "Notes of a meeting on cultural relations with Latin America," November 8, 1943, DEA file 5836-40, and Robert J. Williams, "Cultural Exchanges and Canada," *International Perspectives* (July–August 1987): 21.

60 Robertson to prime minister, April 26, 1946, minuted by Robertson, May 6, 1946, DEA file 19-AK-40. See also Wrong to Pearson, May 27, 1946, ibid., and circular dispatch, October 30, 1946, file 19-AL-40. In 1946, Vincent Massey was made a Companion of Honour by King George VI, an award which the Canadian prime minister only with extreme reluctance allowed him to accept. Claude Bissell, *The Imperial Canadian: Vincent Massey in Office* (Toronto: University of Toronto Press, 1986), pp. 173–75.

61 Rive to Pearson, November 25, 1946, DEA file 19-AK-40.

62 Pearson to Rive, January 15, 1947, ibid. The author of the poem was MacDermot. Several others were composed at the same time and sent to Rive with Pearson's letter. One of these is reproduced in Sidney Friefeld, "The Poets of External." *Bout de Papier* 6, no. 4 (1989): 14–15.

63 J. W. Holmes, "1945: Reflections from Canada House," text of an address at Carleton University, December 5, 1986, pp. 2–4, Holmes Papers, Canadian Institute of International Affairs, Toronto.

Index